HOMES WITH CHARACTER

REVISED EDITION

HOMES

with Character

by HAZEL THOMPSON CRAIG

*Free-Lance Decorating Consultant;
formerly, Head of Home Economics Department,
Gallaudet College, Washington, D. C.*

and OLA DAY RUSH

*Formerly, Head of Home Economics Department,
Public Schools, District of Columbia*

D. C. HEATH AND COMPANY   Boston

Drawings by ROGER H. MARTIN

and PATRICIA CHANDLER

Library of Congress Catalog Card Number 62-9969

Printed in the United States of America (6 I 2)

Preface

In *Homes with Character*, emphasis has been placed on developing within students a greater appreciation of their present homes from the family living, economic, aesthetic, and practical points of view. Consideration has also been given to helping students set up goals for their own homes which they will eventually establish. Organization and content have been selected and arranged to make the book usable wherever and whenever units on the home are taught at the secondary level. Thus the authors feel that the book will be of value to all whether they are enrolled in simple junior high school units or in more inclusive ones in the senior high school or junior college.

Furthermore, the authors recognize that providing a home for a family and living in that home is the prerogative of both men and women. Family needs, manner of living, and the cycle through which a family with children expands and contracts determine the type of dwelling which will be most satisfactory. Aesthetic, economic, and practical concern for the physical setup of the home is necessary if that home is to truly express character.

Food, clothing, and shelter are the three basic material needs of a family. Believing that the areas of foods and clothing have been more adequately cared for in home economics text materials than the area of housing, the authors feel that *Homes with Character* will serve a definite need in the field.

Organized in nine units of work, the text begins with a unit on what satisfactions one should expect to receive from a home and how a family's money must be spent. Units 2 and 3 are concerned with the choice or planning of the structure. Unit 4 presents color and design principles in terms of home decorating. Units 5, 6, and 7 are concerned with interior arrangements and furnishings. Unit 8 presents guides which the consumer will need in making purchases for the home, and Unit 9 deals with management, maintenance, and inexpensive improvements which can be made in the home.

Material in the book may be used in other sequences than in these particular units. For instance, walls, floors, windows, and furniture are discussed in two or three different units. Each approach is from a different angle—in one case, design or style; in another, consumer buying; and in the other, care. Should a class want to study furniture, for instance, the Table of Contents or the Index makes it easy to locate these approaches.

Following each unit a list of books, booklets, pamphlets, and sources from which other materials may be secured is given. At the close of each chapter Suggested Activities are provided to help students choose school and home problems or projects upon which they would like to work. The illustrations, which include sketches and photographs, were chosen to clarify and elaborate the text as much as possible.

In the revision of *Homes with Character*, it has been necessary to condense or delete some of the material in the first edition in order to cover as much new material as possible. The information on color and design has not been changed, because it is basic. However, many of the illustrations have been replaced, and new color pages have been inserted. The sections on home safety, budgets, and home financing have been brought up to date. The original material in the chapter on home architecture has been condensed in order to give space to newer approaches to housing. There is new information on livable floor plans, recommended room sizes, air conditioning, home wiring, and kitchen planning. The sections on floor coverings, paints, lighting, and windows have been completely revised. The chapter on home appliances has been rewritten to include the newer appliances. Textiles are classified according to the Textile Fiber Products Identification Act, which became effective in 1960. Some space is given to selecting stainless steel, plasticware, ovenware, and mattresses. References at the close of each section have been brought up to date.

Perhaps the greatest help to teachers will be the *Charts* to accompany *Homes with Character*. The charts in this guide parallel the book and help to make the material in the text directly applicable to the student's present home.

As in the case of the first edition, it is the hope of the authors that students and teachers will derive both satisfaction and fun from using this book. May there be many homes with improved character as a result.

HAZEL THOMPSON CRAIG
OLA DAY RUSH

Contents

1

Study
your family needs
and consider
what you want
in a home

ILLUSTRATION 1. *Comfort, convenience, and beauty are being planned into this contemporary living area by the family members.*

CHAPTER I

How much satisfaction does your home give your family?

HISTORIANS claim that the stabilizing force of a good home means more to any society than all the scientific achievements in the world. Do you agree? Certainly pleasant family relations and the proper emphasis on values come ahead of the location of the home and its furnishings. Nevertheless attractive surroundings and convenient work areas contribute to personal well-being and make relationships with others more pleasant.

In a study made by Dr. Virginia Cutler some time ago, husbands and wives were asked to rate in order ten values: comfort, convenience, friendship, health, safety, location, economy, personal interests, privacy, and beauty.

At the *upper income level* both husbands and wives emphasized comfort and friendship; at the *middle income level*, comfort and health; and at the *lower income level*, health, safety, and economy. It is not easy to separate values, because the emphasis on friendship and comfort would change if health, safety, and income were threatened.

All of these values influence family relationships. Some are basic and others aesthetic. Beauty and order are aesthetic values, but, consciously or unconsciously, people are affected by their surroundings. Big supermarkets are aware of this when they em-phasize eye appeal in shelf arrangements and provide soft background music.

Although the food, automobile, and other industries have taken advantage of research, home builders have not done so. To stimulate more interest in home planning for better living, the government initiated a "Women's Congress on Housing" attended by over one hundred homemakers. McCall's "Congress on Better Living" has continued these conferences. Builders and equipment manufacturers are now applying some of these homemakers' recommendations.

Among the things women want in a home are: more space indoors and outdoors; at least one full bath plus a washroom near the play area; a definite separation between activity and quiet areas; a kitchen from which to observe children at play; easy-to-maintain floors and counters; adequate storage space for clothing, hobby materials, toys, sports equipment, summer furniture; and fewer built-in luxury items.

★ **WHAT FEATURES PROVIDE COMFORT IN YOUR HOME?**

We may do many routine home jobs in an awkward way. Many of you may study in an uncomfortable position when a table, chair, and lamp for your use every evening could easily be arranged. Everyone may wish there were more really comfortable chairs in the house. When you are at home, go into each room and examine it from the comfort angle.

Working in comfort

Let us begin with the laundry. If you have an old-fashioned basement laundry, a heavy linoleum strip or rubber mat at the laundry tubs will absorb the shock of shoes clicking on a concrete floor. A shelf for soaps, bleaches, and so forth near the tubs or the washing machine will avoid stretching or bending to reach supplies. A carrier on wheels for the clothesbasket saves lifting and carrying wet clothes. Tight clotheslines within arm's reach will reduce discomfort in hanging up clothes. A high stool to sit on while ironing small pieces will save strength for other tasks. Arrangement of equipment is discussed on pages 85–87.

From the laundry let us enter the kitchen. Are table heights comfortable? The average 36-inch height for sink or cabinet may be too high for the short person. The usual 4-inch base for sink and cabinet need be only 3 inches high and still give toe room. The difference of 1 inch may eliminate working with shoulders and arms in a cramped position. Proper lighting, which is discussed further on page 69, is important in the kitchen to create comfortable working conditions.

Another important work area is the study area. Before you begin to study, try out different chairs, tables, and lighting arrangements until you feel that they will create the most comfortable conditions.

Relaxing in comfort

Proper rest each night is necessary if you are to enjoy the following day. A good firm mattress, a fluffy pillow of moderate size, and light warm bedding are more conducive to good rest than a soft mattress, a large heavy pillow, and thick bulky covers. One does not sleep comfortably in a room that is too hot. If bedroom radiators are turned off in the middle of the afternoon, the room will be more comfortable at bedtime.

When you relax by sitting down, you want to be comfortable. It is surprising how few

ILLUSTRATION 2. *A comfortable and an uncomfortable furniture arrangement. At the left the coffee table is so close to the divan and the chairs that people cannot get in and out of the furniture grouping without stumbling over the table. The grouping at the right makes the furniture easily accessible.*

homes have really comfortable chairs. And when a chair is uncomfortable, few people take the trouble to remedy the discomfort. Check your chairs to see whether springs need reconditioning. Make a cushion for a chair that is too deep to sit in comfortably. If your studio couch slides out from the wall when you lean against the cushions, place some rubber casters under the legs. Tables are often an uncomfortable height for the chairs used with them. Try rearranging some of your tables and chairs to find more comfortable combinations. Good lighting for reading, writing, and piano practice saves eyestrain and thereby contributes to everyday comfort.

Eating in comfort

To enjoy fully the pleasure of a meal, one must be comfortable. If the table is too low, place some casters under the legs. If the chairs are too low, add some attractively covered pads. If your junior high school brother cannot eat without practically lying on the table, find out if he is actually uncomfortable sitting up straight. And if so, work out a more comfortable plan. If you are serving refreshments at a party, don't expect to give people a cup of coffee and a plate of salad and have them eat in comfort without tables. Lap trays or nests of tables to supplement end tables will provide your guests with more comfort when refreshments are served.

✶ WHAT PRECAUTIONS ARE NECESSARY FOR HEALTH IN THE HOME?

A strong healthy body, a happy frame of mind, and freedom from emotional disturbances are all necessary to good health. A child may never have a disease and yet always be sick. Family jealousies, nagging, arguing, worry, suspicion, lack of interests, may keep a child constantly upset mentally and emotionally. If parents are happy, understanding, patient, and interested in their children's activities, the mental and emotional factors of health are negligible.

Good health insurance is dependent upon nutritious food, fresh air, proper clothing, adequate housing, restful sleep, personal cleanliness and cleanliness in one's surroundings, good posture, an interest in work and in wholesome recreation, wise safety precautions, and moderate living habits.

Nutritious food

Food is an exceedingly important factor in health. From your courses in food preparation and nutrition, you have learned what foods you need for good health. As a future homemaker you will know how to plan nutritious meals. And from a careful study of this book, you will learn how to plan a kitchen in which you will enjoy working, and how to provide a happy social atmosphere in which to serve meals.

Fresh air and proper clothing

Everyone should spend part of every day out of doors, provided the clothing worn is adequate for the weather. To maintain good health, you should have some ventilation during the night. Avoid sleeping in a draft, but get some fresh air unless your home is properly air conditioned. In wintertime the air in most homes is too dry. Although radiator pans are not the best solution for increasing the humidity, they help to make the air less dry. Some families are equipping certain rooms of the house with plug-in humidifiers that filter, wash, and circulate air. When porches are used as living, dining, or sleeping areas during warm weather, screens eliminate the menace of flies and mosquitoes.

Adequate housing

Space for living, eating, sleeping, and recreation are essential in maintaining good health standards. Living in an apartment is convenient, economical, and easy, but too often it deprives one of freedom and privacy, especially if families are large.

Cleanliness

Hands should always be washed before handling food. Nails should be kept filed and clean because germs remain under the nails and are often transferred to food. Nostrils, hair, scalp, and feet need special care for good health. The annoying housefly and kitchen garbage pail are two of the worst health hazards. Be sure that all screens are tight and free from holes, and swat every fly you see. Keep food covered and in the proper place until ready to be eaten. Wash all foods that are to be eaten raw. Line the garbage pail with a paper bag. Wash and rinse the pail with boiling water, and air it regularly. If garbage is not collected frequently, sprays to control flies and other insects are obtainable.

ILLUSTRATION 3. *For your medicine chest — aspirin, ice bag, witch hazel, oil of cloves, syringe, soda, cotton, bandages, burn ointment, hot water bottle, thermometer, eye cup, eye wash, antiseptic, sterile pads, adhesive tape, medicine dropper, ammonia.*

A first-aid cabinet

Any family is likely to have some sickness and accidents during a year. In many cases the supplies in the medicine cabinet are inadequate to meet everyday needs. Check your medicine cabinet to make sure that it contains the supplies listed in Illustration 3.

ILLUSTRATION 4. *How safe is your room? Long extension cords, sewing equipment left lying around, unanchored scatter rugs, drawers left open, overflowing wastebaskets, all are safety hazards.*

If you have a piano, you need a cabinet within easy reach for your sheets and books of music. And if you have a phonograph, you want a convenient storage cabinet for records. Near your sewing and mending center you need shelves or a cabinet adequate for sewing supplies, patterns, materials, and clothing to be mended. Near your bed, you may need a table with a top large enough for a book, lamp, and clock and with a drawer or extra shelf for incidentals. Consider convenience in letter writing. Have you a convenient place for note paper, writing paper, post cards, pen, eraser, ink, and stamps? Right now, you can make many changes at little or no cost which will add greatly to ease and satisfaction in living.

✶ HOW SATISFACTORY IS THE LOCATION OF YOUR HOME?

Although choosing a homesite is discussed more fully in Unit 2, pages 33–37, a few general questions pertaining to location are raised here. Does the location of your home give satisfaction or dissatisfaction? Is your home located in a satisfying community? Does the neighborhood take pride in the appearance of its homes? Is there a satisfactory place for young children to play? Are there any health or safety hazards or business noises that make living in your community a danger or a nuisance?

Is your home conveniently located in regard to distances from work, school, church, transportation facilities, shopping centers, recreational facilities, provision for fire protection, and other community services? Exposure, space around the home, the type of terrain, are also important in judging a homesite. If you will judge various homes you visit, noting the desirable and undesirable features, you will be in a better position to judge your own homesite now or sometime in the future.

✶ WHAT CONSIDERATIONS INSURE PRIVACY IN THE HOME?

Many young married couples begin homemaking in a one- or two-room apartment. When a baby arrives, the privacy of mother and father is infringed upon. For fear of disturbing the baby, mother and father must share one room evening after evening. Sometimes one or the other would like a little privacy to read in quiet, to listen to a football game, or to have a "hen" or a "stag" party. No matter how much a couple enjoy each other's companionship, there are times when privacy is desired. The wise couple will plan ahead when they anticipate sharing a room with a new member. A high screen will shield the baby's crib from the light of an ordinary lamp. Or a gooseneck student lamp will provide ample light for reading or mending without giving too much light in that part of the bedroom where the baby is sleeping. One of the parents can go to the bedroom for a quiet hour if the radio is disturbing or if callers stop by to visit with the other parent. If some forethought is not given to privacy in the home, either the husband or the wife will start "running out" after dinner to get away for a little while. Soon the "little while" may become an entire evening, and many evenings.

Even a small child enjoys the privacy and independence of his own room, and whenever possible each child should have his or her own room. This is particularly important if the children are of the opposite sex, or if they are of the same sex but of widely different ages and interests. Sometimes families think that a room built as a guest room or a dining room must retain its original purpose, while the house could be made much more livable if it were studied from the angle of family needs and interests. A too large kitchen may be made to include a dining area, thus releasing the dining room for other purposes. Or a much needed laundry alcove may be worked out in the oversized kitchen, so that laundering may be dovetailed with kitchen work.

Suppose a family of four — mother, father, and a growing son and daughter — must live in a five-room house. They need at least three bedrooms. Space for dining, living, and preparing food — to say nothing of other activities — must be provided. How will the family plan to use the rooms in their home?

One family solved the problem by converting unused basement space into quarters for the son. They finished the walls and ceiling of this basement room, and built a double closet with ample shelves, and a bookcase with desk compartments. An alcove in the room served as a workshop for the boy. The addition of a card table, some chairs, a chest of drawers, a studio couch, and a bedside table gave the boy a room that insured privacy and met his needs and interests. Of course a basement bedroom must be dry, so that it is healthful.

Another family decided that a dining room, which would be used on an average of one hour a day, was a luxury they could not afford. They installed a table to drop from the kitchen wall when needed for breakfast and for noon snacks, and bought a good-sized, drop-leaf table to use in the living room for the evening meal. Thus the space intended for a dining room could serve as a bedroom for the daughter, and later as a recreation room for family fun when the daughter left for college.

As teen agers, you fully appreciate the meaning of privacy. You like your own bedroom with an extra bed if possible or extra sleeping space so that you can invite a friend to spend the night occasionally. After you finish high school, if you live at home and work or go to college, you may want to completely redecorate your bedroom to resemble a one-room apartment. A studio couch may serve as a bed and sofa, and a chest of drawers as a dressing table. You may want to replace your study table with a desk and add additional bookcases. To these necessities, you may want to add a fold-away coffee table, a card table, and some easy chairs, end tables, and lamps. Thus equipped, you could entertain privately should your parents have guests in the living room.

Other considerations pertaining to privacy in your home that you as teen agers expect may include the following:

1. A telephone near a door, so that the telephone may be temporarily removed from the room if others are occupying the room. It is assumed that you will not monopolize the telephone.

2. An unwritten law that every member of the family will knock before entering your bedroom, and that no one will enter the bathroom while it is occupied

3. An understanding that no drawer in your bedroom will be opened without your knowledge, and of course, that no mail of yours will be opened or read

If you establish habits now that provide for privacy, you will benefit in the future. There are times in the lives of all of us when we want to be alone, and it is good for us to be alone. Few people realize this, and allow themselves to get on other people's nerves. Of course, respect for privacy calls for the golden rule. One should accord the same consideration to privacy for others in the family that he wants for himself.

✦ WHAT EFFECT DOES ECONOMY HAVE UPON HOME STANDARDS?

In the study by Dr. Cutler mentioned at the beginning of this chapter, the economy value was at the *top* of the list made by wives in the lower-income group and at the *bottom* of the list made by wives in the upper-income group. Wives in the middle-income group rated economy in eighth place. On a low income every cent counts, and as the income increases the economy value is overshadowed by comfort, friendship, and health.

It may be false economy for both husband and wife to work outside the home. This is particularly true if they are letting money "run through their fingers" merely because it is plentiful, or if they are forming bad spending habits that may be hard to break should it become necessary to live on one income. If the two incomes are to be used to buy furniture or a home, to send children to college, or to lay away a nest egg for the future, a working partnership may be good.

In any partnership, particularly that of homemaking, good money management is essential. Every member of the family needs to understand how the family income must be distributed. Good business practices must be followed in record keeping and in locating unwise expenditures. A study of spending the family income is given in Chapter 2, Unit 1, pages 18–24.

People do not learn to manage money without experience in managing it. If children are to learn how to use it, those of junior high school age or even younger should be given an allowance with certain responsibilities for using their money wisely.

You may save several dollars a week on *food* by reading the food store ads and laying away nonperishable food that is on sale; by studying recipes for attractive, economical, and nourishing dishes; by cooking in the proper quantities; and by storing your food to prevent spoilage. You may save a great deal on *clothing* expenditures by removing spots and pressing your own clothing; by learning how to sew and mend; by watching store ads for special sales; and by reading labels and knowing what to look for in buying a new garment. You may clip a few dollars off *other expenses* by turning off light switches and the burners of your range when they are not in use; by repairing the leak in a faucet; by getting proper rest to keep up your resistance to sickness; by patronizing a neighborhood movie instead of a more expensive one downtown; and by waxing your floors and furniture to save wear.

Economy should be a regular practice but not to the extent that all the pleasure of entertaining or buying something new is taken away because you are overly money conscious.

✶ HOW MAY BEAUTY AFFECT HOME ENJOYMENT?

Some people may think that it doesn't matter whether a home is bright and cheerful or ordinary and dull. But brightness or dullness has a psychological effect on everyone. School children quickly notice a bright new dress a teacher is wearing or an interesting new picture on the classroom wall. Those in charge of hotels, restaurants, schools, and factories are becoming more and more aware of the effect cheerful surroundings have upon people. Color and lighting experts are consulted in building or remodeling hotels, schools, and factories.

Color and arrangement have a greater effect upon your daily living than you sometimes realize. A cheerful kitchen, an attractive tablecloth and dishes, and a little extra attention given to serving an attractive breakfast plate certainly starts the day off to advantage. Make dinner a social time for the family. If you have pretty china, silver, glassware, and tablecloths or doilies, use them. Don't wait until the last minute and throw just any old thing on the table. Set the table ahead of time, and occasionally eat by candlelight. Keep a little surprise in store to add an **extra**

ILLUSTRATION 7.   *Greater privacy may be secured with attractive looking and sound-resistant folding doors.*

touch of charm and beauty to the evening meal at least one night a week. Share this responsibility with your young brothers and sisters; let each one have a chance to plan the surprise or new note of interest.

An attractive, orderly living room radiates hospitality. Interestingly decorated windows and attractive lamps lend a final touch to either expensive or inexpensive furnishings. Choose colors that are keyed to each other. And enjoy living with the colors you like whether or not they express the popular trend. Each member of the family is conscious of beauty in the home, and a family consultation should be held when new paper, draperies, a piece of furniture, or a picture is to be bought.

✶ HOW MAY FRIENDSHIPS BE MADE MORE ENJOYABLE IN THE HOME?

Some of the fundamentals basic to any friendship are understanding individual differences, sharing responsibilities, winning each other's trust and confidence, sympathizing with each other's problems, and enjoying similar interests and activities. Parents may encourage friendship with their children by avoiding arguments, by refraining from nagging, by resisting the temptation to delve too deeply into their children's affairs, by allowing them a reasonable amount of freedom, by encouraging them to contribute to the conversation, by listening attentively to them, and by sharing their joys and disappointments. Teen-age boys and girls who share in the family responsibilities by offering to help at home, who respond promptly and willingly when asked to do a favor, who accept the opportunity to go out with their parents, or who share in social events at home are not only building up lifelong friendships with their parents but are better equipping themselves to establish happy homes of their own.

The home in which the family lives can actually interfere with friendship — when there is no provision for sharing interests and activities, when inconvenient arrangements make unnecessary work, when there is insufficient space for necessary privacy, when the home is so unattractive that its members prefer to be elsewhere. Kitchens that are too small for more than one person to work in, that provide no space for the baby's playpen or the older children's toys; living rooms that are too "primped up" to be lived in; or bedrooms that make no provision for an occasional private talk are not conducive to family friendship.

Provision in the home for friendship with those outside the family is also important. Mother and father and brother and sister want to invite their friends in, singly or in groups, for individual or family visits. An atmosphere that makes guests welcome, room for guests at meals, space for visiting, a quiet place for mother and dad when the teen-age group wants to play records or hear a radio program, a place for the rest of the family to gather when sister entertains her date in the living room — these are some of the provisions a home may offer for friendships with those outside the family.

✦ HOW DO PERSONAL INTERESTS INFLUENCE HOME PLANNING?

Happy is the man or woman, girl or boy, who has a variety of interests and hobbies. Parents should encourage their children's

hobbies and interests by providing time and space for them. The small child is content with his toys, but with the school-age child personal interests become more varied. Personal interests of the growing boy and girl run the gamut from collecting insects, stones, stamps, cards, or coins to building model boats or airplanes, painting, sewing, playing or listening to music, making amateur photographs, and so on.

What do members of your family do for fun? Perhaps you or some member of your family would like to develop some interesting hobbies. Examine the following lists, and on a separate piece of paper check the activities you and other members of your family enjoy or think you would enjoy. Do not write in this book.

What *sports* do you enjoy? Indicate (P) if you enjoy them as a participant or (S) if as a spectator.

Archery	Badminton	Bicycling
Golf	Aviation	Boating or sailing
Skiing	Baseball	Hockey
Boxing	Basketball	Hunting
Tennis	Camping	Ice skating
Hiking	Fencing	Swimming
Fishing	Croquet	Roller skating
Riding	Bowling	Horseback riding

What types of *collections* may furnish a hobby?

Bottles	Butterflies	Antique furniture
Coins	Autographs	Miniature furniture
Dolls	Stamps	Rare books
Rocks	Jewelry	Antique glass
Shells	Rare prints	

What types of *handwork* provide interesting hobbies?

Basketry	Block printing
Cartooning	Kite making
Ceramics	Leather tooling
Embroidery	Photograph developing
Sewing	Textile painting
Weaving	Soapbox racer building

Crocheting	Model building
Puppetry	(boats, airplanes)
Metal craft	Soap sculpture
Knitting	Wood carving
Book binding	

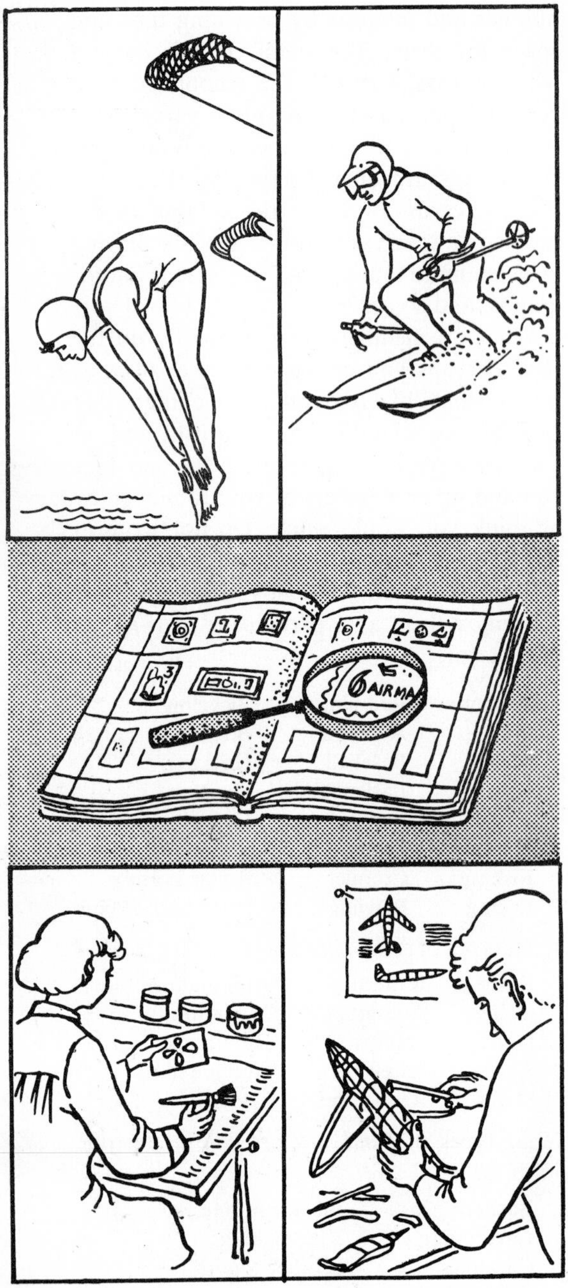

What are your *cultural interests?*

Concerts	Listening to recorded music
Lectures	Oil painting
Dramatics	Piano playing
Photography	Violin or other instrument
Theater	playing
Singing	Water-color painting
Nature study	

What are your *additional interests?*

Bridge	Livestock raising
Bee raising	Magic tricks
Card games	Nature study
Cooking	Pets
Gardening	Radio

Now that you have checked your interests, what provisions can you make to enjoy these interests more fully? You can readily see why hobbies and interests influence home planning. If one family member enjoys ice skating, riding, and skiing; another, bicycling, playing tennis, and fishing; another, playing the violin and oil painting; and still another, developing photographs, space will have to be planned not only for enjoying some of these pleasures but for storing all the necessary equipment.

There is nothing more relaxing and satisfying than to have an opportunity sometime during the week to indulge in your favorite pastime. If you know of some secret urge a member of your family has to try out a new interest, plan to have that person receive a Christmas or birthday gift that will stimulate such an interest. Your mother may help you shift furnishings around a little to provide space for that new interest. Too many people fail to develop interesting avocations or hobbies simply because of lack of encourage-

ILLUSTRATION 8A. *What do you do for fun? Do you swim, ski, collect stamps, paint textiles, build models?*

ment or hindrances of one type or another that can easily be overcome.

If your home can provide all of Dr. Cutler's values discussed above, you may be assured that it will give satisfaction to the entire family, and that it is the kind of home to which children will always want to return.

SUGGESTED ACTIVITIES

1. Decide on the three values you would rate first in the enjoyment of your home. Which of Dr. Cutler's values would you rate last?

2. Study your home, inside and out, to determine the prevailing impression given by its appearance. Is it formal or informal? Is it quiet or gay? Is it spacious or compact?

3. Decide whether or not the prevailing impression given by your home reflects the predominant traits and interests of your family.

4. List habitual or occasional practices of members of your family which are objectionable from the standpoint of respect for the privacy of others. How can you help to correct some of these practices?

5. If you are a baby sitter, tell the class what safety precautions you use with children.

6. Name some of the advantages and disadvantages in the location of your home.

7. Plan what you can do to make better provisions for the development of friendships in your home.

8. Check your home from basement to bedroom, and list some changes that will make your home (a) more comfortable, (b) safer, and (c) more convenient.

9. Rearrange the closet, dresser drawers, and desk or study table in your room to provide greater convenience.

10. Determine how well your home provides for the health of its members.

11. Talk over with your family their special hobbies or interests, and plan how your home can better provide for these interests.

8B. *Or do you like piano playing, gardening, or rabbit raising? Does your home provide space for your hobby?*

CHAPTER 2

How must your family's money be spent?

How difficult it is sometimes to live within our means! No matter how carefully spending plans are made something always seems to come along to "upset the applecart." Even so we must have some basis for distributing the income if it is to meet family needs.

Some of the things we should know in order to spend wisely are the following: (1) why expenditures differ for different families; (2) why expenditures vary during the lifetime of a family; (3) what a budget is; (4) what expenditures a budget must cover; (5) how income is distributed among expenditures; and (6) what sources are included in income.

✶ WHY DO FAMILY EXPENDITURES DIFFER?

A number of factors influence the way various families spend their incomes. Families living in a city will have to pay more rent for the same size and style house than they would in a small town. However, the higher city salaries may not alter too much the percentage of the income spent on a home. A family of six naturally must spend a much larger proportion of money for food, clothing, and rent than a family of three. Prolonged illness, accidents, and the unforeseen responsibility of caring for relatives will knock to pieces any plan for spending. The interests

and desires of the family will also affect spending habits. Some families will curtail present expenses in order to send their children to college. Some families may prefer spending money on entertaining, while others spend money on books, music, and the like. Thus future goals affect immediate practices.

✶ WHY DO EXPENDITURES VARY DURING A FAMILY'S LIFETIME?

In *Houses for Family Living*, a booklet published by the Woman's Foundation, the expansion and contraction of the family unit is interestingly presented. The "early years" of married life is the first stage described. During this period of from one to three years, expenses for initial furnishings are great. The homemaker has a dumbbell-shaped day with activities concentrated in the early morning and late afternoon. Her working week averages about forty hours. This is the period when good housekeeping, marketing, and food preparation procedures should be perfected to make the "crowded years" ahead run more smoothly.

The "crowded years" begin when the first new member of the family arrives and continue until the last child enters school. During this period the workday bulges in the middle and takes the form of an egg. Expenditures on movies, meals out, and new clothes are trimmed to bare necessities, and money spent on food and additional home furnishings is increased. It is during this period, which may begin during the second year and last until the fifteenth year, that the homemaker benefits from her early practices in good time and good money management. With the arrival of the first child, the forty-hour week increases to a sixty-hour week, and as the size of the family increases, the work week may even extend to a hundred hours.

Following the "crowded years" come the "peak years," the period when the children

| EARLY YEARS | CROWDED YEARS | PEAK YEARS | LATER YEARS |
| From 1 to 3 | From 2 to 15? | From 12 to 27 | From 25 to 40 |

ILLUSTRATION 9.   *The family life cycle. Each of the four periods into which a family's life falls has unique characteristics. Demands on the house are greatest during the peak years when the children are growing up and the parents have more freedom, and decline as the children leave.*

are all in school. Household duties become more regular, and each family member usually has some home responsibility. It is a most stimulating period for parents. The mother has more time for activities outside the home and even though the father may feel overtaxed in meeting financial responsibilities, both parents should experience the complete satisfaction of living that comes only to a family with children. The food budget increases. Mother and dad continue to wear last year's clothes, postpone buying a new car, and sacrifice summer vacations in order to see that their children have all the advantages possible. Some parents are prone to mortgage their future by trying to give their children more than they can afford.

The "peak years" represent the climax in the family pattern. When the last child leaves home, the house seems empty, and the long full years are only memories. There is almost too much time on hand especially if the parents have failed to provide themselves with an outlet — some kind of hobby, church or social work, or civic enterprise. The big house is not needed, and is often sold or converted into a two- or three-family house. Financial demands are suddenly decreased. But the earning capacity of the family head has reached its peak, and retirement years are close at hand. The parents realize their mistake if they have not provided for the "late years" both in personal interests and in financial arrangements.

In most cases a carefully planned money and time management budget, faithfully practiced, can provide the necessities for each period as it arises.

✦ WHAT IS A BUDGET?

A budget is a record of past expenditures, an estimate of future expenditures, and an itemization of current expenses over a certain period of time. The budget should be discussed and planned by the entire family, so that each member will understand his responsibility in making it work.

There are a number of steps in making a budget. *First*, record all forms of income; *second*, list all fixed expenses and estimate all anticipated expenses; *third*, study present spending habits and determine where you can wisely curtail expenses; *fourth*, study unusual anticipated expenses to determine whether the satisfaction received will justify the expenditures; and *fifth*, find out the best means of investing part of the income.

The benefits of keeping a budget are that (1) money is set aside for necessities, and future purchases are planned; (2) individual family members understand their responsibilities in sharing income; (3) the wage earner is relieved of the constant strain of meeting family demands; (4) family members learn the value of cooperation; and (5) a record of expenditures is available for future reference.

✦ WHAT EXPENDITURES MUST A BUDGET COVER?

By far the major part of income in most families is spent for essentials. Some of these essential expenditures amount to a definite sum each year or each month, and thus may be called *fixed expenditures*.

Fixed expenditures include rent or payments on a home, taxes, interest, insurance, public utilities (water, gas, electricity, and telephone), fuel, payments on household articles, carfare to and from work, maid service, and church and club contributions. From last year's receipts, it will be easy to list these expenses. Sometimes fixed expenditures may be reduced by finding cheaper rent, conserving utilities, and doing without maid service and club memberships. But on the whole, they cannot be greatly reduced.

Other expenses may vary somewhat from month to month, and may be called *flexible expenditures.* Flexible expenditures include food, clothing, new furnishings, gasoline, personal articles, health (for doctor, dentist, drug, and hospital bills), education, magazine and periodical subscriptions, recreation, charity, and gifts. Of all the flexible expenses, food will vary the least.

The money spent on clothing and home furnishings may vary greatly depending upon how skillful the homemaker is with tools and a needle, and how willing the family is to do without luxuries. Inexpensive wholesome forms of recreation may be found to replace movies and expensive parties.

In attempting to cut down expenses, a family should look for needless expenditures and evidences of waste rather than basically reducing its standard of living unless a basic reduction cannot be avoided.

★ **HOW ARE BUDGETS PLANNED?**

A budget or spending plan is just as necessary for a family as it is for any government or business. When expenses are tailored to income, heavy debts will not be incurred.

It is impossible to establish percentages that will apply to every family because families vary in number and members vary in age; satisfactions expected are never the same; interests, activities, and obligations differ. The editors of *Changing Times* have suggested flexible budget percentages at several income levels as shown in the column opposite.

An interim study of the city worker's family budget was made during the fall of 1959 by the Bureau of Labor Statistics to determine the income needed for a family of four to live adequately in twenty major cities.* This "typical" family included a husband and wife, a girl in grade school, and a boy in junior high school. In all these urban studies,

* "The Interim City Worker's Family Budget," *Monthly Labor Review*, August, 1960

FAMILY BUDGET AT THREE INCOME LEVELS
(after taxes)

Item	$3100 to $5500	$5600 to $9500	$9600 to $14,000
Food	30–40%	18–30%	15–20%
Housing	15–25	15–25	15–20
Household operation	5–10	5–10	5–10
Furnishings	3–4	3–4	4–5
Clothing	10–15	10–12	5–10
Car operation	6–8	4–7	3–5
Medical	5–10	5–10	3–6
Personal expense	3–10	3–7	3–7
Recreation and education	5–10	5–10	5–10
Gifts and contributions	2–5	2–5	4–10
Life insurance	2–5	4–5	5–8
Operating margin	1–15	1–20	1–25

Reprinted by permission from *Changing Times*, the Kiplinger Magazine

the wife was not employed outside the home. "Adequate living" provides a five-room rented dwelling, central heat, bathroom, telephone, television, hot and cold running water, limited entertainment and travel, and a used car every three years.

Sometime during the mid-sixties a more thorough study of the city worker's family budget will be made.

Many factors have made it necessary to update the original budget. The average family income rose from just above $4000 in 1946–47 to over $7000 in 1959–60. (More than one income may be included in family income if more than one family member is employed.) However, the average family income is higher than necessary to provide adequate living even in the most expensive city. This means that more families have greater discretionary income for items formerly deemed luxuries.

Family income has many hidden benefits. Fringe benefits in business and industry provide a yearly average of $980 per employee. These benefits include the employer's share of social security, pensions, paid vacations, sick leave, on-the-job medical care and physical examinations, parking facilities, group health and life insurance, discounts on company products, bonuses, and profit sharing.

Inflation and increased income taxes have caused the dollar to have less buying power than in 1946–47. The cost of goods and services has been increasing at approximately 2 per cent yearly. If inflation continues at this rate, it will take 20 per cent more income in 1970 to maintain the same standard of living as in 1960. Yet the average $7000 family income bought more goods and services in 1959–60 than the average $4000 family income bought in 1946–47.

The income needed to provide the "typical" family with adequate living in *The City Worker's Family Budget* ranged from $5320 in Houston to $6567 in Chicago and Seattle. In this interim study, Washington, D.C., was used as the control city representing 100 per cent with an annual income of $6147. How this income was distributed is shown.

BUDGET FOR A FAMILY OF FOUR IN
WASHINGTON, D.C. — FALL, 1959

Item	Amount	Per cent
Food	$1684	27.4
Housing	1226	20.0
Clothing	676	11.0
Transportation	615	10.0
Medical care	400	6.5
Insurance, occupational expenses, social security deductions	258	4.2
Personal taxes	690	11.2
Other goods and services	598	9.7
Total	$6147	100.0

Food costs in Pittsburgh were 12 per cent higher than in Washington and 24 per cent (a yearly difference of $400) higher than in Houston. Rents, heat, and utilities were 13 per cent higher in Chicago than in Washington and 35 per cent higher than in Philadelphia. The cost of other goods and services ranged from $2175 in Atlanta to $2470 in Chicago. These items included clothing, home furnishings, transportation, medical care, personal care, house operation, reading, recreation, education, tobacco, gifts, and contributions.

The allowance for life insurance was set at $138 and social security deductions at $120 in all areas. Federal, state, and local income taxes were adjusted according to the locality.

It is estimated that a husband and wife can live adequately on 66 per cent of the income necessary for a four-member family; a husband, wife, and one child between 6 and 16, on 87 per cent; and a five-person family, on 120 per cent.

This study, of course, has its limitations. In the first place, only a certain percentage of families would come under the description of the "typical" family. The study assumes that the family will pay rent, whereas many families in this stage of the family cycle are making payments on a home. The twenty cities studied are geographically representative, but not an accurate criterion of living costs all over the country. Over a period of a year living costs will vary considerably, even in one locality. And to be able to live in a larger home, buy a new car, take an extended vacation, give a home to a relative, or educate children beyond high school would require more than the amount allowed in this study for "adequate living." However, the study can serve as a basis in helping city families with school children to estimate a budget within which to live adequately.

✱ **WHAT SOURCES ARE IN-CLUDED IN INCOME?**

Income is generally thought of as money received in salary or wages over a definite period of time — day, week, month, or year. *Salary or wage income* is what most people count on for their living, and will be discussed before other types of income are mentioned. Salary or wage income may be earned by the father, by the mother, by both the father and the mother, or by the father, mother, and one or two older children in the family.

Some workers are employed by the job, and are paid when the job is completed or on a daily basis, or by the hour. Naturally their income varies. Many workers are employed by the week, and under normal circumstances, they can count on a fixed weekly income. Others receive monthly or bimonthly pay checks of a fixed amount. Those who are dependent on the land, such as farmers and cattle raisers, receive their incomes once a year at crop- or cattle-selling time. They cannot predict exactly what their income will be.

Rents are usually paid by the month, and stores and banks send out monthly statements of accounts. In many respects, budgeting is easier when income is on a monthly basis, but the same general principles can be applied to other income bases.

In addition to the regular wage or salary income, a family may have an *occasional income;* an *investment income;* or a *gift* or *inheritance income.* An occasional income may be earned when a member of a family works for short periods — perhaps before or after regular working hours. Part-time selling or working in any business or industry during periodic rush seasons may be the source of this income. Investment income is derived from interest on loans, stocks or bonds or from rent on real estate. Gift or inheritance income is received from others, usually relatives, and is likely to come in a sizable sum. It should be used wisely on such things as canceling debts and making payments on a home, or if there is no immediate need, it should be laid away for the future.

Another source of income, although not often thought of as such, is *home management income* or money saved by the homemaker's work and by her efficient running of the home. If all the meals eaten by the family had to be bought in a restaurant and if all the housekeeping had to be done by a paid employee, the homemaker's contribution would soon amount to a considerable sum. Likewise, money saved by making wise purchases for the family and by economies in operating the home amount to additional income for the family.

SUGGESTED ACTIVITIES

1. List the conditions that will cause the budgets of different families in your class to differ.

2. Divide the expected span of your family pattern into "early," "crowded," "peak," and "late" years beginning with the year your mother and father were married. (Assume that the youngest child in your family will leave home at 18.)

3. If you do not already do so, keep a record of your own expenses. Study your habits of spending money, and plan how you can help stretch your family's income.

4. Make a collection of personal and family expense account books, and arrange a class exhibit.

5. Find out what per cent of your family's income is spent on housing. How does it compare with the percentage spent for housing by the Washington family?

6. Sit down with your family and list all immediate and future sources of income for a year. List your probable expenses for the year, and plan a budget.

SELECTED REFERENCES
FOR UNIT ONE

BOOKS

Bradley, Joseph F., and Wherry, Ralph H., *Personal and Family Finance*. Holt, Rinehart & Winston, Inc., New York, 1957

Duvall, Evelyn Millis, *Family Development*. J. B. Lippincott Company, Philadelphia, 1957

Faulkner, Ray, and Faulkner, Sarah, *Inside Today's Home*, Revised. Holt, Rinehart and Winston, Inc., New York, 1960

Fleck, Henrietta, Fernandez, Louise, and Munves, Elizabeth, *Exploring Home and Family Living*. Prentice-Hall, Inc., Englewood Cliffs, N.J., 1959

Hatcher, Hazel M., and Andrews, Mildred E., *Adventuring in Home Living, Book 2*. D. C. Heath and Company, Boston, 1959

McDermott, Irene E., and Nicholas, Florence W., *Homemaking for Teen-Agers, Book 2*. Charles A. Bennett Company, Inc., Peoria, Illinois, 1958

Rhodes, Kathleen, and Samples, Merna A., *Your Life in the Family*. J. B. Lippincott Company, Philadelphia, 1959

Townsend, Gilbert, and Dalzell, J. Ralph, *How to Plan a House*, Revised. American Technical Society, Chicago, 1958

Troelstrup, Arch W., *Consumer Problems and Personal Finance*. McGraw-Hill Book Company, Inc., New York, 1957

Wilhelms, Fred T., and Heimerl, Raymond P., *Consumer Economics — Principles and Problems*, Revised. McGraw-Hill Book Company, Inc., New York, 1959

CURRENT PUBLICATIONS

Write to the following addresses for current lists of literature, with prices:

ACTION, Box 462, Radio City Station, New York 20, New York (*better neighborhoods*)

Better Light Better Sight Bureau, 750 Third Avenue, New York 17, New York (*home lighting*)

Institute of Life Insurance, 488 Madison Avenue, New York 22, New York (*family protection*)

Metropolitan Life Insurance Company, One Madison Avenue, New York 10, New York (*family protection and home safety*)

Money Management Institute, Household Finance Corporation, Prudential Plaza, Chicago 1, Illinois (filmstrips available too)

Children's Spending
Consumer Credit Facts for You
For Young Moderns
Your Automobile Dollar
Your Budget
Your Clothing Dollar
Your Equipment Dollar
Your Food Dollar
Your Health and Recreation Dollar
Your Home Furnishings Dollar
Your Savings and Investment Dollar
Your Shelter Dollar
Your Shopping Dollar

National Safety Council, 425 North Michigan Avenue, Chicago 11, Illinois (*home safety*)

New Castle Products, Inc., New Castle, Indiana (*Modernfold doors*)

Owens-Corning Fiberglas Corporation, Toledo 1, Ohio (*choosing a home*)

U.S. Government Printing Office, Washington 25, D.C. (*publications for the homemaker*)

2

Learn
how to judge
values
when you buy,
build, or rent

ILLUSTRATION 10. *When arranging for the financing of a home, either ready built or being planned to fit your lot and your needs, consider that the extra money is well spent for such things as sturdy exterior finish, good insulation, and a step-saving floor plan.*

CHAPTER I

How will you finance the purchase of a house?

A HOME represents such a big purchase that buying plans should be made slowly and carefully. Although about six families in ten "own their own homes," the majority of these homes are mortgaged.

✸ WHAT WILL INFLUENCE YOUR DECISION TO OWN A HOME?

The question of whether to own a house or not is debatable. The answer may be *yes* (1) if you run a farm and feel that you will spend your lifetime there; (2) if you own your own business, or if your promotion opportunities are limited to the community in which you live; (3) if you can be reasonably sure that the character of the neighborhood in which you buy will not deteriorate; (4) if you are assured of a stable income; (5) if you can build or purchase a home at a price you can afford; (6) if you prefer to have the greater part of your savings invested in a home; (7) if owning a home will give your family greater security and prestige in your neighborhood; (8) if you are willing to cut down on vacations, travel expense, use of your car, and entertaining to pay for your home; (9) if you are young and can liquidate your mortgage before your earning power decreases; (10) if you desire the independence of owning your own home in your old age.

The answer may be *no* (1) if you are in any position where promotion will change the locality in which you live; (2) if you dislike the responsibility and methodical care and upkeep of a house; (3) if you prefer to live "cramped up" in the winter to save your money for a long summer vacation in the mountains, at the seashore, or traveling; (4) if the character of the neighborhood is apt to be unstable; (5) if you are thinking of trying out a new kind of work; (6) if your income fluctuates.

✸ HOW MUCH DOES IT COST TO OWN A HOME?

If the answers to most of the questions above indicate that you would be a good prospect for home ownership, the next question is "How much can I afford to pay for a house?" Roughly, the answer is two to two-and-a-half times your annual income, if the head of the family has a job that is secure and the income is stable. If the family is large, you naturally spend a larger proportion of income for clothing and food, and therefore you will have less to invest in a home without considerable sacrifice.

If your family's yearly income is $6000, and if you plan to spend two to two-and-a-half times your income on a house, $15,000 maximum cost is indicated. This cost could be met over a period of years without undue hardship. Your family should study its financial situation; list all its assets that can be turned into cash; and then consult banks or other lending agencies for comparative rates and conditions.

Down payment and mortgage

Through the Federal Housing Administration (FHA) and Veterans Administration (VA) home ownership is possible for more people. Mortgage rates for FHA comply with the Housing Act passed June 30, 1961. VA loans will expire after July 25, 1962, unless Congress extends the privilege. The FHA has financed about 27 per cent of home loans in the past 25 years. The down payment on an FHA home loan is much lower than it is on a conventional loan. Some veterans may be able to obtain low- or no-down-payment VA loans. Some agencies will not finance FHA and VA loans.

Although many people like a low down payment and a long term over which to repay a loan, they often do not realize that a low down payment means a larger mortgage involving higher interest costs over a longer period. It is usually advisable to make *as large a down payment as possible*. On a conventional loan the down payment is usually between a fourth and third of the value of the house. The majority of homes are financed by conventional loans.

Through the FHA a family may apply for a loan up to $25,000 for a single-family dwelling. The down payment is determined thus: 3 per cent on the first $15,000 or less; *plus* 10 per cent on the next $5000; *plus* 25 per cent of all over $20,000. The mortgage payments may extend over any period up to 35 years. In an FHA mortgage there is a penalty if the mortgage is paid off before

the contract period expires. Most conventional mortgages are open-end mortgages — which means that the mortgage may be paid off at any time before the mortgage period expires without a penalty.

Let's contrast the down payment on a $22,000 house financed by an FHA and by a conventional type loan. On the first $15,000 of an FHA loan the down payment would be 3 per cent ($450), plus 10 per cent of the next $5000 ($500), plus 25 per cent of the $2000 over $20,000 ($500). Thus the down payment on a $22,000 home financed through FHA would be $1450. For homes costing up to $15,000, the minimum down payment through FHA is $450 with monthly payments of $81.84.

The down payment on a conventional loan for a $22,000 house would be between a fourth and a third of the house cost, or between $5500 and $7333. The total amount of interest paid on a conventional loan would, of course, be much less.

If you are assuming an existing mortgage you should have a lawyer go over all the terms with you. If you are applying for a construction loan (a loan to build), you may be able to arrange to have mortgage payments increased as the building progresses.

Trading a home

About one family in three who buys a new home already has a home but wants a larger or more modern one. It is not as easy to trade a home as it is to trade a car, because few homes are standardized. About one family in every 100 actually trades a house, in contrast to 85 in 100 who trade cars. Home owners between thirty and forty years old with two or three children are the best prospects. Trade-ins may be on a *straight trade-in* the same way a car is traded, on a *guarantee* that the house will be sold, or on a *conditional contract* which reserves the right to eventual ownership after a specified time.

Monthly payments, insurance, taxes

If a new house, appraised at $18,000, is paid for over a period of 15 years, monthly payments will be approximately $140 on an FHA loan (down payment $1400) and $114 on a conventional loan (down payment $4500). To these amounts must be added insurance and taxes.

Home owner's insurance offers the best protection if the owner lives in the house. Under one policy, the owner may obtain fire, theft, and extended coverage (windstorm and hail, flood, aircraft, auto damage, etc.), plus public liability (benefits for anyone hurt or fatally injured on the premises) and insurance on personal belongings. (If a person rents a home, he needs insurance only against fire and theft of personal belongings.) A landlord does not need home owner's insurance if he does not live in the property, but he needs the other two types of insurance.

Taxes are based upon the *assessment*, and the assessment is usually about two thirds of the value of the house. There are county, state, and local taxes. Taxes vary greatly. There is also a transfer tax for the buyer and the seller.

Hand money

You should buy a house only after you have looked around and compared values and costs. After you have found a house you like, you turn over to the home owner or real estate agent a certain amount of money — from a few hundred dollars up. This is called *hand money* or *earnest money*. It temporarily ties up the sale until you can make arrangements for the down payment. You will obtain a sales agreement with necessary signatures.

Contract of sale

This is the document that describes the whole contract between the buyer and the seller. A lawyer should check the contract for errors and loopholes.

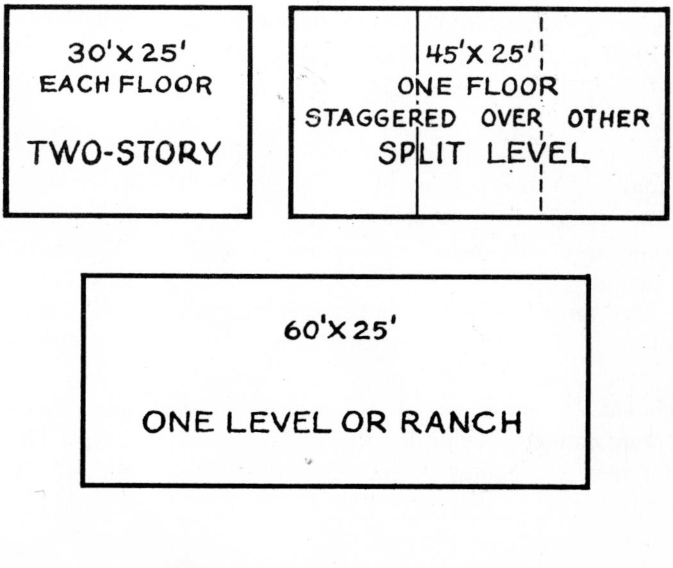

ILLUSTRATION 11. *The two-story house takes just half as much lot space as the ranch house; and the split-level house, from two thirds to three fourths as much lot space. All provide the same number of square feet of floor space. However, actual living space is decreased by stairways in the two-story home and by longer halls in the one-level house.*

30' X 25'
EACH FLOOR

TWO-STORY

45' X 25'
ONE FLOOR
STAGGERED OVER OTHER
SPLIT LEVEL

60' X 25'

ONE LEVEL OR RANCH

ILLUSTRATION 12. *After all financial details have been settled comes the delightful work-fun of planning the decorative details of the new home.*

Deed, certificate of title, and abstract

The *deed*, the official written contract outlining all the details of the transfer, is evidence of ownership. In some states the buyer holds the deed and in other states it is held in trust (escrow) by a third party until the loan is paid. The deed should be registered with the registrar of deeds. The buyer should hold the deed or a copy of it. The deed will bear certain revenue stamps. It should be kept in a safe place with other valuable papers.

The *certificate of title* makes sure that the property is undeniably in your name. Often people desire to take out title insurance, should an unforeseen question arise at a future date concerning the title rights. A fee for title search may be included in closing costs.

The *abstract* is the legal description of the property plus its history of ownership. The abstract should have the deed and the mortgage recorded on it. It is usually held by the lending agency until the loan is paid, but you should read and understand it.

Closing costs

At the time of settlement, people sometimes lose their option on a home because they fail to understand and anticipate closing costs. These costs may run as high as $500 or $600. The major items in closing costs are transfer tax ($\frac{1}{2}$ to 1 per cent of sale), prorated taxes, and insurance. Other less expensive items include search of title, title insurance, service fee, recording of deed, preparation and recording of mortgage papers, and credit report.

✦ HOW MAY YOU KEEP BUILD-
ING COSTS DOWN?

Grading, filling, excavating, sustaining
walls, long driveways, and a long line of steps
to the entrance all add to the total cost without giving very much in living satisfactions.
Special drains and sewer connections also
run up costs. Therefore the grade and location
of the lot are important.

The biggest saving in building comes from
using pre-built components (wall sidings,
flooring, windows, roof trusses, cabinets, and
doors), prefinished floors and prefinished wall
panels, and standard plumbing and wiring.
Dormer windows will cost more than other
types of windows. Aluminum window frames
and marble sills require the minimum of
maintenance. Another big saving comes from
concentrating plumbing in one area — back
to back in two walls, or vertical in two-story
houses.

A square two-story house is the least
expensive to build. A flat, shed, or gable
roof costs less than a hip, gambrel, or mansard roof. Concrete block is the least expensive construction material. Plywood panel
siding, available in many textures, is attractive and not expensive. Well-insulated aluminum siding needs no maintenance. Brick
and stone veneer are in the moderate price
range. Solid brick and solid stone walls are
more expensive.

A slab floor is less expensive than a floor
with a crawl space. A completely excavated
basement is the most expensive foundation,
but it offers valuable space for a recreation
room, laundry, and storage.

Popular roofing materials are summarized
briefly: *Asphalt shingles*, which are flat and
interlocked to resist wind, give a durable, inexpensive roof. *Red cedar shingles*, popular
in red-cedar-growing sections of the country,
give good insulation and add strength to the
roof. *Shakes*, grooved to give a rough texture,
are thicker than shingles and improve in
appearance with age. A *built-up roof* — layers
of asphalt-saturated felt over a plywood base
— is inexpensive and good for roofs with
little or no slope. *Asbestos-cement shingles* are
also inexpensive, durable, and attractive.
Aluminum roofing reflects heat, can be treated
to eliminate surface reflection, and requires
almost no maintenance. A *terne* or alloy-
coated sheet steel roof will last indefinitely if
painted from time to time. *Tile* roofs are distinctive but expensive. Under any roofing
material, roof insulation four to six inches
thick will more than pay for itself in lowering
heating and cooling costs.

Sometimes it is better to weigh present
economies against long-time enjoyment. For
instance, the difference between meeting FHA
minimum requirements and *quality* standards
may be less than a thousand dollars on a
moderate-sized home.

✦ WHAT IS WISE FINANCING?

Sometimes families find that owning property is more complex than they had imagined.
For wise and satisfying home financing and
ownership you should:

1. Make sure you want the responsibility of maintaining property and making periodic repairs.

2. Make as large a down payment as possible
   and borrow as little as possible. Interest is expensive.

3. Do not spend so much for a home that you
   will have to make unnecessary sacrifices or
   fail to make payments.

4. Seek advice ahead of time from a lawyer, a
   lending agency, the contractor, the local
   zoning and engineering department in the city
   hall or borough building.

5. Know where you can obtain hand money and
   down payment, where you can borrow, and
   finally, how you can meet closing costs.

★ DO YOU UNDERSTAND OTHER TERMS IN HOME FINANCING?

AMORTIZE: To provide for the gradual elimination of a debt by making definite payments at stated intervals.

APPRAISAL: An estimate of the value of the property for tax and transfer purposes, or for bankruptcy proceedings.

ASSESSMENT: Value placed on property by a city, county, or state assessor.

COLLATERAL: A security in the form of life insurance, other property, or stocks or bonds to insure payment of a short-term loan.

LIQUIDATE: To settle accounts, distribute assets, and wind up an estate.

MORTGAGE: An agreement to pay a loan over a specified period at set interest rates. On a *straight mortgage*, the borrower pays regular interest rates and repays the entire loan at a final given date. On an *amortized* mortgage, regular monthly payments are made — paying interest and cutting down the principal or amount borrowed at the same time. When the borrower pledges property already mortgaged for a second loan, the mortgage is called a *second mortgage*. The lender earns more but takes a greater risk. An *open-end mortgage* gives the borrower the privilege of paying off the mortgage at any time without paying a penalty. In an FHA loan, there is usually a penalty for paying off the mortgage before the time stated in the agreement.

SUGGESTED ACTIVITIES

1. Find out from home owners in your community their reasons for owning their own homes.

2. Give some good reasons applicable to your town for renting a house rather than owning one.

3. Price a new home in your locality that the average family could afford. Figure the costs on the following mortgage arrangements. You may want to call upon someone who handles mortgages for help. (a) FHA loan over 15 years at prevailing interest rates; (b) FHA loan over 35 years at the same interest rates; (c–d) conventional loans over the same periods and at the same interest rates with one third and with one fourth of the cost of the house as down payments.

4. Compare the necessary down payments and interest rates on a $16,000 house required by several lending agencies in your locality, as well as the mortgage departments of some insurance agencies.

5. Discuss and illustrate the following types of mortgages: amortized, straight, second, and open-end.

6. Bring to class the following papers. You may secure blanks to be filled in. (a) agreement between buyer and seller; (b) application for loan; (c) mortgage; (d) contract; (e) deed.

7. Demonstrate at the chalkboard the steps in buying a house. Determine the cost of the house, amount of hand money, amount of loan and mortgage, down payment, and closing costs.

8. Observe houses under construction. Find out how many are built from precut components. If possible observe the construction of a complete prefabricated house.

9. Select a ranch-style, a split-level, and a two-story house of approximately the same number of square feet and ask an architect, contractor, or representative of a savings and loan association to estimate comparative costs.

10. Select a ranch-style house and compare the cost of different roofs and sidings. Compare the costs of an L-shaped, a U-shaped, and an H-shaped floor plan of about the same number of square feet.

11. Bring to class samples of different roofing and siding materials for study.

CHAPTER 2

What guides will you use in choosing a homesite?

REGARDLESS of whether a family buys, builds, or rents a home, the location of the home must be carefully considered. If a family makes a mistake in renting a home, they are free to move when the lease runs out. But when a family buys or builds a home they may be locating themselves for a lifetime. The location of the home can add dividends of satisfaction or subtract tolls of dissatisfaction and regret. Hence we present a yardstick of considerations for measuring values.

✶ WHAT CONDITIONS AFFECT THE PERSONAL ENJOYMENT OF A HOMESITE?

Neighborhood surroundings; services, location in regard to transportation, schools, church, and shopping centers are important factors in one's personal enjoyment of a homesite. If you are going to take any pride in your home, you will want it to be in a good neighborhood. The interpretation of "good" will vary, but everyone should expect certain things. Since home owners are likely to take care of their property, a neighborhood where other people own their own homes is apt to be more desirable than one in which all homes are rented. The value of your home should be in keeping with the value of other homes in the community. To judge a neighborhood, look for orderly yards, homes with a well-preserved exterior finish, and the absence of unsightly garbage and trash disposal. Find out whether or not juvenile delinquency is a problem. If you are neighborly, you will look for a community where people are friendly.

If you like trees, buy a lot with trees on it because trees do not grow in a few years. Be sure an interesting view cannot be destroyed by future tall buildings. Investigate the neighborhood for marshes where mosquitoes and other insects may breed. Avoid sites near factories because of their disagreeable smoke and odors, near railways and highways because of the noise and vibration which may shake plaster loose. Investigate traffic hazards that may cause sorrow.

For city workers a homesite in the suburbs is ideal provided transportation facilities are available. On a limited budget bus fare for two or three school children is an item to be considered. If the bus or car stop is beyond walking distance from the home, there is the added inconvenience of having someone drive members of the family to and from the bus. Nearness to schools, churches, parks, playgrounds, and libraries adds to the convenience of the homesite and to the parents' peace of mind. Consider how far you must go to buy your groceries and drugs, to have shoes repaired, and to have clothing cleaned. A location too near a business district is not desirable because the noise and traffic may lower the value of the home, but one within ten- or fifteen-minutes walking distance is a convenience. Main highways in a village are to be avoided, since they cause safety hazards for young children in particular.

Other questions may arise in connection with owning a suburban home. How often and at what cost are trash, ashes, and garbage removed? Is mail delivered or is it necessary to rent a box at the post office? Are fire and police protection provided? Is the community free of fire hazards?

A few points should be mentioned about the location of a farm dwelling. For instance, a farm home should be on a good road that connects with a highway (rather than on it), so that there is easy access to school, church, and town. The house should be placed so as to capitalize the point of greatest natural beauty on the farm. Low-lying damp land should be avoided, and the home should not be unduly near the barnyard, chicken yards, or stable. If possible, the home should be in an area that is serviced by rural electrification. And of course, it should be located where there is a supply of good water. Since fire-fighting service may not be available, it is essential that a farm home be as nearly fire-proof as possible.

✦ WHAT PHYSICAL FEATURES ABOUT A HOMESITE SHOULD BE CONSIDERED?

A survey

From the physical and legal angle a survey of the proposed site is desirable. This survey will determine boundaries, and show you whether there are encroachments on your property by adjoining owners or encroachments of your property on that of theirs. Also it will give you a clearer picture of the contour of the land so that the architect may take advantage of the terrain in drawing plans, will determine the extent and probable expense of excavating and the need for retaining walls or for filling in the land, and will reveal the type of soil or foundation on which a house would rest. Clay and sand will support a small house, but a larger house requires gravel or rock. Rock excavating is expensive.

Good drainage

Poor drainage may cause permanent basement dampness. Find out from the city engineer what type of tile to carry off storm and sanitary drainage is under a site you think you might buy. If a small pipe has been used which is closer to the surface than six feet, the lot may have to be filled in so that the foundation for the house will rest above the pipe. If the lot has no sewer or storm pipes, find out who will have to pay for putting them in. Improvements of this type are expensive.

Avoid building at the foot of a hill where your basement might become a basin. Avoid building in a river or lake section unless you are sure that your home will not be surrounded by water during flood seasons. If you would have a dry basement, be sure that the soil does not constantly hold moisture.

Relation of house to lot

If you are certain about the size and type of house you want, don't buy a lot until you are sure it will complement your house. Is the shape of the lot suited to the shape of the house you want to build? Is the space adequate? Will the house complement the con-

ILLUSTRATION 13. *"Falling Water," a world-famous residence in Bear Run, Pennsylvania, shows Frank Lloyd Wright's interpretation of integral planning.*

tour of the land? A Southern Colonial house may require a large oblong site, while an English half-timbered house may fit nicely on a narrower rolling site.

Exposures

It may be very disappointing to buy a homesite and find that you cannot enjoy a terrace in summer because it would get the late afternoon sun, or find that the angle at which you wanted to locate your living room gets all the wintry winds. If you want a sunny kitchen or living room or a porch with a breeze on a hot summer evening, think about these things while your plans are still flexible. The angle at which the sun strikes a sloping back yard may also be important to the gardener.

In home planning modern architects are more and more concerned with solar orientation or the placement of the house in relation to the sun. In order to take advantage of solar orientation, you will need a broad lot which will allow as many rooms as possible to face south. With proper window glass and

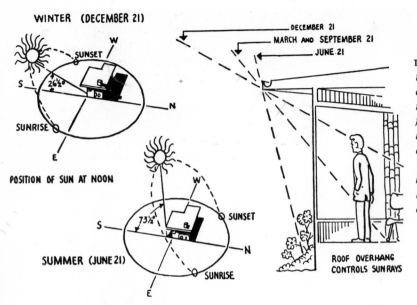

WINTER (DECEMBER 21)

SUNSET

W

S   26½°

N

SUNRISE

E

POSITION OF SUN AT NOON

DECEMBER 21
MARCH and SEPTEMBER 21
JUNE 21

W

S   73½°

SUNSET

N

SUMMER (JUNE 21)

SUNRISE

E

ROOF OVERHANG
CONTROLS SUN RAYS

ILLUSTRATION 14. *Solar orientation. The amount of sunlight entering the house in both summer and winter is controlled by facing the house south, by the large glass areas on the front, and by the overhanging roof. Thus additional warmth and daylight enter the house in winter. Southern exposures in summer are also generally good.*

placement of windows, maximum sunlight is assured in winter, and an overhanging roof reduces the sun glare in summer. Solar orientation cannot control sunlight on east and west windows.

Zoning

You will also want to find out whether or not the lot is in a zoned area. By city ordinance certain districts of cities and towns may be restricted to residential buildings, while others permit commercial buildings, such as gas stations, garages, grocery stores, drugstores, and so forth. If the lot is in a residential zone, you will want to know if the ordinance permits only single-family houses or if duplex and apartment houses are allowed. Zoning laws are intended for the protection of property owners, but they should not be unchangeable. As a city grows it may be advisable to replace single houses with apartment buildings, and additional shopping centers

may be needed. Residents should have an opportunity to vote on whether or not the laws are changed.

In residential zones there may be restrictions on the percentage of a site the house may occupy, a minimum and a maximum limit on the total cost of a house, a limit on the distance between houses across the street from each other or from the side elevation of one house to that of another. There may also be certain fireproofing ordinances with which the house you build must conform.

Improvements

Sidewalks, roads, and connections for electricity, sewage disposal, water, and gas are expensive improvements on a piece of property. An inexpensive lot without them may prove to be more expensive than you can afford. If these improvements are lacking, find out when they will be made, if possible, and who will bear the expense of making them.

✳ **WHAT LEGAL ASPECTS ARE IMPORTANT?**

If you are planning to buy property, you want to be sure that it has a clear title before you make a settlement for it. You do not want to find out after the transfer is made that legal irregularities make the boundaries of your lot uncertain or that you are liable for the payment of back taxes or debts. Attorneys and research agencies will examine title rights, secure a definite statement of boundaries, and locate any indebtedness on the land. Possible hidden defects which may cause serious loss or expensive litigation are outlined by the Lawyers Title Insurance Corporation of Richmond, Virginia.

1. False personation of the true owner of the land
2. Forged deeds, releases, and the like
3. Instruments executed under fabricated or expired power of attorney
4. Deeds delivered after death of grantor or grantee, or without consent of grantor
5. Undisclosed or missing heirs
6. Interpretation of wills
7. Wills not probated
8. Deeds by persons of unsound mind
9. Deeds by minors
10. Deeds by persons supposedly single but secretly married
11. Birth or adoption of children after date of will
12. Mistakes in recording legal documents
13. Want of jurisdiction or persons in judicial proceedings
14. Errors in indexing
15. Falsification of records

When a sale is made, the former owner transfers the property to the new owner through a deed. A deed is the legal document of ownership. The deed should be examined by a title company or an attorney to find out if (1) it is properly prepared, (2) it adequately describes the property, (3) it is signed, sealed, attested, and acknowledged as required by law. The deed should then be recorded in the proper court.

Time spent in talking with people who have recently bought property, in reading books and articles on the subject, and in securing legal advice will pay valuable returns in the satisfaction you will enjoy.

SUGGESTED ACTIVITIES

1. Select a vacant lot in your community, and judge it as a possible homesite for your family from the standpoint of neighborhood, surroundings, services, and location.
2. Judge the same lot from the standpoint of probable drainage, exposures which would be possible for various rooms, and improvements which have been made.
3. Visit your city hall or courthouse and ask about zoning laws in your community.
4. Ask an attorney or some person who has recently bought a lot to tell the class about the legal procedure necessary in a sale.
5. Discuss any trouble acquaintances of yours have had with land titles.
6. Mount pictures of two different styles of home architecture, and describe the kind of site and the size and shape of the lot you would choose for each house.
7. From the homes in your community, select an example of a house and lot that complement each other. Analyze the size, shape, contour, and landscaping of the lot in relation to the size, shape, and architecture of the house.
8. Find out what the average selling price is for homes in your neighborhood.
9. Find out the assessed value of several pieces of property in your community, and determine the yearly *city*, *county*, and *state* taxes. Your city hall or courthouse will give tax rates.

CHAPTER 3

What style architecture will you choose?

IF YOU walk down the street in the residential section of any American city, you will probably spot samples of widely varying architectural styles. Each house symbolizes an architectural trend or a way of living. Styles in American architecture vary more than in any other country because of the varied background of the people and wide range of climate and topography.

Climate and native materials determined the design of early shelters. In New England, early homes were built of logs; in the Middle Atlantic states, stone was used; and in the extreme southern states and the Southwest, clay produced the adobe house.

Influences in home architecture

Early New England houses were simple oblong structures with gabled roofs. This type of house has been the basis for most Early American designs. The Dutch, settling in New York and Pennsylvania, used the same form but built with stone and introduced the double pitch or gambrel roof. Wealthy planters of the South engaged English architects to design their homes. They naturally used the Georgian style as a basis, but added the veranda with two-story-high columns because people in the South spent more time outdoors than did people in England.

Homes along the Gulf coast reflected the French influence, featuring balconies with intricate iron grillwork. The Spanish, settling in the Southwest, built adobe homes with inside courts or patios. Increased wealth and the desire for prestige inspired the many gabled, highly ornamented houses of the late nineteenth century known as the Victorian style. Most Victorian houses violated the principles of good design, and the style was short lived. The mission-type bungalow of the early twentieth century was a contrast to the fussy Victorian house. During the 1920's, Cotswold and English half-timbered houses became popular. The 1930's brought in houses with flat roofs, severe exteriors, sun decks, and an emphasis upon solar orientation. This housing style marked the first complete departure from the traditional designs.

The contemporary trend actually began with Frank Lloyd Wright at the turn of the century, but America was slow to accept his radical changes. Wright has had perhaps the greatest effect on American contemporary architecture of any architect of the twentieth century to date. While other architects were still designing ornamented Victorian houses, Wright was advocating integration of house and land, with emphasis on exposure and view.

ILLUSTRATIONS 15 and 16. *Patios, enclosed courts and gardens, and home swimming pools reflect the trend toward outdoor living.*

ILLUSTRATIONS 17A and 17B. *Four general types of houses are currently popular. Pictured in A is a California-style ranch house and in B, a two-story house—both contemporary.*

17C and 17D.   *C shows a story-and-a-half Colonial-style home with dormer windows and D, a contemporary split-level house.*

Present contemporary houses are not limited to any form. They may be one-story, two-story, split-level, or story-and-a-half, but all contemporary houses stress open planning, window walls in living areas, and outdoor patios or terraces. The so-called ranch house has become the basic one-story style. This rambling house does not always have a functional or contemporary exterior. It may take on architectural features of the classic Cape Cod, Colonial, Japanese (or Pacific), Spanish, or "storybook" (an exaggerated interpretation of the Swiss chalet) styles. Any house with good lines, a limited number of materials in the exterior, and a minimum of frills outlives "fad" houses or very ornate dwellings.

★ HOW CAN YOU LEARN TO COMPARE HOUSE FORMS AND STYLES?

ONE-STORY OR RANCH: This style makes integration of outdoors and indoors easier than any other style. The floor plan is flexible and the exterior design may be varied in line and materials. There are no stairs to carpet, climb, or clean. Traffic circulation is easy and living is informal. Extra rooms may be added without too much trouble.

On the other hand, a ranch house requires a large lot both for floor space and for the outdoor living associated with it. Costs will be higher than for many other styles because more roofing is needed, a larger foundation is necessary (with slab floors the cost may be kept to a minimum), and longer pipelines must be installed for heating, wiring, and plumbing. Sleeping areas are not always as private or as quiet as in the split-level or two-story house. The high windows necessary in bedrooms for privacy and furniture arrangement provide poor ventilation, and they are difficult to decorate.

TWO-STORY: This house is usually the most economical to build, and provides maximum space for the money spent. It provides the most privacy and quiet. This style may be built on a small lot. It lends itself to almost any exterior or interior plan, but it does not adapt itself to outdoor living as well as the ranch or split-level home. In two-level houses, stairways take up floor space, are expensive to carpet, and create an accident hazard for small children and older people.

STORY-AND-A-HALF: Many Cape Cod, Northern Colonial, Dutch Colonial, and salt-box houses are a story and a half. The first floor usually includes one or two bedrooms and a bathroom. Often this type of house will have an unfinished second floor where two bedrooms and a bath may be added at a future date. These styles of houses have charm and are not particularly expensive to build.

SPLIT-LEVEL: The split-level house is designed primarily to take advantage of natural contours. It lends itself well to outdoor living. There are stairs, but not as many as in a two-story house. Sleeping areas are usually isolated and private. The split-level is one of the most complex and most difficult types of houses to design from the angles of function and beauty. It may be very livable and interesting, or it may be a complete failure.

Regardless of the style of architecture, today's houses emphasize outdoor living. Architectural lines harmonize with natural surroundings, and large windows take advantage of the best view. Grillwork of concrete, wood, or metal and tall plantings enclose attractive patios, terraces, gardens, and carports. Solariums and swimming pools are becoming as much a part of the house-and-lot plan as patios and gardens.

Whether you build a traditional or a contemporary house, buy a ready-built house, or buy no house at all, you should be able to recognize basic architectural styles. On the following pages are thumbnail descriptions of the many architectural styles you will find in houses in residential and suburban areas all over the United States.

The Garrison or Early Colonial

The *Garrison* style house is an outgrowth of the early blockhouse. This is a Colonial style, economically constructed, and may be a story and a half or two stories with a gable roof. The upper half may be of clapboard or shingle construction, and usually extends over the lower half which may be of stone or brick. A large stone chimney may be at the center or at the side. The second floor may have dormer or double-sash windows with small panes. Small latticed windows often show the early English influence. This style is so well proportioned and so functional that adaptations are found all over the country.

ILLUSTRATION 18. *The Garrison or Early Colonial*

The Salt-Box House

The *salt-box house* (its name derived from the old salt box of colonial times) has two stories in front and one in the rear. It is characterized by the single gable roof, with the back extending to the ceiling of the first floor. The exterior is of clapboard or shingle construction, and the windows are placed symmetrically. The house has a center chimney. The second floor often extends over the first in front. There is no porch or protection over the entrance. The paneled door is set in a plain frame. Windows seldom have shutters. Originally typical of New England, the style may be found now in nearly every section of the country.

ILLUSTRATION 19. *The Salt-Box House*

ILLUSTRATION 20.   *The Cape Cod Cottage*

The Cape Cod Cottage

The *Cape Cod cottage* is a picturesque low one-story or story-and-a-half house which offers a lot of charm. It originated in Cape Cod, Massachusetts. The roof forms a gable, and there is usually a second floor. The house has dormer windows with small panes. Sometimes full-length windows on one side take the shape of a bay. Windows flush with outside walls have shutters. The shingled roof usually forms eaves or an overhang at the front of the house. The door, framed by square pilasters, resembles the salt-box house door; it has four panels, often with small panes in the upper section. Frequently the door is painted a gay color and ornamented with a large brass knocker.

The Dutch Colonial

The *Dutch Colonial* house originated in New York, New Jersey, and eastern Pennsylvania. The gambrel roof forms eaves over the first floor, and provides more space on the second floor than a gable roof does. The simple Dutch doorway may have an upper and a lower section. The lower part of the house may be made of brick or stone. Shingles or clapboards cover the second-floor walls on the side section. Often the entire house is made of shingles or clapboards, painted. The style appears to best advantage on slightly sloping terrain, and, except for ranch adaptations, is found mainly in cold or moderate climates.

ILLUSTRATION 21.   *The Dutch Colonial*

The Georgian

The *Georgian* house dates from eighteenth-century England and shows a strong classic influence. This perfectly symmetrical style has a central hall containing the stairway, and similar rooms on each side of the stairs. Traffic flows easily through the house. The rear may be L-shaped or oblong. The broad hip roof is flanked on each side with a brick chimney. Shuttered windows are placed symmetrically across the house. A paneled door set between two Doric columns, with a triangular pediment above, is another distinctive feature of Georgian style. Georgian houses are found in all sections of the country.

ILLUSTRATION 22. *The Georgian*

The Regency

The *Regency* house, an outgrowth of Georgian style, developed during the nineteenth century. The exterior may be of brick, frequently painted white, or of stucco or stone. The houses are square and the plans symmetrical. Shutters often reach to the ground on the first floor. Typical of the style is the grillwork at the entrance, with a curved hood or circular balcony over the door. There is often an octagonal window above the entrance. This style is pretentious and requires a large lot. It is usually found in areas with moderately warm climates.

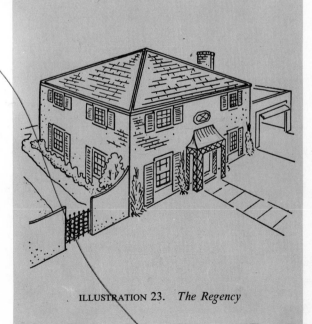

ILLUSTRATION 23. *The Regency*

ILLUSTRATION 24. *The Northern Colonial*

The Northern Colonial

Northern Colonial style combines the features of Garrison and Georgian to produce a rather commodious type of house. The floor plan is usually symmetrical, with symmetrically placed windows which sometimes have shutters. There may be one or two chimneys. The scroll-and-urn pediment is typical of the door framing. The door is paneled and usually recessed to provide protection. The style is adaptable to cold and moderate climates and to slightly rolling countryside. This type of house may be built on a fairly small lot.

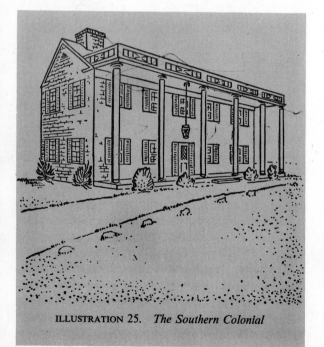

ILLUSTRATION 25. *The Southern Colonial*

The Southern Colonial

Southern Colonial style is a pretentious adaptation of Georgian. It was originally used by the wealthy landowners of the South. Two-story Grecian columns support a high roof with a simulated balcony. The floor plan may be rectangular or L-shaped, with a center hall and a stairway turning at a broad landing. Shutters are used at windows and doors. The broad roof over the veranda or portico provides protection for outdoor living, and the shutters keep the house cool. This pretentious house needs level or slightly rolling ground and lots of open space.

The Cotswold

The *Cotswold* house shows Gothic and Tudor influences. This style has a roof with two or three gables, and a prominent stone chimney; the exterior is usually of stucco or stone, with roughhewn timber at the pitch of the roof. Windows are small with many panes of glass, and there may be some dormer windows on the second floor. There is no porch or stoop. The front door is made of vertical boards ornamented with large iron hinges. The floor plan is informal and interesting. The style is best suited to the rolling terrain of New England and the Central Atlantic states. It is out of place in the open spaces of the Southwest, and not well enough ventilated for warm climates.

ILLUSTRATION 26. *The Cotswold*

The English Half-Timbered

The *English Half-Timbered* house dates from the reign of Queen Elizabeth I. This style is familiar in many parts of America. The roof is shingled and has many gables. The exterior usually has a stucco finish, but it may be stone or brick. The upper half has timber crosspieces, and frequently the second story projects beyond the first. A chimney of heavy stone is on the outside. Windows are not large and have small rectangular or latticed panes. The door resembles the Cotswold style. The floor plan is informal. This house adapts well to a colder climate and a fairly large sloping lot with trees.

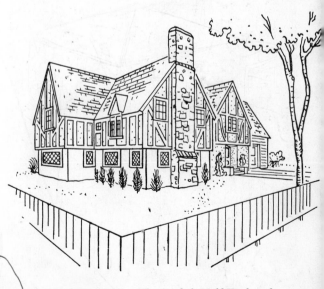

ILLUSTRATION 27. *The English Half-Timbered*

ILLUSTRATION 28. *The French Provincial* ✓

The French Provincial

The *French Provincial* is less familiar in this country than other styles. Originally it was the French farmer's interpretation of the more pretentious homes of royalty. Its distinctive and complicated mansard roof is a rarity today. The house is usually a story and a half. The dormer windows are hooded, and the first-floor window shutters may extend to the ground. The exterior is stone or stucco, and the roof is shingled. The house has a large brick or stone outside chimney; the entrance is usually at the side. The style is suitable for mild climates and a moderate-sized, fairly level lot.

ILLUSTRATION 29. *The Norman French*

The Norman French

The *Norman French* style has a quaintness and charm all its own, whether in a simple structure or a mansion. A steep hip, or modified mansard, roof extends above the first floor on one wing, and fits into a hip roof with a low pitch at right angles to it. Often there is a turret or tower. Hood tops characterize the second floor windows. Grillwork ornaments the shutters and the section above the door. A tall outside chimney flanks one side. The exterior is concrete, stucco, or painted brick. The house adapts itself well to a slightly rolling terrain and moderate climate.

ILLUSTRATION 30.   *The Monterey is an example of the blending of two styles. The charm of Southern Colonial is combined with Spanish architectural features to produce this distinctive style.*

SUGGESTED ACTIVITIES

1. Arrange a bulletin board showing how styles in housing developed in the United States.

2. Give brief class reports describing early home life in different areas of America, and how it influenced architecture.

3. Collect and display pictures of famous houses in America. Consult *House and Garden* and other home, service, and art magazines.

4. Discuss a number of contemporary styles, using illustrations to identify roofs, doorways, and windows.

5. Display a number of Frank Lloyd Wright's designs, and discuss his contributions to present-day architecture.

6. Select floor plans for split-level, ranch, and two-story houses, each with approximately the same number of square feet, and compare the cost of building each. A contractor or architect may help you determine costs.

7. Compare the advantages and disadvantages of the styles mentioned in Activity #6. 42

8. Display illustrations of split-level, ranch, and two-story houses in several different designs — i.e., Colonial, Cape Cod, French, and Contemporary.

9. Discuss the best position on the lot for a patio in relation to the house plan and exposure. For instance, would you want the patio near the living room, bedroom, or kitchen? Would you want to have the patio receive the setting sun? Why or why not?

10. Make a list of roof, window, and door types and identify each.

CHAPTER 4

What information will be helpful in planning a home?

THE PLANS for a home are exceedingly important, for it is here that all the essential elements of a house are brought together. It is here that the family's needs for comfort, privacy, convenience, safety, health, personal interests, and beauty must be met within the limits of the amount of money available.

Since maximum livability at minimum cost is the desire of most families, the services of an experienced and competent architect are considered essential. His technical knowledge makes it possible for him to effect savings that an inexperienced person is unable to make. Usually these savings more than offset his fee, and result in better design and better construction. However, a prospective home owner who understands the principles of home planning is able to talk more intelligently with the architect.

Fundamental principles of home planning are described in the following paragraph taken from *Principles of Planning Small Homes*, a bulletin of the Federal Housing Administration.

Livability of any house is dependent upon adequacy of room areas, relationships of rooms to afford privacy, circulation within and between rooms, room exposures, and equipment [and storage space] that provide for the convenience and comfort of the occupants. Economy in planning requires the elimination of waste space, especially hall areas; rooms planned for dual purposes when possible; and rooms whose shape and wall space permit the use and arrangement of essential movable furniture in a minimum floor area. Economy in planning also is related to the structural elements of the house and the installation of mechanical equipment, especially that of heating and plumbing.

✳ HOW MAY THE BASIC PLAN PROVIDE FOR LIVABILITY?

The basic floor plan of any house must provide for two general needs of the family — living, including cooking and eating, and sleeping. The size of the family affects the amount of space needed for these activities, but whether the family is large or small or whether the house is low or high in cost, the basic needs remain the same.

In Colonial days the family cooked, ate, and carried on much of its social life in the warmth of a big old-fashioned kitchen. In modern planning, when space must be curtailed because of cost, a dining room is considered a luxury. The dining area may be combined with the kitchen or living room, or if space permits, it may be placed in an alcove adjoining either room. If the dining area is placed in the living room, it should be easily accessible to the kitchen.

The sleeping area should be well separated from the living area. If possible, sleeping rooms should be located in corners, so that there are two exposures to insure proper ventilation. Each bedroom should be easily accessible to the bathroom.

In both living and sleeping areas, wall space in relation to doors and windows should be planned so that there is adequate space for large pieces of furniture, such as sofas and beds, and if possible, so that these pieces may be changed about occasionally. It should not be necessary to walk around beds to reach closets and entrance doors, and the enjoyment of the living room should not be destroyed by an arrangement of doors which causes a diagonal passageway across the room. A small front entrance hall relieves the living room of its function as a passageway, but if space must be reduced to a minimum, the hall may be eliminated. In this case the entrance should be at one side of the living room with a door to other parts of the house on an adjacent wall.

Although hall space is desirable to provide privacy and traffic lanes between rooms, for the sake of economy, it should be no larger than necessary. The minimum hall area for a one-story, two-bedroom house is a square with doors to each of the bedrooms, to the bathroom, and to the kitchen or living room opening off the four sides. Additional bedrooms mean that length must be added to the hall. In a small two-story house a first-floor hall is frequently eliminated, and the length of the upstairs hall will be determined by the number of rooms adjoining it.

Storage spaces should be included in every bedroom and kitchen and in or near every other room. Although this topic is discussed more fully on pages 88 to 93, it will be noticed that storage space is provided in each of the basic plans described as follows.

✦ HOW ARE PRINCIPLES OF PLANNING APPLIED IN BASIC FLOOR PLANS?

Let us study several basic floor plans to see how provision for livability is worked out. These plans are selected from the bulletin *Principles of Planning Small Houses.*

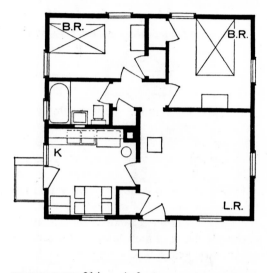

·ILLUSTRATION 31A. *A basic one-story, square house*

Plan A

The first plan in Illustration 31 is for a basic one-story, two-bedroom house. Economy of construction is shown in the use of the square plan, and room sizes are based on using framing materials of standard length. Plumbing is concentrated in one area by having the kitchen and bathroom adjoin.

An entrance hall is eliminated, but closet space is provided at the front door. The living and sleeping areas are separated, thus insuring privacy. The living room is fairly spacious but does not allow much flexibility in the arrangement of furniture.

The bedroom windows provide cross ventilation. Closets may be reached without going around beds, and main traffic areas are not blocked. Even though closets are provided in each bedroom for clothing, in the bathroom for linens, and in the living room for coats, there is an apparent lack of provision for general storage. However, space for this purpose may be provided in the attic, reached through a generously sized scuttle.

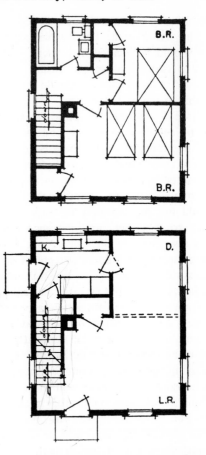

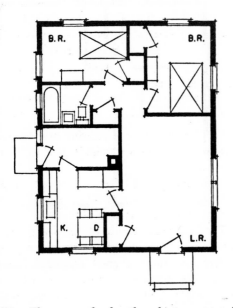

31B.   *The square plan lengthened into a rectangle*

31C.   *A basic two-story, two-bedroom house*

Plan B

The second part of Illustration 31 shows the floor plan lengthened, producing a rectangular shape. In this way living room space is increased, and a utility room is provided between the kitchen and the bathroom. Again, plumbing is concentrated in one area. The kitchen exit is moved, but sink and storage units are still near the exit, and the placement of windows insures good light and ventilation. The living room wall space is a little more usable than that in Plan A. General storage space is provided in the utility room next to the kitchen.

Plan C

This plan represents a two-story, two-bedroom plan with a basement. The side-wall stairway shows economical planning that minimizes stair and hall space. The dining area has one open wall, so that the dining and living rooms may be used as one area on special occasions. The living room has ample floor space and closet space, but the wall area is limited. The upstairs hall occupies a minimum amount of space, yet it provides privacy for the rooms and passage between them. The bathroom door is off line with the stairway, thus increasing privacy. The linen closet and the two bedroom closets are placed where they can be easily reached. A garage or family room may be added at the left, with a third bedroom over it.

✦ WHAT SIZE ROOMS MAKE A HOUSE MORE LIVABLE?

In order to qualify for FHA loans, houses must meet certain *minimum* standards. Somewhat higher standards, to provide greater livability, are set up by the mortgage department of the Metropolitan Life Insurance Company and by the Small Homes Council of the University of Illinois.

Rooms that are too small or not conducive to an easy flow of traffic provide less livability. Often a small additional initial cost will provide for greater comfort and privacy. When this sum is spread over ten or fifteen years it may not be missed. The Small Homes Council recommends 1500 square feet of living space, exclusive of bathrooms and closets, for a family of four. Many homes in the popular price range have not much more than 1000 square feet of actual floor space. You may want to compare the rooms in your own home with *minimum* standards set up by the Federal Housing Administration for home loans, and those set up by a lending agency such as a life insurance company.

FHA MINIMUM STANDARDS

	Three-Bedroom Dwelling	Two-Bedroom Dwelling
Living room	170 sq. ft.	160 sq. ft.
Master bedroom	120 sq. ft.	120 sq. ft.
Other bedrooms	80 sq. ft.	80 sq. ft.
Kitchen	70 sq. ft.	60 sq. ft.

METROPOLITAN LIFE INSURANCE COMPANY'S MINIMUM STANDARDS

Living room	196 sq. ft.
Master bedroom	171 sq. ft.
Other bedrooms	110 sq. ft.
Kitchen	112 sq. ft.

To give rooms more pleasing proportions, even Metropolitan's standards have to be increased.

A minimum of $9\frac{1}{2}$ feet is required on the width of the *bedroom* to allow enough space to move about at the ends of the beds.

The minimum width of the *living room* should be 12 feet, and a minimum length of 17 feet is desirable for good furniture arrangement. The smallest *bathroom* that will accommodate a tub, a toilet, and a washbowl is 5 by 5 feet, but 7 by 8 feet is better. The Cornell Kitchen study recommends 96 square feet as a *kitchen* minimum, with 120 square feet if a wall oven and dishwasher are included in the plan.

31D. *This floor plan, similar to 31C, shows an expanded second floor with an additional bedroom. The new room was built over a garage added to the first-floor plan.*

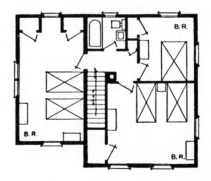

ILLUSTRATIONS 32A and B. *This studio-type apartment provides an efficient and comfortable plan for one person, or a suitable temporary apartment for two people. The sleeping alcove and the kitchen may be closed off when not in use.*

★ **HOW MAY A ONE-ROOM APARTMENT BE PLANNED?**

Many people have third-floor space that may be turned into an apartment for a single person or a couple. Illustration 32B shows how space may be provided for cooking, eating, sleeping, and living, by using folding doors.

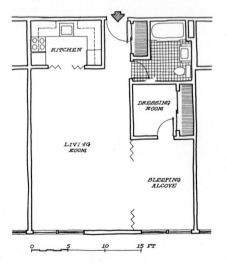

STAGE #1

★ WHAT FLOOR PLAN PERMITS EXPANSION?

Many young couples would like to buy a small home and enlarge it as requirements demand. The house illustrated is developed on the basis of a twelve-foot module. It is made of precut components, and the buyer may do as much or as little of the construction as he wishes. The package with the floor, walls, and roof arrives first. When these parts are assembled, equipment for plumbing, heating, and electrical needs arrives. Costs are distributed in this way.

STAGE #2 FLOOR PLAN

★ WHAT SHOULD YOU KNOW ABOUT THE LANGUAGE OF BUILDING?

In order to understand building plans you must know the meaning of the following terms and symbols.

WORKING DRAWINGS OR BLUEPRINTS: All scale drawings from actual measurements of floor plans, elevations, and details needed to build a house.

PERSPECTIVE DRAWINGS: A pen-and-ink or pencil drawing giving a picture of the house with proposed walks and landscaping.

32C. This precision-cut home may be built in stages. Floor plans and exterior views of both the first and the second stages are shown here.

ILLUSTRATION 33. *A perspective drawing. This kind of drawing gives a picture of the house with proposed walks and landscaping.*

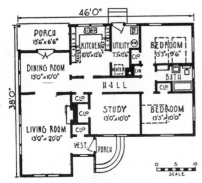

ILLUSTRATION 34. *A floor plan. This is a layout drawn to scale of all the rooms in the house.*

STORY: The portion of the house between floor and ceiling. A house with one floor is called a one-story house, with two floors, two stories, and so on.

SCALE: A unit of measurement used in drawings so that plan dimensions are always in exact proportion to actual dimensions. For instance, one inch on a drawing of a fireplace may represent one foot on the real structure. For house drawings, the usual scale is one-fourth inch equals one foot.

FLOOR PLANS: A layout drawn to scale representing all the rooms of the house. Separate drawings are used to show each story.

ILLUSTRATION 35. *A side elevation. Each side of the house is drawn to scale in a separate drawing.*

ILLUSTRATION 36. *A detail drawing. This drawing shows an enlarged view of the construction details in building the door shown.*

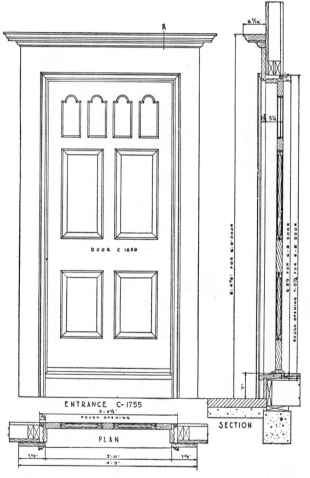

ELEVATION: A line drawing in scale showing a picture of the side of a house. Each side is shown in a separate drawing.

VERTICAL SECTION: A drawing which shows any part of a house as you would see it if you could cut through it

DETAIL DRAWING: A drawing that shows an enlarged view of construction details for cornices, fireplaces, stairways, and any special features

LANDSCAPE DRAWING: A drawing representing the contour of the land, showing place-

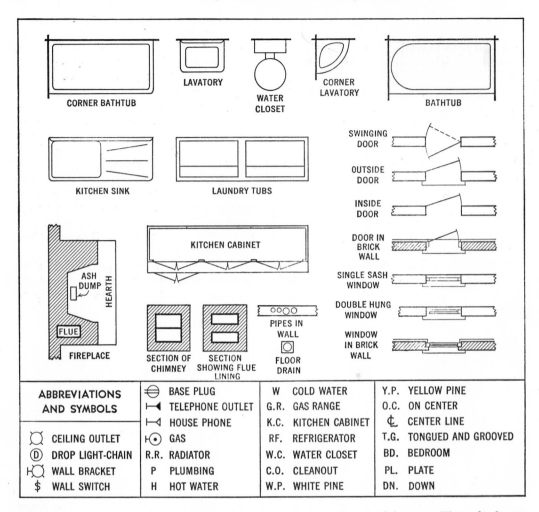

ILLUSTRATION 37.   *Common symbols and abbreviations used in architectural drawings. Ways of indicating different types of doors, windows, building materials, electric outlets, plumbing fixtures, and the like are shown.*

ment of trees, shrubbery, plantings, walks, and walls

SYMBOLS: Abbreviated pictures that represent kind of materials, electrical outlets, stationary equipment, doors, windows, and so forth

SPECIFICATIONS: A written statement which indicates in complete detail such things as excavating and grading to be done; kind of building materials, hardware, cabinetwork, and fixtures to be used; heating, plumbing, and electrical connections and equipment to be installed; and kind of interior and exterior finishing to be done. This lengthy but necessary sheet must accompany the blueprints or working drawings.

SUGGESTED ACTIVITIES

1. From the discussion of floor plans in this chapter, select a plan you like and analyze it according to the following questions.

    (a) Is there adequate space for your present family needs?

    (b) Does the wall space in the bedrooms provide for the placement of beds so that they do not have to be walked around to reach the entrance door, closet, and dresser; so that they can be made up from two sides; so that the head does not have to be situated immediately under a window; and so that there is room for bedside tables? Is there an alternate furniture arrangement for the bedrooms?

    (c) Does the location of the bedroom provide privacy in relation to other rooms, especially the bathroom?

    (d) Does the position of doors eliminate constant traffic through the living room to other rooms?

    (e) Does living room wall space permit at least two different furniture arrangements?

    (f) Is there adequate storage space?

    (g) Are recreational needs cared for?

2. Mount on the board pictures of newly built homes in your community, and if possible find out how much the homes cost.

3. Keep a scrapbook of pictures of some of the features you would like in a home.

4. Obtain blueprints from an architect or contractor, and practice reading the symbols.

5. Ask someone who has recently built a home to show you the sheet of specifications and to tell you some of the building problems involved.

6. Visit several new homes, and compare the livability of the floor plans. Also compare the houses from the standpoint of probable cost.

CHAPTER 5

What heating, plumbing, and electrical provisions will meet your needs?

IF HEATING, air conditioning, insulation, plumbing, and wiring needs are studied carefully before plans for a new home are in the final stage, many economies may be effected.

★ **WHAT WILL DETERMINE THE TYPE OF HEATING SYSTEM TO BE USED?**

The climate and the style and size of the house will influence the type of heating system. For instance, steam is the most satisfactory heat for large buildings, and warm air is adequate for moderate-sized compact homes. In any installation other than floor and ceiling panels, the heating units should be in or near outside walls because outside walls and windows account for 60 to 80 per cent of heat loss.

Heating systems are briefly summarized below.

Warm air

In this system heated air is filtered throughout the house via ducts to registers, baseboard units, tiles under the floor, or baffles in the ceiling. A *gravity warm-air system* is satisfactory for small compact houses, economical to install, and simple to operate; but this system requires a basement, and the large ducts occupy a lot of otherwise usable space.

A *forced warm-air system* may be used in larger houses and those without basements.

Forced warm-air heating is more expensive to install than a gravity warm-air system, but it has a quicker response, lower operating cost, and may be adapted to air conditioning.

Steam

In this system, steam is forced through pipes into radiators. Steam heating usually costs more than warm-air heating. A *one-pipe system* carries both the hot steam and the return condensation. A *two-pipe system* uses one pipe for steam and one pipe for return. In the one-pipe system, temperatures will fluctuate because the house becomes hot when the steam pressure is up and cool when the pressure is released for the return of the vapor. Temperatures remain more uniform with a two-pipe system.

A steam system cannot be adapted to central air conditioning.

Hot water

In this system, water is heated in a boiler and circulated through pipes to radiators. A *gravity hot-water system* is economical to install but responds slowly to temperature changes; moreover it requires a basement and well-insulated pipes. A *forced hot-water system* responds quickly to heat demands, may be installed in houses without basements, and uses smaller pipes without insulation. In hot-water systems, water must be drained out of the pipes if the house is closed in winter. Air conditioning may be adapted to hot-water systems.

Radiant home heating

Ideally, heat for radiant home heating should come from all directions. Generally, radiant home heat is provided by *convection* or *radiation*. Circulation of warm air from baseboard panels — which provides comfort, uniform heat, and quick response to temperature changes — is an example of heating by convection. Ceilings and floors with built-in heating coils exemplify radiation — heat received directly from heated objects. Usually heat radiated from heated ceilings makes rooms more comfortable than coil-heated

floors. Radiant heat facilitates the arrangement of furniture. If radiant home heating is provided by warm-air or hot-water systems, air conditioning may be added.

Temperature zoning

Many people prefer to have bedroom temperatures lower than temperatures in living areas. This may be accomplished by turning off heat in some rooms; however, temperatures may be controlled more uniformly by installing two heating units in a rambling house, by equipping some types of heating systems with two thermostats, or by heating separate rooms by electricity with individual thermostats.

★ WHAT FUEL WILL YOU USE?

The fuel will depend upon availability, reliability of delivery, cost, and efficiency in heating the house. *Gas* is clean, quick, and quiet, but in many areas it is expensive and

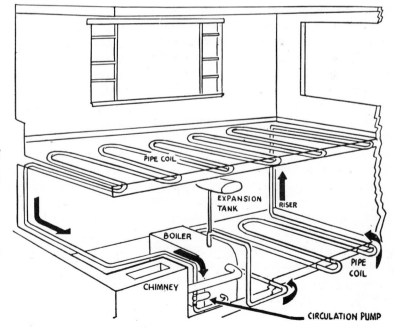

ILLUSTRATION 38. *Panel heating. The building structure itself is heated by pipe coils located beneath the surface of the floors, thus warming the air and the objects in the room. A conventional boiler or furnace produces the heat. No radiators or registers are visible.*

pressure is low at certain times of the day. *Oil* is not quite as clean as gas but it is quick, quiet, and, in many areas, less expensive.

Coal may be the least expensive fuel in some areas. Coal can be treated to decrease the dirt, and a stoker reduces much of the labor. *Electricity* for central heating is available in areas near power projects. It is clean, efficient, safe, silent, and uses no floor space — but the house to be heated by electricity must be well insulated.

✶ HOW WILL YOU PROVIDE FOR AIR CONDITIONING?

Besides controlling temperatures, air conditioning regulates humidity, purifies the air, eliminates drafts, prevents furniture from drying out, and reduces cleaning bills. It is desirable for people with allergies.

Types of air conditioning

Air conditioning may be provided by a central heating–cooling unit, by a separate central unit, or by individual room air conditioners. In new homes it is advisable to provide for future air conditioning when the heating system is planned.

Summer comfort depends upon relative humidity. You feel more comfortable on a hot dry day than you do on a hot humid day. With temperatures between 75° and 80° F. and the relative humidity below 60, the climate is considered ideal.

Air conditioning provides and maintains this ideal climate. With an air-conditioning system, the air is cooled, purified, and dehumidified by means of an *air-cooled* or a *water-cooled* condenser. The air-cooled condenser is seldom used with air conditioners of over 3-ton capacity. A ton refers to the amount of heat necessary to melt a ton of ice in one day. The average home (based upon size, and activities) requires a 3- to 3½-ton unit.

The water-cooled condenser uses from 75 to 150 gallons of water per hour for each ton of cooling. However, a cooling tower may save up to 95 per cent of the water by cooling it and using it over and over.

Good insulation and air circulation inside, plus natural or artificial shade outside, make air-conditioning systems more effective and economical.

The heat pump

Using a heat pump is a newer method of providing year-round air conditioning. This all-electric pump, requiring no water or fuel, is useful for cooling homes and small businesses. Indoor equipment needed includes air circulation fan, filter, combination heating–cooling unit, and auxiliary heaters. The section outdoors contains the refrigerating compressor, air-cooled condenser, and automatic electric controls.

Air conditioning an existing home

Central air conditioning may be installed in existing homes with warm-air or hot-water heating systems. With a *forced warm-air system* a number of methods of installation are possible. The most common is to install the main cooling unit beside the furnace, with the compressor and the condenser outside. Cool air may be diffused through ceiling, sidewall, baseboard, or floor vents. With a *hot-water system*, radiators and convectors are replaced with "remote room units" containing coil, drip pan, air filter, motor fan, and controls.

✶ WHAT PRACTICES WILL GIVE THE BEST RESULTS FROM YOUR HEATING AND COOLING SYSTEM?

The following practices will keep the house warmer in winter and cooler in summer.

1. Insulate well. Insulation comes in roll, sheet, and bulk forms for installation by blowing or pouring. In thickness, roof insulation should be from four to six inches, wall insulation (unless there is a basement), two inches. A vapor barrier is necessary to prevent condensation.

2. Keep blinds and shutters closed on very cold and very hot days. Outdoor shutters are much more effective than shades indoors.

3. Use thicker walls (or thicker insulation and fewer windows) on western exposures to shield the house from sun, and on exposed areas to protect the house from strong winds.

4. Choose the proper heating system in relation to climate and size and style of house.

5. Have the heating and cooling system checked regularly.

6. Avoid having more than five degrees difference between day and night thermostat settings. Keep doors closed when windows are open in winter or air conditioning units are in use in summer.

7. Seal cracks around doors and windows. In winter use storm doors and windows on sides with windy exposures.

8. Understand the heating system's operation.

ILLUSTRATION 39. *Ceiling insulation is a particularly effective way to shut out excessive heat and cold. Mineral wool (shown here in enclosed batts) is one excellent insulating material.*

ILLUSTRATION 40.   *The wall-hung toilet facilitates cleaning, as does the contemporary-style cabinet lavatory, which also provides excellent bathroom storage.*

✦ HOW WILL YOU PLAN YOUR PLUMBING NEEDS?

Plumbing installations must conform with local plumbing codes regarding size and kind of pipes used. However, a minimum amount of material and labor is needed when pipes are concentrated in one area. In a one-story house plumbing for bathroom and kitchen may be placed on a wall adjacent to both rooms. In a two-story house the pipes may be placed *vertically* with the kitchen under the bathroom. It may not always be desirable to economize on plumbing in these ways if such an arrangement interferes with livability.

✦ WHERE WILL YOU PLACE BATHROOM FIXTURES?

The smallest size bathroom that will accommodate a full-sized tub is five feet square. In this area, a small lavatory and a toilet will have to be placed on opposite walls; the door must be centered and open out. A bathroom 5 by 8 feet or larger is more desirable. When the bathroom is long and narrow, the lavatory should be placed between the tub and the toilet. The tub should not be placed under a window if this can be avoided. A tub is preferable to a shower stall if there is only one bathroom. If there is not enough space for an adequate number of bath towels, a portable rack may be a convenience. If the lavatory does not have a counter or a cabinet, there should be a shelf nearby and a medicine cabinet over the lavatory.

If a large bathroom can be divided with a wall separating the tub from the other two fixtures, it may be more useful. A dressing area in the bathroom is attractive if the bathroom serves only one or two people. Having a washer and dryer in the bathroom may be convenient for families with small children, but generally is undesirable.

ILLUSTRATION 41A. *Bathroom 5 by 6½ feet (right). This is the minimum space for fixtures along one wall and for the door to open into the room.*

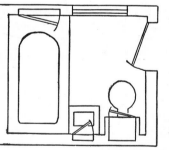

41B. *Bathroom 5 by 8 feet (below). Fixtures are along one wall, and more ample storage space is allowed.*

41C. *A divided bathroom (below). Efficiency in the use of fixtures is comparable to that of having two bathrooms. One-wall placement of fixtures is allowed.*

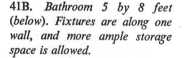

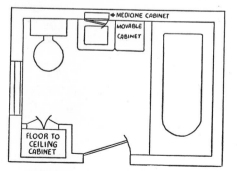

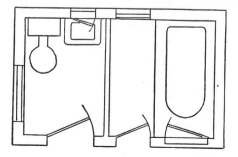

★ WHAT IS ADEQUATE WIRING?

When electric wires are carrying an overload, there are certain warning signals to show that wiring is inadequate. Toast may take longer to brown, the vacuum cleaner may fail to pick up all the dirt, the television picture may flicker, lights may become dim when major appliances are turned on. As a final warning a fuse may blow out or a circuit breaker may be tripped. If this happens frequently, your wiring should be checked to prevent fires.

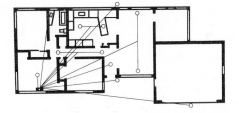

ILLUSTRATION 42A. *From your bedroom or some other convenient central place, you can control lights and appliances in all parts of the house if you have a remote-control wiring system.*

Entrance wires and branch circuits

If a house is adequately wired there should be three heavy wires entering the house from the main power line. These wires will come together at the service entrance and lead to the electric meter. The entrance switch or main circuit breaker should have a capacity of 100 amperes, which is adequate for the average home using approximately 25,000 watts of electricity. The number of watts used is indicated on all light bulbs and most small appliances. One kilowatt is equal to 1000 watts, if power should be listed in kilowatts.

The four types of branch circuits are *general purpose* (115–120 volts), *small appliance* (115–120 volts), *individual* (115–120 volts) for low-wattage large appliances like freezers, refrigerators, circulating fans, and washing machines, and *heavy-duty* (230–240 volts) for major appliances that heat or have heavy motors, such as electric ranges and hot-water heaters, and most electric dryers and air-conditioning units.

★ WHAT IS LOW-VOLTAGE REMOTE CONTROL?

Dial telephones, thermostats on furnaces, and push buttons on elevators operate by *low-voltage remote control*. This wiring system is common to new homes but expensive to

42B. *Fluorescent strips concealed by a wood cornice accent cherry red draperies and decorative wallpaper. A long fluorescent tube is concealed in the bookcase, too. Lamps provide local lighting, while a single ceiling spotlight highlights the dining table.*

install in existing homes. From a central control switch any or all lights in the house may be turned on or off individually or at once. A 24-volt switch and low-voltage wires relay messages to any outlet, and can even turn on the coffee pot. Nine lights may be controlled from one dial and master switch; more dials may be added for more lights. This system is safe, and it gives security from prowlers.

★ **WHAT PROVISION SHOULD BE MADE FOR LIGHTS, SWITCHES, AND OUTLETS?**

Provision should be made for background as well as decorative lighting when the wiring system is planned. For general lighting every room, with perhaps the living room an exception, should have one or more ceiling lights. Decorative lighting plus general lighting and lamps give a room character. Pictures, bookcases, corner cupboards, collections, and plants may be lighted with bracket or recessed ceiling spotlights. Recessed lights in the ceiling may accent the dining-room table, a furniture grouping or arrangement on a buffet, or a special collection. Every work place in the kitchen, laundry, workshop, and sewing or writing area should have good local lighting. For very close work it may be desirable to have an additional spotlight-type lamp.

A lamp on each side of the bedroom mirror and a tubular light on each side of the bathroom mirror will give better lighting than just one light. If the mirror is long, there should be an additional bracket light or local ceiling light. If a light is installed over a tub or in a shower stall, it should be vaporproof. If a bathroom needs additional heat, a fan heater may be installed in the overhead light. Illuminated ceiling panels and ceiling spotlights are increasing in use.

Switches are as important as lights. There should be a two-way switch at top and bottom of all flights of stairs and at each door if a room has two entrances. The switch should not be near the tub or lavatory in a bathroom. Switches may be had to control all the lamps in a room or to dial any degree of light desired. An automatic closet switch is a convenience, but a light with a chain will suffice in a closet.

Outlets should be within easy reach of the average six-foot cord at beds, sofas, and other places. It is hazardous to connect a number of cords to one plug or use numerous extension cords. All cords and plugs in kitchens, utility rooms, workshops, and outdoors should be rubber, and sockets should be por-

ILLUSTRATION 43. *Lighting an upstairs hall. A light switch is placed between the two bedroom doors, so that the hall can be lighted as soon as the occupants leave their rooms. A switch at the head of the stairs is also needed.*

celain for safety. Double and triple outlets are preferable to single outlets, especially in bedrooms where it may be necessary to connect a lamp, a clock, and an electric blanket or heating pad. It should never be necessary to disconnect a lamp to use an appliance. There should be sufficient outlets or an appliance panel in the kitchen and enough outlets near the serving area in the dining room for connecting appliances.

SUGGESTED ACTIVITIES

1. Take a class survey to find out what heating systems are represented. Discuss advantages and disadvantages.

2. List the heating systems that may be used in houses without basements; with basements.

3. Evaluate the heating system in your home from the standpoint of cost of installation, ease of operation, and efficiency in supplying the proper amount of heat. Find out what it costs to heat your home for a year.

4. If possible, find out from home users in your community their opinions as to the advantages and disadvantages of using gas, oil, and coal as a fuel.

5. Find out what it would cost to convert a coal furnace to (a) gas and (b) oil.

6. List the heating systems that may be adapted to air conditioning. Investigate cost of adding central air conditioning.

7. Mount illustrations of different air conditioning systems.

8. Investigate the extra cost of installing and operating year-round air conditioning in the homes of several members of your class.

9. Discuss what you do to keep your house cooler in summer and warmer in winter. What else can you do?

10. Find out what it would cost to insulate an average-priced home to meet FHA requirements and to meet recommendations suggested in the text.

11. On your classroom bulletin board display floor plans showing adjacent and vertical plumbing, and rambling plumbing layouts.

12. From your city or borough engineer find out what you can about the plumbing code.

13. Mount illustrations of well-planned bathrooms.

14. Find out how many amperes you have available to take care of your home wiring needs, and what volt circuits you have in your home.

15. Discuss the signs and dangers of inadequate wiring as applied to your own home.

16. Discuss lighting, switches, and outlets in relation to your own home.

How will you evaluate a ready—built place?

RATHER than build a home, your family may choose to buy or rent a ready-built house or apartment. Knowing how to judge a homesite and understanding the principles of home planning will help you in evaluating a ready-built place. If you are buying a house, you will want to know the quality of its construction and how much necessary repairs will add to the ultimate cost of the house. You may be thinking of remodeling it, and you will want to know whether or not it is worth remodeling. If you are to rent a place, you will want to know the terms under which you are renting and the services you can expect. But whether you intend to rent or to buy, the first consideration is whether or not the place will provide the values you desire in a home.

✱ DOES THE PLACE MEET THE NEEDS OF THE FAMILY?

The following questions will suggest points which must be thought through in judging whether or not a ready-built house or an apartment will meet your family's needs.

1. Is the neighborhood desirable?
2. Is there sufficient bedroom space for the family?
3. Are the work centers well planned? (For example, centers for food preparation, laundry, sewing)
4. Is the place easily accessible to work, shopping centers, school, church, and the like?
5. Is storage space adequate and conveniently placed? (For example, for outer and inner clothing, children's toys, tools, cleaning equipment, kitchen equipment and supplies, games and card tables, trunks, bicycles, fishing and hunting equipment, garden tools)
6. Is the space for eating satisfactory?
7. Are the facilities for recreation, hobbies, and entertaining adequate?
8. Do sleeping areas provide good ventilation, adequate space, and sufficient privacy?
9. Are kitchen and living room exposures desirable?
10. Are bathroom facilities sufficient for family and guests? (If the house is two story, a partial bath on the first floor preferably near the service entrance is a great asset if there are young children in the family and if a first-floor room is ever used for a bedroom.)
11. Is there space for guest accommodations?
12. Will the rooms lend themselves to furnishings already on hand?
13. Are bedrooms accessible without passing through the living room?
14. Is there too much lost hall space?
15. Is there an upstairs exit over the roof or the garage if a fire should block the stairs?
16. What has the present occupant to say about the house?

✦ **IS THE HOUSE WELL CONSTRUCTED?**

If you buy a poorly constructed house, the cost of repairs and improvements added to the purchase price may cause you to overrun your allowance for a house. The following questions will be of help in checking the construction of a house. Some of the questions also apply to renting a house. Those marked * pertain to renting a house as well as to buying a ready-built one. Enlist the help of a qualified person in judging those questions which you cannot decide alone

*1. Is the heating system adequate and in good condition? Can you burn the fuel of your choice? Can you estimate heating costs?

*2. Is the house wired for convenience and special equipment?

3. Will the house require insulation or weather stripping?

*4. Will the roof withstand a downpour of rain without leaking?

5. Are gutters and drain pipes large enough to carry off water during a storm?

*6. Is the basement moistureproof?

7. Are the walls free of termites?

*8. Do all stairways have handrails?

*9. Can flues and chimneys pass the tests of the National Board of Fire Underwriters of the American Standards Association?

*10. Are the floors in good condition?

11. Does all plumbing pass your inspection in appearance and action? (For example, adequate water pressure both upstairs and downstairs, reliable temperature controls, and satisfactory performance of toilet flush boxes, drain pipes, and basement drain.) A qualified plumber should be called to give a thorough inspection.

12. Will the cost of exterior upkeep be high? (A frame structure is more expensive to keep up than brick or stone, though the original cost may be less.)

*13. Are all hinges and locks in good repair? Is the other hardware, such as doorknobs, neat and in good condition?

14. Are the walls free of plaster cracks?

15. Is the floor plan completely satisfactory? (If not, secure an estimate on remodeling and include the cost in the purchase price.)

16. Are joists, posts, and basement beams of good wood?

17. Are the foundation, eaves, doors, and windows level?

18. Does the roof have good gutters, sound leaders, and firm shingles or smooth slate or metal roofing?

✦ **IS THE HOUSE WORTH REMODELING?**

Your family may buy a house with the thought of remodeling it, or you may already own a house which you would like to modernize. Perhaps changing an entrance and adding a terrace, shutters, or new paint will do the necessary "face lifting" if the floor plan meets your family's needs. If the house is too large or too small, it may need more extensive remodeling. Before undertaking remodeling on a large scale, get a fairly accurate estimate of the cost. Find out what repairs, if any, would have to be made to make the house structurally sound. Then decide whether or not your house could be sold if you added the cost of repairs and remodeling to its present sale price. If it would not sell at the new figure, remodeling would be an unwise expenditure.

A few general points to remember if you have decided that the house is worth remodeling are these:

1. Make a complete plan for remodeling before starting any part of it, even though all the work cannot be done at once.

2. Engage the services of an architect for the final preparation of your plans. If it is an

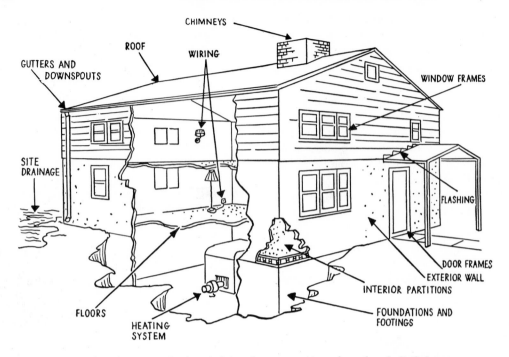

ILLUSTRATION 44.   *Points to check in judging the construction of an already-built house*

extensive job, he will be able to save you money.

3. Avoid changing the plumbing layout, because plumbing changes are costly.

4. Before changing your heating system, make sure that the change will be completely satisfactory and worth the cost involved.

★ WHAT WILL BE SOME CONSIDERATIONS IN RENTING?

Deciding on a house or an apartment to rent presents some special considerations, even though the family must judge the livability of the place in much the same way it judges a house to be built or bought. You must consider the location, how well the house will meet the needs of the family, how well it will accommodate your present furnishings and equipment. Finally, the amount of

the rent must be within your price range. There should be an understanding between tenant and landlord about the following:

1. A schedule for papering, painting, and finishing floors.

2. Responsibility for paying for water, light, and heat.

3. Removal of trash and garbage.

4. Supplying refrigerator, range, washer, and dryer.

5. Cleaning basement and cutting grass.

6. Supplying supplementary heat and extra outlets.

7. Restrictions concerning children and pets.

8. Services included in lease such as washing windows, polishing floors.

9. To whom rent is to be paid and when.

10. Conditions under which lease may be terminated.

✦ **HOW WILL YOU PLAN MOVING?**

Our population has become mobile, with one person in every five moving each year. If you are planning to move, the following suggestions should be helpful.

Arrange to terminate your lease or sell your home as soon as plans are definite. Although real estate agents charge a percentage of a house's selling price, their contacts will facilitate disposing of property.

Contact the moving van company in advance to obtain approximate costs and make sure of the special dates and equipment requested. Arrangements may have to be made for disconnecting and installing major labor-saving appliances.

Prepare a list of friends, relatives, stores, shops, magazine subscription departments, insurance companies (life, fire, auto, liability, hospitalization), and other businesses to be notified of your change of address. Most moving companies will supply printed forms to send.

Terminate newspaper, milk, laundry, and other delivery services.

Write letters requesting that your club and other memberships be dropped or transferred. Church membership should not be terminated until you have located a church in your new community.

Accumulate all valuables: important papers, guarantees, stock and bond certificates, mortgages and other papers relative to real estate holdings, birth certificates, health records, children's school records, valuable jewelry, and furs; have these items sent registered mail. Some people prefer to take these things in the car with them, but this is not always safe. Never send these important and valuable items in the moving van.

Sketch on a floor plan the tentative furniture arrangement for your new home. Tag all furniture and label all boxes. Be on hand when the van arrives to direct the unloading and placement of furnishings.

Contact utility companies to have water, gas, electric, and telephone service discontinued at the old address and to have these services started at the new place.

Take with you a copy of the telephone directory — convenient in checking addresses.

SUGGESTED ACTIVITIES

1. List the general reconditioning which usually needs to be done in a house or an apartment that has been occupied previously.

2. Ask your father or some other well-qualified person to help you judge your house from the standpoint of good or poor construction.

3. If possible, visit some house or apartment which is for rent, and judge the location and floor plan from the standpoint of livability.

4. Bring to class pictures of houses before and after remodeling. Try to relate cost of remodeling to purchase price of house.

5. Select several floor plans of poorly planned homes and suggest improvements.

6. List points important in buying a house which may not be so important in renting one.

7. Give reports on the following: termite control, damp basements, remodeling of plumbing and wiring.

8. Secure a copy of a lease and discuss its provisions.

9. Provide bulletin board displays showing how to get more space or to add a workshop, family room, sewing area.

10. Display illustrations using wall panels or folding doors as room dividers.

11. Discuss experiences members of the class have had in moving. Add your own ideas to the suggestions for moving.

12. Price a new house that can be rented and is also for sale. Compare costs and satisfactions in renting and in buying the property.

SELECTED REFERENCES
FOR UNIT TWO

BOOKS

Beyer, Glenn H., *Housing: A Factual Analysis.* The Macmillan Company, New York, 1958

Bigelow, Howard F., *Family Finance.* J. B. Lippincott Company, Philadelphia, 1953

Dalzell, James Ralph, *Blueprint Reading for Home Builders.* McGraw-Hill Book Company, Inc., New York, 1955

Dalzell, James Ralph, *Concrete Block Construction for Home and Farm.* American Technical Society, Chicago, 1957

Dalzell, James Ralph, *Remodeling Guide for Home Interiors.* McGraw-Hill Book Company, Inc., New York, 1956

Dalzell, James Ralph, and Townsend, Gilbert, *How to Plan a House.* American Technical Society, Chicago, 1958

Eisinger, Larry, *How to Build and Contract Your Own Home.* Arco Publishing Company, Inc., New York, 1957

Fischman, Walter Ian, *The Week-end Builder.* Crown Publishers, Inc., New York, 1954

Kirkpatrick, Waldo A., *The House of Your Dreams — How to Plan and Build It.* McGraw-Hill Book Company, Inc., New York, 1958

CURRENT PUBLICATIONS

Write to the following addresses for booklets, current lists of literature, and prices:

Aluminum Company of America, 1211 Alcoa Building, Pittsburgh 19, Pennsylvania (*building materials*)

American Standard, 40 West 40th Street, New York 18, New York (*plumbing and heating*)

Better Homes and Gardens, Meredith Publishing Co., Des Moines, Iowa (*annual books on home improvement, home building, and remodeling*)

Carrier Corporation, Carrier Parkway, Syracuse 1, New York (*air conditioning*)

Harnischfeger Homes, Inc., Port Washington, Wisconsin (*precut homes*)

Iron Fireman Manufacturing Company, 3170 West 106th Street, Cleveland, Ohio (*heating and air conditioning*)

Johns Manville Corporation, 22 East 40th Street, New York 16, New York (*insulation and building materials*)

Mobile Homes Manufacturing Association, 20 North Wacker Drive, Chicago 6, Illinois (*mobile homes*)

National Adequate Wiring Bureau, 155 East 44th Street, New York 17, New York (*wiring, outlets, and switches*)

National Gypsum Company, Buffalo 2, New York (*walls and insulation*)

National Homes Corporation, Lafayette, Indiana (*precut homes*)

National Housing Center, 1625 L Street, N.W., Washington, D.C. (*general literature on housing and equipment*)

R. O. W. Sales Company, 1365 Academy Avenue, Ferndale 20, Michigan (*windows*)

Swift Homes, Inc., Elizabeth, Pennsylvania (*precut homes*)

U.S. Government Printing Office, Washington 25, D.C.

FHA Home Owner's Guide, Catalogue No. 2.6/6:H 75

Planning the Bathroom, 1952 (Home and Garden Bulletin No. 19)

Remodel, Repay, Repair, Catalogue No. HH 2.2R 28/956

When You Buy a House, Look at the Lot and Neighborhood, Catalogue No. HH 1.2:75

Your Home Buying Ability, Catalogue No. HH 2.2H 75/11

U.S. Steel Company, Pittsburgh 30, Pennsylvania (*steel homes*)

Bette Malone, United Van Lines, St. Louis 17, Missouri (*planned moving*)

Small Homes Council, University of Illinois, Urbana, Illinois (*home building*)

The Wiremold Company, Hartford 10, Connecticut (*wiring and outlets*)

3

Plan
work and storage
centers
for convenience
and efficiency

ILLUSTRATION 45.   *This attractive and spacious dining area is located conveniently near the kitchen—which is well planned so that there is no cross traffic.*

CHAPTER I

How may arrangement of work areas contribute to efficient homemaking?

EFFICIENCY in the arrangement of work areas is as important in the home as it is in industry. Although the amount of work done in the home has decreased through the years, emphasis upon more efficient methods of doing the remaining work has increased. By conserving time and energy spent on household tasks, family members have more leisure hours in which to enjoy companionship. In order to conserve time and energy, home planning specialists have applied principles of good management to the planning of work areas in the home.

The most significant improvements have been made in kitchen planning which has reached a high degree of perfection since the early 1930's when research was begun. Kitchens have become not only efficient food preparation centers but pleasant, convenient, and sanitary places in which to live and work. Laundries are also becoming cheerful, convenient, and efficient work centers. An understanding of the principles underlying efficiency will help you in evaluating and improving the work centers in your home.

✳ WHAT FUNCTIONS MUST THE KITCHEN SERVE?

A homemaker spends a large part of her day in the kitchen. While she is at work, she may need to supervise young children at play. She will have to answer calls at the front door, back door, and telephone. She may have to dovetail her work in the kitchen with that of doing the family laundry, tidying up the house, and preparing the dining room for guests. All these points should be kept in mind in judging the location of the kitchen in relation to the other parts of the house and yard.

Although the kitchen is primarily a food preparation center, it may also have to serve as a full-time or occasional dining area, a laundry, or a daytime nursery. Frequently the ironing, if not the washing, is done in the kitchen. The kitchen often serves as the office in the house where accounts are kept and where market lists and menus are made. With these functions in mind, the kitchen in the home of a family should not be too small. For the sake of efficiency, neither should it be too large. An oblong shape is easier to arrange than a square shape.

✳ WHAT PHYSICAL CHARACTERISTICS SHOULD THE KITCHEN HAVE?

As a work center for the preparation of food, a kitchen must be cheerful, sanitary, well ventilated, and adequately lighted. Surfaces should be durable, nonabsorbent, stain resistant, and easily cleaned. In addition to

ILLUSTRATION 46. *Activities controlled from the kitchen. Ideally the kitchen should be located so that all of the activities which go on in the following centers could be controlled.*

1. *Work area — meal preparation*
2. *Play pen or nook for children's play*
3. *Front door — callers*
4. *Telephone*
5. *Rest area or planning center*
6. *Laundry — ironing*
7. *Back yard — drying clothes, children at play*
8. *Laundry — washing*
9. *Back door — deliveries*
10. *Storage area — cleaning supplies, food, equipment*
11. *Dining area — serving*

these qualities, counter surfaces should be heat resistant. Closets must be verminproof. Cross ventilation is desirable for the comfort of the worker. An exhaust fan is recommended for the removal of odors and some of the cooking heat. Near the kitchen door, there should be a table or counter for receiving and separating produce and groceries. Between the kitchen and living area there should be a closet for cleaning supplies and equipment.

A kitchen needs all the natural light possible. One general rule is to have the window area occupy at least 10 per cent and preferably 15 or 20 per cent of the floor area. A window over the sink where so much of the work is done permits a mother to enjoy a pleasant view while she works as well as to supervise her children at play in the yard. A general ceiling light and a light over each work area are desirable. Kitchen ceilings should be painted a very light color for good light reflection. Good lighting will reduce fatigue and prevent accidents. These are important considerations in any work area.

✦ HOW CAN YOU JUDGE KITCHEN EFFICIENCY?

The kitchen is often thought of as the control center of the house, yet it is frequently poorly located and poorly planned.

A well-located kitchen is (1) convenient to living areas, (2) planned so that its only exit is not through a garage, (3) arranged so that children can be supervised at play, (4) amply supplied with natural light, and (5) near the food-serving areas, so that it is not necessary to carry supplies through other rooms.

The Cornell Kitchen Study sets a kitchen minimum of 80 square feet, but recommends 96 square feet for greater efficiency, and 112 square feet if a wall oven and a dishwasher are built in. To have an eating area in the kitchen, you need a room at least 11 feet by 12 feet.

The Small Homes Council of the University of Illinois recommends a work triangle with from 4 to 6 feet between range and sink (measured from center fronts of the appliances), 4 to 7 feet between refrigerator and sink, and 4 to 9 feet between range and refrigerator. A work triangle with a total distance of from 15 to 22 feet is considered satisfactory.

ILLUSTRATION 47. *Good lighting is of special importance in the kitchen. Notice the broad fluorescent ceiling light, the bracket lights over the sink and the range, and the lighting over the corner work counter.*

For kitchen storage space, the Small Homes Council recommends 20 linear feet of wall space (base cabinets plus wall cabinets) as a liberal amount, $17\frac{1}{2}$ feet for average use, and 15 feet as the minimum for any kitchen. Four feet must be added to compensate for each corner used for storage cupboards.

Desirable counter space should include: 15 inches beside the refrigerator on the side the door opens; 36 inches on the right of sink for stacking dishes; the 30 inches on the left of sink for draining and drying; 24 inches near the range for serving; and 36 inches of unbroken counter space for mixing near the sink.

In analyzing over a hundred kitchens, the Small Homes Council found that the commonest faults were: poorly arranged work triangles, too little counter and storage space, too many doors, and doors opening in the wrong direction.

✦ WHAT IS A DUAL-PURPOSE KITCHEN?

By having the kitchen serve more than one purpose, many activities can be dovetailed for greater efficiency and more personal satisfaction.

Play area: In the home where there are small children, a definite play area with storage shelves is an asset. It should be out of main traffic lanes and the work triangle. The space may be converted to other uses later.

Hobby center: A mother who is a full-time homemaker may want to pursue a hobby or part-time job in the kitchen.

Writing nook: A desk for planning menus and writing letters is desirable if space permits.

Sewing and mending space: Sewing and mending are easier if the sewing machine is near the ironing board.

Gourmet corner: If a person enjoys preparing fancy foods (perhaps for sale), she will enjoy having cabinet space for special ingredients.

Laundry room: Most women prefer having the washer and dryer in or near the kitchen to any other location in the house.

Family room: The big old-fashioned kitchen minus former inconveniences is popular now. A braided rug, fireplace, big table for eating and studying, and television can make the kitchen a true family center. A comfortable chair or two will be appreciated by kitchen visitors.

Dining area: An attractive kitchen can be a very pleasant family dining area. Women at the Congress on Better Living preferred a kitchen table to a counter for eating.

✦ WHAT ARE THE BASIC KITCHEN LAYOUTS?

Many changes have occurred in kitchen layouts since the hospital-like kitchen of the early fifties, but the general layouts are basic: the one-wall, corridor, L-shaped, and U-shaped kitchens. Each is planned around three major appliances — refrigerator, sink, and range. Peninsular and island kitchens are variations of basic layouts.

Logically, the refrigerator and storage space should be near the service door, with a cart or counter for unloading.

Ordinarily the sink comes between refrigerator and range. Work between sink and range requires an absolute minimum of 36 inches. More space is necessary if the sink bowl is recessed in the counter and has no drain.

The *two-wall or corridor kitchen* requires an 8-foot minimum room width to provide 4 feet between counters. In the corridor kitchen, counter space is broken and traffic must pass through the work area. For working efficiency, the sink and range should be on the same wall with a minimum of 30 inches at the end of the sink nearest the wall and a minimum of 24 inches on the side of the range nearest the opposite wall. The length of space between should be 36 inches. On the opposite wall, the refrigerator and the wall oven may be at the ends, and an eating or work area between.

ILLUSTRATION 48. *This island kitchen provides surface cooking units as well as storage and counter space in the middle of the room. The wall oven, installed at a convenient height, and the washing machine and dryer, in space-saving stacked position, give further evidence that this is an efficient and compact work area.*

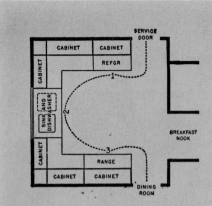

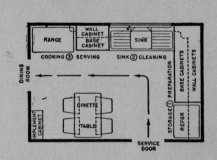

ILLUSTRATION 49A. *The U shape. Work centers are placed around the three sides of the U.*

49B. *The L shape. Again the sink is placed between the range and the refrigerator, but only two walls are used.*

1. *Refrigerator and mixing center*
2. *Sink center*
3. *Range and serving center*

The *U-shaped kitchen* has been popular because it is compact and step-saving. The sink is placed inside the U, with the range center near the dining area and the refrigerator near the outside door. In the U-shaped kitchen, traffic does not interfere. A little space left for a breakfast table makes counter service more feasible. A nearby dining area is desirable. The corner cabinets are not usable unless a set of revolving shelves or a cabinet door with swing shelves is installed. The U lends itself well to a kitchen-laundry combination.

The *one-wall kitchen* is acceptable when space is limited. The sink should be in the center, with the longest counter space between the sink and range for food preparation. The refrigerator may be in one end, with door opening toward work area; and a wall oven may be at the other end.

The *L-shaped kitchen* was found to be the most efficient in the Cornell Kitchen Study. This arrangement provides an uninterrupted work area and leaves two walls free for doors, a cleaning closet, table, and chairs. The washer and dryer, with an additional sink, are often backed against one side of the L to give a peninsular effect. Ample counter space is desirable near the dining area for quick meals and occasional snacks.

The *island kitchen* may be within an L or a U. In some plans the island contains the surface cooking units and a snack bar. In other plans the island contains a trash receptacle, a second sink, and a dishwasher. It actually combines an L-shape and corridor or U-shape and corridor. An island is inefficient when you have to cross the floor between range surface and sink, and hazardous when the range is too near the table.

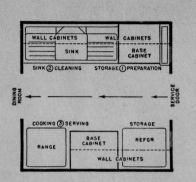

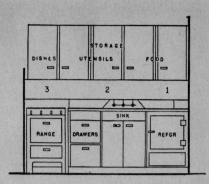

49C. *The two wall. This type kitchen is best adapted to a narrow room since work units must be placed on opposite walls.*

49D. *The one wall. Space for preparing family meals is limited in this compact type of plan.*

1. *Refrigerator and mixing center*
2. *Sink center*
3. *Range and serving center*

The *peninsula* makes use of one arm of the U- or L-shaped kitchen by backing up an eating or laundry area. The peninsula may be a divider between kitchen and dining room with a double-width counter. Cabinets may be suspended from the ceiling back to back to provide storage space for both areas. The space between the wall cabinets and lower cabinets is usually open for a pass-through with a folding or pull-down partition.

★ HOW WILL YOU PLAN YOUR KITCHEN COUNTERS AND STORAGE SPACE?

In planning storage space, a general rule is to store supplies and utensils at their point of first use — in the work center where they will be used. Space in both base and wall cabinets may be used. Where various articles are stored will depend upon such factors as availability of space, frequency of use, and size and shape of the articles. Individual needs and preferences in storing different articles vary, but the following guide may offer suggestions for improving your present storage areas or for planning a new kitchen.

Storage in the sink center

Since the greatest amount of activity goes on in the sink center, we shall begin here. Store (1) fruits and vegetables not requiring refrigeration in well-ventilated bins; (2) dishwashing and cleaning equipment in ventilated cabinets, placing towels and cloths that are in use on racks; (3) clean towels and dishcloths in drawers, placing the towels on the side of the sink where dishes are dried and the cloths on the side where dishes are washed; (4) garbage pail or garbage bags, if the sink has no disposal unit, in cabinet space on either side or under the sink; (5) paring knives, can

STEP SHELF FOR
CONDIMENTS

SLIDING SHELVES FOR
POTS AND PANS

VENTILATED STORAGE BIN
FOR VEGETABLES

METAL-LINED DRAWERS FOR
BREAD AND CAKE

REVOLVING CORNER CUPBOARD
FOR MIXING EQUIPMENT

PARTITIONED DRAWER FOR
TINS AND LIDS

ILLUSTRATION 51. *Convenient accessories for wall and base cabinets. When placed in the appropriate work centers, the accessories shown on this page add to the convenience of the kitchen. They also add to the cost and are secondary in importance to a good basic kitchen plan.*

openers, and other cutlery in small drawers; (6) brushes, strainers, a colander hanging in convenient places; (7) dishes and glasses in a wall cabinet on the side of the sink where they are dried.

Storage in the range or cooking center

Store (1) saucepans and double boiler on sliding shelves or in drawers; (2) lids and cake racks in partitioned cabinets or drawers; (3) spatula, potato masher, cake turner, and ladle in small drawers or on hooks; (4) roaster and frying pan in range or in other cabinet space near range.

Storage in the mixing center

Since the mixing center must be easily accessible to both the sink and the range, store (1) mixer, mixing bowls, and casseroles on adjustable shelves; (2) measuring cups and spoons, shears, biscuit cutter, individual salad molds, and other small equipment in small drawers; (3) muffin, cake, and pie tins in partitioned cabinets or drawers; (4) items such as flour, sugar, salt, tea, coffee, cocoa, baking powder, and shortening in cabinets; (5) spices, seasonings, and flavorings on step-up shelves or in space-conserving racks on the inside of cabinet doors; (6) wax paper, foil, transparent plastic wrap, and paper towels in convenient wall racks.

Storage in the serving center

Since this center is usually adjacent to the range, store (1) such appliances as toaster and waffle iron either on shelves or, if frequently used, on the counter under plastic covers; (2) serving trays in partitioned sections; (3) serving dishes on cabinet shelves; (4) every-day table linens in drawers; (5) bread, cookies, and cakes in jars or boxes or in metal-lined drawers.

✱ WHAT IS THE USUAL LAUNDRY CYCLE?

There are three major activities in the laundry cycle: (1) sorting, stain removal, and washing; (2) drying, and folding no-iron items; (3) dampening, sorting, and ironing the remaining items.

Sorting, stain removal, and washing

Whether this step takes place in the kitchen near the washer or in a separate laundry area, there should be a counter or table for sorting all items. On a shelf near the counter should be absorbents and solvents for removing grease marks and stubborn stains that may not come out in the wash. Lace and sheer garments and garments with seams that may ravel should be placed in a mesh bag before washing. Wearing garments and bedding should be separated from table linens. White items requiring bleach must be washed alone. Dark items should be washed alone to avoid discoloring other items, as well as absorbing lint from light cottons. If a semiautomatic washer is used, dark items should be washed in fresh water because the lint from light items remains suspended in the water.

The directions for using an automatic washer should be studied and followed if the best results are to be obtained. If a semiautomatic washer is used, rinsing must be thorough.

Drying, and folding no-iron items

If clothes are dried outside, it will facilitate work to use a laundry cart with a clothespin bag attached, rather than a clothes basket. Using hangers or drying frames for trousers will eliminate or minimize ironing. Items requiring no ironing, whether dried in a dryer or on the clothesline, should be folded promptly to minimize wrinkling. It is not necessary to iron sheets, underwear, sleeping garments, kitchen towels, and, of course, bath towels. Items that need only touch-up ironing should be folded loosely, also, to avoid unnecessary wrinkles.

The remainder of the laundry items, which need careful ironing, should be kept in a regular place near the ironing board until it is convenient to iron them.

Dampening, sorting, and ironing

Whether items to be ironed are dampened near the sink or in the laundry area, a bottle with a sprinkler top will dampen them more evenly than hand sprinkling.

Where to do the ironing is a matter of space and preference. A complete laundry area is ideal, but many people must do the ironing in the kitchen, sewing room, or bedroom. Some people like to do the ironing where they have a pleasant view, can supervise the children, or watch television.

A flat surface — table or cart — and a folding rack near the ironing board with hangers for dresses, shirts, blouses, skirts, and slacks will make it possible to organize work and sit down while doing most of the ironing. Garments that need to be folded may be removed from the hangers and folded after the iron has been disconnected.

✷ WHAT ARE SUITABLE LOCATIONS FOR THE AUTOMATIC LAUNDRY?

Laundering need not be done hit-or-miss fashion in the kitchen, bathroom, or laundry. Even though you may not have all modern equipment or a separate laundry center, you can work out a convenient plan.

When the laundry can be done adjacent to the kitchen or in a nearby first-floor utility room, other activities may be dovetailed. Perhaps the two disadvantages of having the laundry area in or very near the kitchen are heat and odors. When the laundry is done only once or twice a week, these objections may be ignored.

If the laundry center is in the basement, it may help to have a clothes chute. Many people prefer a basement laundry. They like running water, stationary tubs, space to hang clothes, and a concrete floor for drip-dry items such as outer garments and curtains. Many delicate pieces require careful washing, and only the newest washers and dryers are capable of handling such items.

If floor space does not permit placing the washer adjacent to the dryer, the two units may be stacked. When space is at a premium, a combination washer-dryer may be desirable. Objections to this unit are the extra time required to complete the washing and drying cycles, and the inconvenience of having both units affected in case of a breakdown.

Various locations are suggested for the washer-dryer or combination unit when there is no separate laundry area. These locations are indicated in Illustration 53.

SUGGESTED ACTIVITIES

1. Using scale drawings of kitchens and kitchen equipment, arrange an L-type, a U-shaped, a two-wall, and a one-wall kitchen.

2. Bring to class several types of first-floor plans, and study the location of the kitchen in relation to the front door, the back door, the laundry, the storage centers, and the dining area. Make suggestions that might improve the plans.

3. Collect and mount interesting kitchen and laundry plans. Be able to tell why you like each plan and what type of organization of work centers it represents.

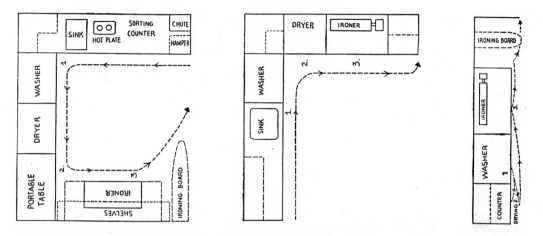

ILLUSTRATIONS 52 and 53. *Basic plans for home laundries or a laundry area. Centers for (1) washing, (2) drying, and (3) ironing are shown at the left in a U plan and at the center in an L plan. The one-wall plan on the right shows how a simple and efficient laundry area can be included in a kitchen or recreation room.*

4. Compare the work centers in your kitchen with those described on pages 79–81. If your kitchen is not arranged efficiently, make plans for improving it. If improvements must be made at little or no cost and if you need extra storage space, perhaps your father or your brother will help you build shelves where needed.

5. Study the storage of equipment and supplies in your kitchen. If improvement is needed, work out with your mother an improved system.

6. From prices secured at local stores or from those given in advertisements, propose a budget for equipping an up-to-date kitchen and laundry.

7. Discuss advantages and disadvantages of each type of kitchen plan, including island and peninsula plans.

8. Discuss the way you do laundry at home and means of improving your laundry cycle. Discuss advantages and disadvantages of various locations for the laundry.

CHAPTER 2

How may adequate storage areas facilitate homemaking?

OVER a period of years family possessions accumulate, for as the family grows, so do its possessions. Confusion and irritation among family members thrive when articles or personal possessions cannot be found, and much time is wasted searching for misplaced items. Accidents often result from awkwardly stored equipment of all kinds. To serve the family well, storage facilities must be carefully planned with adequate space and accessibility of that space in mind.

Storage space must be planned for articles and personal possessions that are used daily, weekly, or only seasonally. Providing space where it is needed and utilizing space which might otherwise be wasted are important considerations. Planning storage space means first of all taking an inventory of possessions to be stored.

Storage space for equipment and supplies used in food preparation and laundering has already been discussed. Articles to be stored and suggestions for storing them conveniently are discussed here in relation to the other main areas of the home.

★ WHAT ARE STORAGE REQUIREMENTS IN THE LIVING AREA?

The living area requires easily accessible storage facilities for a variety of articles which may include coats, hats, umbrellas, toys, books, games, card tables, sewing supplies, magazines, phonograph records, sheet music, musical instruments, and even tennis rackets and golf clubs. The minimum built-in storage space required is a coat closet in the entrance hall or in the living room near the front door if there is no hall. This closet should be large enough to store articles used daily or almost daily. The space should accommodate a rod for coats and a rack along one side for overshoes, with hooks above for umbrellas. Flat hat racks on the back of the door will provide space for hats used daily. A rod for scarfs and a slanting rack for purses and gloves can also be placed below the hat rack on the average door. Shelves above the coat rod may be used for hats, a sewing box, and small games. If card tables, tennis rackets, golf clubs, and the like are to be stored in the living area, a larger closet must be provided or possibly two closets will be needed.

In addition to the built-in closet, book shelves preferably with drawers or a cabinet below for magazines, sheet music, or games; tables and desks with drawers; and cabinets for sheet music or phonograph records will meet the needs of most families in the living area.

COLOR PLATE 1. *Here sectional furniture is grouped together to give storage space in the living room. The grouping also includes space for a desk which can be closed when not in use.*

COLOR PLATE 2. *In this living room, a built-in storage divider wall provides an entry hall and an entry closet — not shown. It also provides ample storage space, including a place for a television set or high fidelity reception equipment.*

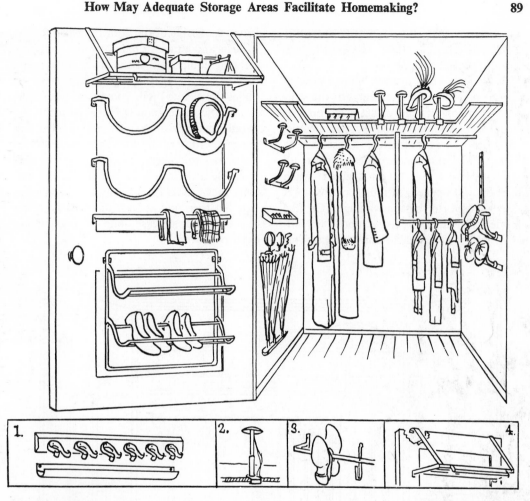

ILLUSTRATION 54.   *An efficiently arranged closet in the living area. The closet provides space for coats, hats, overshoes, and scarfs for both children and adults with ample provision for guests. A rack for dry umbrellas and one for purses and gloves are also provided. Enlarged details are (1) umbrella rack, (2) hat stand, (3) overshoe rack, and (4) utility rack.*

✭ **WHAT ARE STORAGE REQUIREMENTS IN THE DINING AREA?**

In the dining area provision must be made for storing linens, silver, china, and glassware. Frequently space in addition to that available in the usual movable furniture must be provided. Built-in cupboards in the dining room or adjacent to it, with shelves and doors, and a number of shallow built-in drawers for linens will make housekeeping and entertaining run more smoothly. A tarnishproof silver chest or a partitioned drawer lined with tarnishproof material is convenient for storing silver.

✳ **WHAT ARE STORAGE REQUIREMENTS IN THE SLEEPING, DRESSING, AND BATHING AREA?**

The sleeping areas in most houses meet at least the minimum requirements for the storage of clothing if one closet per room is provided. In rooms shared by two people, two closets are preferable. Closets with double or sliding doors are ideal because all the contents are revealed at a glance when the doors are opened. A long narrow closet is never used to best advantage. On the outside of double or single doors, a full-length mirror is an added convenience. This leaves the inside of the door for a rod for ties or belts and a rack or bag for shoes and shoe-cleaning equipment. If the closet is deep and narrow, sliding garment rods that may be pulled out into the room are desirable. A shallow closet may have a garment rod parallel with the door. Plain and padded coat hangers, trousers or skirt hangers, shoulder protectors, and plastic garment bags are other desirable accessories. Shelves above the garment racks should be arranged to accommodate hat trees and at least one hatbox, a frequently used suitcase, and if possible an extra bedcover.

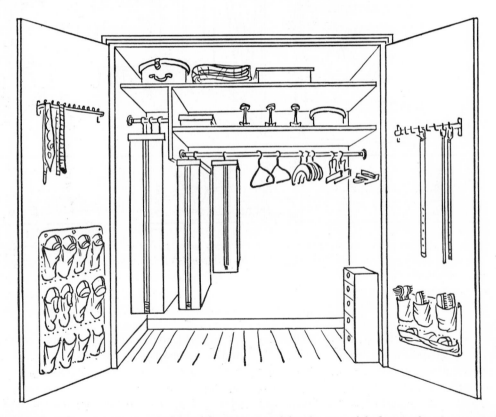

ILLUSTRATION 55. *A convenient bedroom closet. Designed for the owners' bedroom, this closet provides ample space and equipment for two. The double doors make the contents easily accessible.*

ILLUSTRATION 56. *A well-planned linen closet. Space for both clean and soiled linen is provided. The pull-out shelf is especially convenient when fresh linens are being placed in the closet or removed from it. A large house would call for more storage space probably in the hall.*

In planning closets for children, keep rods, shelves, and drawers scaled to the child. Metal strips with adjustable slats may be nailed to the closet walls so that shelves and rods may be raised as the child grows.

Drawers in chests, dressing tables, and dressers are usually spacious enough for flat garments and grooming articles. Partitioned boxes for cosmetics, jewelry, hose, handkerchiefs, and the like make caring for small items easier. A deep drawer in a chest is often a good place for your best hat, shoes, and purse if closet space is limited.

It should be understood whether or not personal possessions, such as toys, books, skates, tennis racket, rainy-day apparel, and the like are to be stored in one's bedroom or in the living area. If large items such as toys are to be kept in the bedroom, storage space should be planned. It might, however, be more convenient to store toys for small children near the living or work areas as well as in the sleeping area.

In bathrooms a medicine cabinet is generally provided for medicines, tooth paste, shampoos, razors, soaps, and the like. In addition it is desirable to have a built-in closet or small movable chest for towels, bath mats, and washcloths.

In some homes a linen closet in the hall may be planned to hold bath linens as well as bed linens. It should be easily accessible to both the bathroom and the bedrooms. A clothes hamper for soiled linens in or near the closet or the bathroom should be provided unless there is a clothes chute.

In the sleeping and dressing area two big storage problems present themselves — where to store winter blankets, and where to store winter clothing. Cedar-lined closets for these purposes are sometimes provided. Cedar chests, garment bags, blanket boxes, and the

ILLUSTRATION 57. *Besides providing storage space on both sides, the efficient and popular pass-through cabinet saves both steps and time. This one is between dining and kitchen areas, but pass-through cabinets are also useful for towel storage — between bathroom and linen closet.*

like may also be used. One or two oblong flat-top trunks have solved this problem in many homes. Trunks are not particularly attractive, but if you will place a pad or folded blanket on top, make a slip cover for the trunk, and stand one or two boxed cushions at the back, you will have an interesting hall love seat or bedroom window seat.

✦ WHAT ARE STORAGE REQUIREMENTS IN THE UTILITY AREA?

The utility area includes storage of cleaning equipment, workshop tools, and garden tools. Cleaning equipment used every day should be stored near where it is used, for example near the working or living areas. In a large house with two floors, a great deal of time and energy may be saved by keeping light cleaning equipment in a second-floor closet and extra cleansers, cloths, and brushes in the bathroom.

A convenient closet for cleaning supplies has shelves on one side for scrub bucket, brushes, polishes, waxes, and miscellaneous cleaning supplies. On the other side are clamps or hooks for hanging a long-handled dustpan, broom, and mop. A larger hook is necessary for the vacuum hose. Floor space is allowed for the vacuum cleaner. The back of the door may have a panel or pockets for whisk broom, cord, sponge, and dustcloths.

The space allotted for tools will vary greatly according to family interests and the size of the home. A small tool kit containing a hammer, a screw driver, pliers, an awl, possibly a small drill, and assorted nails and screws will meet the needs of any family for minor home repairs. The shadow panel shown in Illustration 182A on page 304 is convenient for keeping tools in their proper place.

Garden tools must also be stored conveniently in relation to their use. A partitioned space in the garage, a tool shed, or a section of the back porch are convenient storage places. It is awkward to drag a lawn mower and hose, for instance, up the basement stairs each time they are used. However, if the basement is at ground level on one side, it may be as convenient a place as any.

Storage spaces, particularly closets of any type, are brighter and more sanitary if the walls are painted a light color. It may be desirable to paper bedroom closets. But whether closets are papered or painted, tints may be chosen that tie in with other colors in the room. Hatboxes and other accessories should also harmonize in color. Remember though that convenience and utility are more important considerations than beauty.

SUGGESTED ACTIVITIES

1. Mount pictures of well-arranged closets. Tell why you consider them well arranged, and suggest any improvements that could be made.

2. Make an inventory of articles and equipment to be stored in your room. Judge your present method of storing them, and make any improvements needed.

3. Study the storage of items in the living area of your house. If improvements are needed, enlist your mother's help in making them.

4. Likewise, study the storage of cleaning equipment in your home. If needed, improve the storage arrangements in your cleaning closet.

5. Make closet accessories, such as padded coat hangers, shoulder protectors, dress covers, or shoe pockets, from attractive pieces of dress material, cretonne, or other drapery fabrics.

6. From newspaper advertisements, catalogues, or visits to stores, investigate the accessories for clothes closets which are available. Judge them from the standpoint of cost, durability, and serviceability.

SELECTED REFERENCES
FOR UNIT THREE

BOOKLETS AND PAMPHLETS

Write to the following addresses for booklets, current lists of literature, and prices:

Better Kitchens Institute, 812 Engineers Building, Cleveland 14, Ohio (*Kitchen Planning Book*)

Cleanliness Bureau, 295 Madison Avenue, New York 17, New York (*cleaning closets*)

Douglas Fir Plywood Association, Tacoma 2, Washington (*52 Fir Plywood Home Storage Plans*)

General Electric Company, Major Appliance Division, Appliance Park, Louisville 7, Kentucky (*kitchens and equipment*)

Hoover Home Institute, The Hoover Company, North Canton, Ohio (*closets*)

Hotpoint Company, 5600 West Taylor Street, Chicago 44, Illinois (*kitchens and equipment*)

Knape and Vogt Manufacturing Company, Grand Rapids, Michigan (*closet accessories*)

Masonite Corporation, 111 West Washington Street, Chicago 2, Illinois (*Panelok walls*)

Mullins Manufacturing Company, Youngstown Kitchens, Warren, Ohio (*kitchens*)

Mutschler Brothers Company, Nappanee, Indiana (*kitchens*)

St. Charles Custom Kitchens, 227 Tyler Road, St. Charles, Illinois (*Kitchen Planning Book*)

Small Homes Council, University of Illinois, Urbana, Illinois
  Cabinet Space for the Kitchen, C5.31
  Counter Surfaces, F9.1
  Handbook of Kitchen Design
  Kitchen Planning Standards, C5.32
  Laundry Areas, C5.4
  Separate Ovens, C5.33

U.S. Government Printing Office, Washington 25, D.C.
  Beltsville Energy-Saving Kitchen, 1957 (USDA leaflet No. 418)
  Beltsville Energy-Saving Kitchen, Design No. 2, 1959 (USDA leaflet No. 463)
  Beltsville Kitchen–Workroom with Energy-Saving Features, 1959 (Home and Garden Bulletin No. 60)
  A Step-Saving U-Kitchen, 1952 (Home and Garden Bulletin No. 14)

Westinghouse Electric Corporation, Mansfield, Ohio (*kitchens and equipment*)

Whirlpool Seeger Corporation, St. Joseph, Michigan (*kitchens*)

4

Learn
the basic rules
for using color
and applying
design principles

ILLUSTRATION 58. *Applying art principles in decorating the home. Skillful use of line, shape, texture, and color in this room produces the effect of order and beauty.*

CHAPTER I

How may you use the elements of design to create beauty? in your body?

ACCORDING to Dr. Cutler's study discussed earlier in this book, beauty is one of the satisfactions that people want in their homes. Even so, the opinions of different groups of people may vary as to the importance of beauty in comparison with other satisfactions. Nevertheless, psychologists have proved that people react emotionally to their surroundings. Thus beauty in the home is conducive to individual and family happiness.

Why do some rooms make you stop a minute at the doorway and say suddenly to yourself, "How attractive!" Maybe you think it is the grouping of colorful hunting scenes over the sofa, or the graceful draping of a swag over the window, or the interesting arrangement of pottery and vines among the books on the bookshelves. One thing in particular probably catches your eye and you think, "Ah, there's the secret to a charming and different room." You go home and perhaps cut up some old fabric from a trunk and add swags to your living room windows, or you hurriedly buy some trinkets at the five-and-ten-cent store and scatter them among your books, or you may buy a few inexpensive prints and arrange them in a group almost anywhere on your wall. No one

is impressed with the change, and people who know good design may be annoyed. But what could be wrong? You certainly tried to copy an idea that pleased you!

For one thing the room that impressed you was planned as a whole, so that all the rules of good design — proportion, balance, rhythm, emphasis, and harmony — were observed. Window treatments, picture arrangements, furniture, and wallpapers that are perfect in one type of house may be all wrong in another type. Good basic training in the use of design and color will help you to express good taste.

Technical art terms, such as proportion, gradation, and transition, may seem very vague, and you may want to steer away from them. Yet how will you judge a room without some score sheet or criteria? A knowledge of the elements and principles of good design gives you something tangible with which to work, just as specifications for a house provide directions for the architect. The results obtained through using basic information are as a rule more satisfactory than those obtained through trial and error, although you think sometimes that anyone should be able to copy the ideas of an expert.

ILLUSTRATION 59A. *Confusion in line and shape. Inharmonious use of lines and shapes creates a feeling of disorder in this room.*

59B. *Order in line and shape. The room appears restful when harmonious lines and shapes are used.*

✱ WHAT ARE THE ELEMENTS OF DESIGN?

First of all let us find out what art means because good design is an essential part of art. *Art is a man-made expression of something beautiful.* To the engineer it may mean a steel bridge that spans a wide river; to the sculptor, a powerful statue in bronze; to the painter, a vision on canvas; to the architect, a towering skyscraper; and to the homemaker, a beautiful home. Art is the aesthetic side of science, industry, and everyday living.

The elements of art are the rudiments with which the artist works whatever his category may be. Art elements include *line, form, texture,* and *color.* After discussing the first three, we will consider color separately.

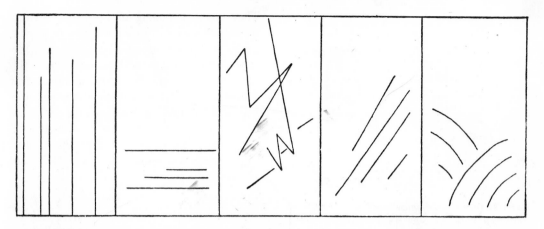

ILLUSTRATION 60.   *The psychology of line direction. Notice how vertical lines suggest dignity; horizontal, repose; zigzag, excitement; diagonal, movement; and curved, gracefulness.*

✳ HOW DOES LINE CONTRIBUTE TOWARD BEAUTY OF DESIGN?

Line is probably the basic element of beauty. Before the artist begins to paint in oil or in water color, he establishes the line directions of his painting on canvas or on paper. He combines horizontal, diagonal, vertical, and curved lines until the effect is pleasing to the eye. Before the dress designer is ready to cut and sew, he determines the predominating lines of the design by sketching with pencil and paper or by draping fabric on a form. Likewise the architect and the interior decorator must organize and combine lines before they can create beauty in a building or in a home.

Lines have certain psychological effects upon the observer. For example, study the groups of lines in Illustration 60, and give one word that expresses your reaction to each group of lines. Block out all the groups except the one you are studying at the time.

In any composition — a painting, a room, or a building — an interesting distribution of line is needed: vertical lines for strength, horizontal lines for repose and tranquility, diagonal lines for action, and curved lines for gracefulness and transition. Understanding the effects of these different kinds of lines will help you to use them to the best advantage in your home.

Vertical lines

These are masculine in effect — severe, strong, direct, disciplined, and militaristic.

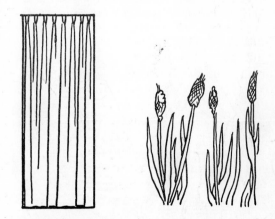

ILLUSTRATION 61.   *Application of vertical lines. Note the dignity in the draperies and in the cattails.*

ILLUSTRATION 62. *Application of horizontal lines. The chest and the sunrise suggest repose.*

ILLUSTRATION 63. *Application of diagonal lines. Note the movement suggested in the diagonal lines.*

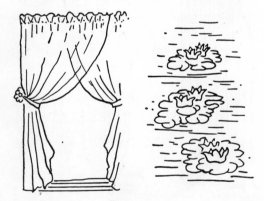

ILLUSTRATION 64. *Application of curved lines. The curves in the lily pads and curtains are dainty.*

They create a feeling of height. In nature these lines may call to mind a row of poplar trees, sunflowers along a country lane, or cattails rising from the low marshlands. In the home the vertical lines of doorways, draperies, secretaries, and highboys give the necessary strength and height to a room. In architecture vertical lines are associated with the spires and Gothic cathedrals of the Middle Ages and with the tall, slender, modern skyscraper.

Horizontal lines

These give solidity, a down-to-earth feeling. They also suggest repose, tranquility, serenity, and relaxation. They help to break the effect of vertical lines carrying one's eye upward, away from the earth. In nature horizontal lines suggest a hazy sunrise over the ocean or a brilliant sunset over the prairie. In architecture horizontal lines predominate in low rambling ranch houses and in many of the modern designs. In the home the horizontal lines of tables, low-back chairs, low bookcases, cornices, and baseboards complement the severely vertical lines in other parts of the room.

Diagonal lines

These are lines of action, disturbing the discipline of straight lines and the solidity of horizontal lines. Forward slanting lines suggest push, and backward slanting lines, pull. Diagonal lines are suggestive also of sophistication and refinement, and arouse interest — sometimes uneasiness. In nature they remind one of a windy day when trees bend toward the earth. In architecture diagonal lines form the slant of roofs and the support of eaves and spires. In the home diagonal lines appear in staircases and in the diagonal plaid of fabrics or wallpapers.

Curved lines

These lines are feminine in effect — graceful, subtle, carefree, youthful, and gay. In nature curved lines are suggestive of clouds, apple trees, rose petals, and winding streams. In architecture curved lines are found in the Taj Mahal — that gem of Indian architecture — and in the domes of Roman buildings, Renaissance cathedrals, and many of our state capitols. In the home curved lines may form a transition between the abrupt joining of vertical and horizontal lines, such as that formed by tie-back window curtains, in arches, and in the graceful curves of furniture.

✷ HOW MAY FORM CONTRIBUTE TOWARD BEAUTY OF DESIGN?

Form and line are closely related. The combination of curved, straight, or diagonal lines to produce three dimensions creates form or shape. Form is something solid and tangible. A combination of horizontal and vertical lines gives rectangular and square forms. A combination of vertical or horizontal and diagonal lines gives triangular, pentagonal, and hexagonal forms. Curves produce oval and circular forms, such as cylinders, spheres, domes, and cones.

Even though beauty in any room requires variety in the type of lines used, a predominance of square and oblong forms and straight lines are suited to a masculine room; and a predominance of oval and semicircular forms and curved lines, to a feminine room.

Shapes or forms may appear small or large by comparison with other forms, such as the size of the room or other furnishings. Shapes may also change their appearance according to the color or material used. A beautifully formed mahogany buffet, table, or secretary is even more handsome if silhouetted against a plain light yellow or light blue-green background than against a floral paper of medium value. A clumsily shaped chair may look even more awkward with a coarse-textured covering silhouetted against a contrasting background. A material which blends in with the background or a striped material discreetly used will make the chair appear more acceptable.

Forms in a room carry the eye from one object to another, and this transfer of attention can be pleasing when shapes are distributed to balance each other and to give transition.

✷ HOW DOES TEXTURE CONTRIBUTE TOWARD BEAUTY IN DESIGN?

Texture immediately suggests fabric — the roughness or smoothness, shininess or dullness, softness or stiffness, and heaviness or sheerness of the cloth in drapery or slip cover material. Texture may also refer to wall finish, rugs, woodwork, an oil painting, a ceramic urn, or the wood in furniture. Texture must be in keeping with style and use of the object or room. Rich Honduras mahogany would not be adaptable to heavy Jacobean furniture, nor would homespun draperies complement fine Georgian mahogany furniture. American beauty roses in a polished silver bowl would provide the richness and dignity that a handsomely set Hepplewhite dining table would require. Likewise an old-fashioned bouquet in a pewter or copper bowl would give unique charm and distinction to an Early American setting.

Texture is just another element that is very useful in achieving beauty in a room.

✷ WHAT ARE THE CLASSIFICATIONS OF DESIGN?

We spoke of the elements of design or art as line, form, texture, and color. These elements produce design that may be classified as either *structural* or *decorative*. For

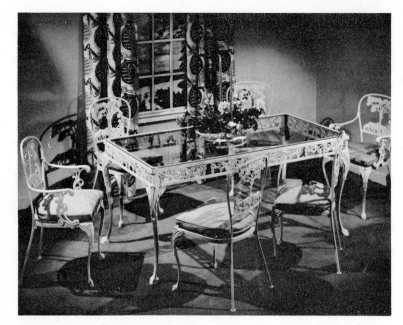

ILLUSTRATION 65A. *Decorative design. This dining room furniture shows decoration throughout its structure.*

65B. *Structural design. Notice the plain, functional aspect in the design of this furniture.*

instance, a chair may be an example of good structural design if it displays good line, form, texture, and color as a result of the way it is made. Another chair may display both good structural and good decorative design if its structure is beautiful and if good ornamentation, such as carving, inlay, or a painted design, has been added.

A criterion closely related to structural design is functionalism. It is possible for a chair to be structurally pleasing without being comfortable, and in such a case the chair's function is not fulfilled. Design which concentrates on function is known as *functional* design. This kind of design is the keynote of modern architecture and furniture. It is an important consideration in the selection of household furnishings, not only of a chair but of a pitcher that will not drip

after pouring or of a lamp that will give adequate light.

As a rule decorative design begins where structural design ends, as was true of the decorated chair. However, some decorative design may be purely ornamental, having no function and no value except beauty. In this sense figurines, ornamental vases, pictures, wall hangings, and the like are examples of ornamental design.

Decorative or ornamental design may be expressed in three styles: *naturalistic, conventional,* and *abstract.* A realistic painting of a bouquet of flowers and a fabric with a photographic print are more or less the exact expressions of something we see in nature, and are examples of naturalistic design. Simplified floral or stenciled designs on wallpaper, fabrics, and rugs illustrate a conven-

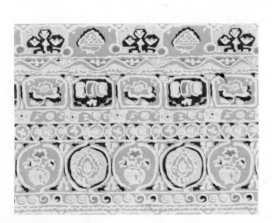

ILLUSTRATION 66. *Naturalistic, conventional, and abstract design. Contrast the realistic flowers in the fabric at the above right with the stylized ones at the above left. Abstract design is illustrated in the fabric at the lower right.*

tionalized approach to decorative design. Plaids, dots, stripes, checks, and geometric patterns in textiles are examples of abstract design. This type of design is also used a great deal in modern paintings.

Good structural design may be judged by the following questions.

1. Is the object useful and suited to the purpose for which it was meant? For example, even though book ends may have good structural lines, they will not be useful in holding books unless the bases are heavy.

2. Is the proportion or relationship of all parts good? For example, a heavy table top supported by spindlelike legs violates one of the basic art requirements.

3. Is simplicity the keynote? For example, a beautifully shaped vase frankly and simply suited to its purpose as a flower container is much more beautiful than one unduly complicated in shape or not entirely honest in purpose.

4. Is there uniformity of idea between choice of materials and expected use? For example, a colonial maple chair would require a homespun or chintz seat cover rather than satin.

Good decorative design may be judged by these questions.

1. Has restraint or simplicity been observed in the application of the design? Decoration that overshadows lovely structural lines defeats its purpose.

2. Is the object enhanced by the addition of decoration? If the decoration is not needed to improve the object, then the effect is poor.

3. Is the decoration in harmony with the style of the object and the background it furnishes? An Indian design on a classic-style ceramic would be out of keeping or out of harmony.

SUGGESTED ACTIVITIES

1. Name the elements of design, and show how each contributes to the beauty of some object.

2. Write a description of a room that has especially impressed you, telling why you think it is beautiful.

3. Bring to class pictures of various types that show interesting line direction, and tell in what direction the most emphatic lines run.

4. Collect pictures of rooms that have a masculine line feeling and others that have a feminine line feeling. Tell how line, form, and texture are used to create these feelings.

5. Assemble three harmonious textures, and suggest their use in a room.

6. Bring to class illustrations that show examples of structural and decorative design. Select the best examples of each type, and arrange them on the bulletin board.

7. Write a criticism on one example of decorative design and one example of structural design using the questions on this page. Select your illustrations from those you have collected or from those on the bulletin board.

8. Collect examples of natural, conventional, and abstract designs. Tell which you think are good and which are poor from the standpoint of design quality.

9. Study your own room. Tell how the structural lines of the room and of the furnishings harmonize. Make suggestions for any improvements needed.

10. Make a study of functionalism in relation to design. For instance, you might study flower containers, book ends, or lamps, collecting pictures or actual examples of those that appear to be good or bad in function and finding out as much as possible about how they really perform in use.

Can you apply the principle of design?

IN THE preceding chapter you learned that the elements or rudiments of design are line, form, texture, and color. These rudiments must be handled in conformity with certain principles or laws that govern their use if beauty of design is to result. These laws or guiding principles are (1) proportion, (2) balance, (3) rhythm, (4) emphasis, and (5) harmony or unity.

The room you observed that made you exclaim, "How beautiful!" must have conformed to these laws, yet you were probably unaware of them. When you tried to copy parts of the room and failed, you were no doubt overlooking some of the laws. In order to make your own room or home more attractive, an understanding of the use of these design principles is essential.

★ WHAT IS PROPORTION AND HOW IS IT OBTAINED?

Proportion is the law of relationships which demands that all space divisions be pleasingly related to each other and to the whole. Whether the interior or exterior design of a house is ordinary and commonplace or attractive and interesting depends to a large extent on space relationships.

The Greek scale

During their civilization, the ancient Greeks learned a great deal about space distribution. They developed a scale of space relationships which we still use today. This scale uses the following ratios in the division of flat areas: 2:3, 3:5, 5:8, and so on. In application to three-dimensional areas, a space division of 5:7:11 is suggested.

In studying these relationships, we realize that unequal space divisions are more interesting than equal divisions, such as halves, thirds, quarters, or eighths. This rule may apply to the spacing of windows in a house. For various reasons, both aesthetic and practical, the windows in a particular group will be the same size. But the space allowed between the windows offers an opportunity for interesting or uninteresting relationships. If the space between is exactly the width of the windows, the result will be less interesting than if the space is wider or narrower than the windows. Windows should be scaled to the width and height of the rooms inside the house as well as to the exterior walls of the house. Very small windows look extremely out of place, as you may notice, on the side or front elevation of many houses.

The Greek scale of space relationships applies to the shape of the room as well as to the size of the furnishings in the room. Square rooms are not only uninteresting to live in, but they are difficult to arrange. Rooms that are too long and narrow are also extremely difficult when it comes to arranging furniture. Very high or very low ceilings indicate that the law of good proportion has

ILLUSTRATION 67A (*above*). *Example of poor proportion. The picture, lamp, and table are too small in proportion to the chair.*

> 67B (*right*). *Example of good proportion. Scale of objects in this grouping is greatly improved.*

ILLUSTRATION 68 (*below*). *Shape ABCD may be enlarged by extending CB and dropping perpendicular lines, YX, at any desired point of enlargement on BY.*

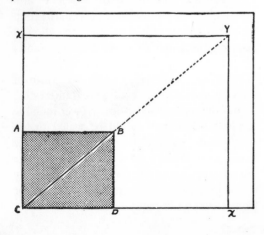

been violated. Proportion is such an important principle of design that it is again referred to in later chapters on the arrangement of furniture (page 186), the laying of rugs (pages 134–135), the treatment of windows (pages 151–158), and the use and combination of colors (pages 119–120).

Reproducing Proportions

If you have ever tried to copy a small picture from a book on a large sheet of paper, you have been confronted with the problem of keeping the proportion correct. You may want to copy some design for your home, and if your copy is not in direct proportion to the length and width of the original, your reproduction will not look right. Study the method used in Illustration 68. Observe that lines drawn at right angles from any point along diagonal CBY will keep your reproduction in proportion to the original rectangle.

✸ WHAT IS BALANCE, AND HOW MAY IT BE SECURED?

Balance is the principle of design that produces a feeling of rest and contentment. Balance may deal with quantity or number, arrangement, color, or the distribution of patterned and plain surfaces. Examples of lack of balance are these: too many windows on one side of an entrance door and too few on the other; heavy pieces of furniture at one end of a room and light pieces at the opposite end; a single bright red chair in a room without a repeat of the color anywhere in the room.

To understand balance, think of the old seesaw illustration. The weights on each side of the center must balance. When two children of the same weight are balancing, each will sit the same distance from the center of the seesaw. This type of balance is known as *even balance*. If one child is heavier than the other and each one sits the same distance from the center, what will happen? The heavy child will be on the ground. Hence if a heavy piece of furniture and a light piece are placed on a wall at equal distance from its center, the side with the heavy piece will appear to be sinking. To obtain balance on the seesaw, the heavy child must move nearer the center, and to obtain balance on the wall, the heavy piece of furniture will have to be moved nearer the center of the wall. We still have balance, but this type is called *uneven balance*.

ILLUSTRATION 69. *Even balance. The symmetrical arrangement on either side of the center of this grouping produces even or formal balance.*

ILLUSTRATION 70. *Lack of balance. This grouping shows neither formal nor informal balance since the apparent weight on one side of the center is much heavier than on the other.*

ILLUSTRATION 71. *Uneven balance. This informal or asymmetrical arrangement is balanced because the apparently heavier object is placed nearer the center than the lighter one.*

Even balance is also referred to as *formal* or *bisymmetric* balance. Uneven balance is referred to as *informal*, *occult*, or *asymmetric* balance.

In decorating a room it is usually a good plan to have at least one wall with formal balance. Two walls may have formal balance but monotony may result if formal balance is used too often. Good informal balance is more difficult to secure than good formal balance. Even though good informal balance is true balance, the effect of this type used on all four walls may not be as restful as that relieved by some formal balance. In using either type, heavy furniture pieces should be placed on walls opposite to windows, fireplaces, built-in bookcases, and so on to insure balance in the room.

The distribution of weight or mass to produce balance should be considered not only from side to side but from top to bottom. We do not like to feel that things are top-heavy. This impression is given when a very low room has heavy ceiling beams or light fixtures, or when a low slender lamp base has a bulky shade.

★ WHAT IS RHYTHM, AND HOW MAY IT PRODUCE BEAUTY IN DESIGN?

Rhythm is the principle of design that suggests connected movement. Not all line movement creates rhythm, since some types of movement express a feeling of confusion instead. Rhythm results when the following types of movement are used in a pleasing manner.

Repetition

Repeating shapes, sizes, lines, or colors will cause the eye to move from one area to another, thus connecting the different areas in a room. This is one of the simpler ways of producing rhythm.

Gradation

A progression in sizes — for instance, in a mantel arrangement with the center object tall and the end objects small — carries the eye gradually from one object to another. Pictures arranged in stair-step fashion also show the use of gradation. However, if the eye travels up toward the ceiling and is not led back to the room, rhythm is broken. When the step arrangement is regular on both sides of the center or when the eye is directed from the top picture to another wall interest, rhythm is retained.

Opposition

This form of rhythm results when lines come together at right angles. Square and oblong furniture shapes, straight cornices over windows with draperies hanging straight below, are examples of rhythm by opposition.

Transition

This form of rhythm carries the eye more gradually from one place to another than it is carried when rhythm results from opposition. Examples of transition are found in arched doors, in curved cornices, and in

ILLUSTRATION 72. *Rhythm by gradation. Progression in height from the chair to the small picture to the larger one and regression back to the floor produce restful rhythm by gradation.*

ILLUSTRATION 73.   *Rhythm by opposition. Many horizontal and
vertical lines come together at right
angles on this window wall to produce rhythm by opposition.*

cantonnières or fitted valances that run
around three sides of a window.

Radiation

This type of rhythm is produced when
many lines extend from a central point or axis.
Radiation is not often found in home decoration, unless it is in bows on dressing tables,
in medallions on furniture or mantel decorations, or in swags over draperies.

✸ WHAT IS EMPHASIS, AND WHY IS IT IMPORTANT?

Emphasis is the principle of design that
centers interest on the most important thing
in any arrangement and that carries the eye
from this point to the related interests. In
a room emphasis may be centered on a painting, on a fireplace, on an attractive window
treatment, or on an interesting furniture
grouping. But no matter where the interest is
centered, all parts must be subordinated to
the most interesting point. Competing centers
of interest defeat the purpose of the principle.

When in doubt, it is better to underempha-
size than to overemphasize. If a mantel
arrangement is composed of a pair of exquisite candlesticks, a pair of beautiful
cloisonné vases, and a lovely antique clock,
the beauty of all three may be lost. The effect
of beautiful figured draperies may be lost if
they are used with a patterned rug or with
patterned wallpaper.

In most room arrangements it is important
though not always possible to make the wall
opposite the door the "picture" wall or the
most interesting wall in the room. Thus the first
impression one gains on walking into the room
is that of the most beautiful spot in the room.

ILLUSTRATION 74.   *Rhythm by transition. The curved lines in the window treatment, the mirror, and the sofa connect horizontal and vertical lines less abruptly than would straight lines at right angles.*

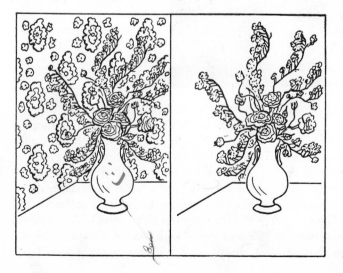

ILLUSTRATION 75.   *Emphasis and lack of emphasis. The sketch at the left shows lack of emphasis caused by equal importance in the background and flowers. At the right the flowers are emphasized by the plain background.*

ILLUSTRATION 76. *Unity. Harmony of line, shape, size, texture, idea, and color in the selection and arrangement of the furnishings in this room produces unity.*

★ **WHAT IS UNITY, AND HOW IS IT EXPRESSED?**

Unity or harmony is the expression of an agreeable combination of parts that produce a connected whole. When all the other laws of design have been obeyed, unity is the inevitable result. Unity or harmony demands that sizes, shapes, textures, colors, and ideas be related. If a room suggests a definite idea, such as that of the rugged outdoors, that of a cozy New England farmhouse, or that of a pretentious colonial mansion, furniture, textiles, and accessories must conform to the idea or character of the room.

A Cape Cod cottage constructed of heavy stone instead of the usual clapboard, or a California mission house of shingles, or a Northern Colonial house with a red hollow-tile roof would look strange because of a lack of unity. A simple copper lamp would be charming in a cottage style home but not in an eighteenth century living room. Classic wallpaper would be beautiful in a dining room with Hepplewhite furniture but not in the dining alcove of a Pennsylvania Dutch cottage.

✶ DOES THE CHARACTER OF YOUR HOME SUIT YOUR FAMILY?

When all the principles of design have been observed and harmony has been achieved, the effect of any room in the home should be satisfying. However, some rooms may fulfill all the principles of good design and yet not be fully satisfactory. In achieving a magazine-cover effect, decorators are apt to overlook the family who will live in the house. Additional criteria for judging the home with character are given as follows.

1. Does the house express your family's personality? Whether the impression given is that of dignity and formality, coziness and informality, simplicity and repose, luxury and richness, femininity and daintiness, or masculinity and severity, the atmosphere of the house should express the predominating characteristics of the family.

2. Are the rooms functional? This means that the living room must be planned for living, not for an exhibit room to show off beautiful furnishings to company; that the writing, sewing, and other work centers must be planned for convenience and comfort; that the dining room must be cheerful and conducive to the full enjoyment of meals.

3. Are the rooms suitable to the occupants? Whether you decorate your home or whether it is done by a professional, the successful decorator considers the people who live in

the home — their tastes and interests — not merely color schemes and furnishings. Anyone who spends a great deal of time reading at home deserves a chair suited to his size, and small children certainly need table and other equipment suited to their height.

4. Is simplicity the keynote? The keynote of the entrance hall may be hospitality; of the living room, graciousness; of the dining room, cheerfulness; of the kitchen, function; and of the bedroom, individuality; but simplicity should be maintained everywhere.

SUGGESTED ACTIVITIES

1. Bring to class pictures of home architecture that show both good and poor proportions.

2. Exhibit pictures of living rooms showing even and uneven balance in the arrangement of furnishings. Show one example of a lack of balance, and explain why balance is lacking.

3. Prepare a bulletin board exhibit showing four ways to obtain rhythm in interior decoration.

4. Bring to class pictures showing emphasis centered on (a) a fireplace, (b) a painting or wall hanging, (c) a furniture grouping, and (d) a window treatment.

5. Select at least one example of overemphasis in interior decoration, and tell why you think it is overdone.

6. Mount pictures of rooms that express (a) formality and dignity, (b) coziness, (c) simplicity, (d) femininity, and (e) masculinity.

7. Look for examples of poor proportion and poor balance in your home, and try to make improvements.

8. Describe one way you could add emphasis to a room in your home which needs it.

9. Name the center of interest in your room. If this center is not easy to recognize, how could you improve it?

CHAPTER 3

Do you know important facts about color?

WE CAN think of at least six different approaches to the study of color in the home — the physiological, the physical, the chemical, the psychological, the aesthetic, and the practical. The *physiologist* studies the effect of color sensations upon the eye, and recommends eye-rest colors for homes as well as factories and offices. The *physicist* studies color according to wave lengths and intensities. He has important contributions to make regarding the light-reflection properties of colors and the amount of artificial light needed in the home. The *chemist* is interested in natural and artificial pigments that are used in dyes and paints. The *psychologist* is concerned with the effect colors have upon people. The artist or the *aesthete* is concerned with beauty in the choice and combination of colors. And last but not least, the homemaker must make a *practical* choice of color for her home, keeping in mind all these contributions.

If you have studied physics, you have probably experimented with light rays by holding a prism in the direct sunlight. Although the glass appeared colorless, by holding it in the sun you found that all the spectrum colors became visible — red, orange, yellow, green, blue, and purple. Perhaps you learned that when a surface appears blue, blue is reflected and all other colors are absorbed. A surface which absorbs all light rays appears black, while one which reflects all rays appears white.

Although the source of color is light, the materials from which paints and dyes are made are of great variety. Color pigments for paints may come from chemicals, such as oxide of lead, ferrous sulfate, and various other substances. Pigments for dyes originally came from berries, bark, roots, foliage, and small insects. Indigo dyes came from the foliage of a plant in India; alizarin, used for red dyes, came from madder grown in France and Belgium; cochineal, used for red and orange dyes, came from the bodies of small insects found in Mexico. Iron scraps have produced buff and rust colors. At present most dyes and paints are synthetic or chemically produced.

Years ago manufacturers of clothing began coordinating fashion colors so that coats, dresses, suits, hats, shoes, and other accessories, although produced by different manufacturers, could be matched. Ten or twelve years ago coordinated colors in home furnishings began to arouse interest. Stores throughout the country were displaying rooms in coordinated colors. Nine basic colors were accepted for backgrounds and accessories.

Using color in the home can be an exciting adventure, but before you can use it successfully, certain fundamental facts should be understood, such as the qualities and properties of color, the classification of colors, the light reflection expected of colors, and certain associations made with various colors.

✶ WHAT ARE THE QUALITIES OR DIMENSIONS OF COLOR?

Hue

This is the name of a color, such as blue, red, or green. Hue is like a family name, for in addition each member of each color family has a special name. In all variations, there are about 150 different hues. A blue may be pure blue, green-blue, or violet-blue, the last two mentioned being obtained by mixing a small amount of green or violet with pure blue. For instance, if pure blue is too cool for a room, a little green mixed with it will produce a warmer blue or turquoise. A yellow that appears too cool in combination with even warmer colors will become more of a butter yellow or a warmer yellow by the addition of a little orange.

Value

This refers to the amount of lightness or darkness in a color, such as a light-blue dress or a dark-blue suit. Light or high values are those above middle value in the value scale shown in Color Plate 5. They may include such commonly known colors as lettuce green, shell pink, sky blue, and sunshine yellow which are called *tints*. These are usually good wall colors. Darker colors, such as burgundy, forest green, and mauve, are below middle value, and are called *shades*. These are good rug colors. Spectrum colors may be made lighter by adding white or water, and darker by adding black.

Intensity

This refers to the brightness or dullness of color, such as bright Kelly green or dull moss green. In mixing paints or dyes, a bright color may be subdued by mixing with it a little of its *complement* or opposite color. In the color circle shown in Color Plate 4, those colors which are directly opposite each other on the wheel are complements. Thus red may be neutralized if a little green is added.

There are thousands of intensities, tints, and shades in every hue. To describe a color accurately you will have to judge it by each of its three qualities. With experience your eyes become trained to see the differences.

✶ WHAT PROPERTIES OF TEMPERATURE AND FORCE DO COLORS POSSESS?

Colors may be grouped according to those that are *warm* in effect and those that are *cool*. Warm colors convey a feeling of warmth and coziness. They seem to advance, thus making a room appear smaller. The warm colors are yellow, yellow-orange, orange, orange-red, and red, with orange or orange-red probably the warmest of all. As a rule warm colors are used best in rooms with a northern exposure. Cool colors convey a feeling of coolness and seem to recede, thus creating an illusion of space. The definitely cool colors are green, blue, blue-green, blue-violet, and violet, with blue being the coolest of all. Cool colors are good background colors for sunny rooms.

Borderline colors such as yellow-green and red-violet may be warm or cool depending upon the amount of yellow or violet in them.

✶ HOW ARE COLORS CLASSIFIED?

Colors are classified as *primary*, *secondary*, and *intermediate*. Primary colors are so named because they cannot be broken down into other colors and because no combinations of other colors can produce them. The primary colors are *yellow*, *red*, and *blue*.

Secondary colors are made by mixing two primary colors — yellow and red to produce *orange;* red and blue to produce *violet;* and blue and yellow to produce *green.*

Intermediate colors are produced by mixing a primary color with an adjacent secondary color. The intermediate colors are *yellow-green, blue-green, blue-violet, red-orange,* and *yellow-orange.* One further distinction can be made. If a color is called yellow-orange, it is understood that orange predominates, or if the color is called orange-yellow, that yellow predominates. Apricot is yellow-orange, and maize is orange-yellow.

The traditional chart in Color Plate 4 is based upon the three primary colors you learned in grade school. The Munsell chart is made up of five principal colors — red, yellow, green, blue, and purple with orange omitted — and five intermediate colors — yellow-red, green-yellow, blue-green, purple-blue, and red-purple. Color harmonies obtained with the Munsell chart are a little less sharp than those obtained with the traditional or Prang chart. For instance, opposite colors on the traditional chart are red and green, and on the Munsell chart, red and blue-green. In this text we shall use the traditional chart.

✳ WHAT LIGHT REFLECTION CAN BE EXPECTED OF THE BACKGROUND COLORS?

A number of large paint companies have spent years of research in taking the guesswork out of the selection and use of background colors. In places where good lighting is necessary, such as in hospitals, industrial plants, schools, office buildings, and homes, color is very important. Paint manufacturers are now producing colors to reduce eyestrain. These colors may not always be of high style, but they are pleasant as well as restful background colors for the home. Some of the paint stores will give you samples of these eye-rest colors upon request.

Light reflection of the various colors is based upon a comparison of the reflection property of a color with that of pure white magnesium oxide. The following light-reflection factors are based upon the experiments of one of our large paint manufacturers.

LIGHT REFLECTION CHART

Name of color	Per cent of light reflected
Color-conditioning white	86%
Ivory	66
Sunlight	68
Peach	61
Tan	23
Light rose	45
Deep rose	16
Very light green	59
Light green	53
Medium green	26
Deep green	16
Very light blue	52
Light blue	42
Medium blue	28
Deep blue	17
Very light gray	58
Light gray	53
Medium gray	28
Deep gray	15

By studying the chart you will notice that in comparison with color-conditioning white, ivory, sunlight (yellow), peach, and light green give the best light reflection and therefore require less artificial lighting. The darker greens, blues, and roses have little light reflection and therefore require much more supplementary light.

✳ **WHAT ASSOCIATIONS DO COLORS HAVE?** *has meant*

Colors have an emotional appeal, and as each different color is mentioned, consciously or subconsciously you associate it with some particular feeling or thing. Let us consider some of the associations with various colors that have been built up throughout the ages.

Black

This is said to be the first color recognized by man. To the Greeks, black symbolized life because out of it was born the day. During the sixteenth century, Anne of Brittany used black for mourning, and this association has existed through several centuries. Black is also symbolic of evil, old age, and silence. It is strong and sophisticated. Its primary use in interior decoration is for small quantities of accent.

Red

According to some, red was the second color primitive man was able to distinguish. Red was associated with blood and therefore life; later it was associated with fire and therefore danger. For instance, the custom of wearing red hunting jackets as a precaution against danger has long been established. In nature a great number of flowers are red or variations of it. Red is the symbol of love, vigor, action, and danger. Bright red is such a forceful color that its use should be limited to small areas of accent in interior decoration. Light values make warm background colors.

Yellow

This color has had many and varied associations. As a color sacred to the Chinese and important to the Egyptians and the Greeks, yellow gradually became a symbol of power, and was therefore disdained by the early Christians. Yellow has been associated with deceit, cowardice, and jealousy as well as with wisdom, gaiety, and warmth. Yellow in its many hues, shades, and values is a very useful color in interior decoration.

White

For a long time white was used as a shroud and was the mourning color of Rome and medieval France. White is symbolic of purity, innocence, faith, peace, and surrender. Off white is used extensively in home decoration.

Blue

This was probably not identified as a separate color for a long time, but was considered a form of black. The Hebrews did not distinguish between blue and purple. Except for the sky, blue is the rarest color in nature — hence the origin of the terms "true blue" and "blue blood." Blue is the symbol of happiness, hope, truth, honor, repose, and distance. Blue in its various forms is employed to a large extent in interior decoration.

Green

This has not always been a popular color, although nature uses it in abundance. Because of its use in pagan ceremonies, green was banned by the early Christians. It was used by Robin Hood and his band, and stands as a symbol of their life and vigor. It became a sacred color to the Moslems. It is associated with luck — particularly that of the Irish. It denotes life, spring, hope, and also envy. It is cool enough to be restful, yet warm enough to be friendly. It is used extensively in home decoration.

Purple

Although purple is an ancient color, it was once a costly color to produce. It became a symbol of royalty, and thus was avoided by the early Christians. Even so, models of the Tabernacle carried through the wilderness in the Exodus of the Jews show purple curtains separating the Holy of Holies from outer chambers. Associated with the spiritual, with mystery, with humility, with penitence, and with wisdom, purple is a dignified color. Mauve, plum, eggplant, and other shades are frequently used in dignified, elegant rooms.

Brown

This was the color designated to peasants during the Middle Ages, and is thus associated with humility. It is reminiscent of autumn, the harvest, and decay. It ranges from yellow to red in cast, and even though it is dark and neutral, it has considerable richness and depth. The wood used in most traditional furniture is brown.

Gray

This is a somber color. It was the color worn by the common people during the time of Charlemagne, and was also worn a great deal by the Quakers. Gray is associated with retirement, sadness, modesty, and indifference. It may have a warm or a cool cast, though it is predominately cool. It is often a good background color in interior decoration.

Color preferences

It is interesting to note that manufacturers are well aware of the color likes and dislikes of the buying public. For instance, reports from rug manufacturers show that tans, greens, and browns are popular rug colors. Black, blue, gray, and green, with maroon gaining in popularity are the best selling colors in the car market. Men as a group are said to prefer blue, and women, red. But in selecting colors for the home or in developing

a wide color appreciation, one should remember that there are great possibilities for beauty in the various hues, values, and intensities of all colors.

SUGGESTED ACTIVITIES

1. Experiment with color by mixing water colors, soft crayons, or chalk to produce secondary and intermediate hues. Also experiment in changing the value and intensity of various hues.

2. Make a large circle like the circle in Color Plate 4. Fill in the various hues using water colors, crayons, or samples of paper or cloth.

3. Select at least ten hues that you like, and tell what associations you have with each hue.

4. Differentiate between warm and cool colors either by marking them on your color wheel or by sorting swatches of colored materials or papers into warm and cool piles.

5. Find pictures of rooms that are predominately cool and predominately warm in color effect. Explain how the effect is produced.

6. Bring a prism to class, and demonstrate how the spectrum colors are reflected.

7. Visit a department store, and investigate coordinated colors in home furnishings.

8. Describe several colors in your classroom, giving their hue, value, and intensity.

9. Collect swatches of cloth or colored paper that show any one hue in several different values and intensities.

10. From your study of color thus far, tell any experience you may have had in discovering a particular hue, value, or intensity that you liked very much.

11. Collect a variety of colors in paint swatches, wallpaper samples, and pieces of cloth, and label each color according to its trade name and to its hue, value, and intensity.

12. From a paint store, secure sample cards of eyestrain-reducing background paints. Compare these colors with background colors in sample cards of other paints.

CHAPTER 4

Can you use color successfully?

COLOR may set you on top of the world or put you down in the dumps. When you feel depressed, you have the "blues," and when you are exhilarated, you are in the "pink." You are in the "red" if you are in debt, and in the "black" if your credit is good.

Color can work magic in a room. It can hide defects or create them. It may enhance beauty or diminish it. Unpretentious furnishings in the right color setting may look like a picture from a magazine, and exquisite furnishings in a poor color setting may look nondescript.

Some people seem to have a natural gift for using color. They can visualize an entire house in new colors, while others appear to be blind when it comes to using and enjoying color. However, the ability to create beautiful color schemes can be developed through study, even though a natural aptitude may be lacking.

✶ HOW DO THE PRINCIPLES OF DESIGN APPLY TO THE USE OF COLOR?

The principles of design apply to the use of color as well as to the use of line, area, and shape. Let us examine the use of these principles in planning color schemes.

Balance

Colors must be balanced to give a feeling of rest. This principle is exemplified in the law of areas — light, dark, and dull colors should be used in the largest areas, slightly grayed colors in the next largest areas, and intense or bright colors in the smallest areas. In addition the small areas of bright colors should be distributed through a room to balance the large areas of dull colors. Likewise, light colors should be distributed to balance dark colors. In strong contrast, a little light blue will balance a large area of dark blue. In combining complementary colors, the law of areas is particularly important, since complementary hues seen side by side make each other seem more intense. The grayed complement should be used in large areas, and the brighter one in very small areas.

Nature illustrates the application of the law of areas in presenting the light blue sky and water in very large areas, the dark green shadows of hills and trees also in large areas, the brighter green plants and grass in slightly smaller areas, and the bright colored flowers in the smallest areas of all.

Proportion

You learned in Chapter 2, Unit 4, that an even distribution of spaces is less interesting than an uneven distribution. This principle of proportion applies to use of color as well, especially if two colors of the same value are used. If you want to use medium blue-green and medium red on four chairs in

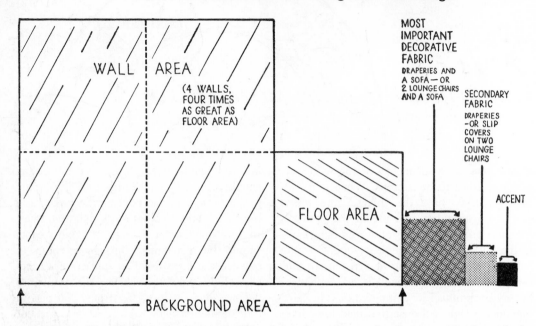

ILLUSTRATION 77.　*Diagram of room areas. This scheme shows floor and wall areas subdued as a back-ground. Interest centers on the most important decorative fabric, which is used at least twice in the room. The secondary fabric is subordinate to the first. A mere dash of accent adds character.*

a room with a gray rug, it may be more interesting to cover two of the chairs in blue-green, one in a soft red, and the fourth in a stripe with red, blue-green, and gray.

Rhythm

For instance, rhythm through *repetition* is shown when the colors in figured draperies are repeated in various ways throughout a room. Rhythm by *transition* in color is frequently used. For example, hall wallpaper with rose and green figures on a light gray background offers an opportunity to use transitional colors in the living room and dining room. The living room walls may be gray. The draperies may repeat the colors in the hall wallpaper, and the rug may be a little deeper green than the green in the wallpaper.

The dining room may have green paper and a rose rug a little deeper than the rose in the hall wallpaper. The transition from one room to the other will then be gradual, and the colors will be keyed to each other.

Emphasis

As you enter a room you should be conscious of one color with other colors subordinated to it. Blue may be the predominating or emphatic color with wine or yellow used as an auxiliary color. Emphasis may be on the background color, for instance, if a pale green is used for the walls and a deeper green for the rug. If the backgrounds are very grayed, emphasis may be gained by a bright accessory color.

If you wish to emphasize the rich warm

COLOR PLATE 3. *The warmth of yellow makes this room sunny and cheerful in spite of the snow outside. The use of green adds character and interest.*

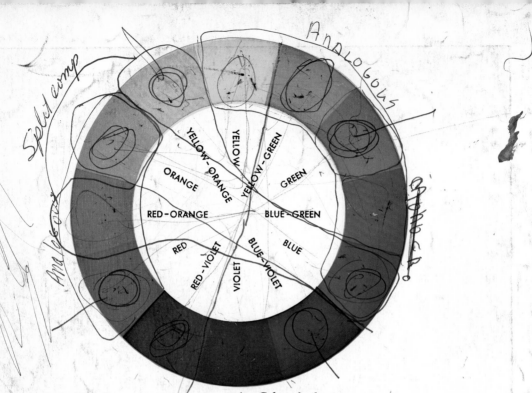

COLOR PLATE 4. *Color wheel*

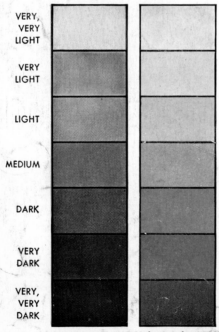

VERY, VERY LIGHT	
VERY LIGHT	
LIGHT	
MEDIUM	
DARK	
VERY DARK	
VERY, VERY DARK	

COLOR PLATE 5. *Value scale*

COLOR PLATE 6. *In this modern room, yellow — as such and in the orange and green — gives a unifying effect. Gray, black, and other neutral colors offset the brighter tones.*

COLOR PLATE 7. *Muted tones and a white wainscoting provide a suitable setting for the eighteenth century mahogany furniture used in this hall.*

COLOR PLATE 8. *The colors in the rug are the basis of the color scheme in this eighteenth century style of dining room. The soft blue of the walls, the rose red of the chair covers, and the neutral tone of the draperies repeat colors in the rug.*

brown of fine mahogany, you will use it against a plain light wall. The blue family adds emphasis to the beauty of rich dark woods because blue is the complement of the reddish browns. Light modern woods become more mellow and lovely against fairly dark walls. Bleached mahogany is beautiful against a rich medium-green paper, but dark mahogany loses character by lack of contrast.

✳ WHAT ARE THE STANDARD COLOR HARMONIES?

Color harmonies may be similar or contrasting. Similar harmonies are restful but sometimes monotonous. Contrasting harmonies are interesting, but sometimes they are disturbing if they are too striking. Similar and contrasting harmonies are described in the following paragraphs. The color masks on this page will help you to understand the harmonies. White, black, and gray may be included in any harmony.

Similar or related harmonies

These are produced from colors that lie near each other on the color wheel, and include monochromatic and analogous harmonies.

A MONOCHROMATIC HARMONY: Means a one-color harmony — *mono* meaning one and *chroma* meaning color. Using several values of one hue, such as light, medium, and dark blue, illustrates this harmony. Hues must match, but value must contrast in a one-color harmony. For example, a light bluish purple should not be used with a dark reddish purple, or a light orange-red with a dark violet-red.

AN ANALOGOUS HARMONY: A combination of neighboring hues that have one hue in common. Ordinarily yellow, yellow-green, and green are more pleasing than yellow-green, green, and blue-green. In other words, the combination of analogous primary, secondary, and inter-

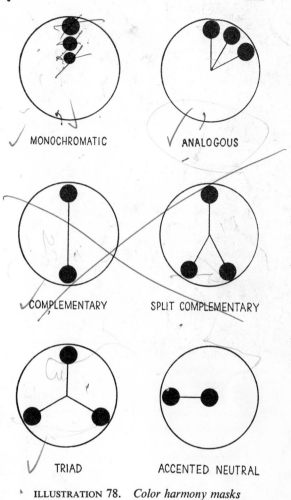

MONOCHROMATIC   ANALOGOUS

COMPLEMENTARY   SPLIT COMPLEMENTARY

TRIAD   ACCENTED NEUTRAL

ILLUSTRATION 78. *Color harmony masks*

mediate colors is more pleasing than the combination of a primary or secondary color with the two intermediate colors on either side of it. This is especially true of red-orange, red, and red-purple. Hold these three colors together, and then hold red, red-orange, and orange together, or red, red-violet, and violet. Determine the effect for yourself. In an analogous harmony, hues should differ in value and intensity for the most pleasing effect. Analogous harmonies show a little more contrast than one-color harmonies.

CONTRASTING HARMONIES: These are produced by combining colors that are far apart on the color wheel. Contrasting colors should differ in value and intensity. The four contrasting color harmonies most frequently used are complementary, split complementary, triad, and accented neutral.

A COMPLEMENTARY HARMONY: Obtained by using the two colors opposite each other on the color wheel, such as blue and orange. A true spectrum blue and orange might be effective in advertising but not in a dress or a room. However, if you lower the intensity and value of the orange to a London tan and soften the intensity of the blue until you have a powder blue, the harmony will be pleasing. Or for the walls of a room, you may use the orange in a light value such as apricot. With a medium rust rug and furnishings in blue of two or three different values, a pleasing complementary harmony will result.

A SPLIT-COMPLEMENTARY HARMONY: Obtained by combining one color such as yellow and the colors on each side of its complement which would be red-violet and blue-violet. The true complement, violet, is omitted. If you apply this scheme in a room, the walls might be light yellow and the rug a medium blue-violet. Red-violet may be used in the furnishings, with all three of the colors appearing in the figured draperies.

A TRIAD HARMONY: A combination of any three colors that form an equilateral triangle on the color wheel. It can be the most interesting of all harmonies, but it requires the most careful study. As you will see, this harmony may combine the three primary colors — red, yellow, and blue — or the three secondary colors — orange, green, and purple — or three of the intermediate colors. You will often find this harmony in printed fabrics, and they will be helpful to you in applying color harmonies of this type in rooms. For example, suppose you choose for draperies a fabric with yellow-orange, blue-green, and red-violet on a white background. The walls may be a very light yellow-orange, the rug may be aqua, and the sofa may be upholstered in a medium, grayed red-violet. Notice that different values and intensities of the hues are used.

AN ACCENTED-NEUTRAL HARMONY: A harmony in which the largest areas of a room are neutral with small areas of a bright color used for accent. For example, the walls, rug, and divan might be gray of different values with occasional chairs of red for accent. A beige costume with Kelly green accessories or a gray costume with red accessories illustrates this harmony in dress design.

★ WHAT ARE SOME GUIDES IN PLANNING COLOR HARMONIES?

Frequently an inexperienced person can plan a color harmony more successfully by following some kind of guide. For instance, a painting, a flower print, a textile, or a decorative vase that you like may become the central idea for your color scheme. If you analyze the colors in the picture or the textile, you will probably find that they illustrate one of the color harmonies just described. But having the harmony already worked out will help you visualize your room and give you something by which to check samples of colors for various furnishings in the room.

If you have a living room with a cool exposure, a landscape painting rich in all the warm colors of autumn — soft rusts and browns, gay yellow and rich greens — can serve as an excellent guide for using these colors in your room. Walls painted a sunshine yellow will bring warmth into the room. A medium green rug will give another good background color. Draperies with cocoa brown, chartreuse, rust, and rich green motifs on a yellow background which matches the wall will emphasize the colors in the painting. Upholstery colors might be green and cocoa brown, and accessory notes might be in rust.

A perky pansy print may be used as the basis for an interesting bedroom color scheme. The orchid and plum tones in the pansy suggest orchid walls with a rich plum

Pacific

rug. Draperies with a soft yellow background and flowers in white, purple, wine, and green would give character to the light orchid walls.

Decorators frequently use a figured drapery fabric as the central idea for a color scheme in a room and key other colors to those in the fabric. It is often easier to find colors in paints and wallpaper that match appropriate colors in the print than it is to select the solid colors for the walls first and then try to find a printed fabric that repeats them. If you are building the color scheme for a room around a figured textile, select the wall color from one of the lighter tones in the drapery fabric and the rug color from one of the deeper tones. Use one of the bright colors for the accessory notes.

The person who has worked a great deal with color may be successful in arriving at interesting color schemes from many sources, but the inexperienced person will benefit by having some simple guide and by knowing how to recognize and apply the harmony it illustrates.

✚ WHAT CONSIDERATIONS WILL INFLUENCE YOUR CHOICE OF COLORS?

Many factors enter into the choice of colors — the likes and dislikes of the family; the exposure, shape, and size of the room; the colors in furnishings already on hand; the effect of artificial light on different textures and colors; and the family's manner of living.

Family tastes

A room such as the living room which is shared by all members of the family should not have colors that appear too strong and masculine or too dainty and feminine. It should represent as nearly as possible a composite of the family's taste. Individual rooms

offer the opportunity for expressing individual tastes. But it should be remembered that some colors are so bright that they are disturbing if used in large areas. Bright chartreuse, burnt orange, and red are interesting colors, but as background colors they are not considered as good as soft turquoise, rose, and wine.

Physical characteristics of the room

You have learned that warm colors, such as the various yellows, beiges, and pinks, are the best wall colors for rooms with a north or northwest exposure and that cool colors, such as the blues, greens, and grays, are best for walls with a south or southeast exposure. A room that receives little sunlight will seem even more dull if decorated entirely with blues and grays. On the other hand, light cool colors tend to make a room look larger especially if the woodwork is painted the same color as the wall. A room with a high ceiling will seem more cozy and less high if the ceiling is painted a slightly darker value than the wall. If a room is long and narrow, it may appear shorter by painting one end wall a warm color in a medium or near medium value because warm colors seem to advance.

Color of furnishings already on hand

It is not always possible to use exactly the colors you want because rugs and draperies cannot be bought every time wall colors are changed. However, it may be possible to exchange rugs or draperies in some of the rooms, and in this way you may have a little more freedom in choosing a color harmony.

Effect of lighting

Artificial light will change the appearance of color. Yellow electric light will fuse yellow

COLOR SCHEME CHART

Type of room and furnishings	Exposure and color scheme	Walls	Rug	Draperies	Upholstery
Large sunny living room with traditional furnishings in eighteenth century mahogany	South exposure. Split-complementary scheme of yellow, blue-violet, and red-purple	Delphinium (light purplish blue)	Burgundy (dark violet-red)	Bold figures in yellow, violet-blue, and red-violet on a cream background	Yellow and blue-violet in striped lounge chairs. Medium blue in plain-colored sofa. Red-violet in plain-colored occasional chairs
Medium-sized, dark bedroom with modern furnishings in bleached mahogany	North exposure. Analogous scheme of yellow, yellow-orange, and orange	Light butter yellow	Sand or old gold	Beige background with yellow, rust, and chocolate in pattern	Rust in plain-colored lounge chairs. Chocolate slip cover edged in gold on sofa. Beige, brown, and yellow in striped or plaid occasional chairs
Medium-sized, medium-light dining room with Duncan Phyfe furniture	Southwest exposure. Scheme taken from the colors in a basket of fruit containing limes, grapes, and apples (split complementary)	Lime-green background with violet figures	Eggplant	Lime-green rayon faille	Lime and red-violet threads in tapestry-covered chair bottoms
Medium-sized, sunny bedroom for a boy. Modern furniture in dark mahogany	Southeast exposure. Scheme taken from a hunting scene in which red-orange, green, and blue predominate (split complementary)	Sky-blue paint or paper	Russet or rich brown	Horizontal-striped homespun with red-orange, green, and blue stripes on a beige background	Bedspread same as draperies. Green slip cover on a chair
Small dark bedroom for a girl. Early American furniture in maple	Northwest exposure. Triad scheme of yellow, blue, and red	Light sunshine yellow with matching woodwork	Grayed medium red and blue in braided rugs	Grayed dark red, medium blue, and light yellow figured or plaid chintz valance and tie backs over white ruffled curtains	Medium blue bedspread with chintz flounce. White dressing table skirt with medium blue swags. Cherry red accessories on dressing table

with any color, making a plum rug look brown, a light blue wallpaper look gray, and lemon-yellow walls appear a rich sunshine yellow. If you are dissatisfied with your wall colors under artificial light, change your bulbs. Bulbs with a blue cast will make pink walls appear slightly orchid, blue walls appear slightly gray-blue, and yellow walls appear chartreuse. Bulbs with a pink cast make pink appear warmer, blue appear slightly lavender, and yellow appear slightly flesh. Of course you do not want to carry these changes to such an extreme that you interfere with good light for reading, sewing, and other close work.

Texture

Colors that seem very good in homespun textures will often appear too strong in smooth or glossy textures. This is especially true of bright blue and rose. Some blue and rose tones seem very harsh in glossy textures, but in rugs or dull-textured drapery material, the same dyes may produce pleasing colors.

Manner of living

Throughout the ages, manner of living has had a definite effect upon the choice of colors. The Egyptians, who lived in the bright sunshine, used colors in their pure spectrum value and intensity. The Greeks, who enjoyed nature and who spent a great deal of time out of doors under shade trees, used lighter, more subtle colors. The Romans, for whom life became more militaristic, strengthened somewhat the intensity of the colors they used. The early Christians rejected the pomp and power of the rich golds, reds, and purples, and used more sombre colors. During the Renaissance, and later as wealth increased, fabrics and colors used gained in richness. Likewise, in modern life manner of

living affects choice of colors. For instance, if a family's manner of living requires a rather formal appearing house, a predominance of subdued but rich colors will be used. If casualness is the keynote, brighter, friendlier colors will predominate.

The chart on page 124 offers a summary of how colors may be used to produce various effects, not only in relation to manner of living but in relation to type of room, exposure, and furnishings.

By studying the color schemes in the chart, you will notice that an attempt has been made to subdue sunny rooms and to brighten dark rooms, to increase the size of small rooms and to decrease the size of large rooms, to present rooms which are rich in appearance and those which are more casual in feeling, to describe a room that will please a boy and one that will please a girl, and to plan a dining room that will be gay and conducive to enjoyment at mealtimes.

SUGGESTED ACTIVITIES

1. Bring to class colored pictures of rooms that show (a) good balance of values, (b) good proportion in the distribution of color, (c) good rhythm in the repetition of color, (d) good transition in the use of color, and (e) good color emphasis. From pictures collected by the class, mount and label the best examples, and place them on the bulletin board.

2. Using wallpaper swatches, select background colors that will enhance (a) dark furniture and (b) light furniture. Test the effect of your selections by holding the swatches behind the furniture.

3. Judge the color harmony or harmonies used in your homemaking department. What types of harmonies are used? Are they good examples of the types? Are they well chosen from the standpoint of use, size, exposure, and

furniture in the room where they are used? Is there transition in color between adjoining rooms?

4. Select colored pictures of rooms that illustrate at least three of the six color harmonies described on pages 121–122. Describe the colors used in each harmony giving their hue, value, and intensity.

5. Describe rooms at home or others with which you are familiar that illustrate at least two of the six color harmonies.

6. Using water colors, crayons, or bits of colored paper or cloth, assemble examples of the six types of color harmonies.

7. Plan how you would apply each of the six harmonies you have assembled in decorating a room.

8. Mount samples of paint from paint sample cards which you would recommend for (a) a large sunny living room, (b) a large dark living room, (c) a small sunny bedroom, and (d) a small dark bedroom.

9. Collect samples of different textures in the same color. For instance, find shiny, dull, rough, and smooth samples of the same hue, value, and intensity in blue. Compare the effectiveness of the samples for use in decorating a room, telling how or how not each might be used.

10. If possible, plan a color scheme for some room which is to be redecorated. Collect samples of all the colors you will use. Discuss your plan and your samples with your classmates and teacher for their criticism or approval. Perhaps you can supervise the redecoration, doing some of the work yourself.

SELECTED REFERENCES
FOR UNIT FOUR

BOOKS

Agan, Lessie, *The House, Its Plan and Use*, Revised. J. B. Lippincott Company, Philadelphia, 1956

Alexander, Mary Jean, *Decorating Begins with You*. Doubleday and Company, Inc., New York, 1958

Austin, Ruth E., and Parvis, Jeannette O., *Furnishing Your Home*, Houghton Mifflin Company, Boston, 1951

Better Homes and Gardens' Decorating Book. Meredith Publishing Company, Meredith Building, Des Moines 3, Iowa, 1956

Brandt, Mary, *Good Housekeeping Book of Home Decoration*. McGraw-Hill Book Company, Inc., New York, 1957

Goldstein, Harriet, and Goldstein, Vetta, *Art in Everyday Life*, Revised. The Macmillan Company, New York, 1954

Hardy, Kay, *Harmonize Your Home: A Practical Guide for the Home Decorator*. Funk and Wagnalls Company, New York, 1955

Hardy, Kay, *Room by Room — A Guide to Wise Buying*. Funk and Wagnalls Company, New York, 1959

House and Garden's Complete Guide to Interior Decoration. Simon and Schuster, Inc., New York, 1953

Koues, Helen, *The American Woman's New Encyclopedia of Home Decorating*. Doubleday and Company, Inc., New York, 1954

Lewis, Dora S., Burns, Jean O., Segner, Esther F., *Housing and Home Management*. The Macmillan Company, New York, 1953

Morton, Ruth, *The Home and Its Furnishings*. McGraw-Hill Book Company, Inc., New York, 1953

Rand, Marcia, *Be Your Own Decorator*. Dodd, Mead and Company, New York, 1959

Rutt, Anna Hong, *Home Furnishing*. John Wiley & Sons, Inc., New York, 1961

Trilling, Mabel B., and Nicholas, Florence, *Design Your Home for Living*, J. B. Lippincott Company, Philadelphia, 1953

Whiton, Sherrill, *Elements of Interior Design and Decoration*, Revised. J. B. Lippincott Company, Philadelphia, 1957

CURRENT PUBLICATIONS

Consult sources in Unit Five

5

Plan
your backgrounds
with confidence

ILLUSTRATION 79. *A formal traditional room. The idea of this room carried out in the wall and floor treatments as well as in the style of the furniture and accessories is formal traditional eighteenth century in feeling. Since a figured rug is used, wall and window treatments are plain.*

CHAPTER I

How will you treat walls, floors, and ceilings?

IN ANY room the large background areas, such as walls, ceilings, floors, and windows, provide a setting for furniture and accessories. These main backgrounds are the "backdrops" for the stage or the home in which family members carry out daily activities. They can make or mar the decorating idea. And once their treatment is decided upon, they are neither easy nor inexpensive to change.

If you are decorating a new house and if cost is of no consequence, your choice of backgrounds and furnishings is unlimited. However, most of us must decorate our homes on a limited budget. As a rule, the floor covering is the most expensive background, but it is also the most permanent one, since most rugs are expected to give nearly a lifetime of service. Wallpaper or paint and window curtains will probably be changed about every five years. Good draperies may last ten to twelve years. But if you are to make wise choices in backgrounds, there are a number of points to consider.

★ WHAT FACTORS INFLUENCE THE CHOICE OF MAIN BACKGROUNDS?

A number of factors will influence your choice of main backgrounds, such as your present furnishings, the idea you want to convey through decoration, the use of the room, the effect upon adjacent rooms, the exposure, the size and shape of the room, and the personalities of the people who will live in the room.

Your present furnishings

These will often limit your choice of backgrounds. Since a rug is more or less a permanent background, the decoration of walls and windows may have to be planned in harmony with the floor covering you already own. On the other hand, your family may have postponed buying a living room rug until other things have been provided, and now you find that they are ready to make this purchase. Let us suppose that you have new draperies and fresh wallpaper and paint in your living room. In this case you will want to select a rug that repeats one of the colors in your present furnishings but one that also will be a good basic color for future color schemes.

The idea of the room

If the idea of the room is formal with traditional or eighteenth century furnishings, rugs should be solid in color or formal in pattern; walls should be plain, striped, or formal in the design repeat. Informal colonial or Early American rooms call for less formal or the handmade type of rugs. Walls may be pine

ILLUSTRATION 80. *In this contemporary room, simple but well-designed furniture, carefully selected accessories, an area rug, and an unusual wall treatment all combine to make a truly attractive living area.*

paneled or papered with small design repeats or plaid patterns. Modern rooms may have solid-colored throw rugs or plain carpeting. The walls may be done in plain-colored, textured paper, in bold-patterned paper, in plain paint, or in light-colored plywood paneling.

The use of the room

Rooms in which you spend the most time, such as living rooms, workrooms, and bedrooms, should have restful lines and colors.

Rooms in which you spend only a little time, such as bathrooms, halls, and dining rooms, may have more pattern and color. Let us consider further suitable backgrounds in relation to the use of each room in the house.

THE ENTRANCE HALL: Used as a passage to other rooms of the house, an entrance hall gives a stranger his first impression of your home. For that reason it should be cheerful and attractive. The colors used in the hall should tie together the colors used in rooms opening off the hall.

ILLUSTRATION 81. *In this Early American room, the braided rug, the maple furniture, the informal patterned wallpaper, and the unique decorating accents are carefully blended to form a restful living area.*

THE LIVING ROOM: Plain-colored paint or paper, or striped, plaid, or textured paper will provide a pleasing background if figured draperies are to be used. A figured paper may be used if the rug and draperies are plain.

THE DINING ROOM: Figured paper may be preferred because only a little time each day is spent in the dining room and because people usually like to eat in a gay atmosphere. A textured or tone-on-tone rug will show food stains less than a plain rug. Linoleum in formal pattern or in a solid color is pleasing and practical, particularly if there are small children.

BEDROOMS: Walls should be pleasing to the occupant in color and design, and for clean-ing purposes, scatter rugs are more practical than large ones. Although wallpaper with pictures may be attractive in the nursery, patterned paper is apt to keep the child's mind too active. Painted walls and a plain wood or linoleum floor are the most practical choices for rooms where small children sleep and play.

BATHROOM AND KITCHEN: Walls in bath-rooms and kitchens should be finished with semi-gloss paint or washable wallpaper. Tile below with paint or washable wallpaper above will give a more colorful, a more easily cleaned, and a more permanent finish to bathroom walls, but of course the cost will be greater than that of plain painted walls. Glazed tile, rubber tile, or inlaid linoleum with a cove base around the walls will give the longest service for a bathroom floor, but when cost is an important consideration, a smooth varnished floor or a printed-linoleum floor with a mat at the tub and lavatory will be satisfactory. Semigloss enamel will give an easily cared for kitchen wall finish, and linoleum or rubber tile, a satisfactory floor covering.

The effect upon adjacent rooms

When rooms open into other rooms or into a hall, the adjoining areas must be keyed to each other by colors and lines. At least one color in one room must be carried over into the color scheme of the neighboring room. Some people use a figured carpet or wallpaper in the hall, and choose rug and wall colors for adjoining rooms from the colors used in the figured hall carpet or wallpaper. In a small house it is usually wise to carpet the hall, the living room, and the dining room alike. And if these rooms are very small, the paper may be the same on all walls. Variation may be obtained by transitional colors used in the accessories and furnishings.

The exposure of the room

Tints of warm colors — yellow, red, and orange — are considered good background colors for rooms with a north exposure, and tints of cool colors — blue, blue-green, and green — are considered good colors for rooms with a south exposure. However, for various reasons, you may not always be able to choose backgrounds according to the rule and will want the next best choice. Then it may be helpful to know that pink, for instance, may be made a little cooler by adding blue, or green a little warmer by adding yellow.

The size and shape of the room

You may increase the apparent size of a room by choosing very light wall colors, by painting the woodwork to match the walls, and by using a wall-to-wall carpet of the same hue as the walls but darker in value. Use a plain-colored drapery material that blends rather than contrasts with the walls, or use a figured material with a background that matches the walls. You may decrease the apparent size of a room by using bold-patterned wallpaper with woodwork that gives some contrast. Or use dark walls with furniture that gives contrast. You may increase the height of a room by using dark rugs, vertical-striped wallpaper without a border, and light ceilings. You may decrease the height of a room by using a slightly darker color on the ceiling than that used on the walls, or by using wallpaper with a horizontal feeling, or by using a chair rail or wainscoting with a solid color below it and with a figured wallpaper above it. A long narrow room will appear wider if one long wall, especially if it is the wall opposite the entrance door, is lighter than the other walls. Using a pronounced wallpaper design or a warm color on one or both of the narrow end walls will make the room appear to be in better proportion. In a square room, a large mirror on one wall or a horizontal striped paper on one wall, especially if it is a modern room, will create a feeling of more depth.

✳ WHAT ARE SOME SPECIAL CONSIDERATIONS IN THE CHOICE OF FLOOR COVERINGS?

Although we have discussed backgrounds in general, there are some special considerations in the choice of floor and wall coverings. A number of things in addition to those mentioned under main backgrounds will enter into the choice of floor coverings. If there are small children and pets in the home, inlaid linoleum, patterned rugs, or bare floors and scatter rugs may be a better choice than wall-to-wall carpet. Floor covering must be evaluated by appearance, use, resistance to soil, ease of maintenance, durability, and cost.

The difference in cost between inexpensive and quality floor coverings in the average-sized home may not be great in relation to the total home furnishings budget. The cost of labor is the same whether the living-room floor is prefinished hardwood or a soft wood, or carpeted wall to wall with wool, nylon, or viscose carpet; whether the bathroom floor is ceramic or asphalt tile; whether the kitchen floor surface is vinyl tile or asphalt tile.

Wood flooring

Many people prefer wood floors with room-size, area, or scatter rugs. There is a wide choice of wood flooring, the most popular of which is *prefinished oak* laid in parallel boards. Sometimes several strips of wood are joined in squares, and the squares are laid with the grain of one at right angles to the grain of the other. This treatment resembles parquetry. True *parquetry*, however, produces an intricate floor pattern by combining inlay blocks of two or more woods of different colors in geometric or other patterns.

ILLUSTRATION 82. *This area rug sets apart one end of the living room for a small conversation group or reading and writing area. Notice the parquetry floors and the entire-wall mirror.*

Especially good with Early American furnishings is *random-width* plank flooring set with wood pegs. A combination of any two woods may be used. Wood floors should be neither dull nor shiny, but they should have a rich patina.

Brick and similar textures

With the emphasis on integrating indoor-outdoor living, brick, stone, terrazzo, ceramic tile, and quarry tile have become popular flooring materials. *Brick* floors are often used in the family room and adjoining patio when the climate permits a long season of outdoor living. Inside floors of brick are less difficult to care for if the brick is sealed and waxed.

Ceramic tile is the best flooring for bathrooms because of its ease of maintenance and its wide range of colors and designs. It is often used in entrances as well. *Terrazzo* and *quarry tile* are reminiscent of floors of ancient Greece and Rome. These materials are used in family rooms and adjoining patios, and in informal living rooms of contemporary homes. *Stone* floors are often interesting, but they appear cold in living areas in moderate and cold climates and they are noisy and hard to walk on. They are fairly expensive to install, but easy to maintain.

Composition or resilient flooring

Linoleum, asphalt, cork, vinyl cork, rubber, vinyl asbestos, and pure vinyl are composition flooring materials of a resilient nature. They differ greatly in cost, use, resilience, resistance to grease, durability, and ease of maintenance.

Each resilient floor material requires its own mastic or cement and special care in handling. Some materials are recommended for above-grade installations, others for on grade or below grade, as discussed on pages 247 and 248.

Carpets and rugs

Carpet gives a floor the appearance of luxury, absorbs shock and noise, and helps to establish a color scheme. It makes a floor warm for children's play. There are fewer falls on carpeted stairs, and falls are less severe. Whether you choose a room-size rug, wall-to-wall carpet, or an area rug will depend upon personal preference, the condition of the floor, and the amount of money available.

Carpets and rugs represent a major item in home furnishing, and a great deal of thought should go into their selection. Before discussing them, let's make sure we understand the difference between a rug and a carpet.

A *carpet* originally meant a floor covering made by seaming together strips of narrow carpet. Carpet is woven on looms varying in width from 27 inches to 18 feet — and of course there is no limit to the length. Carpet woven on 9-, 12-, 15-, and 18-foot looms is called *broadloom carpet*. The bulk of rugs now are cut from 12-foot broadloom carpet.

A *rug* is any floor covering made in one piece. It may have a pattern and a border with fringe, or it may be cut from broadloom carpet.

A *room-size rug* is one that comes to within 12 inches or less from the wall on all sides. When a rug has a wide area around it which is not defined by furniture, the rug seems to float. To give a rug that is too small the effect of wall-to-wall carpet, the floor around it, if it is in poor condition, may be painted or tiled to match the rug. Otherwise the rug should be used as an area rug. Either treatment will secure unity.

An *area rug* is a smaller rug used to define a certain area. In a large room, for instance, area rugs may be used to separate living, reading, and eating areas. Area rugs often have sculptured borders.

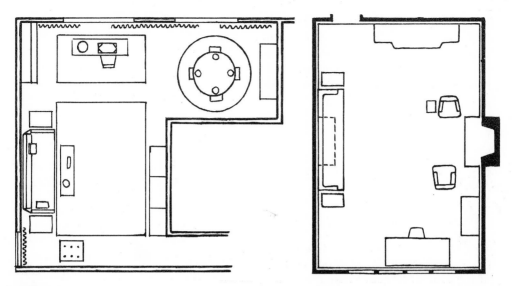

ILLUSTRATION 83.   *In the floor plan on the left, a large room is divided into three separate activity areas by rugs, and yet maintains unity. The rug shown in the right-hand floor plan comes to within a few inches of the walls, yet may be reversed because the cut-out section planned for the fireplace hearth will be covered by the sofa.*

A *scatter rug* is any small rug used to complement a room feature or a piece of furniture — in front of the fireplace, bed, or dresser. Scatter rugs should be well anchored.

An *accent rug* is a small rug with definite color and pattern placed on top of solid color wall-to-wall carpet.

Wall-to-wall carpet increases the apparent size of the room and tends to give furnishings unity. It is considered safer than any kind of rug, it conceals floors in bad condition, and it is easier to clean than a rug with floor around it. On the other hand, wall-to-wall carpet must be cleaned on the floor, and on-location cleaning is seldom as thorough as factory cleaning. Since wall-to-wall carpet may not always be reversed, traffic lanes begin to show. Installation costs must be added to the cost of the carpet. Many people choose a rug that comes within an inch or so of the walls, giving the effect of wall-to-wall carpet.

In instances where a large rug must be cut to fit the hearth, it may be reversed by placing the cut-out area under the sofa opposite the fireplace.

Other rug buying guides are discussed on pages 249–254.

★ WHAT ARE SOME SPECIAL CONSIDERATIONS IN THE CHOICE OF WALL FINISHES?

Wall coverings come under three main groups — paint, wallpaper, and wood paneling. Less frequently used coverings are linoleum, textiles, tile, and simulated tile. The structural finish of the wall may be plaster, concrete block, brick, glass brick, tile, wood, or wallboard. Glass brick and tile are structural finishes requiring no applied decoration. Plaster, concrete block, brick, wallboard, and wood may be painted. Only smooth plaster, wallboard, and canvas-covered wood may be papered. Newly plastered walls should not be painted until thoroughly dry. The time required for drying will depend upon the type of plaster used. When small plaster repair jobs are done, plaster may be given a coat of shellac or special sizing, and the paint may be applied after several weeks. Prefabricated plasterboard panels may be used in place of regular plaster, and painted immediately.

Paint

Whether you are painting walls, woodwork, or furniture, it is important to have clean, smooth surfaces, good equipment, and a good quality paint. If the surface has traces of grease or soap the paint will peel. A more velvety finish may be obtained if fine sandpaper is rubbed over the surface and the dust is wiped off between coats.

In most cases a new surface requires a sealer or primer to fill in the pores and give a smooth painting surface. Some paints will cover with one coat if the surface is well sealed, but other paints require two or even three coats. Many paints take a minimum of 24 hours to dry, while others dry in minutes. Most painted surfaces are washable. Semigloss paint is recommended for woodwork, and semigloss or gloss for kitchen and bathroom walls.

Painting is usually easier than hanging wallpaper. Many people paint over wallpaper with paints recommended for this type surface but painted wallpaper is difficult to remove from the walls.

SEALER AND PRIMER PAINT: A sealer or primer paint is necessary on any new surface — wood or plaster to fill in the pores and give a good painting base.

UNDERCOAT: On nonporous surfaces an inexpensive undercoat gives a good base for the final coat of paint or enamel.

OIL-BASE PAINTS: These come in flat, semigloss, and gloss finishes, and they are usually thinned with mineral spirits or paint thinner. Two coats of oil paint are needed — three coats if a very light color is painted over a dark color. Flat oil paint gives an attractive finish for all rooms except the kitchen and bathroom, but it is somewhat difficult to wash as it absorbs grease and soil. However, flat paint conceals wall irregularities. Woodwork should be painted with semigloss paint. A little clear varnish added to flat paint will give the necessary gloss.

ENAMEL: Enamel comes in high gloss, semigloss, and low gloss. It dries with a very smooth hard finish. Before applying enamel, rub the surface lightly with fine sandpaper and wipe with a cloth slightly dampened with turpentine.

ALKYD: These paints are thinned with mineral spirits, and an undercoat is necessary. This type paint comes in flat, semigloss, and gloss finishes. Alkyd paint is durable, washable, and permanent to light; brush marks do not show.

LATEX: This is sometimes referred to as rubber-base paint, but true rubber-base paint requires a strong volatile solvent. Latex paint is thinned with water. This paint is less expensive than oil-base paint, is easy to use, and dries with a durable finish. It has little odor, does not show brush marks, covers well, and dries in about 30 minutes. Tools clean in soapy water.

VINYL: Vinyl paint is thinned with water. It is washable, easy to apply, dries fast, covers well, and has very little odor.

CALCIMINE: This is a water-soluble paint made of whiting, glue, water, and color pigment. It cannot be washed.

CEMENT: This is a gloss paint which resists the alkali in concrete. Ordinary paints will not hold up on concrete.

VARNISH: Varnish is a colorless liquid which gives a firm hard surface. Varnish comes in dull, semigloss, and high gloss finishes. A special varnish must be used for outside surfaces.

COLOR PLATE 9.   *Painted walls are used as a background in this room. Closely blending figured draperies add an interesting pattern to the plain-colored walls in the room.*

COLOR PLATE 10. *Here figured wallpaper and plain-colored curtains are used. A small allover conventionalized design that is informal in character helps express the decorating idea of the room.*

Varnish should be applied only in dry weather and only when there is ventilation. It takes at least 24 hours to dry. There are clear streakless varnishes that may be applied to wallpaper to make it washable.

SHELLAC: Shellac comes clear and in orange color, and it is thinned with alcohol. It is used as a wood sealer and also as a built-up finish in refinishing furniture. It dries in a few hours.

LACQUER: Lacquer is thinned with lacquer thinner. Like nail polish, it dries very quickly; it is difficult to use by an amateur painter. Lacquer may be sprayed on from a pressurized can. The surface should be smooth or have a lacquer base primer.

TEXTURE: Paints to simulate different textures can be sprayed on or applied with a brush. One coat usually covers. Flecked and crepelike surfaces are obtainable. Rough plaster and other textured effects may be obtained by using special brushes.

Wallpaper

Some people prefer wallpaper to paint because of the wide choice of colors and designs in wallpaper. Wallpaper also gives a room more warmth. Companion wallpapers are available, so that two rooms may have the same basic colors but have varying patterns. A number of the same designs may be had in wallpaper and drapery fabrics. This provides for an interesting use of the pattern in adjoining rooms. One room may have plain-colored walls and printed draperies, while an adjoining room may have plain draperies and figured wallpaper of the same pattern as the draperies in the first room. Wallpaper and drapery fabric of the same design may be used together in a room for an interesting effect.

Wallpapers are printed by machine rollers and by a silk-screen process. Silk-screened

ILLUSTRATION 84A. *Bold simplicity is the keynote of this bedroom-study. Texture plays an important role in this room, too — bamboo draperies, textured plaid wallpaper, and corduroy pillows and spreads.*

wallpapers usually have larger patterns and more versatile designs than roller-printed wallpapers. Many papers are spongeable and others may be washed with care. Truly scrubbable wallpapers are vinyl coated or oilcloth, and they cost more than other wallpapers.

Principles of design must be applied in selecting figured wallpaper — proportion, balance, and harmony of shapes and sizes. You should avoid wallpaper that gives a busy effect or appears spotty. Large repeats should not be used in a room that is cut up with doors, windows, and fireplaces. Scenic wallpaper requires an unbroken wall, and may be used in vertical or horizontal panels.

Ordinarily, designs that are conventionalized are more pleasing than those that are too realistic. Designs that appear to rest flat on the wall are easier to live with than those that have a definite perspective. Scenic wallpapers or those with a three-dimensional effect need space to hold their own. Designs that seem suited to paper are a better choice than those that try to simulate something else such as wood or marble.

Texture is also an important consideration in selecting wallpaper. Overly rough and overly shiny textures should be avoided. Fairly smooth textures suggest elegance and sophistication, and are thus best suited to formal or traditional rooms. Soft, uneven textures suggest simplicity and comfort, and are thus best suited to informal or modern rooms.

Before selecting wallpaper, bring home some long strips of papers you think you like, and stick them on the wall with pins or transparent tape. Live with each pattern a day or two until you are sure of what you want. In studying the effect of wallpaper on your walls, remember that (1) colors will look stronger on four walls than on a single wall; (2) designs will look much larger in a wallpaper book

than on the wall; (3) a wallpaper with a definite repeat is disturbing in a room with many doors and windows, because the repeat is broken too often; (4) small patterns look better in small rooms, and large patterns in large rooms; (5) small over-all patterns help conceal structural irregularities; (6) scenic papers and pictorial panels are best used on only part of the wall area.

Wood paneling

During the Gothic period and throughout the Elizabethan period in England, wood paneling was the principal wall finish.

Precut and prefinished paneling comes in natural wood finishes — walnut, birch, mahogany, pine, fruitwood, maple, and oak. These panels are usually 4 by 8 feet and made to interlock. They give a handsome finish to living, dining, recreation and family rooms, and to the library. Often a wood finish is used only on one or two walls, with an interesting wallpaper on the other walls. True wood paneling is much more expensive than plywood paneling.

Sheets of laminated plastics

Made of synthetic resin, fabric, and paper, laminated plastics are used in kitchens and bathrooms as wainscoting or as an entire wall finish. You are probably familiar with the laminated plastics used in drugstore, restaurant, and theater fronts.

Tiles

Ceramic tile is the most hygienic, most durable, and most easily maintained finish for bathroom walls. Plastic tile which comes in squares and sheets is not as durable as true ceramic tile, but it is less expensive. Dampness may cause it to warp.

84B.   *Interlocking wood panels are not difficult to install. Available in many finishes, they can be installed on one or more walls in a room. Fittings are available for adjustable shelves, too.*

Brick

Brick in beige or red tones is used in fireplace walls or outside walls near the patio. It is popular in family rooms and recreation rooms. Brick may be used in combination with wood paneling, wallpaper, or painted walls. Bricks may be painted with dull finish colors for decorative effects, too.

Glass

Clear glass may be used as an entire window wall, while patterned glass is usually used for a divider wall. Patterned glass walls let in more light than opaque walls, but they are translucent enough to give privacy. Patterned glass comes in plain panels, corrugated, and screen or checked effects.

ILLUSTRATION 85. *For an interior partition, decorative glass paneling is attractive and provides additional light on the stairway. For exterior walls, glass bricks provide the same attractive appearance plus insulation against heat and cold.*

Glass brick

With the development of modern architecture, glass brick is sometimes used as a wall finish. Glass bricks are strong and provide heat insulation. Bricks used as walls are translucent, thus admitting some light but insuring privacy within the area inclosed. Other bricks which are transparent are often etched or painted and used purely as decoration. Glass bricks are best adapted to modern rooms.

Linoleum

As a wainscot finish with a border, linoleum is sometimes used on walls in nurseries, playrooms, kitchens, and bathrooms.

✳ HOW SHOULD CEILINGS BE TREATED?

Ordinarily the ceiling should be very light for the best light reflection. The heavy oak beams in Old English reception rooms and dining rooms are seldom seen now. In some modern homes, living room ceilings are darker than the walls, and are often rather interesting. Lamps placed at strategic places provide light where it is needed, and hence a light ceiling is not needed for light reflection. However, in homes where ceilings are low, a dark ceiling will make one think about Henny Penny and the falling sky.

Many people who do their own papering and painting prefer to paint ceilings because it is difficult for an amateur to paper a ceiling. In rooms of ordinary height — at least nine feet — it is interesting to repeat in the ceiling one of the light colors in figured wallpaper, such as pale sunshine yellow, sky blue, or light dusty pink. For playrooms and music rooms, acoustic tiles made of perforated fiber board may be used on ceilings to subdue noises.

✳ HOW WILL YOU PREPARE WALLS AND MEASURE FOR WALLPAPER?

Preparation of walls

Formerly, newly plastered walls were allowed to dry a year before they were papered, but quick-drying plaster and plaster sealers will permit the application of wallpaper in a much shorter time. Wallpaper applied over several old layers of paper will never be satisfactory. Old wallpaper may be removed by steaming and scraping with a putty knife. Professional steaming units may be rented. Before applying wallpaper to walls that have never been papered before, a good priming coat of sealer should be put on the walls. People who invest a lot of money in good wallpaper usually have a lining paper applied first. If the walls are badly cracked, a muslin base especially for the purpose will prevent the paper from cracking as the plaster expands and contracts. Walls around damp chimneys sometimes need a special moistureproof undercoat to prevent the paper from marking.

Bolt and roll sizes

Before you choose wallpaper you will want to know the width and length of rolls. Ordinary wallpaper is bought by the bolt. A bolt contains three rolls of narrow paper or two rolls of wide paper. Wallpaper widths are 18 inches, 22 inches, 24 inches, and 30 inches. A single roll or half a bolt of 18-inch paper is 7½ yards long; of 22-inch and 24-inch paper, 7 yards long; of 30-inch wallpaper, 5 yards long. This means that a bolt of 30-inch paper will cover approximately the same area as a bolt of 18-inch paper. What is lost in width is gained in length, and *vice versa*. Whether or not a pattern has to be matched is an important consideration in determining the amount needed.

Paneled or scenic wallpaper may be had in rolls or panels. The width of the roll or panel depends upon the design and the type of paper, varying from 18 to 30 inches. The length depends on the repeat of the pattern, but usually there are about 36 square feet in a roll.

Measuring

When you measure for wallpaper, you will want to know approximately how many square feet of wall space must be covered. To find the number of square feet of wall space, add the length and width of the room, multiply by its height, and double the total. Since one roll will cover about 36 square feet, divide the number of square feet of wall space in the room by 36 to find the number of rolls needed. For two average-

sized windows and a door, take off one roll. A bedroom which measures 12 by 14 feet and is 9 feet high, and which has one door and two windows will usually require 12 rolls or 6 bolts of paper.

Papering

If you are planning to do your own papering, assemble the following items in addition to your wallpaper:

> Large table
> Wide brush for pasting
> Pail for mixing paste
> Large dry paper-hanger's brush
> T-shaped support to hold ceiling paper
> Plumb line
> Ladder
> Yardstick
> Old newspapers
> Old rags
> Large scissors
> Sharp razor blade

With the new prepasted papers, equipment for pasting will not be needed. Follow carefully the directions given by the manufacturer for applying the paper.

When using figured paper, plan to center definite repeats over points of interest, such as mantels, large pieces of furniture, and so forth. Drop a plumb line down from the ceiling before you begin, and with a yardstick draw a vertical line along the plumb line. The first strip of paper should follow

ILLUSTRATION 86A. *Steps 1 (above) through 4 (below) in papering a room.*
1. *Measure from plumb to door to see if woodwork is straight. Mark plumb line for starting guide.*
2. *Cut lengths, adding 2–3" surplus to each.*
3. *Remove selvage along lines indicated.*
4. *Place strip on table, and apply paste evenly.*

this line. Lay the paper out on a table, and cut several lengths noting where it is marked "match here." Allow two to three extra inches on each strip. Remove the selvage, since wallpaper should not be overlapped but butt joined. The selvage may be removed with scissors, but you will have a cleaner line if you cut it off with a razor blade held against a hardwood yardstick. Place the paper face down on newspapers, and cover the surface evenly with paste. Lift up the two ends and fold lightly toward the center, allowing the pasted sides to adhere temporarily. This will give a shorter length of paper which will facilitate its handling. Begin at the top, and carefully hold the side of the paper in place along the plumb line. When the paper is lightly in place, firmly smooth the wide dry brush over the entire surface to eliminate bubbles or wrinkles. Work from the top to the bottom, and if wrinkles persist, lift the paper from the bottom and then brush from the center out toward each side. With a sharp razor blade and a yardstick, cut off the surplus paper at the baseboard and at the ceiling. Continue working from left to right, matching figures in the paper as you progress.

If borders are used, it will not be necessary to exercise so much care in having the top edge of the paper even. Borders tend to subtract height from a room which may or may not be desirable. When they are used,

86B. *Steps 5 (above) through 8 (below).*
5. *Fold ends lightly to center for easy handling.*
6. *Start at top, allowing 1–1½" surplus to be trimmed later. Follow plumb line, and if door is not straight, trim surplus paper later.*
7. *Smooth with brush to bottom. Trim surplus later.*
8. *Match pattern and edges on next strip.*

they should be a part of the decorative scheme of the room in feeling, line, color, and design.

The three rooms pictured in Illustrations 79 to 81 will help to summarize the important points discussed in this chapter. Study the captions under the illustrations, and from the Suggested Activities which follow, choose those that will give you more confidence in your ability to select the proper wall and ceiling finishes and floor coverings.

SUGGESTED ACTIVITIES

1. Select a room at home or at school which needs to be redecorated. Study it from the standpoint of present furnishings, decorating idea, use, effect on adjacent rooms, exposure, and size and shape. Plan the redecoration of the room, collecting pictures of various effects you want to carry out and samples of new additions, such as wall finish, draperies, and rug. Talk the plan over with your classmates and teacher and with your mother. Carry out your approved plan. This may be either a class project at school or an individual project at home.

2. Make a large class chart or a set of individual charts showing a good choice of wallpaper, paint, and floor covering for
   (a) a small room
   (b) a dark room
   (c) a formal room
   (d) a large room
   (e) a light room, and
   (f) an informal room.
   You may paint small paper swatches to resemble rug colors or cut small samples from rug booklets.

3. Mount pictures of each room of the house showing suitable floor and wall treatments.

4. Collect booklets and magazine clippings on the selection of wall finishes, rugs, and floor finishes. Make a scrapbook or portfolio of your collection.

5. Recommend the size of a broadloom rug to buy for a room measuring $16\frac{1}{2}$ by 18 feet. Widths of broadloom rugs are 6, 9, 12, 15, and 18 feet.

6. List the special considerations your family would have in choosing rugs for the downstairs rooms and areas.

7. Find out what kinds of rugs are available in the Better Home Furnishings group of coordinated colors.

8. Look for traffic lanes or other spots which are showing wear in the rugs or floor finishes in your home. Try to remedy these situations.

9. Discuss the points made on floor coverings in this chapter with your mother. See if her experience confirms some of the points and adds others.

10. Try out various methods of cleaning painted surfaces in your home or homemaking department. Compare the cost and efficiency of the cleaners used, and notice how satisfactorily the various types of paint respond to cleaning.

11. Obtain samples of asphalt tile, rubber tile, and inlaid linoleum. Compare the cost of buying and laying these finishes in a kitchen.

12. Tack about a dozen wallpaper samples along the blackboard, and discuss them from the standpoint of design, texture, and where they might be used. Compare the papers as to cost and quality.

13. Use the new wallpaper waxes and lacquers on samples of wallpaper, and experiment with washing the treated samples.

14. Measure your bedroom or some other room that needs repapering, and estimate the cost of repapering it. Compare this estimate with the cost of removing the old paper and painting the walls.

15. Plan uses for attractive wallpaper, such as covering boxes for your clothes closet, papering your clothes closet, and lining storage boxes.

CHAPTER 2

How will you give your windows character and interest?

No MATTER how handsomely a room is furnished, the result is not satisfying if the windows are not right. After floors, walls, and ceilings, windows occupy the next greatest area in the room. Not only do they afford light and perhaps a beautiful view, but they may be a source of beauty within themselves. Since window frames usually make a bold contrast to other horizontal and vertical lines in the room, curtains or draperies are used to soften their lines. Well-chosen curtains or draperies that harmonize with other furnishings can do a great deal toward providing beauty in a room.

Windows require careful study if you are to choose the best treatment for them. Those in different styles of houses and in various rooms require different treatment. The proportions of some windows make them special problems. How to select shades and blinds must also be considered. But in order to understand how to decorate windows, you should know first of all what kinds of windows there are and what terms are used in describing their parts.

✴ WHAT ARE THE DIFFERENT KINDS OF WINDOWS?

The newer type windows are available in wood and metal. Wood transmits heat less readily than metal, and moisture vapor from the air does not condense on wood. *Wooden* windows should be treated to resist decay and moisture absorption. About half of all wood windows sold are glazed, weatherstripped, and hung at the factory. *Metal* windows may have thinner frames than wood because metal is stronger. Aluminum windows need no painting, but natural aluminum will oxidize and darken in industrial and seacoast areas; in these areas aluminum windows must be specially treated. Ordinary stainless steel windows will corrode in salt air but treated stainless steel windows will not.

All windows are classified as *sliding*, *swinging*, or *fixed*. There are many combinations. Any window that swings into a room — horizontally or vertically — presents a problem in curtaining or decorating.

Sliding windows include the double-hung type and those that slide horizontally. *Swinging* windows include casement and awning types that swing out, as well as windows that swing in from the bottom (hopper) or from the top (above sinks). *Fixed* windows may have one permanent sash with others that slide or swing. *Dormer* windows may be double-hung or casement or sliding. The *arched* window, found more often in older homes, is interesting but

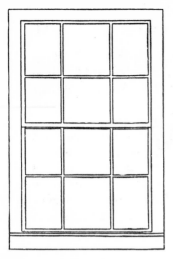

DOUBLE SASH

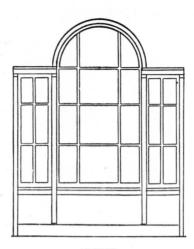

ARCHED

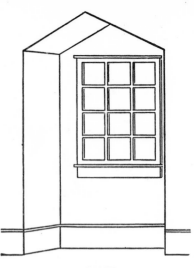

DORMER

PICTURE

ILLUSTRATION 87. *Different kinds of windows. These are the main types of windows, though variation may occur in some instances in size of panes, grouping, and the like.*

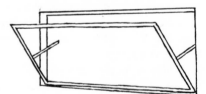

HOPPER

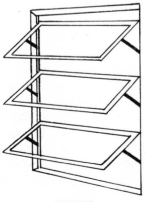

AWNING

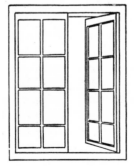

CASEMENT

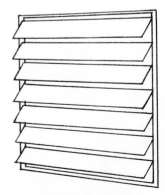

JALOUSIE

difficult to decorate. The large *picture* window, so popular in new homes, is often used with no thought of the outside picture it will frame. Draw curtains or draw draperies are usually hung at the picture window.

✱ WHAT TERMS ARE USED IN DESCRIBING WINDOWS?

Terms related to the parts of a window are *sash*, *frame*, *sill*, and *apron*. The frame and apron outline the window. The sill forms the base of the window, and the sash frames the glass in the window. Though actually a part of the room construction, *baseboard* is a term closely related to window decoration, since it is sometimes a determining factor in curtain or drapery lengths.

Other terms used in describing window treatments are *shade* or *Venetian blind*, the covering used over a window, and *curtain* and *drapery rods*, the supports used for hanging curtains and draperies. *Glass curtain* is a sheer hanging over the window glass, while *drapery* is a heavier hanging at both sides of the window frame. *Cornice*, *lambrequin*, and *valance* are decorative bands of wood or fabric sometimes used across the tops of windows. *Swag and cascades* of fabric are also a decorative finish for the tops of windows. Examples of all these terms are sketched in Illustrations 88 and 89.

✱ WHAT KIND OF WINDOW COVERING WILL YOU CHOOSE?

Most people want a window shade or a Venetian blind to give privacy and to shut out glare. However, there is a growing tendency to eliminate both shade and Venetian

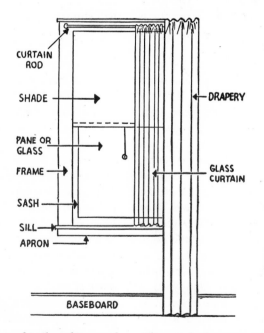

ILLUSTRATION 88.   *Terms used in describing windows. These and other terms shown in Illustration 89 are used in describing window parts and treatments.*

blind, and to use draw draperies on traverse rods. This is especially true if the window is a picture window. The disadvantages of using draw draperies with no shade or blind are the lack of glare control and the lack of privacy during the daytime. These disadvantages are negligible if the window does not face morning or afternoon sun or a scene where people are constantly moving about on the outside. At night, of course, the draw drapery is drawn over the window.

In considering the type of window covering that serves both daytime and nighttime use, the question always arises as to whether to choose a window shade or a Venetian blind. The popularity of Venetian blinds seems to be increasing. The first Venetian blinds were used during the Georgian period, but they nearly disappeared from use until fairly recently. During the Victorian period, shutters were used either inside or outside the windows, and during the first quarter of the twentieth century, nearly every home had green or tan window shades.

Shades are less expensive than Venetian blinds, but they have to be replaced more often. When shades are pulled all the way down, they actually block out more light than Venetian blinds, but shades do not diffuse light as well as partly opened Venetian blinds. Shades as a rule require glass curtains, while glass curtains may or may not be used with Venetian blinds. Even though Venetian blinds control light and ventilation well, they sometimes rattle in the wind. They require considerable care, but this care is little more than that required to wash and stretch or iron the glass curtains generally used with shades. Venetian blinds lend dignity to a room, and are obtainable in a variety of tints which are more apt to tie in with a color scheme. After weighing the pros and cons, whether you choose Venetian blinds or shades

is a matter of personal taste. Windows may be decorated attractively with either. However, before choosing window shades or Venetian blinds, you should know something more about each.

Venetian blinds

These are made of steel, aluminum, wood, or plastic. The American Hotel Association has set up certain specifications for Venetian blinds used in hotels. White cedar is recommended as the best kind of wood, high-quality flexible aluminum as the best kind of aluminum, and flexible steel as the best kind of steel. Plastic blinds are not recommended, since strong sunlight tends to warp the slats and fade the colors, and since the plastic shows scratches. Plastic blinds are also expensive. No doubt they will be improved in the future. Cotton-twill cord is preferred over nylon cord because nylon is hard, stiff, and will slip when the blinds are adjusted.

Window shades

These come in various grades. A good cloth window shade will withstand many washings. Light-colored window shades are preferable to dark ones particularly from the inside of the house, but dark window shades make it possible to darken a room more completely. However, some light-colored washable shades are now treated so that they shut out practically all daylight. Since window shades occupy so much of the wall area, color should be a determining factor in choosing them. Since they are usually considered a part of the background, they should be as inconspicuous as possible. If cream-colored woodwork is used, matching cream-colored shades are a good choice. Since cream is a neutral color, it also goes well with other light woodwork tints. Darker shades may be used with natural or stained woodwork.

Outside effect

In addition to considering the inside effect of window treatments, one should also consider how the windows look from the outside. If the front of the house shows pink ruffled curtains at one window, blue at another, shades at a few windows, and Venetian blinds at others, it will look like "the house that Jack built." From the outside looking in, the effect is more pleasing if all windows on the same side of the house, especially the front, are treated alike. The effect may be acceptable, however, if all the windows on each floor are treated alike. Since draperies may not be seen from outside the house, more variation in them is possible. But a house will look much more attractive if all the windows on the street side are fitted either with window shades or with Venetian blinds and either ruffled or tailored curtains if curtains are used. Merely providing the proper fittings is not enough. Each morning shades or blinds should be adjusted at the same height on all windows.

✦ HOW WILL YOU PLAN GLASS CURTAINS AND DRAPERIES?

Glass curtains

These are used at a window to give a more pleasant diffusion of light by day and to soften the blackness of window openings at night. As has already been said, a glass curtain may or may not be used with a Venetian blind. But if Venetian blinds are used without draperies, full ruffled or tailored curtains are usually used. Though glass curtains are sometimes used with draperies, they may be used without draperies in the following instances: (1) in small rooms, so that the windows will not overbalance the room; (2) in simple graceful rooms where informality

is the keynote; (3) in rooms where there is a great deal of pattern in the wallpaper.

If the window is recessed, the glass curtain will be set against the window — not on the wall. For windows that are not recessed, the rod for a glass curtain is usually hung across the width of the frame and an inch below the top of the frame. The inch heading at the top of the curtain will cover the top of the frame, and the curtain will cover the sides of the frame. An exception to this rule is the very large window or the window with an unusually pretty frame. In this case the effect may be more interesting if the curtain is hung so that the entire frame is visible. Sheer curtains should be two to three times the width of the window and stop at the sill, at the end of the apron, or at the floor — never between the frame and floor. Ruffled glass curtains on very wide windows should be extra full.

Draperies

They may add color and pattern to a room especially if the room is large and the windows fairly large and interestingly spaced. They may be made to hang straight if the room is formal, to be tied back if the room is less formal, or to serve as draw draperies if such service is desired. Most drapery materials will hang better if they are lined. Sateen is the usual lining material whether the drapery is chintz or satin or cretonne. Homespun fabrics need not be lined. Draperies may be topped with swags, a cornice, a lambrequin or shaped valance, a ruffled valance, or a swag and cascades.

If the room is small and the ceilings are low, tailored or straight draperies are best. If the room is of average height, a small cornice painted to match the woodwork or a predominating color in the drapery fabric may add interest. Draperies are usually hung

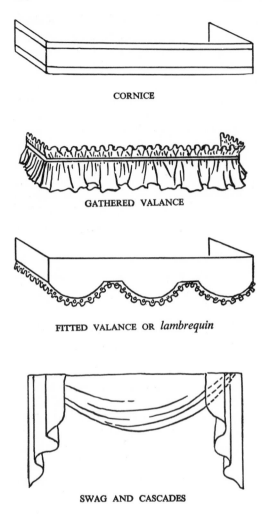

CORNICE

GATHERED VALANCE

FITTED VALANCE OR *lambrequin*

SWAG AND CASCADES

ILLUSTRATION 89. *Decorative finishes for the tops of windows. When they do not overemphasize a horizontal line, these finishes add interest to window treatments.*

so that they completely cover the window frame at the sides. In formal rooms, draperies may be floor length. Sill-length draperies are satisfactory in informal rooms. Draperies may stop at the lower edge of the apron provided the glass curtains also stop there.

Cornices

These may be made of wood, plastic, or mirror glass. Wood cornices are the most frequently used, and a plain wooden board with an interesting molding at the top and bottom is always in good taste. Wood cornices may be finished in their natural wood color, may be painted some other color, or may be covered with cloth, cork, or leather. Sometimes the coverings are edged with brass nails. Cornice board may be bought by the foot in department stores.

Valances

These headings may be made of gathered or pleated cloth. *Lambrequins* have a backing of buckram, plywood, or masonite which is shaped in different designs. These shaped valances or lambrequins may be covered with cloth and edged with fringe, or those with a plywood or masonite backing may be painted to harmonize with the room decoration. While the width of a cornice should be a little less than one-eighth of the over-all length of a floor-length drapery, the width of a lambrequin or a gathered valance should be about one-seventh of the length of the drapery.

Swags and cascades

Headings of this type are appropriate for large formal rooms with high ceilings. They are apt to look too heavy in small or average-sized rooms. If you have any occasion to use a swag and cascades, the sketch in Illustration 93 will help you to cut them. The depth of the swag in the center after it is draped should be about one-seventh of the drapery length or one-seventh of the distance between the top of the frame and the floor. The width of the cascade at the top should coincide with the width of the drapery when hung.

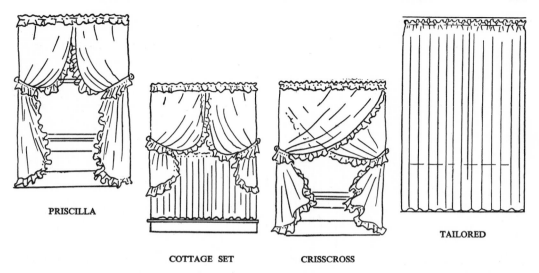

PRISCILLA

COTTAGE SET

CRISSCROSS

TAILORED

ILLUSTRATION 90. *Curtain styles. The purpose of the room and the decorating idea govern the use of curtains and the style selected.*

★ **HOW WILL YOU DECORATE VARIOUS WINDOWS?**

The way you decorate windows will depend upon their appearance from the street, the type and use of the room, the decorating theme, and the type, size, and position of the window. If there is a view, don't destroy it with heavy curtaining. But if the window faces a wall, you will want to minimize the view as much as possible without losing too much light. Illustrations 90–97 offer suggestions for decorating a number of different types of windows.

Living room windows

Because of their impersonal nature, tailored curtains and lined draperies with French pleats are a safe treatment in many living rooms. A wooden cornice with tailored draperies or curtains may be equally good

ILLUSTRATION 91. *Café and tier curtains are particularly adaptable and attractive for many types of contemporary rooms.*

1.

2.

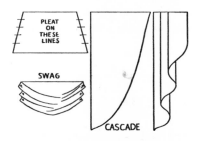

3.

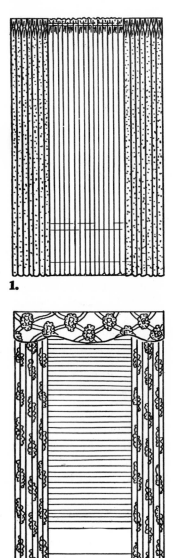

4.

ILLUSTRATION 92. *Formal window treatments. Sketch 1 shows floor length, French-pleated draperies with long glass curtains; 2, floor-length draperies with swag, cascades, and curtains; 3, floor-length draperies with a cornice and sill-length curtains; 4, floor-length draperies with lambrequin and Venetian blind.*

ILLUSTRATION 93. *Swag and cascades. Cut so that center of draped swag is $\frac{1}{7}$ of drapery length; top of the pleated cascade is the width of hanging drapery; length of the cascade is $2\frac{1}{2}$–3 times its finished width.*

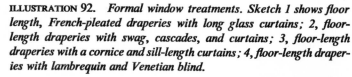

provided the cornice does not shorten the windows too much. Tall windows in large formal rooms will permit a little more dressing. Lambrequins or a swag treatment is interesting if not overdone. Lace curtains with draperies of rayon satin, brocade, or damask belong only in the strictly formal living room. Ruffled curtains are always in good taste in cottage-type or Early-Colonial living rooms. Venetian blinds with draperies of interesting texture, pattern, or stripe, or draw draperies are suitable for modern rooms.

Dining room windows

The treatment of dining room windows follows the same general rules as those for living room windows. If patterned paper is used, plain-colored draperies are usually best. The dinette, if near the kitchen, should carry out the kitchen idea, or if it is a part of the living area, it should carry out the living room idea.

Kitchen windows

Curtains for the kitchen may be as gay and individual as you please, provided they are good in line and color and harmonize with other furnishings. Of course, they should be easy to wash. Gingham or flowered-percale curtains are frequently good. Bands of plain-colored percale joined with rickrack braid make colorful curtains. Fitted oilcloth valances are also good in the kitchen.

Bedroom windows

The *owners' bedroom* should have a window treatment that is neither too dainty nor too masculine. Tailored draperies with a gathered valance may give this in-between look, or tailored draperies with soft crisscross or ruffled curtains may also be used. If the walls are figured, glass curtains without draperies

ILLUSTRATION 94. *Informal window treatments. Sketch 1 shows a swag draped over apron-length tailored curtains; 2, apron-length draperies hung by rings on a pole; 3, apron-length draperies with cornice; 4, gathered valance and tie backs with ruffled curtains.*

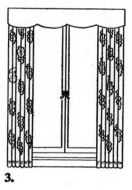

3.

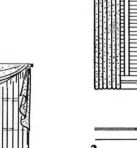

2.

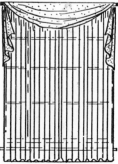

1.

4.

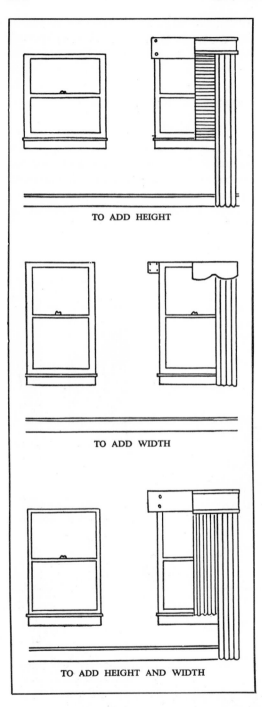

TO ADD HEIGHT

TO ADD WIDTH

TO ADD HEIGHT AND WIDTH

may be a suitable choice. With plain walls, gay figured chintz or cretonne in an in-between design is frequently good.

Guest room windows should also have an in-between treatment. Draperies may be enhanced by adding a plain or shaped cornice, a French pleated or a gathered valance, or a swag effect with heavy cotton cord of a contrasting color. If curtains are used alone, they may be made more interesting by adding a gay pleated or ruffled valance with tie backs to match the valance.

The windows in a *boy's bedroom* should be masculine in treatment. If curtains are used they should be of the tailored type. Many boys prefer striped or plaid homespun fabrics, plain-colored monk's cloth, or denim draperies with no curtains. If figures are used, they will be bolder and more masculine than those chosen by a girl.

The windows in a *girl's bedroom* may be either frilly and feminine or tailored, as the occupant's taste dictates. Priscilla, crisscross, or swagger-type curtains without draperies are frequently a good choice. A plain-colored swag at the top of curtains or daintily figured draperies may also be good.

✶ HOW WILL YOU TREAT PROBLEM WINDOWS?

Awkwardly placed or awkwardly sized windows present problems. In solving these problems, some very interesting effects may

ILLUSTRATION 95. *Problem windows. To add height, place board above window, and use cornice and floor-length draperies. To add width, place wood blocks at sides; hang drapery over wall, and cover with cornice. To add height and width, nail board above and beyond window for drapery.*

result. The well-proportioned double-sash window lends itself to any number of treatments, but the double-sash window that is too small in proportion to the wall on which it is placed, or too long for its own width, or too wide for its length needs special consideration.

Small windows

A window that is very small will need to be made to appear higher and wider. A strip of wood four or five inches wider than the top of the window frame and long enough to extend several inches over the frame at each side may be placed over the window. The resulting cornice is actually higher than the window, and its extra width permits the draperies to extend over on the wall on each side of the window, giving an appearance of additional width. For the greatest effect of height, the cornice should be covered to match the drapery.

To create the appearance of a larger window, fasten a board the width of the window above the window frame. Paint the wood the color of the woodwork; mount a mirror on it if desired. Treat the area as one window.

Long and short windows

If a window is too *long and narrow*, nail small strips of wood to the wall at the top of each side of the window frame, and fasten the drapery rods to these extensions. Use a cornice in a color which contrasts with the draperies to further break the height. If a *short* window needs height, add a shaped

ILLUSTRATION 96.   *One way to treat a problem window, such as this strip window over the bed, is to use patterned fabric matching the wallpaper.*

ILLUSTRATION 97.   *The use of translucent café-type curtains here allows maximum light, unifies the contemporary room's background, provides privacy, and may camouflage an unpleasant view.*

valance above the window so that the lower edge of the valance covers the top of the window frame. Use vertical-striped material for the drapery and as a covering for the valance.

Double windows

These are best treated as a unit. A Venetian blind the width of the two windows may be used, and the windows may be decorated with one pair of very full ruffled curtains tied back from the center, or with full tailored curtains hung on one rod. A drapery on each side of the double window with a cornice, a valance, or a swag running the full width of the two windows will also give an interesting unit. If two windows are close together but not adjoining, they may also look more interesting if treated as a unit. This may be done by placing a window-length strip of mirror from frame to frame between the two windows. The cornice, valance, or swag treatment just described may be used, and if desirable at intervals within the unit, other full lengths of the draperies may be added.

Corner and bay windows

Likewise, corner windows and bay windows should be treated as a unit. For bay windows, full, floor-length tailored glass curtains with colored pliable rayon draped in swags across the top of the windows and allowed to cascade to the floor at each side are attractive. Curving valances or cornices

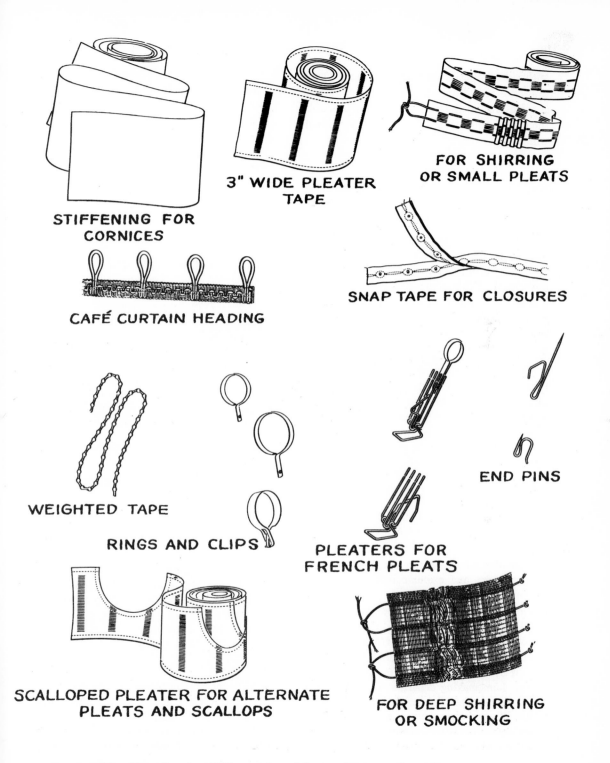

STIFFENING FOR
CORNICES

3" WIDE PLEATER
TAPE

FOR SHIRRING
OR SMALL PLEATS

CAFÉ CURTAIN HEADING

SNAP TAPE FOR CLOSURES

WEIGHTED TAPE

RINGS AND CLIPS

PLEATERS FOR
FRENCH PLEATS

END PINS

SCALLOPED PLEATER FOR ALTERNATE
PLEATS AND SCALLOPS

FOR DEEP SHIRRING
OR SMOCKING

ILLUSTRATION 98. *Examples of available curtain and drapery fixtures and supplies.*

with side draperies may also be used. Draw draperies on traverse rods with a wood cornice around the entire corner is probably the most frequently used treatment for corner windows.

Arched windows

Windows with a glassed arch above them may be draped as a single unit by using an arched rod, and by tying the draperies back. If tie backs are objectionable for any reason, the curved top may be covered with a glass curtain held into a rosette at the center. The lower part of the windows may be treated as a single window with tailored curtains and straight draperies.

Fixtures

The great variety of curtain rods, festoon rings and holders, hold backs, valance pleaters, and cornices on the market make window decoration interesting and fairly simple even for the novice.

SUGGESTED ACTIVITIES

1. Collect and mount on the bulletin board illustrations of interesting window decoration.
2. Collect booklets on window decoration.
3. Visit the window-fixture department of a large store, and examine different kinds of window fixtures.
4. Find pictures of good window decoration for (a) a Cape Cod cottage, (b) a formal Georgian home, and (c) a strictly modern home.
5. Plan and sketch a new window treatment for your living room at home, for some room in your homemaking department, or elsewhere. Submit swatches of materials you would like to use. Buy and make the new curtains or draperies if possible. Directions for making curtains and draperies are given in Unit Nine, Chapter 4.

6. Check your window shades or blinds to see whether the outside appearance of your windows is uniform. Assume the duty of adjusting blinds or shades daily.
7. Study any problem windows you may have at school or at home. Make plans for improving the treatment of them. Carry out your plans if possible.

SELECTED REFERENCES FOR UNIT FIVE

BOOKS

Consult books listed in Unit Four

CURRENT PUBLICATIONS

Floor Coverings and Flooring
　　Armstrong Cork Company, Lancaster, Pa.
　　Bigelow Sanford Carpet Company, 138 Madison Avenue, New York, N.Y.
　　Cabin Crafts, Dalton, Ga.
　　Carpet Institute, Inc., 350 Fifth Avenue, New York, N.Y.
　　E. I. du Pont de Nemours & Co., Inc., Wilmington 98, Del.
　　Firth Carpet Company, Inc., 295 Fifth Avenue, New York 16, N.Y.
　　James Lees and Sons, Bridgeport, Pa.
　　Magee Carpet Company, Bloomsburg, Pa.
　　C. H. Masland and Sons, Carlisle, Pa.
　　Mohasco Industries, Inc., Amsterdam, N.Y.

Walls and Windows
　　Anderson Corporation, Bayport, Minn.
　　Blue Ridge Glass Company, Kingsport, Tenn.
　　Columbus Coated Fabrics Corporation, Columbus 16, Ohio (*wall coverings*)
　　Consolidated Trimming Corporation, 27 West 23rd St., New York, N.Y. (*window treatments*)
　　Imperial Paper and Color Corporation, Glens Falls, N.Y. (*wall coverings*)
　　Kirsch Company, 345 Prospect Street, Sturgis, Mich. (*window treatments*)
　　Libbey Owens Ford Glass Co., Toledo, Ohio
　　Pittsburgh Plate Glass Co., Pittsburgh 19, Pa.

6

Become familiar with furniture styles and arrangements

ILLUSTRATION 99. *Furniture style and arrangement. An example
of modern style, the furniture in this room is grouped for use and
order. Traditional styles are less severe than functional modern.*

CHAPTER I

What are the familiar furniture styles?

ALL the different pieces of furniture we have in our homes today have evolved from four needs of man — a place to sit down, a place to lie down, a place at which to work or eat, and a place in which to store belongings. The first chair was probably hewn from a tree stump; the first table may have been a slab of rock; the first bed may have been a sort of hammock or a pile of leaves; the first chest may have been a hole in the ground or later a crude box. From the first chair have come ladder back, Windsor, rocker, club lounge, wing, Cogswell, button back, and many other styles. The sofa, settee, and love seat originated from the idea of a chair. From the first crude beds have come couches, bed sofas, and beds of all sizes and styles. From the first table, creative man has designed dining, card, tea, coffee, drop leaf, Pembroke, console, and dozens of other styles. From man's first box or treasure chest have come all kinds of chests for every room of the house.

Furniture styles in current use date from the seventeenth century Jacobean period in England. The golden age in furniture was reached during the eighteenth century in England when such craftsmen as Chippendale, Sheraton, and Hepplewhite created the most beautiful furniture forms ever made.

Adaptations of eighteenth century furniture are widely used today. Furniture is now passing through a period of transition. In the modern functional houses, a great deal of furniture is being built in as the house is constructed. And a new type of movable furniture known as the modern style has developed. Simplicity and functionalism are two of its chief characteristics.

Although few of you will ever buy strictly period styles, you should be able to recognize the important features of the principal periods. The court styles of France and some English styles are omitted because they are seldom found in furniture for the home today. A short description of each of the main periods is given, and illustrations show the chief characteristics. In addition, Illustrations 100–102 on pages 162–167 show familiar styles of tables, chairs, and sofas in common use today.

✸ WHAT CHARACTERIZES THE JACOBEAN PERIOD?

The Jacobean period, running from 1603 to 1688, was influenced primarily by the events of the preceding reign, that of Queen Elizabeth. England had gained control of the sea after the defeat of the Spanish Armada in 1588, and with this triumph, she had turned

LOUNGE

COGSWELL

BUTTON BACK

WING

CLUB

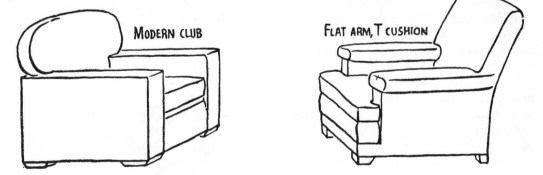

MODERN CLUB   FLAT ARM, T CUSHION

ILLUSTRATION 100. *Styles of chairs. Ranging from upholstered—with varying amounts of wood exposed — to all wood, the present-day chairs shown on these pages exemplify considerable variance in style.*

BARREL BACK

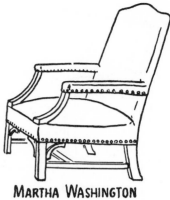

MARTHA WASHINGTON

VICTORIAN CORSET BACK

SLIPPER ROCKER

WINDSOR

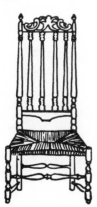

BANISTER BACK

LADDER BACK

LAWSON

CHESTERFIELD

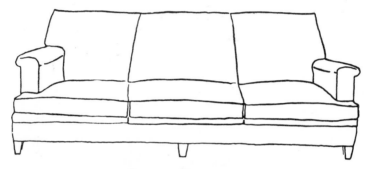

FLAT ARM, T CUSHION

STUDIO COUCH   BED SOFA

ILLUSTRATION 101.   *Styles of sofas. Aside from seating two or more persons, some of the sofas on these pages can also be used as a bed. Uniquely, the modern sectional sofa can be used as separate chairs.*

SECTIONAL SOFA

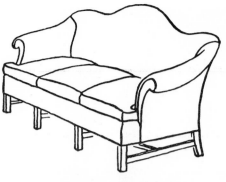

UPHOLSTERED CHIPPENDALE

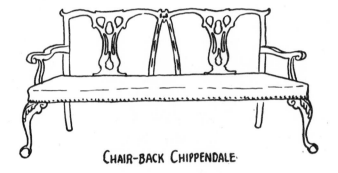

CHAIR-BACK CHIPPENDALE

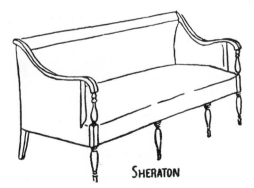

SHERATON

DUNCAN PHYFE CORNUCOPIA

NEST

PEMBROKE

LAMP

TIER

COMMODE   DROP LEAF   CARD OR CONSOLE

ILLUSTRATION 102. *Styles of tables. Throughout the ages man has devised many different*

DRUM

PIECRUST, TILT TOP

STEP

COFFEE

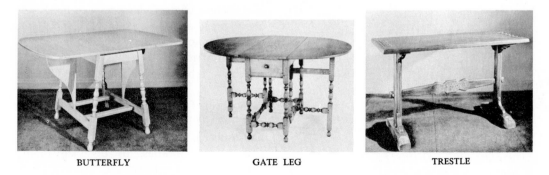

BUTTERFLY   GATE LEG   TRESTLE

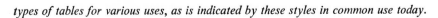

types of tables for various uses, as is indicated by these styles in common use today.

**BULBOUS
OR MELON
LEG**

**FLEMISH-SCROLL
LEG**

STRAPWORK

ACORN DROP

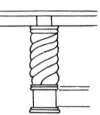

BALUSTER LEG

SPIRAL-TWIST LEG

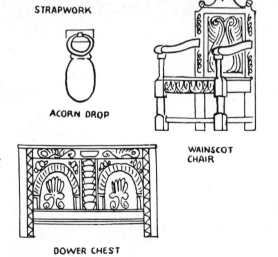

**WAINSCOT
CHAIR**

DOWER CHEST

ILLUSTRATION 103. *Details of Jacobean furniture.
Rectangular and massive forms are characteristic
of this furniture.*

her attention to economic development. As
a further stimulant to progress, many craftsmen and weavers who fled from the continent
to England to escape the Spanish Inquisition
had turned their time and talents to making
furniture.

The Jacobean period covers the reigns of
James I, Charles I, Cromwell, Charles II,
and James II. It was a vigorous, masculine,
somber, and austere period, as a study of the
furniture shown in the accompanying illustration will indicate.

Furniture of the period climaxed the age
of oak. Oak was the most popular furniture
wood between 1500 and 1680. Furniture
forms were rectangular and massive. Moldings
in geometric forms and carving in strapwork
(see Illustration 103), in scrolls, in acorn
leaves, or in geometric designs were the chief
embellishments. The bulbous or melon leg of
the Elizabethan period continued for a while,
but later gave way to the more slender
baluster, Flemish-scroll, and spiral-twist legs.
The spiral turning was of Portuguese influence.
Chairs were improved a bit in comfort, and
sometimes had padded seats and backs upholstered with tapestry and decorated with
fringe. Caning in the seats and backs produced lighter and a little more graceful
chairs. The wing-back chair appeared during
the reign of Charles II, and was first known
as a sleeping chair. Chests included the dower
chest, bread-and-cheese cupboard, and later
the chest-on-chest. Drawer pulls usually took
the form of acorns. The gate-leg and the long
refectory tables are characteristic of the
period.

Jacobean furniture in modified styles fits
well into the larger English Cotswold and the
half-timbered houses or in men's apartments,
oak-paneled libraries, or dignified dining
rooms. It is too large and massive for a
small informal home.

✱ WHAT CHARACTERIZED THE WILLIAM AND MARY PERIOD?

When the Glorious Revolution of 1688 forced James II to flee from England, his daughter Mary and her husband, William of Orange, were invited to become joint rulers. They ruled from 1689–1702. The new rulers introduced a more leisurely and a simpler way of living. William of Orange brought from the low countries many cabinetmakers among whom was Daniel Marot, one-time favorite cabinetmaker of Louis XIV's court.

Queen Mary was a home-loving queen, and the cabinetmakers of the court created furniture for her needs. She had a fine collection of Chinese porcelain, and her cabinetmakers designed cupboards to display this art. The cupboards were decorated with a canopy or hood, a form which has become typical of William and Mary secretaries, chairs, and settees. From the china cupboard developed the first highboy or chest of drawers set on a table. The table had a curved apron or support which carried down to the legs. Chairs became more comfortable and graceful. Typical legs were the cup turned, the trumpet, and the octagonal tapered. A stretcher was used between the legs of tables, chairs, settees, and cupboards. The bun foot — like a flattened ball — was most common, but the Spanish scroll (see Illustration 104) and the ball and claw (see Illustration 104) were also used. The principal surface decoration on all William and Mary pieces was either veneering or marquetry. Fine needle point and lovely tapestries were used for upholstery.

William and Mary furniture may be combined with late Jacobean or Queen Anne. It is adaptable to Early English and Colonial architecture. If you have ever visited the restored homes in Williamsburg, Virginia, you have seen exquisite examples of furniture

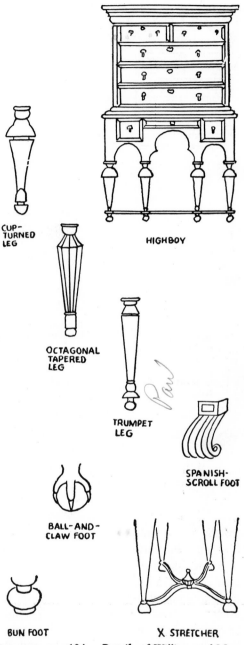

CUP-TURNED LEG

HIGHBOY

OCTAGONAL TAPERED LEG

TRUMPET LEG

SPANISH-SCROLL FOOT

BALL-AND-CLAW FOOT

BUN FOOT

X STRETCHER

ILLUSTRATION 104. *Details of William and Mary furniture. This furniture is less massive and more graceful in form than Jacobean.*

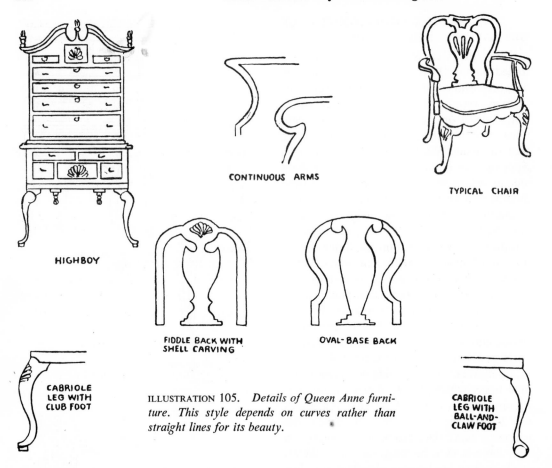

HIGHBOY

CONTINUOUS ARMS

TYPICAL CHAIR

FIDDLE BACK WITH
SHELL CARVING

OVAL-BASE BACK

CABRIOLE
LEG WITH
CLUB FOOT

CABRIOLE
LEG WITH
BALL-AND-
CLAW FOOT

ILLUSTRATION 105. *Details of Queen Anne furni-*
ture. This style depends on curves rather than
straight lines for its beauty.

in the William and Mary style and in subsequent eighteenth century styles.

★ WHAT CHARACTERIZES THE QUEEN ANNE PERIOD?

When William died, Anne, Mary's younger sister, became queen. The period, which ran from 1702–1714, was marked by general prosperity and elaborate entertaining, yet the tastes of Queen Anne were very simple. Except for the characteristic shell carving, furniture depended upon its lines and the grain of the wood used for beauty. Finishes included lacquering, marquetry, and veneer-

ing. The Queen Anne style depended upon curves rather than the straight lines of the William and Mary style, and no stretchers were used between legs. Both the William and Mary and the Queen Anne periods in furniture became known as the age of walnut. However, near the end of Anne's rule mahogany was becoming popular.

Chairs of the Queen Anne period were graceful and often armless to accommodate the ladies' full skirts. The backs of chairs were slightly curved at shoulder height, and a splat down the center of the back was introduced. The fiddle back and the oval-base back shown in Illustration 105 were characteristic shapes. Armchairs were characterized by their continuous arms. The curved or cabriole leg, which had a conventionalized knee-and-ankle form, was typical. The knee was usually decorated with shell carving. The leg terminated in a club or a ball-and-claw foot. The settee was a combination of two or more chairs. Fine needle point and tapestries were used for upholstery. During the first quarter of the eighteenth century, the first Windsor chairs appeared. Though based on the principle of the Queen Anne form, this type of chair developed outside of court circles with variations of its own. This style of chair is frequently reproduced today.

Card playing and tea drinking were favorite pastimes; so naturally a variety of small tables were designed. Drop-leaf tables increased in popularity as well as tilt-top tables with plain tops or raised and carved piecrust edges.

Highboys, cabinets, and china cupboards had carved broken-curve tops or broken pediments. Washstands, wigstands, and tall clocks had characteristics similar to those of other cabinets. Graceful brass drawer pulls and key plates enhanced the beauty of the various types of chests. Drawer handles were frequently pear shaped.

★ WHAT CHARACTERIZES CHIPPENDALE FURNITURE?

With the death of Queen Anne, the court no longer dictated furniture styles. Furniture designs began to take the name of the designer. However, the period from 1720–1810, marked by the reigns of George I, II, and III, is referred to generally as the *Georgian period*. It became known as the golden age of furniture, and mahogany became the principal wood. Of the four names connected with furniture during the period — Chippendale,

Adam, Hepplewhite, and Sheraton — that of Chippendale is probably the most famous.

Chippendale, who lived from 1718 to 1779, was the son of a cabinetmaker and was trained from boyhood in the craft. He understood and used all the furniture embellishments — veneering, lacquering, gilding, marquetry, inlay, turning, carving, and metal mounting. He showed extraordinary ability in his carving. He was one of the few cabinetmakers to become wealthy. His shops were the rendezvous of such famous persons as Horace Walpole, Joshua Reynolds, and Dr. Johnson.

Chippendale designed in four distinct styles as typified by his chairs. At first he followed the general lines of the *Queen Anne* style, using the cabriole leg and the splat back. The splat back was, of course, pierced and carved. The *French* influence, particularly that of Louis XV, was shown in the ribbonlike carving in the splats and in the Cupid's bow top rail of the back.

During Chippendale's time there was a revival of interest in *Gothic* architecture; so

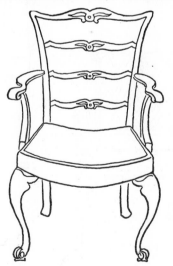

ILLUSTRATION 106A. *Chippendale pierced ladder-back chair*

Chippendale naturally took advantage of it, particularly in his chair designs. Some of the Gothic designs with arched tops, pierced backs, and straight squared legs were good, but others in which Chippendale attempted to duplicate stone carving in wood were not successful.

As trade with China increased, there was a strong *Chinese* influence in Chippendale's designs. The chair backs became more nearly square, and the entire back was filled in with Chinese fret or latticework. Legs were square and straight or resembled several bamboo rods bound together.

Perhaps the three most popular Chippendale chairs reproduced today are the pierced ladder-back chair, the ribbon-back chair, and the wing-back upholstered chair called the "forty-winks" chair. The forty-winks chair is more graceful with the cabriole leg and ball-and-claw foot than it is with the plain straight leg. All of Chippendale's chairs had broad fronts and narrower backs.

Chippendale sofas and settees were of two styles — the all-wood back combining two or three chair backs, and the upholstered serpentine back with rolled arms which is popular today. Legs were either cabriole or straight. Upholstery materials included fine leather, needle point, tapestry, crewel embroidery, and damask.

Chippendale tables were Queen Anne in form — tilt-top types with a center pedestal and three legs, console or wall types sup-

106B. *Other Chippendale chairs. From left to right, the chairs show Chinese influence, Gothic influence, and French influence.*

106C.   *Chippendale break front. Notice the decorated glass doors and the broken-curve pediment and finial urn.*

ported by curved and carved supports, drop-leaf types, and tea and coffee styles. The intricate carving or interesting lacquer made them distinctly Chippendale.

Cupboards, straight or break-fronted cabinets, and desks had paneled and latticed glass doors with symmetrical swanneck decoration. The doors were usually topped with a carved broken-curve pediment and a centered finial urn or eagle. The beautiful brass hardware added a distinctive finish to all cabinet pieces. Chippendale mirrors, either severely plain or elaborately carved, and grandfather clocks are among other cherished pieces of Chippendale design.

★ **WHAT CHARACTERIZES ADAM FURNITURE?**

The Adam period, from 1762 to 1794, is often called the neoclassic period. The revival of the classic influence was stimulated by the excavations of Pompeii and Herculaneum. The Adam brothers, of whom Robert is the best known, were primarily architects concerned with harmonizing exterior and interior decoration. The four brothers became known by the Adelphi, which is a particularly well-designed quarter of London noted for its literary and artistic associations, and which they designed. Catering only to the wealthy, they designed all the decoration of a house

FRET BORDER

HONEYSUCKLE DESIGNS

PATERAE

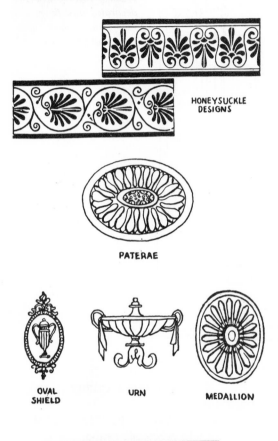

OVAL SHIELD   URN   MEDALLION

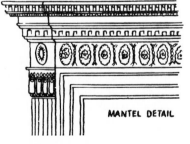

MANTEL DETAIL

ILLUSTRATION 107. *Details of Adam designs. The classic influence is evident in these motifs.*

including the furniture, although they actually made very little furniture.

The Adam brothers discouraged the vogue for wood-paneled walls, and instead they used plaster in delicate tones to serve as a suitable background for the lovely mahogany furniture. They used raised plaster moldings in classic designs around ceilings, as borders, and as panels. Artists were employed to paint appropriate settings within the moldings. Angelica Kauffman was commissioned to do most of the paintings. The brothers also used Wedgwood plaques for ornamentation over doorways and fireplaces. Their mantels were especially beautiful, and were ornamented with classic borders and medallions. Favorite motifs were festoons, frets, honeysuckle designs, swags, paterae or flat circular disklike ornaments, wheatears, husks, urns, and rosettes. The designs of the Adam brothers had a pronounced influence on the cabinet-makers, and many Chippendale, Hepplewhite, and Sheraton designs, particularly in chairs, became known by this Adam influence. The Adam brothers turned to the delicate lines of Louis XVI furniture for much of their inspiration. One of their most important pieces was the dining room sideboard with a commode for wines at each end. On top of each commode was a large carved knife urn.

✳ WHAT CHARACTERIZES HEPPLEWHITE FURNITURE?

The date of Hepplewhite's birth is not known, though he died in 1786. His furniture is often criticized because of its very delicate construction. But what it lacked in strength was made up for in beauty. He constructed a great deal of the furniture for Adam interiors, there being some doubt as to how much of the design was his and how much was the influence of the Adam brothers. Probably his greatest contribution was his large variety of occasional pieces — especially tables. It is a question as to whether Adam or Sheraton designed the first Pembroke table, but this small square four-legged table with drop leaves was one of Hepplewhite's favorite tables. He made many card, end, console, coffee, dining, and side tables.

Like Chippendale, Hepplewhite used chairs as his favorite means of expression. His chairs were small, delicate, and unusually graceful. The most familiar backs were the shield and the camel back. Within the backs he designed urns, Prince of Wales' plumes, and wheatears. Other backs included the oval, the interlacing heart, and the wheel. The legs were always straight, slender, and tapering, and were either square or round. The chairs often had upholstered seats. The sofas and settees had backs that repeated the chair backs.

In addition to beautiful sideboards, Hepplewhite's other pieces included dressing tables with heart-shaped mirrors, roll-top writing desks, washstands, secretaries, clockcases, and four-poster beds with light delicate posts. His wardrobes somewhat supplanted the popular highboys of the earlier periods.

Hepplewhite designed in mahogany and in satinwood. His satinwood pieces were so popular that the latter part of the eighteenth century became known as the age of satinwood. Hardware on Hepplewhite pieces is inconspicuous. Occasionally he employed artists to decorate his pieces with painting. Frequently he used veneers and inlays. His favorite upholstery fabrics were delicate bro-

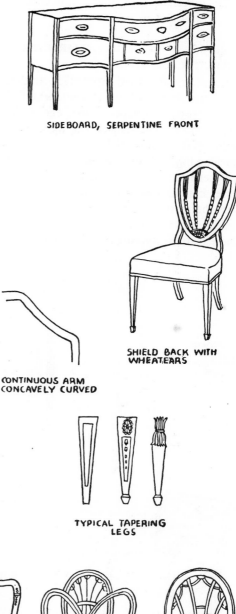

SIDEBOARD, SERPENTINE FRONT

SHIELD BACK WITH WHEATEARS

CONTINUOUS ARM CONCAVELY CURVED

TYPICAL TAPERING LEGS

ILLUSTRATION 108. *Details of Hepplewhite furniture. Curved lines are characteristic of Hepplewhite designs.*

CAMEL BACK   INTERLACING-HEART BACK   OVAL BACK

cades, horsehair, silks, and satins with delicate flowers and stripes.

★ WHAT CHARACTERIZES SHERATON FURNITURE?

Sheraton, who lived from 1751 to 1806, was versatile as well as temperamental. He was a preacher, teacher, artist, and author. His book *The Cabinetmaker and Upholsterer's Drawing Book* published in 1791 had a far-reaching influence on contemporary furniture designers. He had a particular fascination for secret compartments and trick springs, and was the first designer to introduce concealed drawers, panels, and compartments. These features appealed to the ladies. While Hepplewhite's pieces were characterized by curved forms, Sheraton's pieces were more nearly characterized by rectangular forms. He was probably influenced by Louis XVI styles. The fronts of his sideboards combined curved segments with straight lines in contrast to Hepplewhite's curved or serpentine fronts.

Sheraton chairs were delicate in line. Chair backs were characteristically rectangular in shape with vertical balusters, latticed bar work, or ornamental splats between the upper and lower crossrails. Chair arms were delicate and continuous with the front legs and the back. Chair legs were straight and tapering, terminating in a spoon or spade foot.

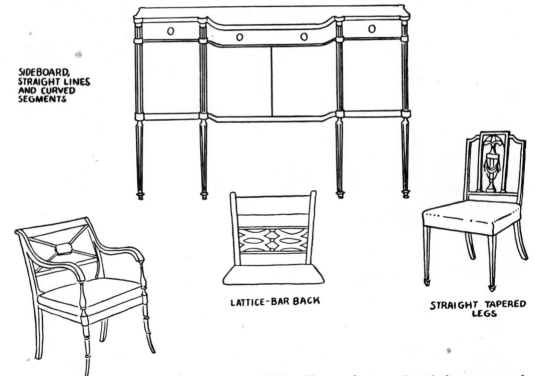

SIDEBOARD, STRAIGHT LINES AND CURVED SEGMENTS

LATTICE-BAR BACK

STRAIGHT TAPERED LEGS

SPLAYED LEGS ON LATER CHAIR

ILLUSTRATION 109A.   *Sheraton furniture. Straight lines more nearly characterize Sheraton furniture than the curved lines of Hepplewhite.*

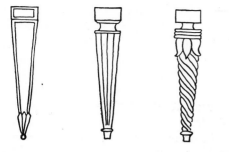

109B. *Typical tapering legs on Sheraton furniture*

Sheraton preferred inlay, painting, and multicolored marquetry to carving. He often bleached and dyed woods for just the right effect in marquetry. His favorite motifs were swags, festoons, urns, cameolike panels, and latticework. He used mahogany, satinwood, sycamore, and tulip wood. If pieces demanded upholstery, he used delicate fabrics and colors.

In addition to his chair designs, Sheraton is well known for his Pembroke tables, his screens on poles with a tripod base, his bookcases with latticed doors, and his swanneck pediments.

✶ WHAT CHARACTERIZES VICTORIAN FURNITURE?

After the great designers during the Georgian period, English furniture design began to decline. We mention rather briefly only one other period.

The Victorian period, from 1837 to 1901, is frequently referred to as a hodgepodge of design. As was true of the times, Queen Victoria herself had little interest in art, and did nothing when she came to the throne to discourage the confusion of prevailing influence — Gothic, Turkish, Venetian, Egyptian, Louis XV, and Empire. However, some Victorian furniture has survived criticism. Occasionally, chairs, tables, and love seats had a homey charm that counteracted a rather uncomfortable style.

The principal woods were black walnut, mahogany, and rosewood. Carved decoration took the form of roses, buds, and fruit. Wood pulls in the shape of carved fruits or pear drops replaced metal. Painting and

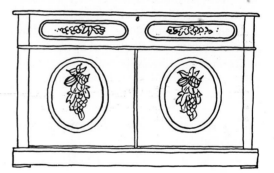

ILLUSTRATION 110A. *Victorian furniture. This sideboard or commode, table, and whatnot shelf are typical Victorian pieces.*

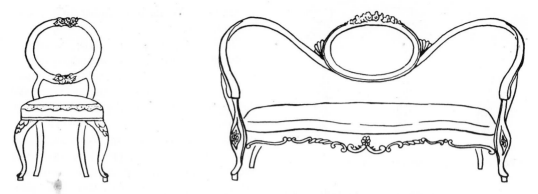

110B. *Victorian chair and sofa. The popular rose carving decorates chair and sofa frames.*

mother-of-pearl were also popular decorations.

Chair backs were usually spoon shaped, and the popular rose carving decorated chair and love seat frames. The legs were a slender cabriole type. Many chairs were tufted and upholstered with plush or horsehair. Other popular pieces were drum-shaped tables, terraced corner tables, whatnot stands, candlestands, and drop-leaf tables with center pedestals.

✶ WHAT IS FRENCH PROVINCIAL FURNITURE?

Since the time of Louis XIV, France has been a leader in artistic expression of many types. The furniture produced during the Louis XIV, Louis XV, Louis XVI, Directoire, and Empire periods affected the styles in other countries at the time, and adaptations are still used in elaborate homes and public buildings. These styles — particularly those of Louis XV and Louis XVI — also influenced the French people outside of court circles, affecting the design of the simpler pieces which they produced for their homes. These styles, which are popular today in simply designed homes, are known as French

Provincial styles. The lines of Louis XV and Louis XVI furniture were simplified and reproduced in local woods, such as pear, cherry, apple, oak, walnut, ash, and elm, and the decoration, if used at all, was much simpler than that of the court furniture.

Present-day chairs, upholstered or made of solid wood, have rather low graceful backs and straight tapering or curved cabriole legs. Gingham or homespun materials are used extensively for upholstery and pads. The large wardrobe called the *armoire*, which was used as a substitute for a closet, is especially characteristic of the style. Hanging shelves for pewter, pottery, glass, and brass are also associated with this style. Early pieces included trestle tables and four-poster beds with valances and draperies.

✶ WHAT ARE THE EARLY AMERICAN STYLES?

The furniture styles in America followed very closely those of Europe except that they were a number of years behind European styles. The Early American or Early Colonial styles of 1620–1725 embrace the period of early colonization up through the first quarter of the eighteenth century. They coincide with

ILLUSTRATION 111. *French Provincial furniture. The wardrobe or* armoire, *the upholstered chair, the wood chair, and the chest and mirror are typical pieces.*

the Jacobean, William and Mary, and Queen Anne styles of England and the Louis XIV style of France.

Our early colonists brought little furniture with them. They constructed rather crude furniture during the first half of the seventeenth century, patterned for the most part after Jacobean pieces. As William and Mary furniture became popular abroad, pieces were gradually imported and copied. Later Queen Anne styles exerted their influence to a more marked degree. The Dutch influence was felt especially in New York, Delaware, and Pennsylvania. Dutch furniture — particularly during the latter part of the eighteenth century — was often painted and decorated in peasant designs. An important piece was the *kas* or large decorated cupboard.

The first settlers used a great deal of oak in early pieces, but as more individuality developed, maple, pine, walnut, cherry, elm, birch, and ash were used. Little decoration except shallow carving was used. Stain and wax were the only furniture finishes until a later date when veneering and shellacking were introduced. Chests were sometimes paneled to relieve the flatness of broad areas.

ILLUSTRATION 112. *Early American furniture. Typical pieces, from left to right, are the Hadley chest, the corner cupboard, the table chair, and the settle.*

Early American chairs were of several familiar styles — wainscot with paneled back, banister back with upright split spindles between the top and bottom crosspieces, ladder back with wide horizontal slats between the back uprights, and Windsor patterned after the English type. Upholstered wing chairs developed in the latter part of the seventeenth century.

Important tables were the butterfly with supports shaped like butterfly's wings for the

drop leaves, the gate leg with legs which could be folded back when the leaves were dropped, and the trestle with trestlelike legs supporting a stationary top. The table chair with the top of the table folding back to form the back of the chair was also used. Hinged-top chests, corner cupboards, Hadley chests with sunflower carving, highboys, lowboys, settles, candlestands, and slant-top desks were also used in Early Colonial homes. Beds had four posters and an over-all canopy or a covering over the head only. Shaving stands and mirrors were used toward the end of the period.

With its unique charm, Early American furniture is especially good in small houses of Cape Cod and Early Colonial style. If you have ever visited Mount Vernon, you have had a splendid opportunity to see some beautiful Early American pieces.

★ **WHAT IS AMERICAN GEORGIAN OR EIGHTEENTH CENTURY FURNITURE?**

The American Georgian period, from 1725 to 1780, parallels the eighteenth century or Georgian period in England and the Louis XV period in France. It follows eighteenth century styles in Europe so closely that repeating all the characteristics is not necessary.

As life in the Colonies became more settled, more formal houses of brick, stone, and wood were constructed. Furniture of the famous English cabinetmakers was both imported and reproduced. Style and beauty were important considerations in selecting furniture, and many new pieces, such as tea tables, china cabinets, card tables, and the like, were introduced. Queen Anne splat- or fiddle-back chairs, tilt-top piecrust tables, kneehole desks and tables, slant-top desks, tall case clocks, banjo clocks, and decoratively framed mirrors with beveled glass were other popular items. Mahogany was the principal wood used, and a lacquerlike finish suggestive of Chinese lacquer came into vogue.

Many beautiful examples of eighteenth century styles may be seen in Williamsburg.

ILLUSTRATION 113A. *American Georgian furniture. Popular items were, from top to bottom, the lowboy, the slant-top desk, and the kneehole desk.*

113B. *American Georgian banjo clock and decoratively framed mirror*

His favorite motifs were the lyre and the acanthus. He also used shells, bound arrows, pineapples, birds, lion's heads, and eagles. Carving was a favorite means of decoration on table and sofa legs, and metal or ormolu mounts usually enclosed the claw feet of the legs. Large areas on chests and drawers were

Good reproductions of American eighteenth century styles add charm, dignity, and personality to almost any home of formal traditional design.

✦ WHAT IS DUNCAN PHYFE FURNITURE?

The Federal period, from 1780 to 1830, coincides with the late Georgian and Regency periods in England and the Louis XVI, Directoire, and Empire periods in France. It found its most aesthetic expression in Duncan Phyfe, who came from Scotland to America in 1794. Phyfe did not originate completely new styles. He merely interpreted the styles of Sheraton, the French Directoire, and the French Empire periods. He gave Americans of the Federal period distinctive and graceful furniture.

Duncan Phyfe worked in mahogany, cherry, maple, and fruit woods, and his tables, chairs, and sofas are some of the most beautiful examples of American furniture.

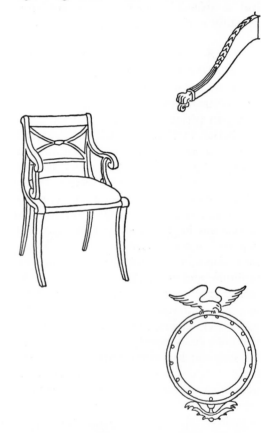

ILLUSTRATION 114A. *Duncan Phyfe. From top to bottom, concave-curved leg with lion's-claw terminal, typical armchair, and eagle mirror*

often veneered with beautifully grained mahogany in a V-shaped pattern called the crotch figure or crotch mahogany. Hardware was used extensively in the form of metal or ormolu tips on legs, brass eagle finials on

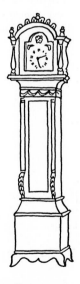

114B. *Other Duncan Phyfe pieces. From top to bottom, lyre-back chair, eagle-finial cabinet, and tall case clock*

desks and mirrors, and metal lion masks and rings as drawer pulls. Toward the end of the period, china and glass knobs replaced brass pulls.

✱ **WHAT IS CONTEMPORARY FURNITURE?**

During the early twentieth century, severe mission oak styles flourished as a reaction to fussy Victorian furniture. During this period, the clumsy Morris chair was a prized possession in many homes.

Toward the end of the first quarter of the twentieth century there was a new conception of furniture styles, referred to as *modernistic* and then *modern*. But present-day architects, decorators, and designers prefer to use the term *contemporary* for the graceful and versatile styles that have been created for today's homes.

Contemporary furnishings represent a fresh approach to the use of space, and feature clear-cut lines and easily maintained surfaces. Functionalism has replaced clutter and stuffiness. Oriental and Scandinavian influences are evident in contemporary furniture styles, fabrics, and accessories.

Inspired by the Paris Exposition in 1925, many designers discarded eighteenth century, Victorian, and mission lines and introduced new shapes. Furniture passed through many stages — from severe, purely functional, box-like forms to styles both functional and graceful.

Characteristic of the contemporary influence is built-in furniture or furniture with separate units that may be grouped or stacked to appear built-in. Contemporary styles depend upon line, form, grain of wood, and texture of fabric more than upon carving or other embellishment.

In general, contemporary furniture styles are low and lines are only moderately curved.

Contour chair shapes are also characteristic. Metals, glass, wood, marble, caning, bamboo, and plastics may be used singly or in combination. Large plants play an important part in the decorative scheme.

Contemporary furniture is especially adaptable to ranch-type homes. Sectional sofas and module storage units lend themselves to versatile arrangements. The wide choice of chairs adds interest to furniture groupings.

★ **HOW MAY YOU COMBINE FURNITURE STYLES?**

Any number of furniture styles may be combined as long as an over-all feeling of unity is obtained. The clever use of color can tie together many styles that have one or

ILLUSTRATION 115. *The simple lines and functional appearance of this attractive contemporary furniture show the influence of Scandinavian designs.*

COLOR PLATE 11. *Notice the simple lines in these contemporary chairs. They combine well with the Oriental-type walls and accessories and the simple design in the rug.*

COLOR PLATE 12. *Functional modern is the keynote of the furnishings in this student's room. The collection of replicas of antique cars adds an interesting note to the contemporary furnishings.*

more characteristics in common — shape, size, texture, or wood. In any room there should be a good balance between wood and upholstered pieces.

All eighteenth-century styles may be combined successfully. A wing chair and a Chippendale or Sheraton sofa fit into any period. Many single pieces of Victorian, French Provincial, or Early American furniture may appear at home in a contemporary setting. If the room is small the wood should be similar in color, but by careful grouping two or three different colored woods may be combined in a large room. It takes skill to introduce brightly painted or black lacquered furniture or pieces decorated with motifs or designs into a setting, but when such unrelated furnishings are used successfully the effect can be boldly dramatic or delightfully charming.

SUGGESTED ACTIVITIES

1. Collect pictures of different types of tables, chairs, sofas, beds, and chests, and bring them to class. Mount the best pictures on a large chart, and label each picture according to its name or type.

2. List table styles that may be used as (a) end tables and (b) console tables.

3. Bring to class illustrations of furniture that represent each of the styles sketched in the text.

4. Collect and mount pictures of living, dining, and bedrooms showing Early American, traditional, and contemporary influence.

5. Identify the style of pieces of furniture you have at home and in your homemaking department.

6. Visit furniture stores to examine furniture and identify woods, fabrics, and styles; report in class discussion.

CHAPTER 2

How may you arrange furniture successfully?

IN YOUR present home you are probably more concerned with arranging furniture than with selecting it. But perhaps someday you will need to select furniture for a home of your own. Since it would be difficult to discuss how to arrange furniture without considering what pieces are needed, we shall consider what the furniture needs are in each room as well as how to arrange the pieces.

The furniture needs of no two families are exactly alike, but basic needs are similar. All families must eat, sleep, dress, and relax. They need similar types of furniture for these activities, and certain principles or truths have been discovered as to how these pieces of furniture can be arranged for beauty and comfort. After understanding these general principles, each family will have to study its own activities and needs in order to make the best selection and arrangement of furnishings.

★ WHAT GENERAL RULES APPLY TO FURNITURE ARRANGEMENT?

Two considerations are important in arranging furniture. They are *design* and *function*. In the composition of a picture, the principles of design must be observed if the effect of the picture is pleasing. A room is a composition of lines, shapes, and colors in its floor, walls, and furnishings. The principles of design must be observed in this type of composition as well as in the other. However, no matter how beautiful a room appears, it is not satisfactory if it is not functional. For example, in addition to being attractive, a living room should provide for the activities the family carry on in the room and should look as though it belonged to the family. A livable, lived-in look is as important as beauty.

Certain rules apply to furniture arrangement in every room in the house.

1. Select furniture that is scaled or in proportion to the room and to the family using the furniture if you expect to be pleased with your arrangements.

2. Select a center of interest, and subordinate all other interests to it.

3. Observe the rules of balance (a) so that large pieces of furniture on one wall balance doors, fireplaces, windows, or large pieces on the opposite wall and (b) so that each wall is balanced from top to bottom. For example, a large picture over a small table will make the wall seem top heavy. Each room is more restful if one wall shows formal balance, but the effect is monotonous if every wall expresses formal balance.

4. Retain good proportions by placing large pieces of furniture on large wall areas and small pieces on small wall areas.

5. Keep traffic lanes in the hall and in each room clear because it is annoying to bump into chairs, tables, or beds when passing through a room.

6. Place all large pieces of furniture parallel with the structural lines of the room.

7. Avoid using too much furniture in a room.

8. Scatter upholstered pieces of furniture among wood pieces.

9. Avoid letting all furniture hug the walls, but at the same time avoid filling too much of the center floor area.

10. Place large pieces of furniture, such as sofas, beds, chests, pianos, and so on, before trying to place small pieces.

11. Arrange all furniture with purpose and function in mind, grouping those pieces which are needed for an activity.

With these general rules in mind, we shall consider what furniture is needed in each room of the house and how to arrange the furniture in each room effectively.

★ **WHAT FURNITURE IS NEEDED IN A HALL?**

Many small houses are built without halls. But if the floor plan permits, an entrance hall offers privacy in the living room and takes much of the traffic away from the main rooms of the house. A hall must have a good storage closet for wraps and other items, preferably built in during the original construction of the house. The very small hall may need no furniture except a mirror, which is a useful item in a hall for both family and guests. The medium-sized hall may need a small table, a mirror, and possibly one or two chairs. Large halls may require two tables or one table and a chest, two or three chairs, and a mirror. The mirror is usually placed over the table, and the arrangement of

ILLUSTRATION 116. *This charming entrance sets the keynote to the entire house. The family room adjoining is functional and attractive.*

other furnishings should in no way interfere with passage through the hall. Wall brackets or pictures may be used on the walls over the furniture. If the front door has vertical glass windows on each side of it, glass shelves for plants and vines or colored glass may be more interesting than curtains or blinds.

★ HOW WILL YOU ARRANGE FURNITURE IN THE LIVING ROOM?

Furniture needs

First of all let us consider what furniture is needed in the living room. If new furnishings must be bought, avoid buying living room suites. Living rooms are much more interesting with mixed pieces of furniture if these pieces are well chosen. A sofa is considered a primary need. There are four general choices — the traditional sofa in many styles, the bed sofa, the sectional sofa of modern design, and the studio couch. Examples of these types are shown on pages 164 and 165. With traditional furnishings, one of the traditional sofas is usually the best buy. Bed sofas, now designed along less bulky lines than formerly, are convenient when the living room must be used as an emergency guest room. Sometimes young housekeepers who expect to expand their houses prefer to buy a well-constructed studio couch to use at first in the living room and to use later in a den, on a sun porch, or in a playroom. Sectional sofas are a good choice especially if the theme in furnishings is modern. They may be arranged to fit into nearly any wall space.

The next need is chairs. For the first year in a newly furnished home, two allover upholstered chairs — wing, club, barrel, or button back — may suffice. These chairs need not be identical, but they should be similar in size and character. Two additional dining room chairs may be used temporarily in the living room, and as the budget permits, one or two occasional chairs may be added.

The living room that also serves as a dining room will need a fairly large drop-leaf table which will accommodate four or six or eight persons. The couple starting on a limited budget may keep an attractive card table and two straight chairs set up beside a living room window. When company arrives, they may place a matching card table at one side, thus providing dining space for six persons.

Small tables are necessary to provide a place for reading materials, for lamps, for ash trays, and so on. Tables with drawers, such as the drum table, the Pembroke table, and the butterfly table, provide extra storage space which is helpful if other storage space is limited. Other table choices are rectangular end tables with or without drawers and shelves, tilt-top and piecrust tables, and tier or step tables. A coffee table is considered a necessity in many living rooms. However, a coffee table may overcrowd a small living room where center floor space is needed for ordinary traffic. An improvised coffee table may be made by using a large tray supported by a folding suitcase rack.

Some provision for books may be the next need unless bookcases are built in the wall. Unpainted book shelves come in many heights and styles, and may be painted to match the woodwork. Secretaries provide storage space for a limited number of books. They, as well as other types of desks, provide a place for writing. Some families may prefer to use card tables as temporary desks, and purchase instead some other item for the living room. If a desk is bought, it should be one with spacious drawers. Although less expensive than other types, the four-legged desk with only one drawer may be an expensive purchase in the end because it will give no more service than a table with a drawer.

Knee room is important for comfort in writing.

Arrangement of furniture

Now let us consider the general rules in furniture arrangement as they apply to the living room. As we said before, first impressions are always important; so it is desirable to make the wall opposite the entrance door look like a picture. Of course, this is not always possible. Suppose you want to center emphasis on a fireplace which may or may not be on the wall first seen from the door. If the room is narrow, a mirror over the fireplace is a better choice than a picture. Accessories important in completing the wall composition may be wall brackets, silhouettes, candle sconces, candlesticks, a bowl, book ends, or ceramic figures. Fireside chairs with a swing-arm or bridge lamp for each chair and a coffee table between the chairs make an interesting furniture grouping below the mantel. Two chairs with end tables and table lamps give another satisfying combination from the standpoint of design and function. Study the fireplace wall shown in Illustration 117.

A good balance of shapes both vertical and horizontal is necessary. The horizontally shaped sofa will be among the first pieces to place. It may be on the longest wall and opposite a group of windows, a fireplace, or an entrance door to balance weights. It may be placed on the wall with the windows if the opposite wall is needed for some other large piece. One living room wall or possibly two walls should have formal or even balance. Even balance on all walls is apt to become monotonous. Vertical pieces of furniture, such as highboys, secretaries, and break-fronted cabinets, should be on walls opposite vertical doors or windows or vertical furniture. If they are placed on walls opposite to

those with horizontal furniture, such as a sofa or a book shelf, the wall composition over the horizontal furniture may be built up with a group of pictures of the same size, a large picture flanked by small ones, or a large mirror and wall brackets or candle sconces.

Four typical living room wall compositions in Illustration 117 show formal balance — a fireplace wall, a window wall, a sofa wall, and a bookcase wall. Four typical wall compositions in Illustration 118 show informal or uneven balance — a window at one side of a narrow wall, a window at one side of a long wall, an off-center fireplace, and a corner window.

All large pieces of furniture, such as upright pianos, secretaries, break-fronted cabinets, desks, large radio-phonograph cabinets, and sofas, must be placed so that they follow the structural lines of the room. This means that none of these pieces should be placed diagonally across corners. A grand piano should be placed with its longest side parallel to the wall, thus permitting the pianist to face the room. Chairs and accompanying end tables may be an exception to the rule, being placed at an angle to the wall and thus facilitating conversation groupings. In a small or even an average-sized living room, the center of the floor should be kept clear. If the living room is very long and narrow, it may be desirable to have a sofa, a book shelf, or a low desk placed at a right angle to the wall to divide the living room into two units — dining and living, conversation and reading or writing, or conversation and sewing.

Study the four ways of placing living room furniture shown in Illustration 119. Notice that the laws of balance are observed, that traffic lanes are clear, that there is no overcrowding, that too much furniture does not hug the walls, and that tables and lamps are

Fireplace as center of interest

Windows as center of interest

Sofa as center of interest

Bookcase as center of interest

ILLUSTRATION 117. *These living room wall compositions show symmetrical or formal balance.*

Window at one side of a narrow wall

Window at one side of a long wall

Off-center fireplace

Corner windows

ILLUSTRATION 118. *These living room wall compositions show asymmetrical or informal balance.*

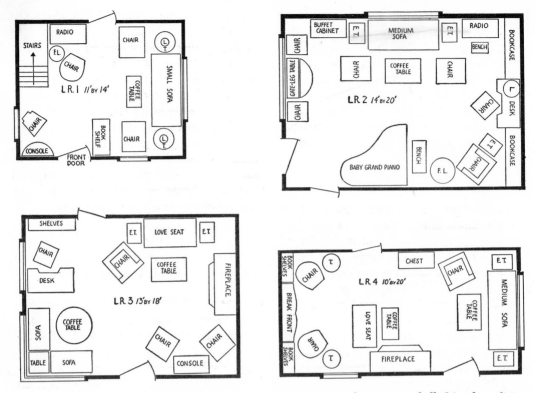

ILLUSTRATION 119.   *Living room 1 is a small room with a stairway and no entrance hall; 2 is a large living-dining room; 3 has the problems of a corner window and an off-center fireplace. In long narrow 4, heavy furniture is placed on the narrow walls to give a feeling of breadth.*

placed so that they are accessible to chairs and sofa. Notice also that there are centers for conversation, for reading, for writing, for dining in some instances, for listening to music, and so on.

★ HOW WILL YOU ARRANGE DINING ROOM FURNITURE?

Dining rooms have lost much of their former importance in our present-day mode of living. A dining area may be provided in the living room or kitchen, or if there is a separate room for dining, it may serve other purposes as well. In many modern homes where a great deal of entertaining is done,

people prefer to have the dining room and living room adjoin, so that there is a larger space for entertaining.

Furniture needs

Dining room furniture is frequently bought in suites, but need not be. Chairs without arms are more satisfactory than those with arms, though the host's chair frequently has arms. There are many styles of dining room tables. It should be possible to extend the seating capacity of a dining table either with leaves or with extension end tables. Corner cupboards are interesting if the space is just right for them, but they do not fit into all houses. The storage units in the dining room should have many shallow pull-out drawers or trays so as to avoid piling up linens and getting them wrinkled. Every dining room needs serving space, either in the form of a serving table or a nearby shelf. Although somewhat out of style at present, a tea wagon is a wonderful convenience when there is no maid. Pick-up stands with several shelves may also be used.

Arrangement of furniture

The arrangement of dining room furniture in the separate dining room is more or less stereotyped, with the table in the center of the floor, the buffet on the largest wall space, the serving table near the kitchen, and the chairs along the wall. If figured paper is not used, the walls may be decorated with matted and framed fruit or flower prints, a mirror and candle sconces, wood or gilt wall brackets, groups of interesting plates, or even a shadow box with vines or figurines. Plants are especially good in dining room windows.

The dining room table need not always be in the center of the room especially if the room is very small. Illustration 120 shows the dining room table (1) in a bay window,

(2) at right angles to the wall, and (3) in one corner of a room with corner windows. Two or four dining room chairs may be kept at the table. The seats should extend about halfway under the table. Corner cupboards may take the place of a buffet.

Less formality in the arrangement of furniture is possible when the dining room doubles as an occasional sleeping room, as a sewing room, or as an additional sitting room. In such a case, a drop-leaf table is best, and furniture should be arranged so that the room looks more like a sitting room.

✴ HOW WILL YOU SELECT AND ARRANGE BEDROOM FURNITURE?

Furniture needs

In selecting bedroom furniture, the first requirement is a good place to sleep. Many people prefer single beds, but when two people share a room, the cost of two single beds and two sets of bed furnishings is nearly twice that of a double bed and one set of bed furnishings. A good double-bed frame mounted on four metal or wooden legs, good springs, and a good mattress are a worth-

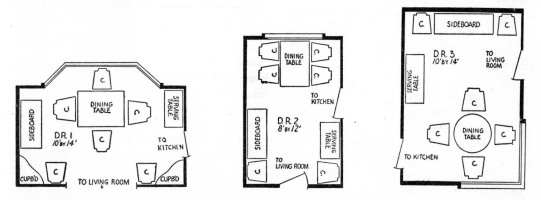

ILLUSTRATION 120. *Dining table placements other than centered. Dining room 1 shows the table placed in a bay window; 2, at right angles to a window wall; and 3, in a corner window.*

while expenditure. The bed may be used without a headboard, with an improvised one, or with one which is bought and applied later. Each occupant of a bed whether it is double or single needs a table and a lamp. The next need is a chest of drawers for each person in the room. Modern designers have introduced twin chests that may be placed side by side to conserve space. One long mirror or two small ones may be placed over the chests. In some modern homes, a closet with drawers and space for garments is built in the length of one entire wall, and only beds, tables, chairs, and a dressing table are needed. Girls and women usually like a dressing table where they may sit down to primp.

Every bedroom is more complete if there is a full-length mirror in the room. It may be on the inside or the outside of a closet door. In addition to one or two straight chairs, one easy chair in each bedroom is an added comfort. Many people still like the old-fashioned idea of a bedroom rocker.

Twin beds are desirable in the guest room. But often the first double bed is moved into the guest room and replaced by twin beds in the owners' bedroom. The guest room does not need as large a storage space as the owners' bedroom, but a closet and some kind of chest are necessary. Again each twin bed needs a night table, and each double bed, two night tables.

The guest room is one of the places where you can use an improvised dressing table that may be interestingly decorated. Dressing tables may be made from old kitchen or library tables. Remember that guest rooms are used by men overnight guests as well as by women party guests; so the decorations should not be too feminine. A boudoir chair, or a rocker, or a padded and skirted chair improvised from an old rocker, and

one straight chair provide enough seating space. More tables and chairs or a desk or a chaise longue may be used in a large room. A convenient piece of furniture for every guest room is a folding suitcase stand.

The children's bedroom is often planned without realizing that children grow up. Children's needs change every few years. Too many parents forget this and buy child-size furniture that must be discarded all too soon. The most desirable plan is to give each child his or her own room, but this is not always possible. Frequently two boys or two girls share a room. In any case it is desirable that each child have his or her own bed, bedside table, chest of drawers, table or desk, and chair. When the crib is discarded, a standard single bed is a better buy than a junior bed. If there is only one closet, there should be an understanding about the dividing line. Two additional upholstered chairs are desirable if space and the budget permit. A double-deck bed, if acceptable, gives more floor space for other furniture. Boys may be more apt to like double-deck beds than girls.

The large bedroom may have space for the occupant's hobbies. Hobbies require storage space as well as working space. Few bedrooms have enough storage space for all the things that growing boys and girls accumulate. Built-in shelves or cabinets with sections closed by doors are excellent for storage. Every girl or boy needs a bulletin board in his room for his keepsakes, pictures, snapshots, party favors, and so forth. Many a wall has been ruined that a bulletin board might have saved.

Arrangement of furniture

The principles of design and function also apply to bedroom furniture arrangements. The bed or beds should be placed first and

ILLUSTRATION 121.   *Multipurpose rooms offer facilities for studying, sleeping, or entertaining guests.*

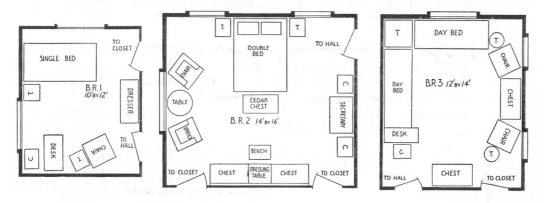

ILLUSTRATION 122.   *Bedroom 1 shows an arrangement for a small single room; 2, for a large double bedroom; 3, for a medium-sized bedroom sitting room for two.*

on the longest wall. It should be possible to place the bed out of drafts and out of line with the morning sun. This is important in rooms with an eastern exposure. If twin beds are used, less wall space will be filled if the beds are placed side by side with the

heads of the beds against the same wall. A table and reading lamp may be placed on the outer sides of each bed. One table and lamp between the beds does not as a rule give enough reading light for two persons, and if one person wishes to sleep, the light

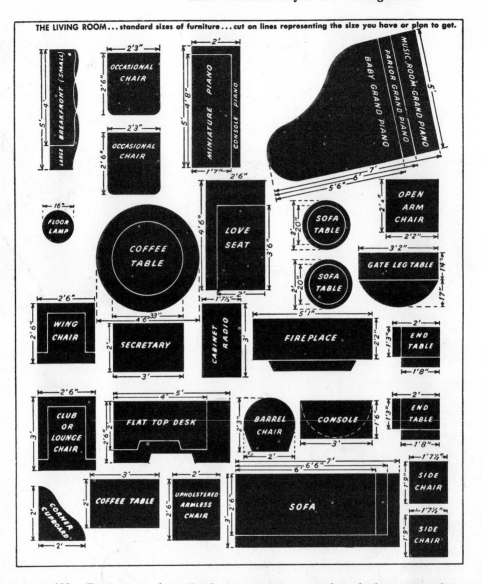

ILLUSTRATION 123. *Furniture templates. On these two pages are templates for living room, dining room, and bedroom furniture. The scale they are drawn to is ¼" equals 1'. When planning a furniture arrangement, draw the room measurements on graph paper to the same scale as the templates. Trace the templates needed, and cut out the tracings. Thus, without moving furniture unnecessarily, the best placement of each piece can be determined on paper.*

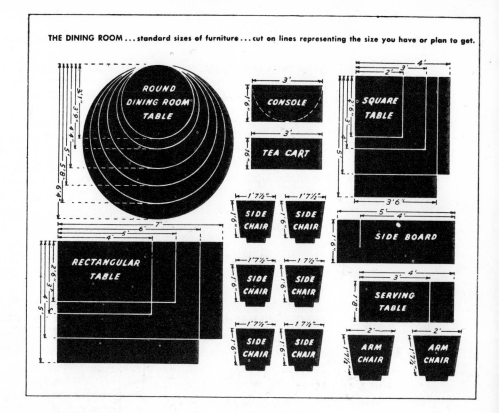

THE DINING ROOM...standard sizes of furniture...cut on lines representing the size you have or plan to get.

ROUND DINING ROOM TABLE

CONSOLE

TEA CART

SQUARE TABLE

RECTANGULAR TABLE

SIDE CHAIR

SIDE CHAIR

SIDE CHAIR

SIDE CHAIR

SIDE CHAIR

SIDE CHAIR

SIDE BOARD

SERVING TABLE

ARM CHAIR

ARM CHAIR

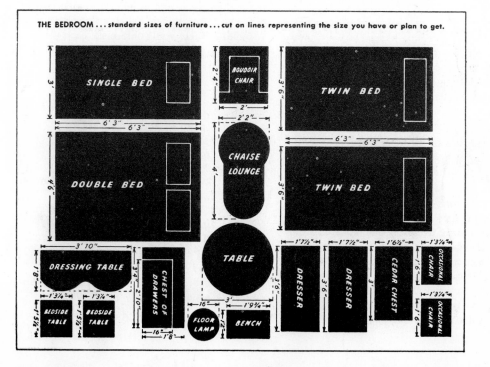

THE BEDROOM...standard sizes of furniture...cut on lines representing the size you have or plan to get.

SINGLE BED

BOUDOIR CHAIR

TWIN BED

DOUBLE BED

CHAISE LOUNGE

TWIN BED

DRESSING TABLE

CHEST OF DRAWERS

TABLE

DRESSER

DRESSER

CEDAR CHEST

OCCASIONAL CHAIR

BEDSIDE TABLE

BEDSIDE TABLE

FLOOR LAMP

BENCH

OCCASIONAL CHAIR

may be disturbing. The beds should be at least 16 inches apart to permit each bed to be made from both sides. If one side of a bed is near a side wall, there should be enough space between bed and wall to make bed-making easy. To conserve floor space, twin beds with low headboards and footboards may be placed at right angles along two walls with a square table in the corner. Beds should be placed so that there is a clear traffic lane to the entrance door and between the dressing table and the closet.

Chests and dressing tables should be placed near the closet to make dressing easy. Wall lights give better lighting at dressing tables than boudoir lamps. The light on mirrors or dressing tables is better when the tables are placed on walls adjacent to window walls than when they are placed on the window wall or opposite the window wall. Desks, tables, lamps, and chairs may be grouped to form a center for reading, studying, or sewing.

SUGGESTED ACTIVITIES

1. Collect pictures of living rooms which show good examples of (a) conversational groupings, (b) reading centers, (c) formal and informal balance, and (d) centers of interest on fireplaces or on windows.

2. Collect pictures of bedrooms which show good examples of (a) double-bed placement, (b) centers of interest on beds or on windows, (c) dressing centers, and (d) reading or study centers.

3. Draw your own bedroom to scale on graph paper using half an inch to represent a foot. Obtain furniture templates or silhouettes from furniture advertising booklets or from the U.S. Department of Agriculture, Bulletin M622, *Your Farmhouse: Cut Outs to Help in Planning.* Experiment with different furniture arrangements which would improve the design and function qualities in your room.

4. Select a floor plan of a small house which would be suitable to some family you know. Draw the living room, dining room, and one bedroom to scale using half an inch to represent one foot. Arrange furniture templates until you are satisfied with the arrangement. Draw in your furniture pieces, and color them a solid color. Ask the family to judge the plans and make any suggestions for improvement.

5. Study the activities your family carry on in the living room. Then study the furniture arrangement in your living room, and make any improvements needed from the standpoint of both function and design.

6. Select a picture of a small child's room that may be rather easily converted into a teenager's room. Tell what changes you would make.

7. Make a chart showing the essential living room furniture needed by a new homemaker. Cut your pictures from magazines or newspapers, and consider the function and design qualities of each piece. Secure probable prices for each piece, and estimate the total cost of the new furnishings. Select a floor plan, and indicate where you would place each piece.

8. Make a similar chart for a bedroom.

SELECTED REFERENCES FOR UNIT SIX

BOOKS

Aronson, Joseph, *The Encyclopedia of Furniture.* Crown Publishers, Inc., New York, Revised 1952

Davis, Frank, *A Picture History of Furniture.* The Macmillan Company, New York, 1958

Gottshall, Franklin H., *Heirloom Furniture.* The Bruce Publishing Company, Milwaukee 1, Wisconsin, 1957

Truman, Nevil, *Historic Furnishing.* Pitman Publishing Corporation, New York, 1950

Consult Unit Eight for additional references

7

Let
your accessories
express
your
individuality

ILLUSTRATION 124. *These simple but attractive dining areas show clearly the importance of well-chosen accessories for traditional and contemporary rooms.*

CHAPTER I

What pictures and wall accessories will you choose?

SOME people use no pictures or other wall decoration for fear of doing the wrong thing, while other people unhesitatingly hang just anything on the wall. Perhaps it is better to hang no pictures at all than to hang them indiscriminately. But those who use no wall decorations are missing an opportunity for beauty and pleasure. Pictures, wall hangings, brackets, and mirrors should be chosen to complete a decorative idea and to be enjoyed. The Chinese often hang a single picture and enjoy it for a period, retire it, and then hang another. In some communities in this country, there is a picture exchange where people may borrow pictures, use them for a period, and then exchange them for others.

Some original oil paintings, water colors, and etchings are envied possessions but too expensive for most people to own. When well framed, good reproductions are in much better taste than cheap originals, and the choice of subject and medium is unlimited. The art of reproduction has been so perfected that it is difficult to distinguish some water colors and etchings from the originals. Not all original paintings are good, and few of the so-called great paintings are meant for the home. For the sake of distinctiveness and individuality, it is wise to avoid using copies of the extremely popular reproductions, such as Rembrandt's *Mill* or Whistler's *Mother* or Gainsborough's *Blue Boy*.

✦ **HOW WILL YOU DECIDE WHETHER OR NOT TO USE A PICTURE?** Before choosing a picture, ask yourself the following questions:

1. Does the wall space need a picture to complete its composition?
2. Will a single vertical, horizontal, square, round, or oval shape fill the need, or is a group of pictures a better solution?
3. What subjects would give me the greatest pleasure and at the same time be suitable to the room?
4. Will a black-and-white, a gray-toned, or a colored picture be most appropriate?
5. What mediums, such as oil, water color, or etching, will fit best into the room, considering the furnishings and other pictures in the room?

Unless you have a cherished picture around which you are planning your room, pictures should be one of the last purchases made. The picture should be in harmony with the room in idea or subject, in texture or medium, in color, in shape and size, in framing, and in placement on the wall. Last but by no means least, pictures should express the personal tastes of family members.

✹ HOW MAY THE SUBJECT OF THE PICTURE BE KEYED TO THE IDEA OF THE ROOM?

Landscapes

These are universally liked, and the choice is unlimited. They are particularly suited to living rooms. *Seascapes* and winter landscapes are especially fitting for a room done in cool colors, whereas autumn scenes harmonize with rich warm room colors, such as rust, yellow, and brown. Summer landscapes with rippling streams, rolling hills, and occasionally a house may be in keeping with any room in which rich greens or soft blues are repeated. Some of the well-known landscape artists are Corot, Lorrain, Rousseau, Constable, and Turner. Van Gogh and Gauguin landscapes are especially good in rooms of modern decoration. Landscapes may be combined with seascapes or architectural pictures, such as pictures of famous buildings or homes.

Flower prints

These are probably next to landscapes in popularity. Flower prints should be matted and then simply framed. They may be hung in groups over the sofa, mantel, or bookshelves in the living room and over a low chest

ILLUSTRATION 125. *A beautiful landscape. The pure bright colors of Vincent Van Gogh's* Vegetable Gardens *make it especially suitable in a modern room. (Artists and Writers Guild Inc.)*

ILLUSTRATION 126. *An interesting group-ing of flower prints. Since the furniture grouping occupies a corner, the flower prints are placed on both sides of the corner.*

ILLUSTRATION 127. *A Currier and Ives print.* New England Winter Scene *is the name of this print which is suitable for use in an informal room.*

or bed in the bedroom. They may also be used in halls and in dining rooms.

Domestic scenes

Paintings of this type, characteristic of Greuze and Vermeer, and *outdoor scenes,*

typical of Currier and Ives prints, are suitable for walls in informal living rooms, in halls, and in bedrooms. Currier and Ives prints are reproduced from original lithographs of mid-nineteenth-century America made by the two artists.

ILLUSTRATION 128. *A domestic scene. Soft muted tones and beautiful light and shadow are characteristic of Vermeer's* Young Woman with a Water Jug. (*Courtesy of the Metropolitan Museum of Art*)

ILLUSTRATION 129. *An interesting still life.* The Sentinels *by Alexander Brook is a distinguished example of still-life painting.* (*Collection of Whitney Museum of American Art*)

Peasant and folklore scenes

Those similar to the paintings of de Hooch, Millét, and Bruegel are especially good in cottage-type homes or in any room furnished with Early American or French Provincial furniture. This type of picture may be combined with domestic scenes. However, scenes with people in them are apt to become tiresome, especially if they are in rooms that are used all the time.

Still-life pictures

Showing groupings of books, flowers, musical instruments, bowls, vases, and fabric, pictures of this type may be used in any living room or bedroom if the picture is pleasing and if the colors fit especially well into the color scheme. Still-life pictures do not draw upon the imagination as much as the other pictures mentioned, and are apt to become a little monotonous.

Realist pictures

Depicting dramatic scenes in everyday life, such as the bold paintings of Bellows, Grant Wood, and Curry, or the lithographs of Daumier, realist pictures must have just the right setting to be a part of home decoration. They reflect so much action and color that they are apt to compete with most furnishings. In the home they are best suited to library or den walls, and occasionally they look well in a hall.

Animal pictures

These are more appropriate for children's rooms and dens. There are many beautiful paintings of dogs and horses in particular. Somewhat stylized pictures of animals are more appropriate for home decoration than those which are too realistic.

Hunting scenes

These may be akin to landscapes or animal scenes, and provided the colors and sizes harmonize, hunting scenes may be combined with landscapes or animal scenes.

Portraits

Those painted by the old masters, such as Rembrandt, Rubens, and Hals, or by the English masters, such as Gainsborough, or by our contemporary American painter Eugene Speicher, and family portraits are restricted to use in formal living or dining rooms where dignity is the keynote.

Godey prints

These prints showing the ladies' styles of the midnineteenth century are always bedroom favorites, especially for girls' rooms and guest rooms.

Audubon bird prints

These prints are aquatints made from the lovely engravings in Audubon's extensive collection. Audubon prints combine nicely with flower prints and water-color landscapes.

★ **HOW MAY THE TEXTURE OR MEDIUM OF THE PICTURE BE KEYED TO THE ROOM?**

Perhaps you have never thought of a picture as having texture, but the medium used or the process by which a picture is made gives the impression of either a delicate or a heavy texture.

Delicate textures

Pictures that have delicate textures include (a) fine *wood engravings* which were developed to their highest degree by the German artist Albrecht Dürer, (b) *steel or copper line en-*

ILLUSTRATION 130. *A lovely portrait*. Mlle. Romaine Lacaux *by Renoir is suitable for use in a delicate formal type of room. (Courtesy of the Cleveland Museum of Art, gift of the Hanna Fund)*

gravings, (c) *mezzotints* in gray tones and *aquatints* in color effects, (d) *pen-and-ink line drawings*, (e) *water colors*, and (f) *etchings*.

Bold textures

Pictures that have a more or less bold or heavy texture include (a) *block prints*, (b) *stencils*, (c) *silk-screen prints*, (d) *oil paintings*, and (e) *wood* and *ceramic plaques*.

Use in rooms

Photographs of scenes, buildings, and people may appear delicate or bold according to the subject chosen. As a rule, portrait photographs should not be hung on living room walls. However, a grouping of individual family photographs may be effective on some walls especially if the walls are patterned and other types of colored paintings are omitted.

Wood engravings, steel or copper engravings, etchings, and water colors, being delicate in texture, may be combined in the same room. They harmonize well with medium or light colors and furnishings. They are frequently used in living rooms, and since they require a picture mat, they may be used on

patterned backgrounds if the background is not too strong for them.

Oil paintings require rich colors and textures in furnishings and plain backgrounds to show to best advantage. A fine large original oil painting may be lighted, but a reproduction is usually not lighted. Oil paintings may be combined with wood prints, water colors, or etchings if these delicate types are rather bold in treatment.

Bold block prints and silk-screen prints, stencils, and wood and ceramic plaques are best used in informal rooms with coarser textures, such as cretonne or sailcloth.

✶ WHY IS IT IMPORTANT TO CONSIDER COLOR IN A PICTURE?

Not only is it important to choose a picture with good coloring, but it is also important to choose one with colors in harmony with the room. Living rooms with plain-colored walls offer the greatest opportunity for using pictures. When the backgrounds are com-

pleted and the room is furnished, it is necessary to study the blank wall areas where a picture might improve the furniture grouping. If the wall area is between two windows with colorful draperies, the best picture choice may be a black-and-white etching, engraving, block print, or scenic photograph. If there are already too many pictures in a room, a mirror, a hanging shelf, or a wall bracket may be a better choice.

For balance, the wall opposite the colorful window draperies may need to repeat the colors in the drapery. This wall may have a plain-colored sofa repeating one of the drapery colors, or a sofa with a slip cover to match the draperies. Above the sofa may be hung one large reproduction of an oil painting, a water-color painting, or a group of colorful flower prints which repeat the drapery colors. If a drop-leaf table is on the wall opposite the window, it may be interesting to place a hanging shelf directly above the table with a vertical row of suitably colored

ILLUSTRATION 133. *Delicate texture. Fine black lines are characteristic of etchings and dry points as this dry point,* Un Orage *by Alphonse Legros, shows. (Albert H. Wiggin Collection, Boston Public Library)*

ILLUSTRATION 134A. *Unrelated sizes and shapes. The vertical picture is not related in size and shape to the horizontal wall space above the sofa.*

Currier and Ives or even Godey prints along each side. Objects on the hanging shelves may also repeat the drapery colors.

A picture will always look as if it is a part of the room if the colors are in harmony with the color scheme in the room.

✴ WHAT RELATION SHOULD THE SIZE AND SHAPE OF A PICTURE HAVE TO THE WALL SPACE?

Again the principles of design must be applied. Since pictures are a part of the composition formed on a wall, they should conform to the size and shape of the wall area. If the wall area is vertical, for instance narrower than it is high, a vertical picture, a vertical grouping of small horizontal pictures, or an oval picture will be needed to retain good proportion. If a low sofa, which is horizontal in shape, is placed opposite a break-fronted cabinet or a secretary, the composition of the sofa wall will need to be built up. This may be accomplished by using three vertical pictures of the same size or one fairly large vertical picture flanked by two smaller vertical pictures of the same size, subject, and medium. Often one large horizontal picture over a sofa is flanked by vertical groups of small oval pictures.

As a rule, hanging pictures stair-step fashion is a violation of the principles of design because the eye is carried away from the center of interest in the room. However, a blank wall along a stairway may sometimes be made a center of interest by hanging flower or bird prints up the wall.

✴ HOW SHOULD PICTURES BE FRAMED?

Many pictures are improperly framed and thus lose much of their effectiveness. A few general suggestions for framing pictures are as follows:

1. Oil paintings require wider, heavier frames than water colors or etchings. Dull bronze tones that harmonize with the rich colors of the oil painting are usually better than bright gold frames. The frame should form a suitable background for the picture rather than vie with it in importance. The larger the painting, the wider and heavier should be the frame. Original oil paintings are nearly always framed without glass. Reproductions may be framed with or without glass.

2. Water colors, pen-and-ink sketches, block prints, etchings, and most lithographs are usually framed with glass and usually require a mat of somewhat darker value than the

lightest value in tne picture. Occasionally this type of picture may be framed without a mat if the picture is very large or has large open areas. A pure white mat board is nearly always too white for any picture. The slightly cream or slightly grayed-whites are suitable if the picture is very light and delicate. Sometimes colored or even black mats may be used. For texture interest, fabric mats are sometimes effective. Bold black prints and embroidered or stenciled pictures may be matted with homespun, monk's cloth, or velveteen mats. Gingham mats may be effective with nursery-rhyme pictures.

3. A mat on a picture should be shaped according to the law of margins. In *vertical pictures* the bottom of the mat should be the widest, the top next in width, and the sides slightly narrower. In *horizontal pictures* the bottom should be the widest, the sides next in width, and the top the narrowest. In *square pictures* the bottom should be the widest with the top and the sides equal in width.

4. Photographs may be framed with or without a mat depending upon the size. A tinted scenic photograph may be enhanced by using a mat,

whereas a portrait photograph may look better without a mat.

5. Select frames for pictures by trying different pieces of molding on the picture. Sepia photographs may look best with bronze or gilt frames, and gray-toned photographs may look best with silver frames. Narrow frames usually look best on pictures with mats.

134B. *Related sizes and shapes. The groups of pictures over these sofas are arranged horizontally to correspond with the horizontal wall space above the sofas.*

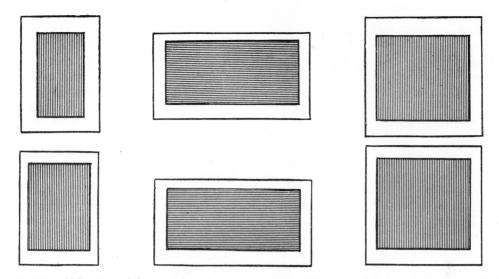

ILLUSTRATION 135.   *From left to right — above, incorrect, and below, correct — a vertical picture should be matted with the bottom margin widest, the top next, and the sides narrowest; a horizontal, bottom widest, sides next, top narrowest; a square, bottom widest, top and sides equal.*

Frequently a little lighter color than the darkest color in the picture is satisfactory for the frame. However, a black frame is often good on etchings and prints. The frame may repeat other woods used in a room. Matted Currier and Ives prints look especially well in fairly broad mahogany frames when other dark wood is used in the room. Bleached wood makes attractive frames on medium walls if the bleached tones are repeated in the picture.

✳ WHAT SHOULD YOU KNOW ABOUT HANGING PICTURES?

If you are sure about your choice of a picture and a frame, you are ready for a few pointers on hanging pictures. Most pictures should be hung so that the center of interest in them is at eye level. It is usually desirable to have the lower edges of all the pictures in a room the same distance from the floor. Pictures over mantels and very large portraits may be exceptions to this rule. Pictures are interesting hung in groups. Odd numbers symmetrically arranged are more desirable than two pictures staggered in height. Hang pictures on regular picture hooks rather than on wires extending from the picture molding. Attach the wire near the top of the picture back, so that the picture will hang flat. If for any reason picture hooks cannot be used, run wires to the molding parallel with the sides of the picture rather than in a V shape.

Here is a secret that will help you avoid having to hang your picture several times before it is right. Have someone hold your picture until it is in exactly the right place, and with a pencil, lightly mark a line on the wall along the lower edge which you can erase later. Find the center of this line and mark it. Lift the picture away from the wall, and hold the back toward you. Push a yardstick firmly up against the wire, and note how far above the lower edge of the frame it extends. Mark this distance on the wall above the center of the line, and hammer in the hook.

✳ WHAT OTHER ACCESSORIES MAY BE USED ON WALLS?

Shelves, brackets, and the like

Too many pictures in a room may become monotonous. If the room is large and the walls are plain, pictures above furniture groupings on every wall may give the impression of a picture gallery. There are many other interesting wall accessories. Hanging shelves of walnut, mahogany, or maple on which are placed small decorative objects or bowls of vines often give needed height to a radio cabinet or a drop-leaf table against a wall. An old gilt picture frame made into a shadow box and hung above some low piece of furniture may help to balance a fireplace on an opposite wall. Gilt, walnut, or mahogany wall brackets on which may be placed bowls of vines or ceramic figures break the monotony of too many pictures. Candle sconces, plates, textiles, or trays also may be used to fill in empty wall spaces.

Mirrors

In modern rooms frameless mirrors sometimes cover the upper half of one entire wall. Mirrors give the impression of more space in a room, and this point should be considered in placing a mirror. Mirrors are usually placed over sofas, mantels, or tables. The hall mirror is nearly always placed over a table.

ILLUSTRATION 136A (*above*). *For a small hall, this space-saving three-way mirror and the wall shelf with small drawers are most useful.*

136B (*left*). *This attractively framed mirror would be most suitable for a traditional bedroom or hallway.*

ILLUSTRATION 137. *Exquisite inlay work makes this matching clock and barometer set an artistic as well as a useful wall decoration.*

In choosing mirrors, it is important to know something about the quality of the glass used and the quality of the mirror finish. Some inexpensive medicine-cabinet mirrors are made of window glass. But good mirrors are made of plate glass, which is thick polished sheet glass, free from noticeable irregularities. The finish usually consists of silvering and a coat of protective paint. A more expensive though more durable finish is the copper-back finish in which the glass is silvered, given a copper coating, and then painted as a further protection. This latter finish is

usually guaranteed for a period five times as long as that of the former finish. Some plate glass for mirrors is tinted flesh to give a warmer glow, and some is tinted blue to subdue reflections. Some mirrors are coated with gold instead of silver. Gold gives a warm light amber glow, while silver may appear cold.

In choosing a mirror, the area in which it is to be hung should be studied to determine (1) what proportion of the area the mirror should cover; (2) whether a vertical, horizontal, round, or oval mirror should be considered; and (3) whether or not the mirror will need pictures, wall brackets, or candle sconces to complement it. The rules of design governing the size and shapes of pictures also apply to mirrors. The space between the mirror and the piece of furniture below it is an important consideration in obtaining good proportion. A picture hung high over a low sofa, table, or mantel destroys unity. Mirrors are part of a unit and should be placed so that they appear as such.

Mirrors of eighteenth century design, such as the Martha Washington, the urn, the gold bar, the Chippendale, or the convex with a heavy gold frame, are especially good in traditional rooms. Convex mirrors give depth to a room, and are interesting in traditional dining rooms. However, they give distorted reflections.

Mirrors in broad frames of maple, pine, or cherry are good in Early American rooms. The unadorned Chippendale mirror may also be used in informal rooms.

Frames on mirrors may repeat other wood in the room, or if they are gold leaf or gilt, they should tie in with other tones of bronze or brass in the room. Modern mirrors are frequently unframed.

SUGGESTED ACTIVITIES

1. Bring to class pictures which exemplify as many different mediums as you can find. Give individual reports on how the various effects, such as block printing, etching, wood engraving, and so on, are produced.

2. Bring to class a picture with warm coloring and one with cool coloring, both of which are suitable for use in a living room.

3. Visit an art supply store, a department store, or a furniture store to see pictures and other wall accessories available.

4. Collect pictures of wall accessories, such as wall brackets, hanging shelves, hanging plates, and so on, from newspaper and magazine advertisements. Judge them from the standpoint of design quality and suitability for use in various rooms. Arrange a bulletin-board display of the better examples.

5. Mount clippings showing pictures, mirrors, and other wall accessories well chosen for the space they occupy.

6. Make a collection of pictures of mirrors, and determine where each should be used.

7. In your library at home, at school, or in your community, look at books on famous paintings. Select some picture which is appealing to you in subject and which might be used at home or at school. Show the picture to the class, and tell the group about the artist and the painting.

8. In some of the better magazines, look for flower prints or other reproductions worthy of framing and suitable for use in your room or in some other room at home or at school. Choose a mat for the print, and cut it according to the law of margins given on page 210 and in Illustration 135. Using an old frame at home which you may refinish if necessary or an inexpensive ten-cent-store frame, frame and then hang the picture.

9. Study the pictures and other wall accessories in your home and at school. Make any needed improvements in the way they are placed or hung. If a new picture or other type of accessory is needed, as a class project, select and hang it.

10. If a suitable old frame is available and if an accessory of this type is needed, make a shadow box for plants out of the frame.

CHAPTER 2

How will you choose lamps and other accessories?

THE exquisite candelabra, chandeliers, and wall sconces of former years were chosen as a part of the decorative scheme of a room, but little thought was given to the effect of the light on eyesight and on colors and contours of the room. Now a decorator must consider all phases of proper lighting. Lamps must not only be a part of the decorative scheme, but they must furnish the proper amount of well-diffused light at the places where it is needed in a room.

Well-placed lamps, clocks, books and book ends, bowls of vines, and the like give a room a cozy hospitable air when they are well chosen from the standpoint of good design and of suitability to their purpose and to the decorative idea. They are as important to a room as a hat and a purse are to a suit, and the effect of many a room or a suit has been spoiled by poorly selected accessories.

In an earlier chapter, pages 66–69, you learned something about basic wiring needs for proper lighting. Now we are concerned with the selection of accessories to furnish the light needed. General illumination is supplied by ceiling and wall lights and large floor lamps. But table lamps or other good spot lighting is needed for sewing, reading, writing, playing bridge, playing the piano,

and dressing. With so much emphasis on adequate, properly placed lighting, let us consider lighting needs.

✦ WHAT ARE YOUR SEEING NEEDS?

If you are in doubt about the benefits you are receiving from the lighting in different areas in your home, you may have your lighting checked by a home-lighting consultant from one of the utility companies. This service is available in most cities as a good-will gesture. The home-lighting expert will use a light meter to measure light in terms of foot-candles. A foot-candle is the degree of light reflected on a flat surface one foot away from the direct flame of a candle. If you sit in the direct sunshine, you may receive something like 10,000 foot-candles of light. If you read under a shade tree on a sunny day, you will have between 500 and a 1000 foot-candles of light. Near a window on a sunny day you will have about 200 foot-candles of light.

The following table, adapted from material developed by one of the big electric companies, will give you some idea of how lighting in your home in terms of foot-candles should check with a light meter.

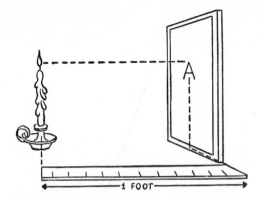

ILLUSTRATION 138. *A foot-candle is the amount of light at point A on a surface 1' distant from and perpendicular to the rays of the candle.*

FOOT-CANDLE NEEDS

Close sewing, drawing, fine needlework	100 foot-candles
Studying, prolonged reading, writing, average sewing on light materials, kitchen work, at bathroom mirrors, for the workbench	50 foot-candles
Casual reading and sewing, at dressing tables	20 foot-candles
General kitchen activities, playing cards and other games	10 foot-candles
General lighting for halls, stairways, and rooms for conversation	5 foot-candles

You may ask how foot-candle requirements may be measured in terms of bulbs of different watts, or why bulbs of different watts rather than foot-candles are not recommended. Here are some reasons why the number of foot-candles rather than the number of watts is given: (1) a 100-watt bulb in one type of lamp will give a different amount of light than a 100-watt bulb in another type, depending upon the type of shade and the height of the bulb from the base of the lamp; (2) the colors in some rooms may absorb much more light than those in other rooms; (3) the lighting load or number of other lights in a room may affect the amount of light received from one particular bulb; (4) the distance at which you are working away from the lamp will change the amount of light you receive; and (5) the same bulb will give different amounts of light in direct

ILLUSTRATION 139. *At the left, direct light causes a glare; at the right, light is well diffused.*

and indirect lighting. Direct and indirect lighting are shown in Illustration 139. Many lamps have a combination of direct and indirect lighting. They may have six-way lighting, with a center bowl giving three degrees of indirect lighting and with individual bulbs giving three degrees of direct lighting.

★ **WHAT POINTS WILL YOU CONSIDER IN CHOOSING A LAMP?**

There are a number of points to be considered in choosing a lamp.

COLOR PLATE 13. *The accessories used in this Early American room help to define its character. Ceiling spotlights illuminate the yellow sofa and the mantel and show off the accessories. Valance lighting also augments the lamps in the room.*

COLOR PLATE 14. *Notice the effective use of accessories in this room. Since the room is small, walls, floor, and furniture are closely blended in color for a more spacious effect. Accessories in keeping with the personality of the room provide accents of color.*

1. *Good function:* Provide a suitable lamp for each lounge chair, desk, piano, or single bed, and two lamps for each sofa or double bed — one for each side. Place lamps so that shadows are eliminated.

2. *Maximum light:* Select lamps tall enough to conform with recommendations in Illustration 141A. Select light shades with white lining and a large enough lower diameter to give a wide circle of light. Three- and six-way bulbs offer flexibility of light for various activities.

3. *Prevention of glare:* Use a diffusing or reflector bowl or a frosted bulb. Adjust lamps so that the lower edge of each shade is between 40 and 42 inches from the floor. Balance the distribution of light throughout the room so that the eyes do not have to adjust constantly to highlights and shadows. Avoid strong contrasts between work surfaces, e.g., dark desk and white paper. Use bullet-type lights only to supplement other lights for very close work.

4. *Color harmony:* In each room or area, use shades that are similar in texture and color to avoid spotty effects. When colored shades are used, group them to complete a color harmony unit. Make sure the linings are white. Use tinted bulbs with caution. *Pink* tints tend to enliven red and rose tones, and enrich walnut and mahogany furniture. *Blue* bulbs flatter the complexion, make blues more intense and greens slightly more blue-green. *Yellow* bulbs brighten reds, yellows, and greens, and enrich maple, pine, and fruitwood. *Green* bulbs make green in plants and furnishings more intense.

5. *Good design:* Consider the style of furnishings in the room and furniture group with which you will use the lamp. Choose the shade and base as a unit, and make sure that the two harmonize in texture, color, and form. If a shade appears to be too low for a base, raise it with a harp. Make sure no part of the fixture shows above or below the shade.

ILLUSTRATION 140. *Some basic lamp styles are floor, table, and wall lamps; adjustable wall or ceiling bracket lights; and small bedroom lamps.*

✶ HOW MAY LAMPS CARRY OUT
THE DECORATING IDEA?

The choice of styles in lamps is unlimited.

If you are furnishing a traditional room, choose the more formal types of bases — urn, fluted column, or vase-shaped — in brass, china, glass, silver, or alabaster, with silk, rayon, or parchment shades. Figurines are sometimes used as lamp bases in period rooms, but urn-shaped lamps with good lines are a better choice in most traditional rooms. Novelty bases should be used cautiously.

In *Early American* and *French Provincial* rooms, lamps should be less formal than those in eighteenth-century or traditional rooms. Pottery, pewter, wood, colored glass, hobnail glass, brass, and copper make good bases. Shades may range from the unadorned parchment type to frilly checked-gingham types, depending upon the scheme of the room.

In *modern* rooms the lamp base is usually of polished wood, spun aluminum, brushed brass, pottery, leather, or an exotic fabric. Shades are usually fairly simple and depend mainly upon texture for their interest.

✶ HOW MAY OTHER DECORATIVE
LIGHTING BE ACHIEVED?

Better light for living means decorative as well as functional lighting. Decorative lighting includes background, local, and accent lighting.

Background lighting

Lighting in the center of the ceiling is the most familiar type of background lighting. But background lighting may be obtained in a number of other ways. *Luminescent ceiling panels* may be set flush with the ceiling to light the entire ceiling, or to light only sections over mirrors in the bathroom, bedroom, and entrance halls, or over work centers in the laundry, kitchen, or workshop. An entire wall may have an illuminated panel to provide more light or to give a decorative effect.

Cove, cornice, or valance lighting provides background light and adds interest to a room. Cove lighting may be set into a cove near the ceiling on one wall or around the entire ceiling. However, cove lighting tends to emphasize ceiling irregularities. Cornice lighting may be used over a work area in the kitchen or over draperies in other rooms in the house. In covered patios, light tubes may be concealed in the beams.

Local lighting

Floor, bridge, swing-arm, and torchère lamps, suspended-fixture lamps, and lighted wall brackets may provide both background and local lighting, depending upon how the light is adjusted. Local lighting is necessary for activities such as playing cards, preparing meals, laundering, casual reading, sewing, and craftwork. Local lighting needs vary from a minimum of 20 foot-candles for casual reading and sewing to 100 foot-candles for close or prolonged reading, sewing, and drawing.

In addition to background and local lighting, extremely close work demands supplementary lighting focused directly on the activity. Bullet-type lights give concentrated light, but they should not be used unless there is sufficient additional light. They should be turned so that the glare will not interfere with the comfort of others in the room.

Accent lighting

This type of lighting is supplied by a recessed ceiling fixture or spotlight, and it is used to highlight an item or an area of special interest. Small accent ceiling lights are used to emphasize the table during dinner, an attractive wall hanging or painting, the piano or desk area, or an interesting grouping of wall accessories.

Electroluminescence

Perhaps the greatest advance in lighting is still not fully developed — *electroluminescence*. In this kind of lighting, electricity is directly converted into light by exciting a thin filament of phosphors with alternating current. The phosphor film is sandwiched between two surfaces (at least one of which is translucent) that will conduct electricity. When this lighting principle is perfected, light of any color may be dialed off and on at will. It will be possible to have enlarged vacation slides as illuminated wall panels. Television sets will be no thicker than picture frames. Draperies or an entire wall may be made to glow. Already cars have this type of lighting on dashboards, and glowing tables and panels give unusual home decorating effects.

ILLUSTRATION 141.   *Contemporary blends with traditional in this beautifully furnished and lighted room. Special lighting is focused on the decorative fireplace wall. Classic lamps flank the sofa, and a tall lamp serves the wing chair. Lamps and shades are properly selected to give good light for reading.*

✳ WHAT OTHER OBJECTS GIVE CHARACTER TO A ROOM?

Other accessories, such as clocks, books and book ends, candleholders, wall brackets, bowls, figurines, and cigarette boxes, should be chosen with regard to their value in carrying out a decorative idea or a color scheme in a room.

Clocks

People often overlook clocks as decoration, especially since small electric clocks have become so popular. Clocks that are good with *traditional* furniture are the bracket type, the Chippendale, the tall shelf clock, the banjo wall clock, the grandfather's clock if space permits, and the mantel clock if it is of traditional design. In *informal* rooms or in

ILLUSTRATION 142. *Candlestick and oil-lamp reproductions complement provincial furnishings. Lamps with figurine bases are suitable for period rooms. Urn shapes are formal and traditional in character.*

ILLUSTRATION 143.   *Types of clocks. From left to right and top to bottom are a banjo wall clock, an Early American shelf clock, and a modern table or desk clock.*

rooms of *Early American* character, simple clocks in a wall bracket or on a shelf, or wall clocks, banjo clocks, and cuckoo clocks add charm to the room. Clocks used in *modern* rooms are extremely plain and angular, and dots or squares often replace the usual numbers.

Books

Many people push books back into book shelves without thought of their value as decoration. When placed on a table between attractive book ends, a two- or three-volume set of lovely leather-bound books or several

ILLUSTRATION 144.
Books as decoration. When books are arranged according to size and color and when other decorative objects are used with them, they add character and interest to a room.

colored clothbound books repeating the colors in the room add a decorative touch. If books are arranged according to size and color in shelves with ceramic figures, colored glass, or bowls of vines scattered among them, the book shelves cease being commonplace and take on character.

Small table objects are discussed in the next chapter as accessories to flower containers.

SUGGESTED ACTIVITIES

1. Bring in magazine pictures showing well-chosen lamps in relation to the background and in relation to seeing needs.
2. Visit lamp departments, and price table, floor, and bridge lamps. Find out some of the things that are apt to make some lamps more expensive than others. In what instances do you think the additional expense may be justified?
3. Investigate certified lamps and shades.

4. Secure a light meter, and test the daylight and artificial light in various work centers in your homemaking department and at home. Plan what might be done to improve the lighting if improvement is needed.
5. Ask a home-lighting specialist to give a talk on proper home lighting.
6. Look at the lamp shades at home and in your homemaking department. If new ones are needed, use the selection and purchase of them as an individual or a class problem.
7. Make a collection of pictures of clocks, and tell where each might be used.
8. Collect pictures showing books and other accessories used as decoration.
9. Find at least one example of poor design and one of good design in (a) lamps, (b) clocks, and (c) book ends. Be prepared to tell the class why you consider each example good or poor.
10. Experiment with the arrangement of books and other accessories in your homemaking department and at home to see whether you can make new and improved arrangements.

CHAPTER 3

How will you use flowers and plants?

WELL-ARRANGED flowers, plants, sprays, twigs, or leaves add interest and beauty to a room. It is not enough merely to pick a bunch of flowers and jam them into a vase. There is an art in arranging flowers, but like any art its principles can be learned by study and experience. Studying pictures of interesting arrangements in books and magazines will help you gain ideas, but experience in actually arranging flowers is essential.

Equipment needed for arranging flowers, selecting the container for an arrangement, points on making an arrangement, accessories that complement flower arrangements, and the use of plants are discussed in this chapter, but first, let us consider where to use flowers.

✷ WHERE WILL YOU USE FLOWER ARRANGEMENTS?

Flower arrangements are usually used on tables, mantels, or window sills, and if space permits, a suitable arrangement is appropriate in almost any room in the house. The color of the flowers should be in harmony with the colors of the room. If you grow your own flowers, consider the colors in your rooms and plant flowers that will be in harmony with these colors. Flowers show off to better advantage against plain-colored walls and draperies than against patterned ones. Only large flowers in bold arrangements may be strong enough to stand out against figured backgrounds. If you must place daintier flowers against patterned walls or fabrics, use a plain copper, brass, silver, or wooden tray back of the arrangement, or arrange a mass of green leaves as a frame for the flowers.

✷ WHAT EQUIPMENT IS NEEDED FOR FLOWER ARRANGEMENT?

Flower arrangement is easier with the proper equipment. You can avoid undependable crisscrossing of stems, and you can achieve the effect you want in a much shorter time. The equipment listed below is all inexpensive and may be stored in a market basket.

NEEDLE-POINT HOLDERS: Several sizes of holders of this type will give you better control over the angles stems take than will glass holders. If you use lead holders in metal containers, place a thin layer of cotton under the holder to prevent rust.

MODELING CLAY: This is indispensable as a base or holder in arranging heavy flowers or weeds, such as milkweed or thistle. Modeling clay may also be used to keep needle-point holders in place.

MESHED CHICKEN WIRE: When crumpled up, meshed wire is extremely helpful as a holder in arranging flowers in tall vases, in jardinieres, and in round bowls.

MILLINER'S WIRE: Wire with a green covering and *green raffia* may be used to tie small clusters of flowers in place, for instance clusters of violets or pansies among larger flowers. *Transparent tape* may also be used for this purpose.

TWISTEMS: These long pliable wires and *pipe cleaners* painted green will hold up limp stems.

A SHARP KNIFE: This is necessary for trimming leaves and stems.

HEAVY SHEARS OR WIRE CUTTERS: These are needed to cut heavy stems and wire.

✳ WHAT FLOWER CONTAINERS ARE NEEDED?

The container is an important part of a flower-arrangement composition. Off-whites, soft greens, and earth colors make good color backgrounds for flowers. Unless strong-colored containers repeat the colors of the flowers, they are apt to detract from the arrangement. Elaborately decorated containers present a competing center of interest with the flowers. Low containers are best for dining tables. High containers and tall arrangements on mantels may lead the eye too far away from the center of interest in the room. Tall containers are attractive against vertical wall areas if the tops of the flowers are not above eye level.

The usual types of containers include urns, trays, flaring oblongs, tall cylinders, narrow-necked vases, flat round dishes, horizontal pillows, upright pillows, and low round bowls. Each of these shapes is made in a variety of materials and textures.

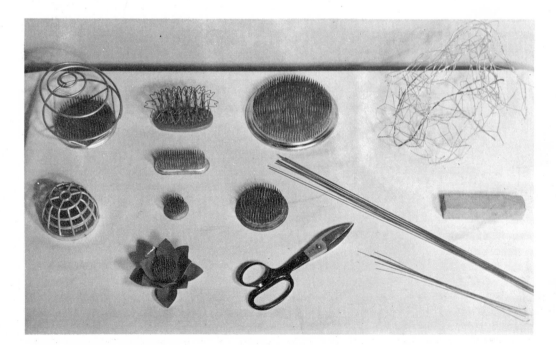

ILLUSTRATION 145. *Equipment needed for arranging flowers. Various types and sizes of holders, meshed chicken wire, milliner's wire, twistems, modeling clay, and heavy shears are shown.*

ILLUSTRATION 146. *Types of flower containers and an appropriate line arrangement for flowers in each type of container are shown.*

Tall cylinder	*Pedestal bowl*	*Upright pillow*
Urn	*Narrow-neck vase*	*Flaring oblong*
Round low bowl	*Flat bowl or tray*	*Horizontal pillow*

✶ **HOW MAY FLOWER ARRANGEMENTS CARRY OUT THE DECORATING PLAN?**

In traditional or formal rooms

Most of the usual containers mentioned are good in formal rooms, provided the texture of the container is not coarse. Smooth pottery, china, alabaster, glass, and silver are all suitable textures, and of course, the flowers used in them must also be delicately textured. Formal or nearly formal balance is usually the best arrangement in tall containers or bowl-shaped containers. Shallow round or oblong containers usually lend themselves best to off-center or informal arrangements.

In informal or Early American rooms

All the standard shapes may be used in these rooms, but the containers should be made of such materials as pewter, copper, pottery, hobnail glass, or handblown glass. All the old-fashioned flowers are good in Early American rooms because the varied colors often repeat the colors in chintz or gingham or cretonne in the room.

ILLUSTRATION 147A. *The delicately textured roses in the onyx pedestal bowl make this arrangement suitable for use in a formal traditional room.*

147B. *The sunflowers informally arranged in the brass container are suitable for an Early American room.*

In modern rooms

Simple rectangular containers, tall or low, with a few big bold flowers are usually best in modern rooms. Three or five large iris blooms with their pointed leaves, a few calla lilies and their leaves, or a single magnolia blossom dramatically arranged — these may be particularly suitable in modern rooms. Large dried leaves, seed pods, and grass plumes also make effective arrangements.

✳ WHAT ARE SOME RULES THAT APPLY TO FLOWER ARRANGEMENT?

A few general rules about arranging flowers are given as follows.

1. Be individual but not eccentric in your arrangements.
2. Select your flower colors to harmonize with room colors, and select your container to harmonize with the flowers and with the decorative idea of the room.
3. Keep good proportions between the sizes and shapes of the flowers, the lengths of their stems, and the size and shape of the container in which they are placed. In general, small short-stemmed flowers require a low bowl, but long-stemmed flowers may be arranged either in a high vase or in a low bowl or tray provided the bowl or tray is broad enough to balance the height of the flowers.
4. Observe the rules of balance in the flower arrangement. Both *formal* and *informal* balance may be used. In formal balance flowers radiate from a central axis, and must be placed so that the radiation is alike or almost alike on all sides. In informal balance the axis is usually off center, and the radiation is unlike but balanced. Informal and formal balance are shown in Illustration 147B and C.
5. Let each arrangement have emphasis either in color or in line. Whether they are all of the same kind or a combination of different kinds, flowers arranged in a mass give *color emphasis*. Such an arrangement should not be so crowded that each flower cannot be seen by itself. When combinations of flowers are used in a mass, large bright- or dark-colored flowers should be placed near the center or at the lower part of the arrangement for color balance. And small flowers placed in groups

147C. *The simple container and the two bold amaryllis blossoms set against the symmetrical radiation of leaves are suitable for a modern room.*

ILLUSTRATION 148. *Line emphasis in the Japanese manner predominates in this informal arrangement of magnolias and redbud sprays.*

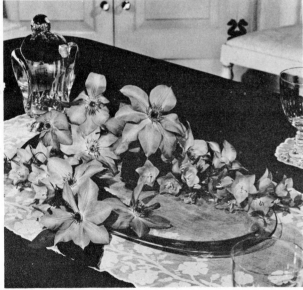

ILLUSTRATION 149. *Because of the massing of blossoms in this dining table arrangement of clematis and Pomona, color emphasis predominates.*

throughout the arrangement give a more interesting color effect than when they are singly placed. *Line emphasis* predominates when only a few flowers of the same kind are informally arranged, when a few sprays of fruit blossoms are used, or when a few dried grasses or leaves are combined.

6. In arranging flowers, work with the container at the height at which it will be used. For a dining table, flowers should always be below eye level; so it is safe to work on your arrangement at table height. Flowers for a mantel will give a different effect when placed on the mantel if they have been arranged, for instance, on a chair. However, if flowers are to be used on a coffee table, a chair may furnish a very good surface for arranging them.

7. Take advantage of pussy willow and forsythia in the spring for arrangements in tall containers or in low bowls. In the fall or late summer gather thistle, bittersweet, pine cones, milkweed pods, cotton pods, and gourds for colorful or subtle but interesting dried arrangements in shallow containers. Weeds are sometimes effective when painted with tempera or enamel paints.

8. Avoid using paper or other artificial flowers. A plant or vines on the dining room table will always be in better taste than artificial flowers.

✳ WHAT ACCESSORIES COMPLEMENT FLOWER ARRANGEMENT?

If you have ever visited a flower show, you may have noticed that small decorative objects supplement many of the arrangements. On each side of an arrangement in a china or alabaster urn, a Dresden china figure might be placed. Or near an arrangement in a copper bowl, there might be copper candlesticks and a copper candle snuffer. With a modern arrangement, you might see a very modern cigarette box and lighter. These little accessories or small decorative objects lend an extra note of interest if they are well chosen. Of course, the accessories must be good in design and must be related in idea, texture, color, and line to the flower container and the arrangement.

Some accessories for the *traditional* room are brass, bronze, or silver candlesticks; ceramic, brass, or polished-wood cigarette boxes; ceramic birds or figures; ornamental clocks or candy jars. Interesting accessories for the *informal* or Early American room are ceramic or carved-wood figures; copper, brass, ceramic, or wrought-iron candlesticks; colored tiles or attractive earthenware plates; an hourglass, a candle snuffer, or a trivet. In *modern* rooms bold ceramic birds, animals, or figures; sleek metal, wood, or ceramic cigarette boxes; or even a mask may be used.

✳ HOW WILL YOU USE PLANTS?

In every part of the country plants, leaves, and vines are available. They not only give a fresh note to a room, but they last a long time. Plants are effective on a dining table, on a mantel, on a dressing table, on any living room table, or on window sills or shelves. Plants are like babies in that they require regular tender care. Proper light, the proper

ILLUSTRATION 150. *The upper arrangement and accessories are suitable for an informal room; the lower grouping is formal traditional in character.*

amount of water, fertilizer, and cultivation are all necessary for good results. Some plants require surface watering, while others must stand in a saucer of water. Direct sunlight will kill some plants, while others require a lot of sunlight. If you buy plants for Christmas, Mother's Day, or merely to have in the house, ask your florist how to take care of them. Poinsettias, azaleas, tulips, hyacinths, and many other plants will bloom again next year with proper care.

SUGGESTED ACTIVITIES

1. Make a display of necessary equipment for arranging flowers, giving an estimate of the price of each piece and the total cost.
2. Classify a collection of containers into those which are primarily suitable for (a) a formal room, (b) an informal room, and (c) a modern room. Tell what kind of flowers you think would be good in each container, and whether you would use a formal or an informal arrangement.
3. Bring some flowers to your homemaking department, and make an arrangement (a) for a formal living room, (b) for a cottage dining room, and (c) for a modern living room. Criticize the arrangements according to the rules given in this chapter.
4. Volunteer the services of your class to arrange flowers for the school, for the churches, or for other organizations in your community.
5. Collect pictures of interesting flower arrangements.
6. Gather weeds, grasses, or seed pods, and make interesting winter arrangements for school and home.
7. Visit ten-cent stores, flower shops, and department stores to see the types of flower containers available. Compare them as to cost and design quality.
8. Collect pictures of interestingly arranged accessories used in formal, informal, and modern rooms.

SELECTED REFERENCES FOR UNIT SEVEN

BOOKS

Consult books listed in Unit Four

Biddle, Dorothy, and Blom, Dorothea J., *New Flower Arrangement for Everyone*. M. Barrows & Co., Inc., New York, 1951

Cyphers, Emma H., *Modern Art in Flower Arrangement*. Hearthside Press, Inc., New York, 1959

Dunlop, Hazel P., *Flower Arranging for Fun*. The Viking Press, Inc., New York, 1959

Köhler, Walter, and Luckhardt, Wassili, *Lighting in Architecture*. Reinhold Publishing Corp., New York, 1959

Nightingale, Frank B., *Garden Lighting*. Knight Publishing Co., Skyforest, California, 1958

Roberts, Patricia E., *The Book of Table Arrangements with Flowers, Fruit, and Other Elements*. Crown Publishers, Inc., New York, 1958

Rutt, Anna H., *The Art of Flower and Foliage Arrangement*. The Macmillan Company, New York, 1958

Webb, Lida, *Popular Styles of Japanese Flower Arrangement*. Hearthside Press, Inc., New York, 1959

CURRENT PUBLICATIONS

Write to the following addresses for current lists of literature and visual aids (with prices):

General Electric Company, Large Lamp Division, Nela Park, Cleveland 12, Ohio (*home lighting*)

Home Industries, 331 Athens Street, Jackson, Ohio (*catalogue of wall ornaments*)

Lightolier, Jersey City 5, New Jersey (*home lighting*)

Old Guilford Forge, Guilford, Connecticut (*catalogue of Early American reproductions*)

Syracuse Ornamental Company, Syracuse, New York (*wall accessories*)

Westinghouse Electric Company, Lamp Division, Bloomfield, New Jersey (*home lighting*)

8

Study
buying guides
and become
a wise consumer

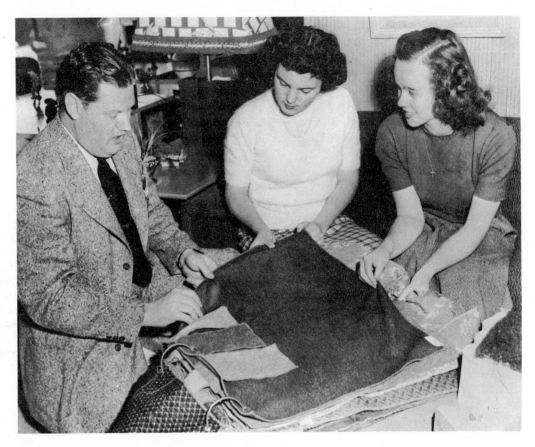

ILLUSTRATION 151.   *These girls are learning how to be wise consumers by listening to an explanation of how to judge quality in upholstery fabrics.*

CHAPTER I

What points will you consider in choosing laborsaving equipment?

A RANGE, a refrigerator, a freezer, a washer, and a dryer, plus other laborsaving equipment and small appliances, represent a large investment. If you want to get the most benefit from your equipment dollar you should know how to select and use electrical equipment most homemakers eventually buy.

The following suggestions will be helpful to you as potential consumers.

1. Study the women's magazines and consumer bulletins and reports. Look at displays and compare performances of different models. Make a note of the features you like and do not like. Write down the model number, suggested performance, and other points so that you can make exact price comparisons.

2. Compare prices, servicing, and guarantees at appliance stores, utilities companies, department stores, and discount houses. If you buy at a discount house or secondhand store, find out about the extra costs such as delivery, installation, and service.

3. Study the guarantee, make sure you understand all the terms, and file it with similar papers. Customers seldom bother to read the guarantee, but blame the dealer when repairs are needed after the guarantee's time limit has expired.

4. Read the directions for use and ask all the questions you can think of when you purchase a piece of equipment. Post the directions near the unit. From 20 to 40 per cent of service calls come from persons who are careless about reading directions or who fail to use common sense. Often an appliance is not plugged in properly, a fuse has blown, or a safety device has not been released.

5. Buy brand-name equipment and make sure service is available. Remember that service calls cost more when made from distances or when parts must be sent away to be replaced or repaired.

6. When your equipment needs servicing, call a reputable person and get a satisfactory explanation of what is wrong and what the cost will be. Get an itemized bill and be sure you understand the charges.

7. Remember that courtesy on the telephone and toward the repairman on the job will secure better service. You can be firm without being demanding.

8. Give your equipment proper care. Soap and water do the best cleaning job on all baked-in enamel surfaces. A very fine cleansing powder may be used for stubborn stains and grease, but cleansing pads and most abrasive cleansers harm the finish. Fruit and acids discolor enamel finishes, so spills should be wiped off immediately. Never clean any appliance while it is warm. Always disconnect small appliances before cleaning.

✱ HOW WILL YOU JUDGE A RANGE?

Gas and electric *ranges* have comparable features in regard to performance and appearance. Surface electric burners are as fast as gas, and gas burners have the desirable control features of electric surface cooking units. The real determining factors in making a choice will be cost of installation and cost of monthly bills. Electric ranges require a 220-volt circuit, and gas ranges with electric controls require a 110-volt circuit — the type necessary for all small appliances. Homemakers accustomed to either range will have little difficulty adjusting to the other. Ranges come in a choice of a dozen or more colors.

In addition to gas and electric ranges, there are electronic ranges which cook foods in minutes without heating the cooking containers. These ranges are expensive, and although they reduce cooking time to a frac-

tion they may have certain disadvantages. Foods will not brown or crust unless the element for browning is turned on; this heats the utensil, thus defeating one of the big selling points. Only china, glass, or paper cooking utensils can be used in electronic ranges, because the radio waves that cook the food do not penetrate metal.

One of the first questions to settle is whether to choose a complete range in the traditional enamel — white or colored — or a wall oven with a surface cooking unit. All of the special features may be had in either model.

Separate ovens make a kitchen look attractive, but if wall space is limited or if the homemaker uses the oven almost as much as she uses the top burners, a complete range is recommended. When a wall oven is used, it is often placed outside the recommended

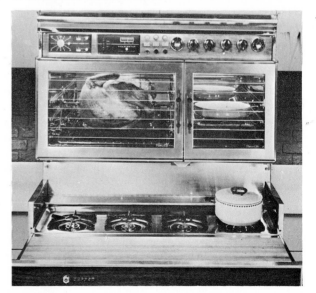

ILLUSTRATION 152A (*left*). *For large families, or those who do much entertaining, stacked electric wall ovens provide plentiful baking space.*

152B (*below*). *This versatile, fully automatic gas range can be hung on the wall or built into it. Usually the range is mounted on a base cabinet.*

work triangle. There should be a heatproof surface at least 24 inches wide adjoining oven, on which to rest hot utensils. The oven should be placed low enough to avoid burning your arms. The oven should be large enough to hold a large roasting pan and should have its own broiling pan. Another desirable built-in feature is a drawer for keeping dishes warm. All ovens should be well insulated, and gas ovens as well as gas surface units should be well ventilated for safety. Avoid placing the range or wall oven next to the refrigerator, for efficient operation of both appliances.

Ranges come in many widths, the most popular of which are the 38″ to 40″ sizes and the 20″ width for apartment houses. Models are available with one oven and a storage compartment; one extra-large oven for baking and broiling and no storage space (few people want to pay for storage space in a range unless other storage facilities are limited); one oven plus a separate waist-high broiler; two ovens with one or two broiling units.

Some desirable features are:

THERMOSTATIC CONTROLS: A control panel across the back should have clearly indicated heat and time controls for surface and oven units. Be sure the controls are easy to operate and are placed to avoid accidental burns from pots, steam, and heat. Most gas and electric ranges have at least five settings for degrees of heat. A simmer control is important.

OVEN TIMER: This device may be set to start the oven and turn it off at any time, whether you are at home or not.

ROAST THERMOMETER: Attached to the oven by a cable, the thermometer may be inserted in poultry or a roast to eliminate guessing at the degree of "doneness."

BROILER: A waist-high broiling unit is preferable to a low broiler unless its location reduces the size of the oven. Some broilers are vertical so that meat may be broiled on two sides

at once. Some ranges have broilers that give a charcoal effect.

ROTISSERIE: A rotisserie may be had in the oven, broiler compartment, or on top of the range. Check the instruction book carefully for its operation, because this feature will vary in performance.

BUILT-IN GRIDDLE: A griddle is built into the top of some range models, but is not needed if you have a separate electric griddle. A range griddle should have thermostatic control, be removable for cleaning, and be dripproof.

SURFACE UNITS: Most women prefer surface units grouped so that work space is either at the side or in the center. Some ranges have units across the back — a good arrangement when there are small children in the family.

Other features that may be included on ranges are a glass oven window, a deep-well cooker, an appliance outlet, panel lights, and pull-out ovens.

Use and care

Smooth exterior and interior surfaces and removable units and trays facilitate cleaning. Some ranges have removable ovens, doors, and entire tops that lift out. When the range is cool, lift out all removable parts and wash with soap and water. Use a brush for stubborn spots. Mild cleaners will do no harm. Clean top, bottom, and sides of the oven regularly, and dry well. Use a brush or fine steel wool to scrape off food. Do not use a knife.

When grease accumulates the oven will lose its efficiency and may smoke. Commercial oven cleaners do a good job if directions are followed. If aluminum foil is used under the broiler pan rack, discard the foil after use, cool and clean the broiler pan, and store the pan far below the heat source. Never line the bottom of the oven with foil, because it may fuse to the surface.

ILLUSTRATION 153A. *Modern refrigerator-freezers bring to homemakers many convenience features plus attractive interior and exterior styling.*

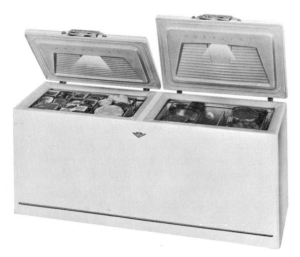

✦ HOW WILL YOU JUDGE A
REFRIGERATOR, REFRIGERATOR-FREEZER, AND FREEZER?

Refrigerators and *refrigerator-freezers* come in gas and electric models and in a wide range of sizes.

Refrigerators differ greatly from refrigerator-freezers in cost and in temperature controls. The combination type with 0° F. freezer temperature costs much more than a similar-sized model with a top freezer unit holding temperatures just below freezing. The refrigerator-freezer has two sets of controls, and will quick-freeze and keep food fresh for a long period. The refrigerator has only one set of temperature controls, but it may have as large a freezing unit as a refrigerator-freezer. This refrigerator will not quick-freeze, and frozen foods should not be kept in the freezing compartment more than three or four weeks. Many foods lose color, texture, and flavor unless they are quick frozen and held at near zero temperatures.

Freezing compartments may be above, below, or at the side of the main space. Refrigerators may be obtained with door openings on either side, and some open from both sides. Some doors open by pressing a foot pedal. It is desirable to have a refrigerator on rollers so that it can be pulled out for cleaning.

Refrigerators and freezers may be built into the wall vertically at any height or suspended horizontally like wall cabinets. One big objection to wall-cabinet installation is the difficulty in reaching foods.

153B. *If you have floor space available for it, you may use a chest freezer. It has the advantage of counter-height work space.*

Some of the things you should consider in choosing a refrigerator are:

CAPACITY: An 8-cubic-foot model will be adequate for a small family; 10- to 14-cubic-foot, for the average family; and a 16- to 20-cubic-foot size is desirable for the large family or a family that does much entertaining. Some space claimed by the manufacturer may be unusable because of poor planning.

DOOR STORAGE: Make sure items stored in door racks may be lifted and replaced easily. Extra deep troughs and many lids can be a nuisance.

DEFROSTING FACILITIES: Automatic defrosting in the main space is standard equipment. Some refrigerators have a forced-air system to draw off moist air and prevent frost formation. Although many units are totally self-defrosting, most people prefer to remove stored foods occasionally, wipe frost from boxes, wipe inside shelves and walls, and reorganize items.

SHELVES: It should be possible to adjust all shelves according to storage needs. If shelves pull out or swing out, make sure they do not catch on items below and upset them. More expensive models have revolving shelves that may be raised or lowered by pushing a button.

ICE TRAYS: Make sure you have sufficient ice trays with easy release. Some freezer compartments freeze water, eject ice cubes, and store them automatically. Some models have no-spill ice trays. This feature prevents layers of ice from accumulating in the unit.

MEAT STORAGE DRAWER: An air-tight drawer in a colder area of the refrigerator will keep meats fresh longer.

Food freezers come in upright and chest models. Most people prefer the upright type, with door space for storage. However, a chest freezer provides counter space, and is almost as easy to use as an upright.

Whether or not you should buy a home freezer may be determined by asking the following questions.

1. Do you actually need it? If you shop once a week, an extra large refrigerator-freezer with a large freezing compartment may be adequate and will cost less to buy and operate than two units.
2. Have you sufficient space? The most convenient place is the kitchen. A chest freezer requires more floor space than an upright model, but it can fit under a window.
3. Is your present location permanent? Moving costs are high and your new home may not accommodate a freezer.
4. Is your electric power dependable? A freezer full of food represents a big financial loss if food spoils while the power is off. A few hours without power will have little effect if doors are kept shut, but a long power shortage may cause food to spoil.

Some desirable features in an upright freezer are: library-type storage space on doors; automatic juice-can rack with separate compartments that load from top and dispense cans from the bottom; easily removable trays. A chest-type freezer should have wire baskets that glide and lift out easily, so that all food may be visible.

Use and care

Load refrigerators and freezers according to the manufacturer's directions. Engineers have worked out scientific food storage plans for best circulation of air and for suitable storage temperature for different foods. Clean the main space regularly. Remove foods and wrap to avoid thawing. Clean as quickly as possible with lukewarm water and mild suds or baking soda solution. Wipe with a rinse cloth and dry well. Wipe all door surfaces inside and out, and the gasket around the door. Avoid sharp instruments in releasing food boxes or ice trays, or in scraping off frost. Do not place hot foods in either freezing compartment or main space.

★ HOW WILL YOU JUDGE WASHERS AND DRYERS?

Washers and dryers are complicated machines, and every time new devices are added there are more things that can go wrong. Perhaps the most important consideration in buying a washer or dryer is to choose a standard brand and make sure it can be serviced nearby. Find out what friends have to say about different models.

The *wringer washer* may have two-speed wash action, timer, wringer with built-in cold rinse (desirable for wash-and-wear items), and lint filter. Many people who own an old wringer washer keep it to use in conjunction with a new automatic machine, to dovetail laundry activities and also for small wash loads. If one must make a choice between a new automatic washer, continuing to dry laundry outdoors, *or* a new dryer, continuing to wash with a wringer model, the latter choice will save more time and energy.

An *automatic washer* that loads from the top has agitator action, and one that loads

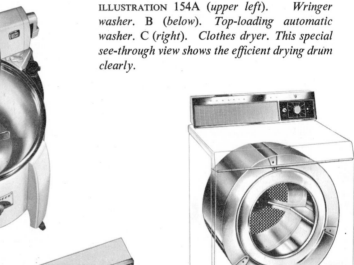

ILLUSTRATION 154A (*upper left*). *Wringer washer.* B (*below*). *Top-loading automatic washer.* C (*right*). *Clothes dryer. This special see-through view shows the efficient drying drum clearly.*

from the front, tumble action. Each has a choice of water temperatures, spin speeds, and washing cycles. Controls may be marked for all types of garments, from extra dirty clothes to delicate wash-and-wear garments.

Here are some special features to consider in choosing an automatic washer:

CONTROLS: Dial or push-button controls should be conveniently placed and easy to read. There should be a water saver control for a small wash, and controls to interrupt a cycle without disturbing the mechanism.

FILTER: Most washers come with a top tray or an underwater filter for lint.

DISPENSERS: Automatic dispensers for detergent, bleach, and fabric conditioner save guesswork, but care must be taken not to bleach colored garments.

An automatic washer must rest level on the floor for efficient operation. Proper care will insure long life for an automatic washer.

Use and care

Before loading clothes into the washer, all garment pockets should be checked to see that they are empty. After the clothes have been removed from the washer, the lid should be kept open until the washer cools to prevent a musty odor. Occasionally the agitator should be removed and cleaned, and the drum of the tumble-type washer should be washed and wiped dry.

Overloading creates a strain on the motor. When garments are crowded they neither wash well nor rinse well. Most washers have suggested load sizes printed inside the lid. White and colored clothes should be washed separately, and as a rule nylons should be washed alone because nylon acts like a magnet — attracting dirt from other fabrics. To minimize wrinkles in wash-and-wear garments, the load should be only about half normal size; the final rinse should be cool, and garments should be removed immediately at the end of the cycle.

A clothes *dryer* is perhaps the biggest labor saver since the semiautomatic washer replaced the washboard. Clothes dryers come in gas and electric models. A dryer should have controls for fluffing, as well as for drying heavy-duty items, ordinary clothes, and wash-and-wear garments. Dryers come with and without vents. In no-vent models, heat, moisture, and lint are handled internally. These models are best for inside rooms and apartments. Lint and condenser chambers must be emptied regularly in vented models.

Electric dryers run on a 110- or a 220-volt circuit, and gas dryers need a 110-volt electric circuit for thermostatic control. Electric models operating on a 110-volt circuit require more than twice as much drying time as those using a 220-volt circuit, and therefore are expensive to operate.

Before putting garments into a dryer, be sure to tie apron strings, fasten zippers, and remove heavy buttons. It may be necessary to experiment with time settings for small loads and items that are not to be completely dried, as well as for heavy bedding or rugs.

Models in washers and dryers change like car models, but if directions for operation are put into practice, there should be little need for servicing for a long time.

A *combination washer-dryer* has advantages and disadvantages over two separate units. The combination type takes up less floor space and costs less than two separate units. When such a unit is set under the kitchen counter or back in one corner of the U-shaped kitchen, laundry and kitchen activities may be dovetailed with little time lost. However, if washings are large, separate washing and drying units will reduce the total time spent in laundering activities.

✶ HOW WILL YOU JUDGE A VACUUM CLEANER?

There are three types of *vacuum cleaners* — tank or canister type with straight suction, upright with motor-driven brush or motor-driven agitator, and the small bag-type cleaner for cleaning stairs and upholstery. For heavy-duty rug cleaning, the upright cleaner with motor-driven agitator brush usually does a better job, but the above-the-floor cleaning tools may be inconvenient to use. The American Carpet Institute recommends seven passes over a rug area with an upright cleaner for thorough cleaning (four forward and three back). The brush should be adjusted to the thickness of the rug. With a tank or canister cleaner, eleven passes are necessary for the same degree of cleaning. On the other hand, a tank cleaner does a better job on hard-surfaced floors, and the above-the-floor tools are easier to use.

Many new homes have built-in plugs for tank cleaners. The dirt is sucked up and travels through tubes in the wall to a dust receptacle in the basement.

ILLUSTRATION 155A. *A canister vacuum cleaner*

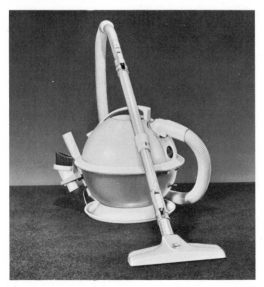

Use and care

To obtain maximum use from a vacuum cleaner, you should learn to use the floor brush, dusting brush, upholstery brush, crevice tool, flexible hose, and extension tubes for all types of household cleaning.

Care will differ with the type cleaner. Many cleaners come with disposable bags inside the dirt-collecting area. In whatever way dirt is collected, it must be removed frequently to permit a free flow of air. Worn brushes and belts should be replaced. Filters on a tank cleaner should be replaced regularly. The revolving brush should be kept free of hair and string. Before running a vacuum cleaner, pick up pins and other sharp objects by hand. Avoid twisting or jerking the cord either at the handle or at the electric outlet.

✶ HOW WILL YOU JUDGE A POLISHER-SCRUBBER?

A *polisher-scrubber* will clean floors quickly, spread wax evenly, and polish floors smoothly. It is effective on asphalt, linoleum, all resilient tiles, brick, concrete, and terrazzo tile. The finish may be restored between scrubbings by buffing the surface. With care, wood floors may be cleaned with a polisher-scrubber. Water should be wiped up quickly.

Designs in polisher-scrubbers include single-, twin-brush, and triple-brush models. A triple-brush is best for heavy-duty cleaning. Each model may have a set of interchangeable brushes — one for scrubbing and one for waxing, and additional attachments for cleaning rugs. An entirely automatic polisher-scrubber will dispense the suds water from one container, scrub and suck up the dirty water in another container. Attachments may be had to clean rugs, treat wool rugs with a moth preventative, and restore the nap.

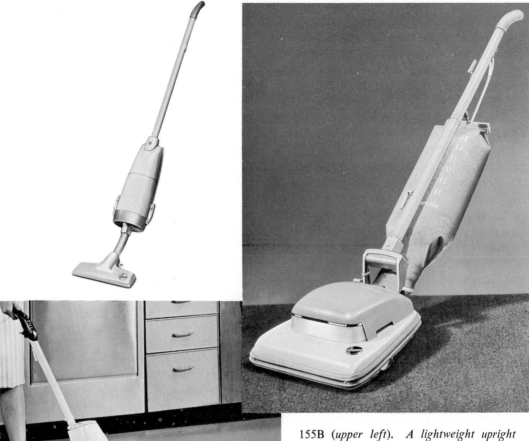

155B (*upper left*). *A lightweight upright vacuum cleaner (sometimes called an electric broom) is particularly convenient for daily cleaning.* 155C (*upper right*). *A standard upright vacuum cleaner, with agitation plus suction, is most efficient for cleaning rugs and carpets.* 155D (*below*). *An electric floor washer or rug shampooer wets floors with clean water and detergent, scrubs them thoroughly, and suction-dries the floors.*

✳ HOW WILL YOU JUDGE AN IRON?

Practically all hand and steam *irons* have temperature controls for all fabrics. Most hand irons weigh slightly over three pounds. Slots in the sides of the soleplate facilitate ironing garments with buttons.

Steam irons may be used as dry irons. Select a steam iron that is easy to fill and empty, and one that is not easily harmed by tap water. Ordinarily, the mineral content of tap water builds up a sediment inside a steam iron, eventually clogging up the holes. Tap water may be filtered with commercial compounds for the purpose of lessening clogging. Commercial solvents may be had to clean a steam iron after it becomes clogged.

ILLUSTRATION 156 (*above*). *An automatic iron;* (*below*) *a steam iron which may also be used dry.*

✳ HOW WILL YOU JUDGE A DISHWASHER?

Dishwashers come in three models — under-counter, free-standing, and portable. Except for installation costs, built-in models are the most satisfactory. A portable dishwasher needs storage space; and each time it is used the faucet hose must be attached and the drain hose must be placed in the sink, thus interfering with sink operations.

Some dishwashers are loaded from the top and others have pull-out racks accessible from the front. Both types are satisfactory. You should be able to load the upper racks without first loading the lower racks. There should be two cycles — utility and ordinary. Some dishwashers have a special cycle for plastic dishes and extra fine china. Capacity is an important selling point in a dishwasher. Some models will hold many more dishes than others, because of spray placement and arrangement of basket partitions.

Machine dishwashing has certain limitations. Extra large and odd-sized dishes and utensils are difficult to stack. Few dishwashers clean residual bits of sticky food, gravy, or egg unless dishes are thoroughly scraped. Rubber, bone, or wood utensils and silver knives with handles cemented on should never be washed in the dishwasher. Aluminum and copper utensils discolor in the dishwasher, and some plastic dishes may not wash successfully. Harsh detergents will discolor or fade fine china.

It is extremely important to follow the directions for stacking dishes in a dishwasher and for operating it. A low-sudsing detergent especially designed for dishwashers must be used, and used in the correct amounts. A temperature of 140° to 160° F. is required, and water pressure should be 30 pounds per square inch. However, most dishwashers will operate at pressures of between 15 and

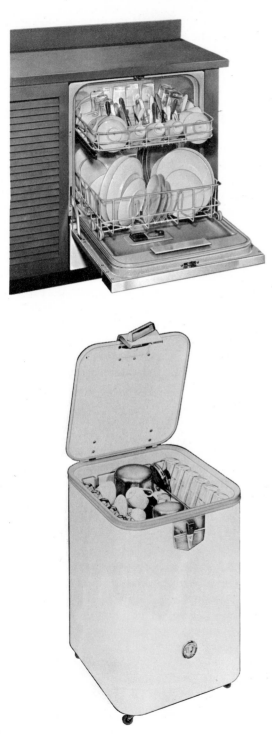

20 pounds per square inch. A very important thing in dishwasher efficiency is proper loading. The soiled sides of dishes must be placed where water can reach them. Items must be evenly distributed for good balance.

★ HOW WILL YOU JUDGE A FOOD DISPOSER?

Food disposers are almost indispensable in apartment houses. The two basic kinds are the continuous-feed and the lock-cover types. The first is faster and more convenient, but often silverware or paring knives get in by mistake. The lock-cover type is safer. The life of the average food disposer is about ten years. The ideal disposer should be able to handle quickly any food that fits into it, and then clean itself thoroughly. Many people abuse disposers by ignoring directions for use and by dropping kitchen utensils into them. A disposer may be installed in any standard sink, but the drain line may need to be reamed out. Some disposers have removable blades that may be reversed for self-sharpening. Usually electric appliances used near water create a shock hazard, but as a rule disposers are electrically safe.

ILLUSTRATION 157A (*upper*). *This built-in dishwasher loads from the front, and has usable counter space above it.*

157B (*lower*). *This portable dishwasher is convenient, as it loads from the top and can be used in various locations.*

⭑ HOW WILL YOU JUDGE SMALL APPLIANCES?

A certain number of small appliances are necessary for kitchen efficiency, but if you have too many appliances you may have insufficient storage space or too few electrical outlets.

A single thermostatic control for a group of appliances may solve the outlet problem. Frying pan, saucepan, griddle, and coffee percolator may be operated from one master control. Wiring should be checked before using all appliances at one time. Small appliances that may be completely immersed in water are easy to clean.

The *electric mixer* is perhaps the most frequently used small appliance. The stand-mounted type with detachable head and ten or more speeds is the best choice. The head should not weigh much over three pounds. The speed controls should be accessible. The mixer can be one of the most dangerous of all household appliances. To avoid accidents, turn the motor off to stir mixtures or scrape the sides of the bowl, and remove the beaters and disconnect the appliance immediately after use. *Portable mixers* are less efficient and have fewer speeds than stand-mounted ones, but they cost less, require less storage space, and do well for most jobs. You should choose a portable mixer that will stand on end as well as hang up on the wall.

The *blender* liquefies, chops, shreds, crumbs, blends, and beats, but it does not perform beating jobs as well as a mixer. The liquid in a blender must be controlled to prevent overflow. Liquid spilled on the motor creates a shock hazard.

Electric coffeepots include percolator and vacuum models. Coffee can be made in from twelve to fourteen minutes in either. Percolators have controls for mild, medium, and strong brews and a temperature control for simmering. The vacuum type has no controls for strength, and the holding temperature is lower than in the percolator coffeepot.

ILLUSTRATION 158.   *An electric mixer*

ILLUSTRATION 159.   *An electric blender*

A completely automatic *toaster* will give successive slices of uniformly brown toast. The mechanism should raise the toast quietly; a dial should control the degree of brownness. Some toasters for home use will make four slices at one time. There may be a tray to keep toast hot. Check to make sure that the bottom of the toaster is well insulated to avoid marking tables. Never place buttered toast in the toaster. Remove the crumb tray occasionally and wipe off dust and crumbs. The heating element should be self-cleaning. Never immerse the toaster in water. Avoid wrapping the cord around it.

Waffle bakers vary according to shape and number of automatic features. A square waffle iron that will bake four waffles at once is the most popular. The outside should be nontarnishable metal, and the grids should be solid cast aluminum. The tray should be wide and deep enough to catch overflow batter, and the handles should be heatproof. There should be a dial to control brownness and a light or bell to indicate when the waffle is done. Never use harsh abrasives on a waffle baker. If waffles stick, brush off the crumbs and read the directions before baking another waffle. The grids may have to be seasoned again.

Electric *frying pans* or skillets are among the most popular electric appliances. They come in several sizes and with glass or metal lids. There should be a dial control for various temperatures, and the pan should be immersible. The pan should not be cleaned with harsh abrasives, and grease should be kept off the bottom.

A number of agencies rate major home equipment and small appliances regularly. Before buying a new appliance, you may want to ask your city librarian to let you see some of these consumer reports and ratings.

ILLUSTRATION 160.   *A separately wired appliance center may well take care of many kitchen appliances at once, without reducing the supply of electricity in other parts of the house.*

SUGGESTED ACTIVITIES

1. Ask your homemaking teacher or a demonstrator from a utility company or a department store to demonstrate how to use and care for any of the following types of equipment with which you are not familiar: (a) a washer, either automatic or manual or both; (b) an ironer; (c) a steam and a cordless iron; (d) an electric and a gas range; (e) a toaster; (f) a waffle baker; (g) a mixer; (h) a vacuum-type coffee maker and a percolator; (i) an upright and a tank-type vacuum cleaner.

2. Interview a number of homemakers who own various pieces of the equipment listed above to find out (a) their reasons for liking or disliking the equipment, (b) the cost of operating it, and (c) the ease with which it is used.

3. Collect pictures of the various types of equipment discussed in this chapter. Secure prices for the various types if possible.

4. List in order the modern laborsaving equipment you would choose. Give your reasons for your choice and rank.

5. Plan appliances for a modern kitchen, and estimate the cost.

6. Make a list of the electrical equipment you have at school or at home, indicating the brand, cost, and date of purchase. Check each piece of your equipment from the standpoint of probable length of time it will last, yearly cost including operation cost, and efficiency of operation.

7. Demonstrate to the class how to defrost an electric refrigerator or how to clean an. electric or gas stove.

8. Give a debate on "A combination refrigerator and home freezer is more satisfactory for the average city family than a separate refrigerator and a separate home freezer."

9. Compare time, labor, and costs involved in using a home-owned automatic washer, in using rental services in an apartment or a community center, and in using commercial laundry services.

10. Compare de luxe models with regular models of ranges and refrigerators to determine whether the additional performance justifies the difference in cost in terms of your needs.

CHAPTER 2

What should you consider in buying floor coverings?

THE FLOOR is a big area, and one that plays an important part in the decorating scheme and in the home furnishings budget. For many years linoleum was the standard resilient floor covering and wool the accepted carpet fiber. Modern chemistry and technology have changed former conceptions of acceptable floor coverings, and expanded our choices.

✴ WHAT ARE RESILIENT FLOOR COVERINGS?

Resilient floor coverings include those made mainly from linoleum, cork, vinyl, asphalt, and rubber. These composition materials may be laid over new wood floors, wood floors in poor condition, or concrete floors in any room in the house. Resilient floor coverings are durable, versatile, colorful, and easy to install and maintain. Some types come in both tile and sheet form. Thickness for home use varies from $\frac{1}{16}$ to $\frac{1}{8}$ inch.

Whether the covering is installed *on grade*, *above grade*, or *below grade* will determine the covering and mastic to be used.

Kinds of resilient compositions

ASPHALT: This is the least expensive of all resilient floor coverings, but it also has the least resilience and the lowest acoustic quality, and dents are permanent. It is especially good for below-grade floors because it resists the alkaline in concrete. Asphalt tile is affected by changing temperatures, and under heavy traffic will tend to chip. Regular asphalt tile is not recommended for kitchens, but grease-proof asphalt tile may be used. Some cleaning preparations and waxes will soften asphalt tile and cause it to bleed. Soap and detergents may be used in cleaning, but only *self-polishing wax* is recommended.

LINOLEUM (inlaid or tile): Linoleum is moderate in cost, durable, and easy to maintain, repels grease, has good acoustic qualities, and comes in a wide range of colors and surface effects. In inlaid linoleum (sold by the square yard) the design runs from top to bottom. In printed linoleum the design is on the surface only. Linoleum tiles come in one thickness but inlaid comes in many thicknesses. Inlaid linoleum and linoleum tile may be used in any room in the house if colors and design are appropriate. Linoleum should not be used on floors below grade.

VINYL SHEETS AND TILES: Vinyl is the best all-round resilient floor covering because it is durable, attractive, and dent- and grease-resistant. Vinyl tiles and sheets come in a wide range of color and surface variations, but vinyls vary greatly in quality and cost. Vinyl sheet, usually bonded to a backing, is recommended only for floors above grade. When bonded to an alkali-resistant backing, it may be used below grade.

VINYL ASBESTOS: This is more resilient and more lustrous than asphalt tile, but less resilient than true vinyl, linoleum, or cork. It costs more than asphalt but less than solid vinyl; is acid- and grease-resistant; may be laid below, on, or above grade; and is easy to maintain and wears well.

RUBBER TILE: Rubber tile has the greatest resistance to denting and ranks next to cork in comfort and quietness. It is almost as expensive as pure vinyl, and care is a little more difficult. *Self-polishing wax* is recommended after a thorough scrubbing with detergent. An occasional buffing with fine steel wool helps rubber tile maintain its luster. It may be used anywhere.

CORK: Cork comes in light, medium, and dark tones. It is recommended for the den, library, or living room. It will not take heavy traffic in areas such as entrance halls or recreation rooms. It absorbs grease and dirt. It must be laid on dry surfaces only, because dampness will cause it to crumble and come up. It has good acoustic qualities. It is not recommended for below grade use. *Vinyl-cork* is more dirt- and grease-resistant and will take heavier traffic, but it is not as resilient as cork.

✷ HOW WILL YOU JUDGE RUGS?

When you shop for a rug you will want one that is durable, resilient, abrasive-resistant, colorfast, and easy to care for; one that will not pill (show pill-like or beadlike formations on top), shed lint, show tracking, or crush. Furthermore, you will want one at a price you can afford. You will also want a rug the right size for your room and one that will fit into your decorating plan.

Wool has always been the most acceptable carpet fiber. The goal of all synthetic carpet yarn manufacturers has been to produce a yarn as strong, as resilient, and as luxurious looking as wool at a price comparable to cotton and rayon.

The best course to follow in selecting carpet or rugs is to buy from a reputable dealer. Don't be fooled by magic words and superperformance predictions. For instance, the early, much-praised rayon carpeting became unpopular even though it was blended with nylon. The small percentage of nylon did not counteract rayon's natural weakness as a carpet fiber; the carpet soiled, crushed, and did not wear well. A more durable blend of rayon or viscose is now available which is far superior to the original rayon carpet fiber.

No fiber is perfect. Wool is resilient, soft, and springy, but wool attracts moths, and good wool is expensive. Nylon is durable, abrasive-resistant, and easily cleaned; but nylon often acts like a magnet to attract dirt, and it tends to pill. Rayon and acetate are produced in beautiful clear colors but lack the strength and resilience of wool. Because of the high cost and scarcity of good wool, substitutes and blends are becoming not only acceptable but desirable as carpet fibers.

You can judge blends only if you know the properties of the different fibers. To obtain the desired end results, it is as necessary to use the proper proportions in blending fibers as it is to know the proper measurements in making a cake. For instance, some fibers require more nylon than others to increase their wear. Less than 20 per cent nylon seldom increases the durability of any weaker fiber. A 70-30 wool-nylon blend produces a durable, resilient carpet.

Since March, 1960, the Federal Trade Commission has required that all carpets and rugs be labeled with the generic names of fibers as well as percentages in the blends. If reprocessed wool is used in place of virgin wool in a blend, the label must say so and state the amount. If a rug passes certain cleaning tests by the Institute of Laundering and Dry Cleaning it will carry a cleanability label — symbol of protection against shrinkage and change of color.

Rug fibers

WOOL: Wool is durable, resilient, warm, luxurious. It comes in an unlimited color range and many weaves and surface effects, cleans well, and can be made permanently moth-resistant. For wool rugs and carpets now in use, a moth repellent may be added in the cleaning process to provide this moth-resistance for a year. Wool-twist carpet is nondirectional, meaning that it may be pieced in any direction without shading. Wool's greatest disadvantage is high cost.

COTTON: Cotton dyes well, comes in many beautiful colors, and is low in cost. Cotton is not resilient, so a plush pile will show traffic and will crush. Cotton sheds lint on dark clothing if children play on the rug, and fuzzes, therefore attracting soil and grease. Grease is difficult to remove unless the rug can be taken up and cleaned. But cotton is a good buy, even in wall-to-wall carpeting, in rooms where there is little traffic, especially in bedrooms.

RAYON: Rayon cannot be judged on its past performance as a rug fiber. Many of its objectionable points have been overcome — low resistance to wear and soil, high luster, atmospheric fading, and crushing. Its good points have been retained — low cost, bright clear colors, and resistance to moths and household stains. Rayon carpet often comes in a loop pile or a tweedlike effect to offset the undesirable qualities of crushing, affinity for soil, and tendency to show wear.

ACETATE: Acetate dyes well, is moderately resilient due to a heat-set twist, and sheds soil readily. Acetate is not harmed by mildew, moths, or ordinary spillage, but acetone (nail polish remover) will dissolve it. Blended properly with nylon, its wearing qualities are increased and softness and low cost are retained.

NYLON: Nylon has enjoyed prestige as well as abuse. Before the fabric labeling act nylon carpet sometimes had only a trace of nylon pres-

ILLUSTRATION 161A and B. *Contemporary broadloom rugs. The rug shown in A, with its color shading and heavier texture, would be suitable for an informal room and would not show soil easily. Rug B, although of the same good quality, is softer and lighter in color and texture, and suitable for formally decorated rooms.*

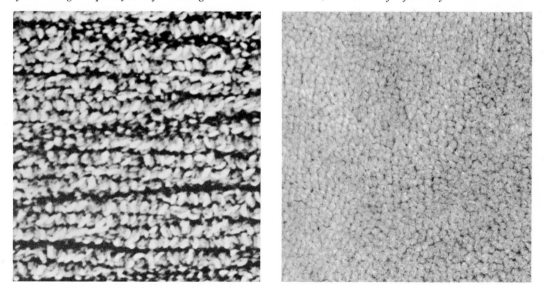

ILLUSTRATION 162. *Rug construction. The close-ness of tufting can be tested by folding a rug sample with the pile side out. Of these three, the folded sample at the top will wear best, because it has the greatest twist and density.*

ILLUSTRATION 163. *Twist and density being equal, the carpet with deep pile (right-hand sample in this illustration) will outlast carpet with low pile, and also will feel more resilient as you walk on it.*

ent, or it might have had even the nylon fiber which was supposed to have been produced purely for wearing apparel and household textiles. Textured filament nylon rug yarns have overcome most of nylon's shortcomings — affinity for soil, pilling, and static electricity.

ACRYLICS: Acrilan (Chemstrand), Dynel (Union Carbide), Verel (Tennessee Eastman), and Creslan (American Cyanamid) are some of many acrylic rug fibers available. Acrylic fibers most nearly resemble wool in resilience, warmth, bulk, and appearance, and blend well with wool and with each other. Acrylics are more durable than most other synthetics, and have less artificial sheen. Acrylics are also nonabsorbent, so water will not cause shrinkage. Unless specially treated for flammability, however, all-acrylic rugs of loose construction may present a serious fire hazard. The fibers are not fuzzy, so soil will not cling to them. Acrylics are nonstatic and mildew- and moth-repellent.

OTHER FIBERS: Warm-weather rugs are made of braided vinyl, straw matting, and woven plasticized kraft paper. They are inexpensive and cool but not very durable.

Rug construction

The weave, backing, and thickness of pile are important considerations in the choice of rugs. A close weave will wear longer than a loose weave, other factors being equal. When you bend a rug at 180 degrees you should not be able to see the backing.

For years, common rug weaves were Wilton, Axminster, velvet, and chenille. The bulk of rugs now produced are tufted.

TUFTING: Tufting has been used on wool carpet only since 1954. In this process, pile yarns are sewn to a jute or canvas base by multiple-needle machines. A coating of latex is sprayed on the back to secure the tufts. Very little flexibility of design is possible, but tweed, loop, motif, border, and sculptured effects may be obtained. A jute backing is often bonded to the latex back to eliminate buckling.

WILTON: Wilton rugs are made in subdued colors on Jacquard looms. Motifs are frequently Oriental. Better-grade Wilton rugs are made of longer and more firmly twisted worsted yarns. In this weave, the ends of each tuft are looped and buried in the background to form a cushion. This construction gives durability and resilience. The Wilton weave is used on more expensive solid-color wool rugs. *Brussels* carpet, associated with the Victorian period, has Wilton construction. Many sculptured and carved effects obtained by cutting sections of pile and leaving other sections in loops are often achieved with Wilton construction.

AXMINSTER: Axminster rugs were originally designed to imitate Oriental rugs. Motifs are larger and colors more vivid in Axminster rugs than in Wilton rugs. Tufts are tied into a coarse, stiff jute back, and no yarns are buried as in the Wilton construction. An Axminster rug may not be rolled up crosswise.

VELVET: This weave is best adapted to solid colors but it may be used for limited pattern effects. The pile is short but dense; it is woven in loops which are tied into a jute backing with linen thread; the loops are cut to form a pile. Straight yarns give a plush or velvet effect, and twisted yarns give a textured effect.

CHENILLE: In the true chenille process, much of the tying is done by hand to give a luxurious deep pile. Designs and colors are unlimited. Good chenille rugs are costly, handsome, and durable. Imitations do not wear well.

Rug cushions

Rug cushions absorb shock and extend the life of the rug. They are available in jute, hair, and rubber, in varying thicknesses. Rugs with short pile require heavy rug cushions and rugs with deep pile need light rug cushions. A heavy rug cushion and a deep-pile rug can be an accident hazard unless the carpet is laid wall-to-wall.

Whether to choose a rubber or a hair rug cushion is a matter of choice. The average

ILLUSTRATION 164. *Types of rugs or carpets*

TONE-ON-TONE AXMINSTER

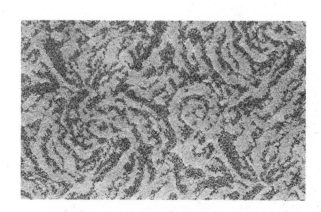

CARVED WILTON

TEXTURED VELVET

LEAF-DESIGN AXMINSTER

CARVED CHENILLE

ILLUSTRATION 165. *Types of rugs or carpets*

rubber cushion is not recommended under small rugs, especially scatter rugs, because the rug will creep off. There are netlike rug cushions and other types of rug cushions that are creep resistant. A good waffle-weave rug cushion made of 40-ounce hair is superior to similar, cheaper rug cushions that are made of a blend of hair and jute. This blend is less resilient than 40-ounce hair, and will not keep its shape. An all-hair rug cushion with a rubberized top is easier to clean than an all-hair cushion without a top.

✯ WHAT ARE ORIENTAL RUGS?

Salesmen of Oriental rugs spend a lifetime learning their business. Oriental rugs are expensive and prized possessions, but they require furnishings in keeping with them in color, in design, and in quality. The term "Oriental" may be applied only to hand-woven rugs that have been made in or near the Orient by the same methods used hundreds of years ago. There are two main types of handmade Orientals — the knotted and the flat or tapestry-woven rugs. Some of the earliest knotted rugs were made by the Moors and the people of Turkey and Persia (Iran). The flat-woven rugs are the *Sumak* rugs which are made in the Caucasus and the *Kilim* rugs which are made in Turkey, Caucasia, and Turkestan.

Yarns for Oriental rugs are carefully prepared and dyed with secret dye formulas. Each knot is tied by hand, and a definite pattern is followed. An expert weaver may tie 8000 to 12,000 knots a day. The colors and designs show through on the back of Oriental rugs; the nap runs in one direction, and a fringe — really an extension of the warp — extends beyond only one end of the rug. Six types of Oriental rugs are described briefly.

Persian

Rugs from Persia are probably the most popular of all Oriental rugs in use in America because they are of excellent workmanship, and are individual and distinctive in design. Many of the patterns start from a center medallion. The subordinate designs are small conventional flowers, vines, leaves, and often small birds and animals gracefully arranged to cover the entire surface. The colors are subtle, and green seldom appears. Most Persian rugs are named for the city in or near which they are made.

Mention is made of a few of the more familiar names of Persian rugs. The *Kirman* weavers use floral forms, particularly roses. *Kashan* rugs are characterized by the use of foliage motifs. *Sarouks*, the most popular of Persian rugs in the United States, are very heavy and durable, a 9 by 12 rug sometimes weighing as much as 100 pounds. They are distinguished by their floral motifs on a deep rose or blue background. The cypress tree or the tree of life is a familiar motif. The *Lilihan* rugs are woven by people of Armenian heritage. These rugs resemble the Sarouks, but the weave is neither as fine nor as soft. The *Kirmanshah*, although similar in name to the Kirman, is a rarer type. These rugs are often distinguished by the use of an eight-pointed star and undulating leaves. Real Kirmanshah rugs are fifty years old or older and are cherished as semiantique possessions because few rugs, except for local use, are made in that section today. Kirman rugs are often mistaken for true Kirmanshahs.

Chinese

Next to Persian rugs, Chinese rugs are in the greatest demand in the United States. In China rug making is concentrated in three areas — Tientsin, Peiping, and Kalgan. In China, unlike Persia, rugs are made in large modern workrooms under supervision rather than in small communities by individual families or groups of families. Chinese rugs are easily distinguished. A large portion of the background is usually of a solid color — a lustrous shade of gold, tan, copper, rust, rose, or blue. The Chinese weaver is content with four or five colors in contrast to the dozens of colors used in Persian rugs. Designs are usually concentrated in the corners with or without a border, and take the form of twin fish (symbol of marital happiness), a canopy (emblem of sovereignty), a lotus flower (symbol of purity), or a dragon (symbol of the universe and the Emperor). Enduring in structure, simple in pattern, and lustrous in texture, Chinese rugs have always been a favorite with Queen Anne and Chinese Chippendale furniture. Of all Oriental rugs, they are perhaps the most adaptable to modern-type homes in the higher price range.

Turkish

The rug industry in Turkey suffered greatly when the Armenians and Greeks, who made most of these rugs, were persecuted and had to vacate their homeland. Most of the rugs made today are *Anatolian* in type, and are woven in bold colors. Other Turkish rugs are known by the names *Hereke*, *Siva*, and *Smyrna*.

Caucasian

In a section of Russia north and east of Iran where 700 years ago Genghis Khan ruled nearly all of the known world, many rugs are still produced. The designs reflect the bold, sturdy, and wild character of the people who weave them and of the bleak, precipitous peaks in the mountainous area in which they are woven. Caucasian rugs are marketed under the names *Shirvan*, *Kabestan*, *Kazak*, and *Karabagh*. With the exception of Karabagh, Caucasian rugs are made in scatter sizes and runner lengths.

Turkestan or Turkoman

These rugs come from the great sandy desert in central Asia. The most familiar type is commonly called *Bokhara*. These rugs usually have a background of plum or red with natural, black, or yellow in large areas. Octagonal or tribal seals are evenly placed over the surface. These rugs may also be used with modern furniture.

East Indian

Many American and British companies maintain workrooms in Indian cities, such as Amritsar, Srinagar, Agra, and Lahore. Many of the weavers in these workrooms are descended from the weavers of the familiar Cashmere shawl. Because of a famine in 1840, the weavers of Cashmere fled their homeland and settled in or near Amritsar. As the demand for shawls declined, these immigrants turned their attention to rug weaving. The designers of Indian rugs try to reproduce in their designs the world about them. Flowers, plants, and even roots are used as motifs. The colors are somewhat lighter than those used in Persian rugs. Unlike Persian rugs, Indian rugs are sold under trade names designated by the importers.

To meet the demand for solid-color rugs, a recent development in rug weaving in India is a rug with a beautiful sculptured surface. Rugs of this type, which may also be had in patterns, are sold as *Taj Mahals*. Some Indian rugs may be copies of the delicate and expensive French Aubussons or Savonneries. The Indian rugs are beautiful for bedrooms and retail at a price much lower than the French originals. The Indian rug market is an expanding one.

Make a few mental notes about Oriental rugs, and plan a trip to a large store to see some of them. Ask a competent salesperson to explain the characteristics of these fine rugs. You will have an experience similar to that of visiting a large art gallery. Each rug will tell a story.

✦ WHAT CARE DO ORIENTAL RUGS REQUIRE?

Although most Oriental rugs will take much abuse, they require special care. Many people in the Orient remove their shoes before treading on a rug — not because of the friction but because of the grit which becomes embedded in the rug and cuts the strands of wool. It is advisable to use a suction-type vacuum cleaner on an Oriental rug at least once a week with a carpet-sweeper cleaning daily. It is also recommended that rugs be taken out doors several times a year, laid on the grass, and beaten firmly but not hard with an old-fashioned carpet beater. This operation should be repeated on the back of the rug. Once a year an Oriental rug should be cleaned by a reliable rug cleaner.

SUGGESTED ACTIVITIES

1. From a department store or a floor covering store, obtain samples of battleship, inlaid, and printed linoleum and asphalt tile. Study their characteristics until you are able to easily identify each.

2. Compare linoleum with asphalt tile as to cost, use, durability, and beauty.

3. Ask a qualified person to give a talk on how to lay linoleum.

4. Ask a qualified person to give a talk on how to lay asphalt tile.

5. Arrange a field trip to a store, and have a salesperson in a rug department show you Oriental rugs. Ask him to tell you something about the history of each rug.

6. For class use, obtain swatches of Wilton, Axminster, velvet, and chenille rugs including as many variations of each weave as possible. Study the pile, back, and weave of each swatch until you can easily identify the weave. Also study each swatch to determine its quality.

7. Visit a rug department, and ask a salesperson to show you various machine-made rugs. Ask the salesperson to tell you about the quality, size, and price of the rugs.

8. List the types of rugs you would consider for your home, and give the approximate price of each. Tell why you have chosen the rugs listed.

9. Identify the kinds of rugs you have at home or in your homemaking department.

10. Supposing that new rugs are needed, measure your living room and dining room at home or at school, and tell what size rug each room should have if the rug is to come within six to twelve inches of the wall. Check on standard rug sizes and broadloom widths in making your recommendations for sizes.

11. Measure a rug that is now being used without a rug cushion under it. In a store's rug department, compare the cost of suitable rug cushions made of various materials.

12. List the uses you make of linoleum at home and in your homemaking department.

CHAPTER 3

What guides will give you greater satisfaction in buying furniture?

BUYING furniture represents a large item in the family budget, and taking time to study all you can about buying it will pay dividends. You will need to consider wise buying practices in determining where, when, and how to buy. You will need to know what kinds of woods are used in furniture construction, and how these woods compare in appearance, durability, and cost. You will need to understand how the construction of upholstered furniture affects its durability. And last but by no means least, you will need to consider how the different pieces you buy will harmonize with other pieces and with the decorative idea of your room or home. Since furniture styles and furniture selection and arrangement are discussed in Unit Six, pages 159–198, this chapter will deal primarily with how to judge durability in furniture and with what practices are advisable in purchasing it.

★ WHAT ARE SOME GOOD PRACTICES TO FOLLOW WHEN BUYING FURNITURE?

If you know furniture values thoroughly, there may be times when the following general buying practices will not be applicable. Even with experience, however, some furniture qualities are difficult to judge. Since furniture is usually a lifetime investment, it is advisable to buy with caution.

1. Buy from a well-established firm. So-called "wholesale" houses claiming to sell to individuals at cost may merely be offering good bait to unsuspecting customers.

2. Shop at several different stores before you buy in order to compare prices, quality, guarantees, payment plans, and the like.

3. It is usually best to buy furniture as it is needed rather than because it is a bargain. In this way you avoid the temptation of buying something that is not quite right merely because it appears to be inexpensive.

4. If you buy at sales, judge values carefully. Compare sale pieces with regular stock. At the semiannual sales of reliable firms, you may be able to get regular stock at a considerable saving. However, in some sales, inferior furniture may have been bought to sell at a sale price.

5. Read any and all labels on furniture carefully, and study and ask questions about the wood and the type of construction used in order to determine whether or not a piece is a good buy for the price. Save all labels and guarantees.

6. If furniture is not labeled, ask the salesman to write a description of it on the sales ticket. For instance in buying an upholstered chair, you will thus have a record of such items as

kind of wood, kind and number of springs, type of filling, and various points about the upholstery fabric should the chair not wear as well as you expect and should you desire to make a complaint.

7. Paying cash for furniture eliminates any carrying charges and prevents any tendency to overbuy. However, it is sometimes necessary and desirable to buy furniture when payments must be deferred. Be sure that you understand the store's credit plan thoroughly, and weigh your ability to pay any extra charges.

8. Decide on the general style of furniture you want before you go to a store to shop. That is, if you want a sofa, decide whether it should have straight or curved lines, whether it should be massive or delicate in design, whether it should be largely of exposed wood or completely upholstered. If you want an upholstered chair, decide whether it should be high or low in style, and rectangular or curved in line. If you are buying dining room chairs, decide whether they will be traditional, Colonial, or modern; whether they will be of a dark or a light wood; whether they will have wood or upholstered seats. Decide what colors will interest you most. The more information you can give the salesperson about your needs, the more apt he will be to show you what you want. Also, you will be less likely to make a poor choice in style and color.

✦ WHAT ARE THE FAMILIAR FURNITURE WOODS?

Kinds of wood

A hardwood is desirable for furniture because it does not dent easily with long wear. Walnut, mahogany, hard maple, oak, and gumwood are the five hardwoods most commonly used for furniture. Other hardwoods are beech, birch, ash, and cherry. Walnut and mahogany in the natural finish are found in traditional furniture; maple, walnut, pine, cherry, and oak are found in Early American furniture, and modern furniture may come in any of the woods in a natural or bleached finish. Oak and mahogany are the woods most frequently bleached. Walnut is sometimes bleached. Birch is naturally light.

Gumwood, which dents more easily than some of the other hardwoods and which is also less expensive, is often stained to resemble mahogany, walnut, or other woods. If you place a piece of mahogany next to a piece of mahogany-stained gumwood, you will soon be able to distinguish between the two. Gumwood has very fine pores which can hardly be seen; mahogany and walnut have much larger pores. The finish on the mahogany-stained gumwood will not be nearly so rich and mellow as that on real mahogany or walnut. Nevertheless, gumwood is very satisfactory in moderate and low-priced furniture, making good styling and good construction possible at a reasonable price.

Solid wood or veneer

Furniture may be constructed of solid wood or veneer. Solid wood is most suitable when rugged lines or intricate carving is desired. When the surface of solid-wood furniture is worn, it can be refinished by planing or sanding, and it will not chip off. Veneering is cut in thin sheets from the sections of a tree where growth is irregular and where a beautiful pattern or design is formed. These thin sheets are glued over plywood which may be of varying thicknesses, three, five, and seven ply being the most common. A good, well-applied veneer may be stronger than solid wood of the same thickness, but a veneer poorly applied over a weak base may deceive the buyer. Good veneers are less likely to shrink or swell than solid woods, and they will not warp. Though veneers cannot be carved, inlays of brass, silver, mother-of-pearl, and contrasting woods can be beautifully worked out.

Labels

In cooperation with the Federal Trade Commission, the furniture industry has established rules regarding statements which can be made on labels and in advertising as to the kind of wood used in furniture. If only one wood is used, a piece of furniture may be designated by that wood, but if more than one wood is used, the label or advertising must list all of the woods. However, manufacturers and retailers are not forced to use labels. If they so desire, they can avoid a misstatement about woods used by making no statement.

Some tags indicate the type of finish used without mentioning the kind of wood on which the finish was applied. Glancing at a tag and not noticing the word "finish," a customer might think a piece of furniture was made of mahogany, walnut, or whatever finish the tag indicates.

The American Walnut Manufacturers Association and the Mahogany Association promote the use of tags designating the kinds of wood used in walnut and mahogany pieces. A piece may be labeled "solid" if all exposed surfaces are of solid walnut or mahogany. It may be labeled "genuine" mahogany or walnut if the frame parts, such as legs, posts, and panels, and the plywood faces for the larger surfaces, such as panels and table tops, are also made of mahogany or walnut.

✳ WHAT WILL YOU LOOK FOR IN WOOD FURNITURE?

Kind of wood and finish

Suppose you want to buy wood furniture without upholstery. Find out what kind of wood has been used, so that you can judge its quality in relation to the price of the piece of furniture. Then examine the finish on the wood. Rich mellow finishes are expensive because much hand rubbing is necessary to produce the effect. Avoid a finish with streaks and patches or a muddy appearance which

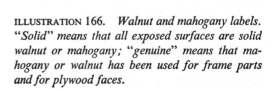

ILLUSTRATION 166. *Walnut and mahogany labels. "Solid" means that all exposed surfaces are solid walnut or mahogany; "genuine" means that mahogany or walnut has been used for frame parts and for plywood faces.*

does not allow the grain of the wood to show through. If the finish becomes sticky when rubbed warm with a finger, it is not durable.

Solidity

Next examine the piece for solidity. Make sure that a chair or a table or a chest stands firmly on a level floor. If a chair has a caned seat, make sure that the weave of the cane is very close because caning will stretch out of shape quickly if it is not firm. Rush-bottom seats are stronger than caned seats, but as the rush dries out, the chair tends to squeak.

Joints

Examine the underside of furniture to determine how the joints are made. Joints that are merely glued together will loosen during changes in temperature. One very good joint is the *dowel* joint shown in Illustration 167A. A dowel pin with spiral glue grooves will hold more firmly than a smooth dowel pin, and a double-dowel joint having two pins and two holes is more substantial than a single one. The *mortise and tenon* joint is a bit more substantial and more expensive than the dowel joint, though either type indicates good construction. In the tenon joint a wood tongue or tenon is cut away at the end of the piece to be joined. It is glued and inserted into a socket or mortise. This type of joint is shown in Illustration 167B.

Support for joints

All good furniture — tables and chairs especially — will have triangular corner block supports under the upper surface to hold the joints in place. These blocks should be glued and screwed rather than nailed or glued in place. In less expensive pieces, nailing may be satisfactory if the wood has not been splintered or cracked. Corner blocks (see Illustration 169) are necessary especially if the chair or table has no stretchers.

ILLUSTRATION 167A. *A double dowel joint*

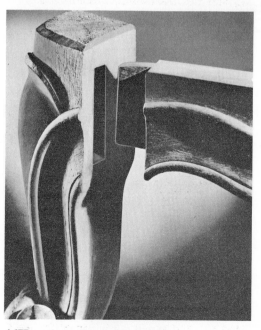

167B. *A mortise and tenon joint*

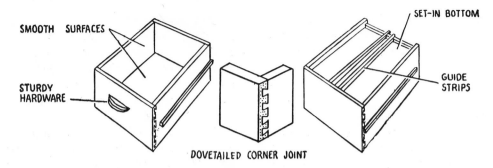

ILLUSTRATION 168. *Points to look for in judging drawer construction*

Operation

If a table or chest has drawers, pull out a drawer and examine it. A well-constructed drawer will have a *dovetail* joining rather than a straight nailed joining. The teeth in the joining should interlock very closely, poor fit being a mark of shoddy construction. Turn the drawer upside down, and see that the four side rails extend below the bottom of the drawer. If the drawer is wide, make sure that there is a groove or guide strip in the center of the bottom to prevent slipping and jamming. If the drawer is narrow and long, make sure that there are guide strips at the sides. Both the inside and outside of the drawer should be shellacked, varnished, or waxed to protect the wood from warping during temperature changes and to make the drawer more easily cleaned. There should be a wood panel beneath the drawer to make it dustproof and to prevent interference from objects in drawers above or below.

Pull out table legs and leaves and open and close doors to check for smooth operation.

Examine hinges, pulls, and brackets. Be sure that the hinges on drop-leaf tables are strong and that drawer pulls are firmly attached. Avoid buying furniture with thin stamped-out metal drawer brackets and thin metal hinges that will not withstand wear.

★ WHAT POINTS WILL YOU LOOK FOR WHEN YOU BUY UPHOLSTERED FURNITURE?

Comfort

If you are buying an upholstered chair or sofa, try it out by sitting down in it to see whether it is comfortable, easy to get in and out of, and the right height from the floor. Most furniture is designed for the average person, five feet eight inches tall. The chair seat is usually 18 inches from the floor in front, slanting down slightly at the rear. The average depth of the seat is 19 or 20 inches, although some cushioned seats are 22 or 24 inches deep. A chair back should be at least 17 to 19 inches above the seat to support the shoulder blades; the arms of a chair are usually comfortable when they are about 7 inches above the chair seat. A living room should have at least one comfortable upholstered chair for a man and one for a woman, in addition to a sofa and pull-up chairs. A large living room may have one or two love seats and additional lounge or pull-up chairs.

Construction

The exposed wooden parts of a chair or sofa may be of any of the woods previously mentioned. If these parts are carved, be sure that the carving is not so shallow as to cheapen the appearance of the furniture. The unexposed wooden parts should be of a kiln-dried hardwood to prevent warping and to prevent screws or nails from loosening. In expensive chairs, ash, hard maple, or birch may be used, and in moderate-priced furniture, gumwood, elm, and mahogany may be used. In less expensive furniture, softwoods, such as poplar and pine, are frequently used. The joints and corner blocks should be constructed like those described under wood furniture on page 259. A frame that is merely nailed and glued together is not durable.

Springs give a chair resilience. The most popular types of spring construction are illustrated. All springs should be made of heavy-gauge steel tempered and treated to eliminate rust. The first chair has *coil construction*. A high-grade chair may have as many as 16 coils, but 9 or 12 are more common. The springs should be tied in eight directions for comfort and durability. Coils should be supported by closely woven burlap webbing crossed under each spring and tightly stretched. *Covered coil springs* come in units of different sizes for seat platforms, chair backs, and cushions. *Flat zigzag springs* often are found in lightweight chairs; they have somewhat less resilience and strength than coil springs.

Filling and *padding* cover the seat platform, back, arms, and cushions in spring construction. The best filling is curled horsehair or horsehair blended with rubberized moss. Dacron fiber filling is popular in moderate-priced furniture; it is resilient, nonallergic, and light in weight. Hogshair, sisal, and excelsior are used in less expensive furniture. Layers of cotton felt, or a thin layer of foam rubber between the filling and a firm muslin cover, give a chair or sofa firmness.

Many people prefer solid *foam-rubber construction*. Foam rubber makes neat corners and retains its shape. Cushion covers tend to creep on foam rubber, but this feature may be overcome by reversing the cushions regularly. Upholstered foam-rubber chairs should be shampooed and not dry-cleaned, because

ILLUSTRATION 169. *Cutaway diagrams showing upholstered chair construction. Important features to have in upholstered furniture are sturdy hardwood frame; firm, well-attached webbing; closely placed, tempered steel springs; and good-quality upholstery material.*

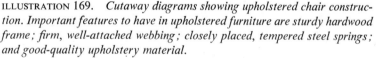

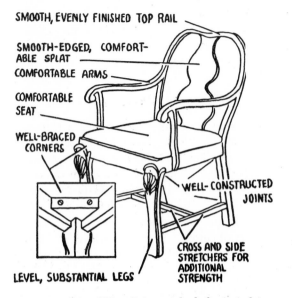

SMOOTH, EVENLY FINISHED TOP RAIL

SMOOTH-EDGED, COMFORT-
ABLE SPLAT

COMFORTABLE ARMS

COMFORTABLE
SEAT

WELL-BRACED
CORNERS

WELL-CONSTRUCTED
JOINTS

CROSS AND SIDE
STRETCHERS FOR
ADDITIONAL
STRENGTH

LEVEL, SUBSTANTIAL LEGS

ILLUSTRATION 170. *Points to look for in judging the construction of a wood chair*

dry-cleaning fluids cause rubber to become sticky. Heat will also harm foam rubber. Down-filled cushions are comfortable, but they must be kept fluffed up to look attractive. A combination of feathers and down will outlast all-down cushions.

Furniture *upholstery fabrics* include cotton, denim, tapestries, plastics, pile fabrics, brocade, and damask. An upholstery fabric must be firmly woven and fairly heavy to hold up well. Nubby effects and threads floating on top catch on nails, rings, and rough objects. Smooth solid-color upholstery is difficult to clean. Figured fabrics, textured weaves, and brocaded effects in nylon, cotton, rayon, and blends treated for soil- and stain-resistance stay fresh looking.

Plastics such as Saran and Trilok and plastic-coated fabrics such as Naugahyde are excellent upholstery fabrics in rooms receiving hard use.

✴ WHAT WILL YOU LOOK FOR IN SPRINGS AND MATTRESSES?

When you buy a mattress and springs, quality and comfort come before cost. The average person spends a third of each day in bed, so a good mattress is a "must." Many people, attracted by bargain sales, buy mattresses that wear out in a year. A good mattress and companion springs will remain as firm as new for ten to fifteen years. Many people use springs and mattresses a lifetime.

If you buy a good mattress you can prolong its life by turning it from side to side and end over end at least once every few weeks. Foam-rubber mattresses need not be turned.

Points to check in a mattress

Mattresses come in a bewildering assortment of sizes, prices, types of construction, and covers. Do not judge a mattress by its cover. A pretty cover may contain inferior materials. Don't just sit on a mattress to test it; stretch out on it. Buy from a reputable dealer. Save all guarantees.

FIRMNESS: Firmness means equalized support so that the body will not sag in any one spot. Almost all brands come in a number of degrees of firmness.

SIZE: Popular mattress sizes for adults are 72 by 39 inches for a single bed and 72 by 54 inches for a double bed. King-sized or custom mattresses may be purchased in longer lengths and various widths and shapes.

CONTENT: In general you have a choice of innerspring, foam-rubber, curled-hair, and cotton-felt mattresses.

TUFTING AND BORDERS: Tufting prevents the contents of a mattress from shifting. Tufting must go through the mattress from top to bottom. The mattress sides should be reinforced so that there will be no sagging or bulging if a person sits on the edge.

HANDLES: For easy turning, a mattress may have plastic, steel, or cord handles firmly attached to facilitate handling.

The *innerspring* mattress is the most popular and the most difficult to judge. One type innerspring mattress has several hundred small coils individually wrapped in heavy fabric cylinders, each stitched to its neighbor. Other types have fewer and larger coils held together by metal bands and springs. The number of coils is not as important as the quality of materials and construction. A heavy and a light person should be able to sleep on a double mattress without causing a noticeable sag. For solid support, the topping should be at least 50 per cent hair.

The *foam-rubber* mattress should be about four inches thick and have a ticking covering secured to the foam rubber at enough points to prevent slipping. Foam-rubber mattresses are not tufted.

A *hair* mattress is made of hair from horses, cattle, or hogs. If a large percentage is hogs' hair, the mattress will be less resilient and may pack and sag.

A *cotton-felt* mattress is suitable for lightweight people, but will not stay firm for long.

Points to check in springs

Covered box springs are preferable to uncovered springs because they are dust free; they protect sheets and blankets from tearing, and they give a neater appearance to a bed. Foam-rubber mattresses should have deeper box springs than those used with innerspring mattresses, to compensate for the less thick foam-rubber mattress. Uncovered bedsprings are less expensive and they are satisfactory under innerspring mattresses. They should be made of heavy-gauge metal tied in four or eight directions, or bound with metal on small horizontal springs. Flat or expandable bedsprings are less resilient and less desirable than good coil springs.

SUGGESTED ACTIVITIES

1. Make a list of the reliable furniture stores in your community (a) for moderate-priced furniture and (b) for high-grade furniture.

2. Make a collection of furniture displays from newspapers and magazines. Study the information given about the furniture for helpfulness in buying.

3. Make a list of woods used for traditional, Early American, and modern furniture. Exhibit samples and become familiar with different woods.

4. Ask the industrial arts teacher to demonstrate how the different kinds of joinings used in furniture are made.

5. Check the construction of one of your dining-room chairs according to the diagram in Illustration 170.

6. Check the construction of an upholstered piece of furniture according to Illustration 169.

7. If you have an heirloom, such as a very old table or a chest of drawers, compare its construction with that of a modern piece.

8. Visit a furniture store where a well-informed salesman will show you high-priced, moderately priced, and inexpensive furniture which he considers good buys for the money. Ask him to explain his reasons in each instance.

9. Assemble newspaper clippings of mattress advertisements on the bulletin board. Discuss in relation to experiences you have had with mattresses.

10. Discuss various upholstery fabrics in relation to ease of care. Compare nylon upholstery with other fabrics that have been treated to give ease of care.

CHAPTER 4

What should you look for in buying household textiles?

NEW DRAPERIES, a new slip cover, or new upholstery may lift a room from the commonplace into the decorator's realm. The satisfaction your purchases give will be determined by your ability to select pleasing colors, textures, and designs in harmony with other furnishings in your home, and by your knowledge of quality and durability in fabrics. Durability in textiles is affected by the type of fiber used, the way the yarn and cloth are made, and the kinds of finishes applied.

★ **HOW DO PROPERTIES OF FIBERS AFFECT END USE?**

Textile engineers must know the limitations and possibilities of each fiber under varying conditions in order to produce a yarn for a particular end use.

Fibers are classified generally as natural and synthetic (man-made). Natural fibers include *animal* fibers such as silk and wool, and less frequently used ones such as alpaca, camel's hair, and mohair. *Vegetable* fibers include cotton and linen as well as hemp, jute, and ramie. *Mineral* fibers are asbestos and glass. Practically all other fibers in use come from a test tube. Rayon was the first synthetic fiber to be produced. Acetate followed, and then nylon, Orlon, Dacron, Dynel, Acrilan, Arnel, Fortisan, Verel, Saran, and many other fibers which are of fairly recent origin. *Plastics* are nonwoven materials and come in unsupported and supported forms; i.e., with or without a woven or knitted cloth laminated to the plastic.

No one fabric can be said to be the best. By knowing the properties of each and the end use, textile engineers can blend two or more fibers to produce the best fiber for any particular use. By understanding something about fiber properties yourself, you can become a better judge of household textiles.

Silk has natural luster, length, and strength, and is wrinkle-resistant and possesses good draping qualities. One of silk's disadvantages is high cost.

Wool is warm, resilient, and cleans easily; but wool will shrink, pill, and attract moths unless it is specially treated.

Cotton is absorbent, hygienic, soft, and launders well, but cotton absorbs grease and releases lint. Heat and dirt are harmful to cotton. Cotton fabrics wrinkle easily.

Linen is naturally lustrous, cool, absorbent, and hygienic, but is expensive and wrinkles easily unless it is treated. Linen is unequaled for embroidery and cutwork.

ILLUSTRATION 171. *Ease of fabric care would be a major consideration in a typical Early American bedroom decorated in this fashion.*

Rayon is inexpensive and may be made to resemble almost any other fiber, but is naturally weak — more so when wet. It has low dimensional stability but good draping qualities. Fortisan is an extra strong rayon, but it comes only in very fine yarns and will not take dark dyes.

Acetates and *triacetates* have many of the qualities of rayon, but look more like silk and drape better than rayon. Acetate will dissolve in nail polish remover; it is thermoplastic, making permanent pleats or crinkle possible.

Nylon is the most abrasive-resistant of all fibers, and adds strength to other fibers in blends, provided the percentage of nylon is sufficient. In a nylon-wool blend for carpet, for instance, nylon should make up 30 per cent of the blend to add greater wear to wool. A lower percentage will greatly strengthen rayon, because rayon is a weak fiber.

The *polyester fibers* (of which Dacron was the first) can be used to produce extremely crease-resistant fabrics. Even a little polyester fiber will increase cotton's resistance to creasing. In a Dacron-wool blend, over half of the blend must be Dacron to improve the crease resistance of wool, because wool is naturally resilient and crease resistant.

Orlon, Acrilan, Dynel, Creslan, and Zefran belong to the *acrylic* family. A close kin, Verel, is classified as a *modacrylic*. All of these fibers are soft, bulky, warm, resilient, and shrink- and moth-resistant, but they are affected by heat. A hot iron will cause the fiber to shrink and pucker. Dynel and Verel are the most fire-resistant of the acrylic family.

Fiberglas is the only fireproof fabric. For this reason it is popular for theater curtains and on shipboard. Fiberglas comes in clear bright colors and attractive prints. But Fiberglas will disintegrate under any kind of friction. Glass fibers are never blended.

To create a fabric that is absorbent, textile researchers might start with cotton. If the end fabric needs greater strength, they can add some nylon. If it needs to be crease-resistant, Dacron fibers can be added. This is what we mean by engineering fibers toward end use.

✳ HOW DOES THE YARN AFFECT THE FABRIC?

No matter what fiber is used, it must be spun or twisted into yarn before it is woven into cloth. Fabrics that are to withstand much strain should be made of tightly twisted yarns. Loosely twisted yarns will absorb more moisture which is important in toweling, but they are also likely to cause a fabric to stretch or shrink. They produce a more lustrous fabric than tightly twisted yarns, but they may cause a fabric to catch and pull on rough objects. Irregularities in the size of yarns tend to reduce durability in a fabric, since the pull of heavy yarns against light yarns is likely to cause the light ones to break. Yarns that are even in size produce a smoother as well as a stronger fabric.

✳ HOW DOES THE WEAVE AFFECT THE CLOTH?

The kind of weave used has a decided effect on the durability of cloth, since various weaves differ considerably in their strength. The kind of weave used also affects the appearance and texture of a fabric. Let us review the common weaves you may have learned in textile study.

Plain

This weave is produced by the regular lacing of a filling yarn over and under the warp yarns across the width of the cloth. It is the weave used in hand-loomed, home-spun materials and in imitations of them woven on power looms. If the plain weave is close and the yarns are firmly twisted, the material will be durable. Household textiles having this weave are scrim, taffeta, gingham, muslin, voile, sailcloth, organdy, and some cretonnes.

Basket

In this variation of the plain weave, two or more filling yarns cross two or more warp yarns. The basket weave is a rather loose weave, and the threads are apt to pull out of place. Thus fabrics of this weave are not suitable for slip covers. Monk's cloth is an example of this weave.

Corded

Still another variation of the plain weave is made by having some of the yarns heavier than others. The warp yarns may be heavier than the filling yarns, or the filling yarns, heavier than the warp yarns. This variation weakens the fabric, since the small threads may break where they cross the heavier threads. Examples of the corded weave are rep, poplin, faille, and bengaline.

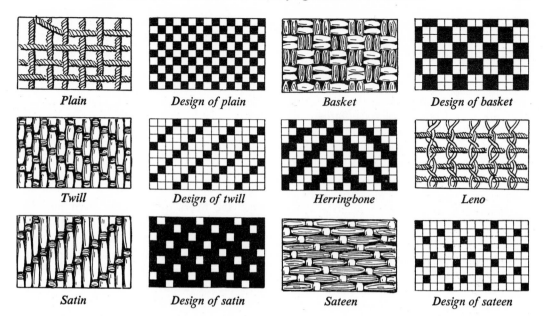

Plain | Design of plain | Basket | Design of basket

Twill | Design of twill | Herringbone | Leno

Satin | Design of satin | Sateen | Design of sateen

ILLUSTRATION 172.   *Sketches of common weaves and diagrams of the design produced are shown.*

Twill

This is an interlacing of one filling yarn over groups of warp yarns with each filling yarn splitting the group of warp yarns crossed in the row above. The progression of one yarn at the point of interlacing in each row produces a diagonal effect as shown in Illustration 172. This weave produces a most durable cloth. Typical fabrics are gabardine, denim, and drill.

Herringbone twill

This variation of the twill weave is sometimes called the chevron weave. Warp and filling threads are interlaced so that the diagonal runs in one direction for a while; then it reverses and runs in the other. The design produced resembles the spine of a herring. This weave is very durable. Fabrics of this weave may be found in solid colors and prints for slip covers and draperies.

Leno or gauze

In this weave pairs of warp yarns are made to cross over each other as the filling yarns pass through. An openwork effect is produced which lets the light pass through. This weave is used in fabrics for glass curtains, such as marquisette and curtain madras.

Satin

In this weave, at irregular intervals, one filling yarn passes over one warp yarn and then under a number of warp yarns. Thus expanses of warp yarn float over the filling yarns on the right side of the material, giving a smooth lustrous effect. Materials made by this weave are less durable than those of the twill type. Silk and rayon satin are examples of this weave.

Sateen

This is a variation of the satin weave in which the filling yarns float over the warp yarns. The sateen weave may not be as firm as the satin weave. Cotton sateen, plain or printed, is an example of this weave.

Rib

Piqué is a typical example of the rib weave which is made of one set of warp yarns and two sets of filling yarns. One set of filling yarn forms a rib and then runs behind the next rib which is formed by the other set of filling yarns. In some piqués a filler yarn runs between the rib and its backing, thus making the ribs more prominent.

Other weaves

These include the *lappet* weave found in dotted swiss when the dots appear to be embroidered into the fabric and both sides of the cloth look practically alike, and the *swivel* weave found in dotted swiss when the extra filling thread which makes the dots is clipped at each edge of the dot. Some so-called dotted swisses have printed dots rather than woven dots. When the dots are woven with the lappet or swivel weave, they will not wash off. However, the cut threads in the swivel-woven dots may pull out easily. When you buy dotted swiss or dotted voile curtains, make sure that the dots are woven rather than printed on, so that the curtains may be washed.

The various figured patterns woven into cloth are made with a Jacquard or a dobby attachment. Among these are *huckaback* used for huck toweling, *damask* in which the pattern shows on both sides, and *brocade* in which the design is formed only on one side. Another weave is the *pile* weave which uses two sets of warp threads, one being looped up in weaving to form the pile and the other being woven with the filling threads in a twill weave to hold the pile in place. Examples of fabrics with cut pile are velvet

and velveteen. Turkish toweling (terry cloth) is an example of uncut pile. Blankets are made with a double-cloth weave using two sets of warp threads and two sets of filling in two interlaced fabrics woven at the same time.

✴ HOW DO FINISHES AFFECT THE CLOTH?

Dyeing

A cloth may be dyed after it is woven, or either the fibers or the spun yarn may be dyed before weaving takes place. *Yarn or fiber dyeing* is much more likely to be color-fast than piece dyeing. *Vat-dyed* and *vat-printed* cottons and linens are fast to washing and some are fast to sunlight. Synthetic fibers that are guaranteed colorfast are *solution dyed*. Rayons so dyed are labeled by such terms as Coloray, Jetspun, and Colorspun; acetates, by such terms as Celaperm, Color-sealed, and Chromspun.

Printing

Direct printing — passing the cloth between rollers, each set carrying a separate color — is the most common method. *Screen printing*, which is actually stenciling through a sheer, strong material tightly stretched over a frame, is used for almost all large designs. *Warp printing* is printing the warp before the filling yarns are woven in, to give a more subtle pattern. *Flock printing* is accomplished by printing an adhesive in any desired motif and blowing minute filaments into the adhesive to produce a suedelike finish. *Discharge printing* is done by passing the cloth between rollers that carry a chemical to discharge dye in a regular design. *Resist printing* is the opposite of discharge — a design is printed with a paste or wax that resists color on the rollers. The waxy substance is later dissolved.

Sizing

Loosely woven fabrics are sometimes sized to give the appearance of better fabrics. The sizing will wash out, leaving a flimsy, loosely woven fabric. Silks are sized or weighted with a metallic substance to give extra weight; extra metallic weighting in time will rot the silk. When silk carries a *pure dye silk* label, it has only the minimum of weighting.

Napping

Napping is a finish given to materials to make them fluffy and warm. Blankets and flannels are examples of napped household textiles. Excessive napping weakens the fabric.

Crease resistance

Dacron or other polyester fiber is frequently blended with other fibers to increase resistance to wrinkles. Cotton, linen, or rayon may be blended or treated with synthetic resins to increase resistance to wrinkling.

Shrinkage resistance

Shrinkage control is important in selecting materials for curtains, draperies, and slip covers. The most familiar label for cottons is *Sanforized*, and for rayons, *Sanforlan*. Fabrics with these labels will shrink no more than one per cent. Wool may also be made shrinkage resistant.

Water repellency and spot resistance

Upholstery and slip cover fabrics may be treated to repel water and to resist spots and soil. Familiar labels indicating this finish are *Syl-mer, Cravenette*, and *Zelan*.

Other finishes

Cotton is *mercerized* or treated with caustic soda to give it more luster and strength. Or-gandy and sheer fabrics may be given an antiwilt finish under such labels as *Wat-a-set* and *Bellmanized*. A *permanent glaze* is often given chintz and sateen. A *coating of phosphorescent and fluorescent pigments* can be applied to a heavy-weight material to illuminate it at night, as a safety measure or for theatrical effects. A *permanent moire finish* may be given to acetate fabrics because acetate is thermoplastic. Other finishes are *moth-, mildew-*, and *fire-resistant*. These are only some of the special finishes that add beauty or strength to fabrics, or make them safer to use or easier to maintain.

✶ HOW MAY YOU TEST FOR FADING AND SHRINKING?

After reading the labels, if you are in doubt about using any material for slip covers, draperies, or curtains, it is wise to buy an eighth of a yard and test it for fading and shrinkage. To test a piece of cloth for *colorfastness to washing*, launder a sample of it, dry the sample in the shade, and compare the sample with the original piece. To test for *colorfastness to sunlight*, cut a piece of cloth about two inches by four inches in size, and place it between two pieces of glass, covering half the cloth with heavy black paper. Place the glass-covered cloth in a sunny window for a week or two. Compare the color of the two halves. The piece will not fade appreciably in the sun if little or no difference can be noticed in the two halves.

To test for *shrinkage*, cut a piece of cloth at least two inches wide and three inches long, and outline the edges on paper. Wash, dry, dampen, and iron. Lay the patch on the original outline. The amount of shrinkage can be estimated for a drapery length by finding the amount of lengthwise shrinkage per inch and multiplying by the number of inches in the drapery.

★ WHAT FABRICS WILL YOU CHOOSE FOR CURTAINS?

Curtain fabrics should be sheer enough to let in the light but opaque enough to give privacy. The weave should be firm so that the yarns will not slip. If the yarns in curtain materials separate when you pull your thumbnail over them, the cloth will not hold up under many launderings. All of the newer curtain materials require care in washing, drying, and ironing. Fabrics may melt under a hot iron and hems may pucker.

Curtain materials are made of the following fibers:

FIBERGLAS: Glass fiber fabrics have high resistance to the effects of sunlight and heat. They are flame resistant, will not shrink, and need no ironing. But their abrasive resistance is low, so Fiberglas curtains must be hung where they will not rub against Venetian blinds, radiators, or window sills. They must be washed carefully by hand. They should not be wrung, twisted, or pinned with clothespins. Fiberglas comes in mesh, marquisette, and bouclé weaves, and in prints.

FORTISAN: Fortisan is an extra strong rayon yarn used mainly in the warp with other fibers in the filling. Curtains of 100 per cent Fortisan are very sheer, because Fortisan comes only in fine denier yarns and in light colors. Fortisan fabrics will wear, drape, and clean according to the other fibers in the blend. Lurex, a metallic, tarnishproof, washable thread, is often used with it. Fabrics made of all Fortisan require gentle washing and ironing. Dry cleaning is usually recommended.

DACRON: Dacron is wrinkle resistant and is not readily harmed by sunlight. It will not shrink or stretch, but is sensitive to heat so hot water and a hot iron should be avoided. Wrinkles set by heat or pressure are difficult to remove. Dacron washes easily and needs little or no ironing. It is especially good for ruffled curtains.

ARNEL: Arnel resists shrinkage and wrinkles, and it may be ironed with a warmer iron

than most synthetics; steam ironing is preferable. It comes in sheer weaves.

ACETATE: Acetate comes in pure white and in colors. Colors in most acetates are fast because they are solution dyed. Acetate has excellent draping qualities and its draping quality may improve when used in blends. A hot iron or nail-polish remover will melt acetate.

RAYON: Rayon curtain fabrics have many of the qualities of acetate and require about the same care. They do not have the dimensional stability of curtains made from many other fibers, especially when wet. Rayon lace and net curtains are available.

NYLON: Nylon is less popular as a curtain fabric than as an upholstery fabric. Dacron and other fibers are less expensive, and wrinkles are less likely to set.

COTTON: Perhaps the most popular cotton curtain fabric is *organdy*. Permanent-finished organdy sheds soil, retains its crispness, and makes attractive bedroom and cottage curtains. *Lawn* is similar to organdy but less sheer. *Dotted Swiss* is similar to lawn but it has woven or printed dots. Printed dots wear off. *Dimity* is a sheer fabric with a heavy yarn used at intervals to give the effect of stripes or bars. *Marquisette*, although a traditional cotton weave, is also available in Dacron, rayon, Arnel, and acetate curtain fabrics. *Net* is a sheer material with a fine or a coarse mesh. Most cotton fabrics have a permanent finish so that they retain their freshness after washing.

★ WHAT FABRICS WILL YOU CHOOSE FOR DRAPERIES?

Choose plain-colored drapery material if you have a great deal of pattern in your walls or rugs. With lace curtains, solid colors in rayon rep, brocade, damask, faille, poplin, or taffeta offer the best choices. If you live in an industrial city where draperies soil quickly, by all means buy colorfast, washable material. Drapery material may be less firmly woven than slip cover material because it is **not subjected to friction. However, it must be**

POTTERY DISH INSPIRING
FABRIC AT LEFT

MODERN
DESIGN

MODERN
TEXTURED
FABRIC

FORMAL
TRADITIONAL   INFORMAL
DESIGN   DESIGN

CHINESE VASE INSPIRING
FABRIC AT LEFT

ILLUSTRATION 173.   *Drapery fabrics. The style of design in these fabrics makes them suitable for rooms of corresponding character. In some instances design inspirations are shown.*

durable in order to withstand the cutting effect of the dust it will collect, the more or less constant exposure to the sun, and the cleaning or laundering necessary. Many draperies hang better if lined, and a lining lessens the possibility of fading caused by the sun. Familiar drapery materials and their characteristics are as follows.

BROCADE: A fabric woven on a Jacquard loom in an allover design of raised figures or flowers. The design appears only on the right side. This elaborate fabric is appropriate only in formal rooms.

CHINTZ: A light-weight, plain-weave, cotton material, usually printed and glazed. A permanent-finish chintz will keep its glaze after washing. Chintz is appropriate for bedroom windows and in rooms with Early Colonial or French Provincial furniture.

CRASH: A plain-weave fabric with coarse uneven yarns and rough texture, available in plain or printed patterns. It may be made of linen, cotton, rayon, or a mixture.

CRETONNE: A firmly woven material with plain or twill weave. Cretonne is similar to chintz, though usually heavier and printed with larger designs. It is appropriate in many different types of rooms.

DAMASK: A material with a woven pattern which shows on both sides. The pattern is flatter than in brocade and only one or two colors may be used. Drapery damasks come in cotton, rayon, silk, wool, or a combination of any of these. Damask is appropriate for formal rooms.

GABARDINE: A firmly woven material with a twill weave. It is usually plain colored, though it may be printed. Cotton gabardine is excellent for slip covers.

GINGHAM: A plain-weave, cotton material woven in checked, striped, or plaid designs. Yarns are dyed and then woven to produce the design effect. Gingham is attractive at cottage windows in kitchens, bedrooms, and the like.

MOIRÉ: A rayon or silk material with a waved or watered effect engraved on the surface by rollers. The pattern is not permanent except on acetate rayon. Materials of this type are effective with eighteenth century or traditional furniture.

MONK'S CLOTH: A basket-weave, heavy cotton material usually found in beige and tan but available in other colors. Sometimes flax or jute is mixed with the cotton. The fabric is best suited for informal rooms.

PAPER: Though not a woven fabric, readymade paper draperies are available. They are inexpensive, colorful, and easily cared for, but of course, they must be replaced much more frequently than fabric curtains.

PERCALE: A closely woven, plain-weave cotton material available in plain colors and prints. Small allover printed designs of the old calico type are especially appropriate in Early American or cottage-type homes.

PIQUÉ: A heavy rib-woven cotton with ribs running the length of the cloth. Piqué may be smart in bedrooms for draperies, bedspread, and dressing table covers.

PLASTIC: An unwoven sheet-form material or a plastic-coated woven fabric. The new plastic materials may look like chintz, cretonne, or taffeta at the window. Plastic drapery material may be washed in the washer, rinsed by hand, and shaken but never wrung. Wrinkles dry out. Fabrics may be noninflammable and impervious to mildew, acid, alkali, and alcohol. Some types will not crack, rot, or peel.

REP: A heavy material with heavier yarns used for the filling threads than for the warp threads, producing a horizontal ribbed effect. It may be made of silk, rayon, cotton, wool, or a mixture.

SATEEN: A soft material with a high luster, usually used as a drapery lining. Printed sateen is good for bedroom draperies.

TAFFETA: A crisp, plain-weave, rayon or silk material usually with a sheen to its surface. Taffeta draperies require an elaborate setting and luxurious furnishings.

VELVETEEN: A pile-weave cotton material for use in formal rooms. Velveteen collects lint and dust very easily.

✳ **WHAT FABRICS WILL YOU CHOOSE FOR SLIP COVERS?**

Slip-cover fabrics must be firmly woven, have a smooth surface, and be guaranteed against shrinkage and fading. If there is any doubt about the fabric's shrinking, wash it before it is made into slip covers. The following fabrics are recommended: chintz, corduroy, cretonne, damask, denim, gabardine, gingham, percale, piqué, rep, sailcloth, and ticking.

If slip covers will not stay in place, strips of Velcro tape may be attached to the underside of the slip cover and upper side of the sofa or chair cover.

✳ **WHAT MATERIALS WILL YOU CHOOSE FOR UPHOLSTERY?**

Suitable upholstery textures for *formal rooms* are damask, brocade, and velvet, preferably in nylon. For *less formal rooms*, chintz, cretonne, sailcloth, corduroy, and rep are suitable. These materials will wear longer and clean better if they have a soil- and water-repellent finish. Frieze wears well but it tends to be scratchy, and slip covers creep on frieze upholstery. Supported plastics such as Naugahyde come in smooth and textured finishes, and are excellent upholstery materials where there are children or where a room has hard use.

✳ **WHAT WILL GUIDE YOU IN BUYING BED LINENS?**

Sheets

When you buy sheets you will want to know something about types, sizes, fabrics, and construction.

Fitted and flat *types* of sheets are available. Fitted sheets make bedmaking easier, and they stay smooth. The lower sheet has four fitted corners, and the upper sheet, two.

Mattresses vary in thickness, so sheets should either be bought or altered to fit the mattress. A fitted sheet that is too tight will cause the mattress to buckle, and it will also wear out faster. If sheets are bought in the proper *size* for the mattress, the sleeper will be more comfortable and bedmaking will be easier. A sheet should be long enough to tuck in on all sides, and should adequately cover the blanket at the top — about 24 inches wider and longer than the bed. It is easy to find the right sheet quickly in the linen closet if the corners of single, double, and special sheets are marked with different colors of bias tape.

The *torn size* indicated on the sheet label is not the actual size. Hems and shrinkage must be subtracted from the *torn size*. A sheet marked 108 inches in length will actually be about 96 or 98 inches long. You should choose sheets that are torn rather than cut, so that the hems will be even and smooth after laundering.

FLAT SHEET SIZES

Bed	Mattress size	Sheet size
Crib	27″ × 52″	42″ or 45″ × 77″
Youth	33″ × 66″	54″ × 90″ or 99″
		63″ × 99″ or 108″
Twin *	39″ × 75″ or 76″	72″ × 99″ or 108″
Double *	54″ × 76″	81″ × 99″ or 108″
		90″ × 108″

* For extra long beds, sheets 120″ long are available.

Fabrics for sheets include muslin, percale, knitted cotton or nylon, and woven nylon. Muslin sheets come in light, medium, and heavy weights. Light and medium weights are preferred for home use — heavy weights for hospitals. Percale sheets are made of finer cotton yarns than muslin sheets. Percale sheets are easier to handle in home laundering than muslin sheets.

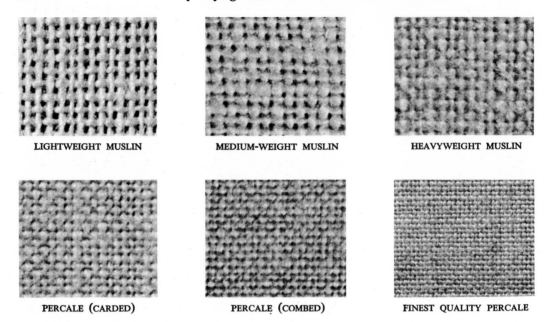

| LIGHTWEIGHT MUSLIN | MEDIUM-WEIGHT MUSLIN | HEAVYWEIGHT MUSLIN |
| PERCALE (CARDED) | PERCALE (COMBED) | FINEST QUALITY PERCALE |

ILLUSTRATION 174. *Magnified weaves of various types of sheets. To make a thread count, weave is magnified under a pick glass, and the number of lengthwise and crosswise threads in an inch of the material are counted. The count per square inch is then calculated.*

Muslin and percale sheets are judged by tensile strength and thread count. Tensile strength refers to the number of pounds of pull necessary to break an inch of fabric as recorded on a special machine. For instance, a sheet with a tensile strength of 70 is stronger than one with a tensile strength of 50. A heavyweight muslin sheet may have a thread count per square inch of 140; a medium-weight, a count of 128; a lightweight, a count of 112. Fine percale sheeting will have a thread count of 180; extra fine percale sheeting will have a thread count of 200 or more. Make a habit of reading labels on sheets.

Whether you choose sheets in white, in pastel tints, in prints, or with decorative borders is a matter of taste. Hemstitched sheets, however, tend to pull loose at the hems before the sheets wear out.

Knitted sheets come in cotton, nylon, and nylon blends. Knitted sheets with fitted corners are excellent for cribs, and many adults like knitted sheets in winter. Woven nylon sheets are lightweight and easily laundered, and require little or no ironing. Ticking on pillows will show through nylon pillow cases.

To test for sizing, rub the sheet between the fingers over a dark fabric. Heavily sized sheets become flimsy after laundering and are not good values. Examine the selvage for firmness and flatness.

Sheets will wear longer if they are: used in rotation; not ironed with an extremely hot iron; reversed from top to bottom; not laundered with strong bleaches; and folded differently each time after ironing. A fold pressed in the same place week after week causes a break along the fold before the sheet is worn out.

You should allow six sheets for each bed in regular use — two on the bed, two in the wash, and two on the shelf. If you customarily drop the top sheet and put a fresh one only on the top, or if you have an automatic washer and dryer, you can get along with four sheets per bed.

Pillowcases

Usually pillowcases should match the sheets in color and material. Standard-sized pillows are 21 by 27 inches, and require pillowcases 42 by 36 inches or 42 by 38½ inches. Larger pillows (22 by 28 inches or 23 by 29 inches) require pillowcases 42 by 36 inches, 45 by 36 inches, or 45 by 38½ inches. When on a pillow, the pillowcase should be a little wider than the pillow and 6 to 10 inches longer.

Blankets

When you buy a blanket, you want one that will look attractive, give warmth, and wear well. Blankets and sheets come in companion colors and prints. In blankets you have a choice of wool, Acrilan, Orlon, rayon, nylon, Dynel, cotton, and any number of blends. The fiber is of less importance than the construction. A lightweight, closely woven blanket with a deep fluffy nap will give more warmth than a firm, heavy blanket. It is the air held in the nap that gives warmth.

Fiberwise, a good wool blanket is the warmest for cold climates, but wool blankets are expensive. Blankets of Acrilan, Orlon, and blends of rayon-nylon-Orlon are lightweight, mothproof, and warm; they do not shrink or felt in laundering. Cotton or lightweight rayon blankets are summer blankets. The original nap soon packs down. An all-rayon blanket, even in a heavy weight, will not stay as fluffy as a wool blanket or one made of an acrylic fiber such as Acrilan,

Dynel, or Orlon. The binding on a blanket should be firmly stitched. Acetate and rayon bindings are soft, but nylon bindings wear longer without fraying. Read blanket labels to determine fiber content and care.

Blanket sizes are: twin beds, 65 by 90 inches; double beds, 80 by 90 inches. Blankets for an extra large bed are 90 by 108 inches. Blankets should always be long enough to stay tucked in at the foot of the bed.

Electric blankets come in sizes 66 by 84 inches for twin beds, 72 by 84 inches for full-size beds, and 103 by 86 or 95 inches for king-size beds. Electric blankets should *never be dry cleaned*. They must be washed according to directions that come with the blanket.

When washing blankets, spot-clean with a liquid detergent. Fill washer with *lukewarm* water and add detergent. A fabric conditioner will keep the blanket fluffy. Immerse blanket in sudsy water and let stand five to fifteen minutes, depending upon degree of soil. Wash *one minute*. Spin water from washer. Rinse well in lukewarm water. Spin three minutes, and hang over two parallel lines to dry. Dry on a clear day in the shade. Shake well, press bindings with a steam iron, and fold. Spray with moth preventive, cover, and store in a cool closet. If you use a dryer to dry a blanket, read directions carefully. It is always a good idea to toss three or four bath towels in the dryer with the blanket, and to remove the blanket before it is too dry. To avoid wrinkles, do not allow a blanket to remain in the dryer after it is dry.

✶ WHAT LINENS ARE NEEDED FOR THE BATHROOM?

Towels for the bathroom include bath towels, face towels, guest towels, and finger towels. Bath towels and face or hand towels receive the hardest wear, so they should be carefully chosen for durability. Guest and

Closeness of background weave indicates strength.

Examine background weave in plain portion.

Feel towel to judge weight and grade.

Fast selvage   Overcast selvage   Hemmed selvage

Hold towel to light to judge closeness of weave.

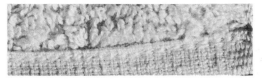

Look for close-stitched hems, backstitched at ends.

finger towels may be as fancy as your taste permits.

Bath towels

Bath towels must be *absorbent* as well as *durable*. Cotton Turkish toweling or terry cloth woven with uncut loops in a pile weave is used. The thickness and spacing of the loops on the surface control absorbency, and the ground weave controls the wear. The loops should be set close together, and for absorbency, they should be moderately long. Loops that are quite long may catch and pull out, thus lessening durability. The background must be firm and close to hold the loops in place. As shown in Illustration 175, the background weave can best be studied by examining it where there are no loops near the hem or the selvage. Other ways to judge closeness of weave and durability of selvages and hems are also shown in the illustration. Elaborate patterns in the weave usually increase cost and may decrease absorbency if large unlooped spaces are part of the design.

In addition to weave, size is important in buying towels. Extra-large bath towels may be 36 by 68 inches or 38 by 72 inches. These are more like beach towels. Some people like to wrap up in one after a shower, but towels of this size cost more than other towels and are heavy to handle in laundering. Large bath towels are 24 by 40 up to 28 by 52 inches. It is wise to stock some of the large towels for the men in the family. Medium-sized towels are 20 by 40 up to 22 by 44 inches. This is the size for general family,

ILLUSTRATION 175. *Ways of judging quality in terry towels. A close weave and well-constructed selvages and hems indicate durability.*

hotel, club, and hospital use because the lighter weight of the towel makes it easy to launder at home and economical to have laundered. Face towel sizes are 16 by 26 up to 18 by 36 inches. The most popular size in wash cloths is 12 by 12 inches, and bath mats, 22 by 36 inches.

Face towels

Many people prefer terry cloth face towels, and of course quality is judged as it is for bath towels. Hand towels also come in a variety of other fabrics. They may be all linen, all cotton, linen and cotton, or rayon and cotton. The weave may be plain, twill, damask, or of the type commonly known as huck. The roughness of huck makes it quite absorbent. Hand towels like bath towels are not compulsorily labeled. If there are no labels, you are your own judge of quality. Linen or linen and cotton absorb moisture better than all cotton; rayon is the least absorbent. A close weave, the absence of excess sizing, firm selvage edges, and if readymade, substantial hems with close stitching are points to look for in judging quality.

✦ WHAT LINENS ARE NEEDED FOR THE DINING ROOM?

Many people prefer using plastic or cork place mats for informal meals, especially breakfast and lunch. Linen or lace rather than cork or plastic mats are used for the formal luncheon. Be as individual as you care to be in serving informal meals, but when you serve a formal dinner, a tablecloth is proper. The cloth may be damask, lace, or embroidered linen. Organdy or unusual tablecloths are better for the buffet supper.

Damask tablecloths are made of linen, cotton, rayon, or a combination of any of these fibers. A good quality of linen gives the most satisfactory cloth because it wears well, launders well, does not absorb stains readily, does not leave lint, and retains its whiteness. However, it is expensive. The better cotton damask tablecloths are given a permanent finish to resemble linen. These cloths are crisper and less full of lint than untreated cotton cloths. Rayon cloths may have a higher luster than cotton and linen ones, and are less easily laundered. Combinations of linen and cotton produce a moderately priced cloth which may be more satisfactory than a poor-quality linen cloth.

Damask comes in standard tablecloth sizes or by the yard. You save a little when you buy damask by the yard and make the hems yourself. When used to describe damask, *single* and *double* refer to the number of filling threads used. Single damask has one set of filling and one set of warp yarns, while double damask usually has 50 per cent more filling threads than warp threads. Cotton damask is usually, though not always, a single damask. A single damask will have a maximum of 175 yarns per square inch, and a double damask, a minimum of 185 yarns per square inch. A low-count double damask will not be as durable as a high-count single damask because too many loose yarns float on the surface. A good double damask is firm and durable, and the pattern is more distinct than in single damask.

After washing, a tablecloth should extend at least 6 inches below the edges of the table all around. Damask widths are 36, 45, 54, 58, 64, 72, 80, and 90 inches, the most popular width being 72 inches. Your own table will determine the length you need. Readymade cloths come in the following sizes: 36 by 54, 45 by 54, 54 by 54, 64 by 72, 72 by 90, 90 by 108 inches. Napkins come in the following sizes: 24 by 24, 22 by 22, 20 by 20, 18 by 18, 15 by 15, and 12 by 12 inches. The most usual size for dinner napkins is 22 by 22; for breakfast napkins, 18 by 18; for tea or luncheon napkins, 15 by 15; and for tea napkins, 12 by 12 inches.

✴ WHAT LINENS ARE NEEDED FOR THE KITCHEN?

Kitchen towels should be at least 18 by 30 inches in size. An all-linen dish towel is absorbent, lint free, drys quickly, and keeps a good color. However, long-fibered linen towels are expensive. Short-fibered towels are less expensive, and when closely woven, they are fairly durable. A part linen and part cotton towel which contains at least 25 per cent linen has greater absorbency than an all-cotton towel. To be labeled "pure linen," an article must contain no less than 95 per cent linen. If an article contains less than 5 per cent, it may not carry any kind of linen label. Beware of the label "pure-linen decoration" because only the colored thread in the border may be the decoration.

To determine whether or not the towel is heavily sized, hold it over a dark surface and rub it between your fingers. The sizing will become powdery and fall out. To determine the closeness of the weave, hold the towel up to the light and note how closely the yarns are woven. A loosely woven towel will give poor service. Also check for firm selvages and durable hems if the towel is readymade.

✴ WHAT WILL YOU INCLUDE IN YOUR HOUSEHOLD LINEN WARDROBE?

The following lists suggest a rather generous number of the various kinds of household linens which may be needed. The number of bedroom linens is based on changing the two sheets on a bed each week, and the list allows two towels for each person per week. The number may be reduced when only one sheet

per bed and one towel per person are laundered weekly. The number in the family, where meals are served, and the amount of entertaining done will affect the number and kinds of table linens needed. The estimate for napkins is low, since it is assumed that paper napkins will be used for many meals.

FOR THE BEDROOM (*per bed*)

6 sheets
3 pillowcases for each pillow
2 mattress covers (1 permissible)
2 mattress pads (1 permissible)
2 blankets
1 quilt
2 spreads (1 permissible)

FOR THE BATHROOM

6 bath towels per person
6 face towels per person
4 washcloths per person
2 mats

FOR THE DINING AREA

2 tablecloths (lace, damask, or linen)
3 sets of place mats and napkins
2 dozen tea napkins
4 breakfast cloths (if breakfast and luncheon are eaten in the kitchen)
2 or 3 bridge cloths
1 dozen dinner napkins

FOR THE KITCHEN

1 to 2 dozen dish towels
4 pot holders
2 or 3 dishcloths

SUGGESTED ACTIVITIES

1. Collect fabrics which show as many of the different weaves as possible. Mount them attractively on the bulletin board, and label each.

2. List materials suitable for ruffled curtains, and obtain as many samples as possible for your own collection.

3. List materials suitable for tailored curtains, and obtain several samples.

4. On the bulletin board, mount and label drapery fabrics suitable for (a) an Early American living room, (b) a modern living room, (c) a traditional living room, (d) a dark dining room, (e) a boy's bedroom, and (f) a girl's bedroom.

5. Check the suitability and the wearing qualities of household fabrics in your homemaking department.

6. Obtain a piece of drapery fabric for testing. Cut two pieces four inches square. Test one for colorfastness to sunlight and the other for shrinkage. Mount a labeled exhibit of your tests on the bulletin board.

7. Collect materials that might be used for slip covers. Rate them excellent, good, or poor according to their probable ability to withstand friction.

8. Plan a renovation project with your mother or with your classmates for replacing draperies, making a slip cover, recovering a chair, or the like at home or at school.

9. For class study, secure from a department store three well-labeled sheets — one heavy muslin, one lightweight muslin, and one lightweight percale. Read the labels, and explain what the specifications mean. Tell what sheet would best meet your family needs and why.

10. Ask a well-informed salesperson to show the class various qualities of blankets, explaining why the qualities differ. Be sure that you understand what any labels on the blankets mean.

11. Investigate the cost, use, and care of electric blankets.

12. Bring to class a bath towel of poor quality and one of good quality. Compare the selvages, loops, weaves, and appearance of the two towels when held up to the light.

13. Observe the towels in your home, and decide whether they are good or poor in quality.

14. Study the household-linens section of a mail-order catalogue. From the information given about towels, sheets, and the like, pick the best buy so far as durability is concerned.

15. Using swatches of damasks, compare linen, linen-finished cotton, untreated cotton, and a mixture of cotton and linen for (a) ease in laundering, (b) appearance after laundering, and (c) the amount of lint shed.

16. Take an inventory of all the linens you have at home, and compare the list with the suggested lists on page 278. If improvements can be made in any of the lists, make suitable suggestions.

17. Measure the length and width of your sheets at home, and separate them according to double- or single-bed widths and long and short lengths. Mark the top-hem ends with different colors of thread to indicate single—long; single—short; double—long; and double—short. Dark blue may indicate double—long, and light blue, double—short. Red thread may indicate single—long, and pink, single—short.

CHAPTER 5

What will determine your choice of tableware?

WHETHER you live in a cottage in the country or in a large house in town, in a one-room apartment or in a spacious hotel suite; whether you go to school, work at home, or work out of the home, your activities are all centered around three meals a day. Since a great deal of time and money go into preparing these meals, they should be served as attractively as possible. Dinnerware, silverware, and glassware need not be expensive to be attractive, but thought should be given in applying the principles of design to their selection and use. If your best dinner service is to be fine china, you will naturally choose fine crystal, sterling silver, and a linen or lace cloth. However, your table will be in just as good taste if you choose ten-cent-store dishes with good lines and colors appropriate to the room, inexpensive but well-proportioned glassware, and a simple pattern in plated silver. Your tablecloth may be a pretty cotton, rayon, or linen crash. Pleasing lines and harmonious colors may be found in all grades of china, and interesting shapes and designs are available in all grades of silver and glass. Delicate china is out of place with thick, heavy glass; sturdy pottery does not belong with fine crystal. In planning your table service, remember the principle of harmony as it applies to color, texture, line, shape, and idea.

The evening meal should be anticipated by every member in the family not merely to satisfy his hunger but to enjoy happy companionships. To be thoroughly satisfying, the evening meal should be eaten in comfort, with leisure, and in an atmosphere of contentment and sociability. Clean attractive linens and interestingly chosen dinnerware, glassware, and silverware contribute to this atmosphere.

You may have occasion now to help your mother buy some new dinnerware or glassware, and in the not too distant future, you may be thinking of what your own home needs will be for serving enjoyable meals.

✳ WHAT DINNERWARE WILL YOU CHOOSE?

Dinnerware includes two general classifications — porcelain and earthenware. Earthenware may be subdivided into semiporcelain and pottery, semiporcelain being a superior ware to pottery. The first porcelain was made in China, hence the term *china* for general dinnerware. However, more properly speaking, china refers to porcelain ware.

Porcelain

This ware is made from kaolin or China clay and other materials such as feldspar.

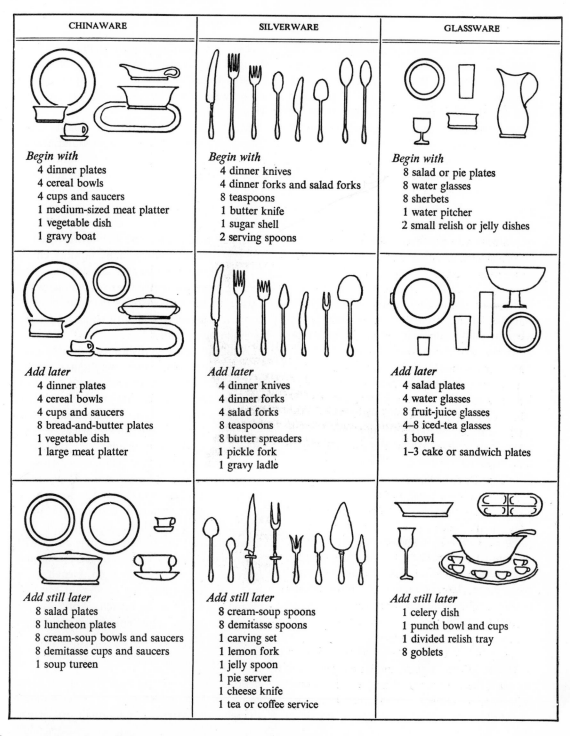

CHINAWARE	**SILVERWARE**	**GLASSWARE**

Begin with
- 4 dinner plates
- 4 cereal bowls
- 4 cups and saucers
- 1 medium-sized meat platter
- 1 vegetable dish
- 1 gravy boat

Begin with
- 4 dinner knives
- 4 dinner forks and salad forks
- 8 teaspoons
- 1 butter knife
- 1 sugar shell
- 2 serving spoons

Begin with
- 8 salad or pie plates
- 8 water glasses
- 8 sherbets
- 1 water pitcher
- 2 small relish or jelly dishes

Add later
- 4 dinner plates
- 4 cereal bowls
- 4 cups and saucers
- 8 bread-and-butter plates
- 1 vegetable dish
- 1 large meat platter

Add later
- 4 dinner knives
- 4 dinner forks
- 4 salad forks
- 8 teaspoons
- 8 butter spreaders
- 1 pickle fork
- 1 gravy ladle

Add later
- 4 salad plates
- 4 water glasses
- 8 fruit-juice glasses
- 4–8 iced-tea glasses
- 1 bowl
- 1–3 cake or sandwich plates

Add still later
- 8 salad plates
- 8 luncheon plates
- 8 cream-soup bowls and saucers
- 8 demitasse cups and saucers
- 1 soup tureen

Add still later
- 8 cream-soup spoons
- 8 demitasse spoons
- 1 carving set
- 1 lemon fork
- 1 jelly spoon
- 1 pie server
- 1 cheese knife
- 1 tea or coffee service

Add still later
- 1 celery dish
- 1 punch bowl and cups
- 1 divided relish tray
- 8 goblets

ILLUSTRATION 176. *Build your dinner service gradually.*

Fine bone ash is sometimes used, hence the term *bone china*. Porcelain is fired at very high temperatures. Because it becomes hard, nonporous, and nonabsorbent, it is called vitrified. It may be distinguished from all other wares by its translucency when held up to the light. When tapped, porcelain or china has a clear resonance. A break in porcelain is clear, nonabsorbent, and the same color all the way through. A few famous porcelains are Royal Doulton, Spode, Wedgwood, Haviland, and Lenox. Porcelain is the finest of all wares, is expensive, and demands fine accompaniments.

Earthenware

Fired at less high temperatures, earthenware is distinguishable by its opaqueness when held up to the light. When tapped it has a flat sound. A break in earthenware is rough, porous, absorbent, and of a dull color. Very high-quality earthenware dishes made of refined clay and fired to a hard state at high temperatures (but still somewhat porous) are referred to as *semivitreous* or *semiporcelain* ware. Two well-known names associated with this fine quality are *Spode* and *Wedgwood*. Poorer qualities of semiporcelain make up many of the popular-priced dinnerware sets.

Pottery

Made from coarsely sieved clays which are not fired to a hard state, pottery is opaque, uneven, and sometimes only partially covered with glaze. Its crude charm, obtained by texture, color, and decoration, calls for an informal setting.

Plasticware

Plastic dishes entered the dining room through the back door. They were first used in canteens and cafeterias; then more attractive designs found their way to breakfast nooks and patios. The designs of Russel Wright and George Nelson have promoted plastic dishes to a position of importance in dinnerware. They fit easily into our informal way of living.

Most plastic dishes in the quality class are made from a chemical compound known as melamine. This material is lightweight, durable, thermoplastic (can be heat molded), and will not bend or ignite. The compound may be colored and printed, and may be given a glossy, dull, opaque, or translucent finish. Plastic dinnerware lends itself well to the type of entertaining many families enjoy. It is at home with pewter or stainless steel serving pieces, with ovenware or woodenware, with reed table accessories (such as baskets, trays, and servers), and with bamboo, plastic, or linen place mats.

Although plastic dishes can be dropped without shattering, they may crack. When exposed to high temperatures they will melt or burn. Sharp knives may mark the surface, but since the material is nonporous, stains will not show in the tiny crevices. Plastic plates have "built-in insulation" and never become as cold as porcelain, earthenware, or pottery plates. They do not attract lint or dust. Most plasticware may be washed in automatic dishwashers in temperatures up to 270 degrees Fahrenheit. You should first, however, read the directions that come with your plasticware. Coffee and tea stains may be removed with an oxygen bleach, sold under various trade names. Avoid abrasive cleaners and chlorine bleach. Abrasion will leave scratches, and chlorine produces a chemical reaction.

Ovenware

Porcelain-glazed pottery and stone china come in an assortment of oven-to-table shapes and sizes — individual casseroles, platters, bowls, and large serving dishes. The colors and designs are permanent to heat. Oven-to-table dinnerware makes it possible to serve piping hot food, and eliminates extra serving dishes.

✸ HOW WILL YOU CARE FOR YOUR CHINA?

You may be a very careful and thorough dishwasher, but do you know how to take the best care of fine china? Sudden changes in the water temperature or very strong soap may cause any kind of dinnerware to crackle or craze. Grease and acids left on dishes overnight may leave stains. Delicate cups should not be hung by their handles, because the handle is the weakest part. Cups should never be stacked in groups of more than two. Cups are safest placed flat on a narrow shelf or tray. Plates should be dried one at a time, because the rim under the plate is rough and may scratch the top of another plate. Real porcelain or extra fine earthenware plates should be stacked with a small circle of felt between each plate. Dinnerware that is not used frequently may be stored with plastic covers over each stack of plates and over each nest of bowls. Flat covers may be used over cups.

✸ WHAT GLASSWARE WILL YOU CHOOSE?

When you buy glassware, you will need a basis for judging its quality. Knowing something about how it is made will be helpful.

Ingredients used in glassmaking

Glass is one of the oldest of man-made materials. It is made by combining sand or silica with an alkali, and heating the mixture until a molten liquid is formed. Other ingredients may be added, depending upon the kind of glass being made. Glass containing a great deal of *lime* is the least expensive to manufacture; it is brittle, and is usually pressed into shape. It is not suitable for cutting or etching. Glass containing a great deal of *lead* is expensive to manufacture, but a glass with a high luster suitable for fine tableware is produced. Glass may be colored by the addition of certain chemicals to the other ingredients.

Shaping

Glass is shaped either by *blowing* or by *pressing*. In shaping pressed glass, the molten liquid is forced into an inner mold which may be hinged or in one section. An inside mold or plunger forces the hot glass into the crevices of the center mold. Large pieces are frequently molded in two or more sections which are then fused together. The seams of the mold may be visible on the finished glass. In hand-blown glass, the beauty of the shape depends upon the blower's skill. A mass of hot glass on the end of a blowpipe is blown and gently rotated until the desired shape is formed. Whether thin or thick, hand-blown glass is more fragile than pressed glass. It is also more lustrous. *Crystal* glass — the very best quality of plain glass — has a clear bell-like ring when it is tapped.

Decorating

Glass may be decorated by one of four methods: etching, cutting, carving, and hand coloring as shown in Illustration 177.

In addition to these four general methods, various other treatments produce surface variations. *Frosted* glass is produced by sand blasting; *bubble* glass, by filling liquid glass with air bubbles; *cameo* glass, by fusing a light glass over a dark glass and incising or carving through the first layer; *hobnail* glass, by pressing small bumps over the surface.

Famous names

Other terms associated with glass are the following: *Sandwich* glass, which was manufactured very early in the United States and which is now an antique item; *Waterford*, which was originally made in Ireland and which is a cut glass with an iridescent finish; *Orrefors*, which is a Swedish glass that is modern and distinctive in design. The finest and most unusual glass made in America today is *Steuben* glass. Collections of Steuben glass are often exhibited in museums and art galleries.

Tests for quality

There are several tests for judging the quality of glassware. Hold the glass up against a white background. Good glassware is fairly clear and lustrous; poor glassware is slightly colored and cloudy. Feel the edges for

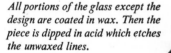

All portions of the glass except the design are coated in wax. Then the piece is dipped in acid which etches the unwaxed lines.

Enamel colors or liquid gold are painted on the glass. Then the color is fused to the glass by slow firing.

The design is cut into the glass by holding the piece against a rapidly revolving abrasive wheel.

ILLUSTRATION 177. *Four ways of decorating glass. Hand-colored (left), etched (center), and cut glass (right) are shown on this page. Carved glass is shown on page 285.*

All parts of the glass except those which are to receive the design are masked out with heavy tape. An abrasive is blown against the uncovered parts until it erodes the design.

a smooth even finish. Poor glass may have a rough or wavy edge. Tap the glass with your fingernail or with a pencil; good crystal will have a resonance. Study the design for grace, suitability of decoration, and evenness of application.

✴ WHAT FLATWARE WILL YOU CHOOSE?

Some of you may have already started a silver service. If you have not started one and if you know what pattern you want, perhaps you can accumulate a number of pieces as birthday and other gifts. If you are undecided about your final choice of a pattern, you might accumulate odd pieces, such as serving spoons, pickle forks, and other individual pieces in a pattern you like. Later you may buy the place settings in the same or in a harmonious pattern.

Your choice — whether stainless steel, sterling silver, or plated silver — will be determined largely by how much money you can afford to spend, your own tastes, and the general character of your home and dinner service. Stainless steel fits in well with a modern setting. Sterling silver and silver plate may be obtained in patterns for any setting. Sterling pieces are often passed down as heirlooms from one generation to another.

Stainless steel

Stainless steel flatware, once associated with hospitals and restaurants, has won a place at the dinner table on its own merit. Because steel is very hard and difficult to die-stamp, all knives, spoons, and forks were formerly of the same thickness throughout. Now pieces are molded for better "feel" and a more attractive appearance. Enamel inlay may be used effectively. Stainless-steel flatware harmonizes better with contemporary dinnerware and crystal patterns than with traditional styles.

Stainless steel has a grayish and cool appearance, resembling polished pewter more than silver. It has a high resistance to corrosion or rust and to food stains from eggs, mustard, and vinegar. It comes in lustrous, satin, and dull finishes. Most people prefer the satin finish.

Sterling

There is only one grade of sterling silver, the quality being established by federal law. All products marked STERLING must contain $92\frac{1}{2}$ per cent pure silver, the remaining $7\frac{1}{2}$ per cent being chiefly copper. Pure silver is too soft to be practical, so just enough copper is added to make it firm. Formerly staple pieces came in two or three weights, but now only the medium weight is produced in most flat-silver patterns.

ILLUSTRATION 178. *Various items in flat silver*

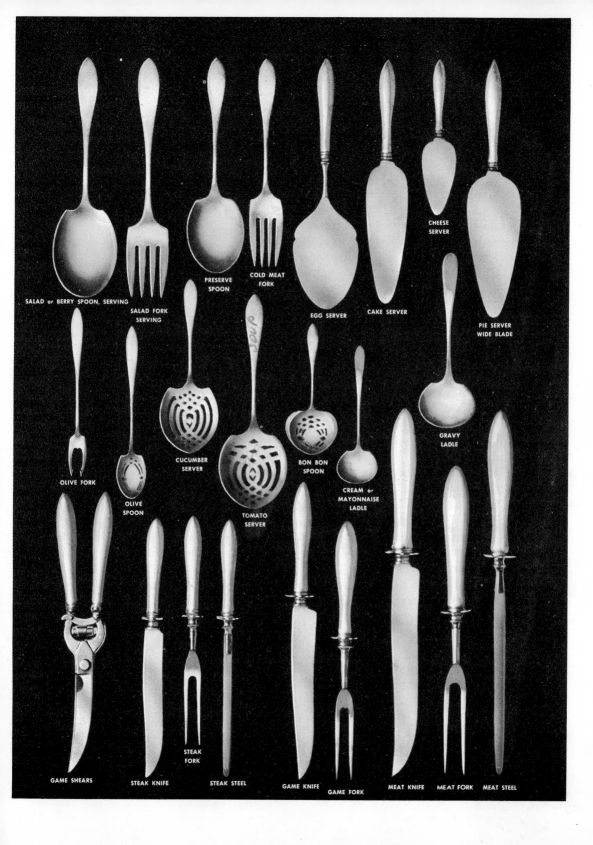

SALAD or BERRY SPOON, SERVING

SALAD FORK
SERVING

PRESERVE
SPOON

COLD MEAT
FORK

EGG SERVER

CAKE SERVER

CHEESE
SERVER

PIE SERVER
WIDE BLADE

OLIVE FORK

OLIVE
SPOON

CUCUMBER
SERVER

TOMATO
SERVER

BON BON
SPOON

CREAM or
MAYONNAISE
LADLE

GRAVY
LADLE

GAME SHEARS

STEAK KNIFE

STEAK
FORK

STEAK STEEL

GAME KNIFE

GAME FORK

MEAT KNIFE

MEAT FORK

MEAT STEEL

Plated silver

Plated silver refers to a base metal molded into spoons, knives, forks, bowls, trays, cups, and other pieces, upon which one or more coatings of silver is placed. Both the quality of the base metal and the weight of the plating affect durability. If you are buying plated silver, be sure to buy the heavily plated quality, because it is more durable, the choice of patterns is greater, the designs are more distinctive, and the teaspoons, tablespoons, and salad forks are reinforced at the points of greatest wear. The silver on lightly plated pieces will wear off in a very short time.

Points on buying

A 52-piece set of stainless steel or silver plate will include 8 forks, 8 knives, 8 cream-soup spoons, 8 salad forks, 16 teaspoons, 2 serving spoons, 1 butter knife, and 1 sugar spoon.

There is a wider choice of patterns in sterling than in silver plate or stainless steel. Sterling silver is usually bought by the place setting, which includes a knife, fork, teaspoon, cream-soup spoon, butter spreader, and salad fork. Many people prefer two teaspoons per setting, omitting cream-soup spoon or butter spreader.

In buying sterling, plated silver, or good stainless steel, it is well to buy the product of a reliable firm from a reliable dealer. The pattern you choose is largely a matter of taste. However, it is a good idea to check the pattern for comfort and balance in the hand; for strength of fork and spoon handles, fork tines, and bowls of spoons; and for well-attached stainless steel knife blades. Although fancy patterns may be popular when you buy your silver, remember that you may tire of this type much more quickly than you might tire of a simple pattern.

✶ WHAT CARE WILL FLATWARE REQUIRE?

Unlike good glassware, china, and linen which are usually saved for special occasions, sterling silver should be used and enjoyed. The initial small scratches soon wear down and result in a nice patina. Good quality plated ware will also withstand daily use. Silver should be rotated in its use to give all pieces equal wear.

Soiled silver will stain and tarnish if allowed to stand overnight. Silver should be washed in warm soapy water immediately after use, rinsed in hot water, and dried promptly with a soft towel. Keep a little silver polish near the sink, and rub stains off pieces used for eggs and salads after each meal. Avoid jamming silver in a rack, and dry each piece individually. When you polish silver, use a good silver polish and rub each piece lengthwise. A soft brush may be used if the design is raised. A tarnishproof silver chest provides a more convenient storage place for flat silver than that provided by rolls with individual pockets.

Stainless steel will not tarnish, but it should be washed promptly and dried thoroughly. Knives, either silver or stainless steel with soldered-on blades, should not be washed in an automatic dishwasher or allowed to stand long in hot water.

SUGGESTED ACTIVITIES

1. Examine a piece of porcelain, of semiporcelain, and of pottery. Tap each piece, and hold it up to the light. Describe the differences.

2. Visit a china shop or a china department to see what kinds of dinnerware are available. See what marks or labels are given on the bottom of the china. Make a list of the makers of porcelain, semiporcelain, and pottery.

3. Arrange a glass display showing as many different kinds of glass as possible, such as Sandwich glass, etched glass, cut glass, frosted glass, and so forth.

4. Write to well-known silver, china, and glass manufacturing companies for booklets on these wares. Study the information given, and report to the class any especially helpful buying hints.

5. At school and at home, look for examples of (a) blown glass and pressed glass, (b) sterling silver and plated silver, and (c) porcelain dishes and earthenware dishes. Explain the differences between the two types of each ware.

6. Compare a piece of crystal glass with a piece of inexpensive pressed glass. Notice the difference in the clearness and luster and in the sound when the glass is tapped.

7. Arrange a display of silver including as many of the following pieces as possible: (a) dinner knife and fork, (b) teaspoon, (c) dessert spoon, (d) serving spoon, (e) salad fork, (f) ice-cream fork, (g) cocktail fork, (h) after-dinner coffee spoon, (i) mayonnaise ladle, (j) olive fork, (k) butter spreader, (l) sugar spoon, (m) jelly server, (n) iced-tea spoon.

8. Investigate the methods used in caring for and storing silver at school and at home. Make suggestions for improvements which will save work and keep the silver ready for use.

9. Plan family gifts to provide missing links in the family silver.

10. Bring to class an interesting piece of china, silver, or glass. Tell the class how long it has been in your family, where it came from, or any other interesting information about it.

11. Collect pictures of attractively set tables.

12. Assemble as many different types of china, silver, glass, and place mats or tablecloths as you can, and arrange them into harmonious place settings.

13. Using the suggestions in Illustration 176, page 281, for a beginning table service, esti-mate the total cost of the pieces in a pattern you would like to have.

14. List ten of the most important points to remember in caring for dinnerware, silver-ware, and glassware.

SELECTED REFERENCES FOR UNIT EIGHT

BOOKS

Ehrenkranz, Florence A., and Inman, Lydia L., *Equipment in the Home.* Harper & Brothers, New York, 1959

Kiplinger's Family Buying Guide, edited by Arnold A. Barack. Prentice-Hall, Inc., Englewood Cliffs, New Jersey, 1959

Peet, Louise Jenison, and Thye, Lenore Sater, *Household Equipment.* John Wiley & Sons, Inc., New York, 1961

NOTE: Consult issues of *Consumers' Research Bulletin* and *Consumer Reports* too

CURRENT PUBLICATIONS

Write to the following addresses for current lists of literature and prices:

Appliances and Equipment

Frigidaire Division of General Motors Corporation, Dayton, Ohio

Good Housekeeping Bulletin Service, 57th Street at Eighth Avenue, New York 19, New York (*buying guides*)

Hotpoint Company, 5600 West Taylor Street, Chicago 44, Illinois

Kelvinator Division, American Motors Corporation, 14250 Plymouth Road, Detroit 32, Michigan

Money Management Institute, Household Finance Corporation, Prudential Plaza, Chicago 1, Illinois (*Your Equipment Dollar*)

The Tappan Company, Mansfield, Ohio

Westinghouse Electric Corporation, Electric Appliance Division, Mansfield, Ohio

Whirlpool Seeger Corporation, R.C.A. Whirlpool Home Appliances, St. Joseph, Michigan

Bedding and Household Textiles

Cannon Mills, 70 Worth Street, New York 13, New York (*sheets and towels*)

Dundee Mills, Inc., 1075 Avenue of the Americas, New York 10, New York (*towels*)

National Association of Bedding Manufacturers, 724 Ninth Street, N.W., Washington, D.C. (*bedding*)

Carpets and Floor Coverings

Consult list in Unit Five

Dinnerware

Copeland and Thompson, Inc., 206 Fifth Avenue, New York 10, New York (*Spode*)

Lenox, Inc., Mount Vernon 10, New York

Meaken & Ridgway, Inc., 129 Fifth Avenue, New York 3, New York (*Minton*)

Syracuse China Company, Syracuse 1, New York

Josiah Wedgwood and Sons, 24 East 54th Street, New York 22, New York

Flatware and Hollow Ware

The Gorham Company, Providence, Rhode Island

International Silver Company, Meriden, Connecticut

Oneida Silversmiths, Inc., Oneida, New York

Sterling Silversmiths of America, 551 Fifth Avenue, New York 17, New York

Towle Silversmiths, Newburyport, Massachusetts

Furniture

American Walnut Manufacturers' Association, 666 Lake Shore Drive, Chicago 11, Illinois (*Furniture Fashion Portfolio*)

Baumritter Corporation, 145 East 32nd Street, New York 16, New York (*photographic catalogues*)

Daystrom, Incorporated, Furniture Division, Olean, New York (*Family Center Kit*)

Drexel Furniture Co., Drexel, North Carolina

Fine Hardwoods Association, 666 Lake Shore Drive, Chicago 11, Illinois (*Know Your Hardwoods*)

Flex-O-Lators, Inc., Carthage, Missouri (*Guide to Buying Bedding and Upholstered Furniture*)

Hekman Furniture Co., Grand Rapids, Michigan

Heywood-Wakefield Company, Gardner, Massachusetts

Kent-Coffey, Lenoir, North Carolina

Mahogany Association, Inc., 666 Lake Shore Drive, Chicago 11, Illinois

Money Management Institute, Household Finance Corporation, Prudential Plaza, Chicago 1, Illinois (*Your Home Furnishings Dollar*)

National Retail Furniture Association, 666 Lake Shore Drive, Chicago 11, Illinois

North Hickory Furniture Company, P.O. Box 785, Hickory, North Carolina

The Seng Company, 1450 N. Dayton St., Chicago, Illinois (*Seng Furniture Facts*)

White Pine Furniture, Mebane, North Carolina

Widdecomb Furniture Company, Grand Rapids, Michigan

H. Willett, Inc., Louisville 11, Kentucky

9

Reduce
the cost
of maintaining
and improving
your home

ILLUSTRATION 179A. *Knowing how to make slip covers is one way to reduce the cost of improving your home.*

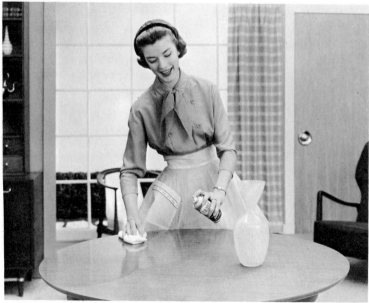

179B. *Keeping the furniture you have attractive and new looking is another important way of improving your home inexpensively.*

CHAPTER I

How will proper care save wear on your home and furnishings?

WHEN you have an attractive home, you want to keep it attractive. With all the efficient modern appliances and small gadgets, housekeeping has ceased to be the chore it was even a generation ago. The homemaker's work is lessened if each person in the family keeps his or her personal belongings in place and assumes some little daily task. Picking up and putting away often consume as much time as cleaning.

Knowing what care floors, rugs, walls, woodwork, furniture, and shades or blinds require is essential in keeping a house attractive. Schedules and various methods of simplifying work make housekeeping much easier. Let us examine these points more carefully.

✦ HOW MAY HOUSEKEEPING BE SIMPLIFIED?

Keeping dirt out

One way to keep a house clean is to keep as much dirt as possible from getting into the house. If sidewalks, steps, and porches are swept each morning, dirt will not be tracked in over the rugs during the day. A stiff bristle mat outside each door and a washable rug inside each door will catch a great deal of the outside dirt and will save the floors and rugs.

Very fine mesh screens in windows or doors that are opened every day will help to block out some of the dust and soot. If there are cracks around the windows or doors, seal the cracks with puttylike tape. On rainy days or if members of the family have been working in the garden, shoes or overshoes should be removed before entering the house. A receptacle for wet umbrellas should be placed near the door. Old-fashioned umbrella receptacles are no longer in vogue as a permanent piece of furniture in the front hall, but in bad weather a tall metal wastebasket serves the purpose very well.

Storing supplies conveniently

A first-floor cleaning closet between the work areas and the living areas of the house will save many steps. If you do not have space for a closet like the one described on page 93, stock a chip basket or a divided wooden tray with cleaning supplies, and keep it in a convenient place.

Using schedules

It is good planning to have a daily and a weekly housekeeping schedule, and every member of the family should share in the

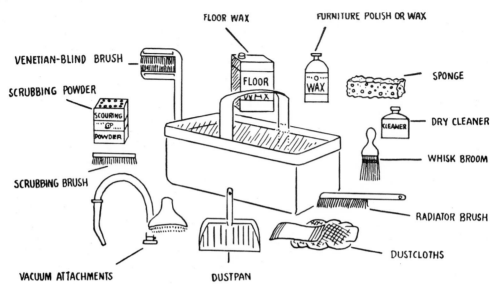

FLOOR WAX   FURNITURE POLISH OR WAX

VENETIAN-BLIND BRUSH

SCRUBBING POWDER

SPONGE

DRY CLEANER

WHISK BROOM

SCRUBBING BRUSH

RADIATOR BRUSH

DUSTCLOTHS

VACUUM ATTACHMENTS   DUSTPAN

ILLUSTRATION 180. *The cleaning basket. A large market basket stocked with these items and kept in a convenient place will save many steps in house cleaning.*

responsibilities. Some tasks performed *daily* are cooking, serving, and dishwashing; bedmaking, straightening up, and light cleaning; bathing, feeding, and caring for small children. *Weekly* or *semiweekly* tasks include marketing, laundering, mending, thorough cleaning, baking, and special cleaning jobs, such as cleaning closets and blinds or shades. On any work schedule, time must be allowed for rest and for personal pursuits.

Schedules will vary in different homes. Here are just a few hints to cut corners in almost any home. Before you go to bed at night, see that things are picked up off the living room floor and tables, and that your clothes and personal belongings are in order in your bedroom. When you wash the evening dishes, set the table for breakfast, and eliminate putting the dishes away and getting them out again. As you finish your breakfast, carry your dishes to the sink, thus saving your mother extra steps. On washday start the

washing while you are washing dishes or tidying the house. As soon as the clothes are dry, fold all pieces that require no ironing and put them away. Before dampening them, fold sheets twice with the smooth side of the hem out, so that only half of one side needs be ironed to give a fresh-looking hem. On baking day make several pie shells at a time; store them in cellophane bags, and place them in the icebox to be filled and used later. Plan a roast to serve three meals — once as a roast, once as cold cuts, and finally as hash in a casserole recipe. Use large trays for carrying dishes in order to save steps back and forth to the dining table. You can probably add many other step-saving ideas to this list.

Some people prefer a year-round cleaning schedule, and reserve one day a week for general house cleaning. Jobs, such as floor waxing, wall cleaning, window washing, and drapery cleaning, are listed and rotated throughout the weeks, so that there is no need for seasonal cleaning. Other people prefer to work very hard for two or three weeks in the spring and in the fall, so that they may relax between times. Whether you work on a year-round or on a seasonal schedule is for you to decide. Either type of schedule is effective if it is made and followed carefully.

✶ WHAT CARE DO FLOORS REQUIRE?

Treatment of floors

Floors will look better and wear longer if they are properly treated.

WOOD: Hardwood floors are easier to care for than softwood floors. Any new wood or newly sanded wood — hard or soft — needs two coats of penetrating sealer. After each coat the floor should be buffed to a soft gloss. Some people use a third coat of floor varnish. The varnish should not have a high gloss. Each coat of varnish should be allowed to dry thoroughly. The floor should be buffed by hand or with an electric floor polisher with very fine steel-wool pads. Solvent-based paste wax is best for wood floors. Self-polishing and water-based waxes should be avoided. There is an old adage: "Water and wood — no good." Water penetrates wood, leaving cracks and crevices to attract dirt. Several times a year a wood floor should be stripped of wax with a floor cleaner and then rewaxed.

ASPHALT TILE: Asphalt tile should set about a month before waxing, and only damp mopping should be done until the mastic is set. Use only water-based paste or liquid wax. Wash in small areas and wipe up water quickly. Remove old wax before rewaxing. Avoid using oily dust mops and solvent-based waxes or cleaners because they dissolve the asphalt and cause it to streak. If two coats of wax are applied over a very clean surface, mopping with a detergent solution may suffice for a long time.

RUBBER TILE: Clean with a mild detergent and rinse with cold water. Rub stubborn spots with fine steel wool. Use self-polishing or water-based wax, and buff occasionally with a floor polisher, using extra fine steel-wool pads. Avoid scouring powders, coarse steel wool, stiff brushes, strong soaps and detergents, and solvent-based cleaners or waxes. A commercial benzine compound used carefully will remove black marks left by shoes on the floor tiles.

VINYL (sheet or tile) and VINYL-CORK: Allow about ten days for the mastic to set on new floors. Clean with a mild detergent or special floor cleaner, and rinse well. Apply a thin coat of self-polishing or water-based wax modified for light-colored floors. Waxes, other than those recommended for vinyl, will cause light vinyl floors to darken or yellow. The benzine compound mentioned above will remove shoe marks from vinyl flooring.

CORK TILE: Apply a penetrating sealer after installation, followed by several coats of wax and a good buffing. When cleaning soiled cork, scrub with a mild detergent, using only a little water and covering a small area at a time. Rinse well with clear water. Water affects cork as it does wood. Use solvent-based paste or liquid wax, and buff with cloth or lamb's-wool pad on an electric floor polisher. Avoid harsh detergents and soaps.

LINOLEUM (inlaid or tile): Ordinary cleaning may be done with a wax cleaner. Alkalies in water dissolve the oil in linoleum and cause it to crack, so constant washing with strong agents should be avoided. When heavy cleaning is necessary, use suds of mild soap or detergent. To remove old wax, add a recommended solvent to the water. Rinse in clear water. Use solvent-based liquid or water-based wax. Avoid abrasive cleaners.

CERAMIC TILE: Avoid all traffic for at least three days after installation. Cover with boards if the area must be used. Use damp mop and light suds of soap or detergent to clean. Periodically ceramic tile floors will need a scrubbing. Ceramic walls may be cleaned with a sponge dipped in no-rinse cleaner. Avoid abrasive cleaners.

ILLUSTRATIONS 181A and B. *Efficient window and wall cleaning is simplified with the use of proper tools.*

STONE and BRICK: Clean thoroughly with detergent and water and apply a recommended sealer. Use a self-polishing or water-based wax. Paste wax may be used on stone.

TERRAZZO and MARBLE MOSAICS: Apply a penetrating sealer to new floors. Dust and damp-mop to clean. Avoid strong alkalies, because they cause rough spots.

✴ WHAT CARE DO RUGS REQUIRE?

You may be amazed to learn that over a period of one year 108 pounds of dirt are dragged into the average six-room house. Fine particles of cinders, sand, and dirt gnaw away at rug fibers and cause them to break. It is wise to keep as much dirt out of the house as possible, by keeping sidewalks and entranceways swept and by placing rugs at outside doors.

Vacuum cleaning will not injure well-made rugs. In heavy traffic areas a thorough daily vacuum cleaning is necessary. A light daily cleaning in living areas, with vacuum cleaning twice a week, is usually all that is necessary to keep surface soil from penetrating deeply.

Almost as important as regular cleaning is regular care. Avoid placing leftover pieces of carpet over other carpet unless there is a piece of felt between. Use casters and plastic wheels under heavy furniture. Keep some moisture in the air, and occasionally use a brush with firm plastic teeth to loosen and revive the nap. Always use a rug pad. Move heavy pieces of furniture, such as chests and pianos, frequently, and clean and spray well to prevent moth damage.

When there is anything spilled on a rug it should be wiped up immediately. Use clean unstarched cloths or paper towels to blot up liquids, and a dull knife to scrape off food. Work from the outside toward the inside, to prevent stains from spreading. Avoid soak-

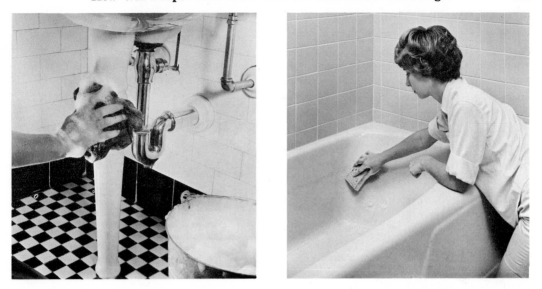

181C and D.   *An abrasive scouring powder may have to be used to remove stubborn stains on porcelain or metal.*

ing the rug or harsh scrubbing. Lukewarm water will usually remove stains from coffee, tea, soft drinks, blood, egg, gelatin, food-stuffs, fruit, fruit juices, milk, and ice cream. A solution of one part white vinegar and three parts warm water will remove traces of bever-age, egg, and iodine stains. Lemon juice and water will neutralize urine stains. A dry-cleaning solvent will remove chewing gum, cosmetics, grease, oil, and traces of ice cream, butter, or cream. Ink stains are often difficult to remove, because of the wide variety of inks in use. Some may be removed with a good commercial dry-cleaning preparation.

Commercial carpet cleaning — either fac-tory or on-location cleaning — is usually superior to home cleaning, but you can clean a rug well yourself if you have proper tools, enough time, and patience *and* if you follow directions. Oriental rugs should always be sent to a plant for cleaning.

An electric rug cleaner that dispenses suds, scrubs, and sucks up the dirty suds facilitates rug cleaning. There are many good rug shampoos on the market, but you should follow directions carefully. Avoid soaking the rug, and never use ammonia. A moth pre-ventive can be added to the water to be used for cleaning wool rugs, or may be sprayed on after cleaning. Powders and dry-cleaning fluids are satisfactory for light soil. In heavy traffic areas, more frequent cleaning with powders will prevent local soiling and fiber packing. After a rug is cleaned, the nap should be gone over with a stiff brush, espe-cially in spots where furniture has rested, and on stairs.

All three types of cleaners are safe for all-wool rugs and on wool blends, rayon, acrylics, and other synthetics. Small cotton rugs may be washed in a washer. If the pile is not deep, large cotton rugs can be shampooed on the floor; but cotton rugs with a deep pile should be sent to a commercial cleaning company. Avoid dry-cleaning solvents on cotton, because they may cause the latex backing to deteriorate and discolor the cotton. Sisal, kraft paper, and hemp rugs may be shampooed.

A rug is an expensive possession, and it may be wiser to have large rugs, especially those in living areas, cleaned commercially.

✷ WHAT CARE DO WALLS AND WOODWORK REQUIRE?

Whether walls are papered or painted affects the way they must be cleaned. Those painted with a water-base paint may need to be cleaned differently from those painted with an oil-base paint. Water-base and oil-base paints are described on page 136. Wallpaper cleaners are satisfactory to use on water-base paints that will not withstand washing. Woodwork and Venetian blinds may be cleaned in the same way that other surfaces painted with an oil-base paint are cleaned.

Painted walls

One secret in keeping painted walls fresh is cleaning or washing them before they become excessively soiled. In dirty industrial cities it may be necessary to wash walls twice a year, whereas in nonindustrial sections a wall may stay clean for two years.

A number of paint cleaners are available in various forms, such as powders to be dissolved in water, liquids, pastes, and gels which may or may not require further dilution. Powders are generally more economical than liquids. A paint cleaner should not be so strongly alkaline that it will injure the paint or the user's hands, yet it should be effective in removing the soil from the paint.

You may make your own liquid paint cleaner by dissolving $\frac{1}{2}$ ounce of trisodium phosphate in 2 gallons of water. A soft soap compound good for walls and woodwork may be made by dissolving 4 tablespoonfuls of pure soap flakes in $1\frac{1}{2}$ gallons of boiling water; then allow the solution to cool, and add $2\frac{1}{2}$ cupfuls of whiting.

Some wall cleaners require one operation, while others require two. On very dirty walls, two operations are always necessary. Mix the solution according to the directions given, and with a synthetic rubber sponge, wash off the dirt. Wring an old bath towel out of clear softened water, and wipe the area clean and dry. Some people prefer to wash from the top down — others from the bottom up. Professional wall washers start at the bottom and wash up to avoid having the water drip over the dirty surface forming streaks that are sometimes difficult to remove. There are arguments on both sides. Wash in a circular motion, and let the areas overlap as you proceed to avoid water marks. A coat of self-polishing wax applied to the clean wall will make it stay clean longer and make the next washing easier.

Papered walls

Using a wallpaper cleaner is usually safer than washing for cleaning papered walls. If the cleaner leaves a dirty mark, it may be wiped off with a sponge wrung nearly dry in mild suds. Rinse well and avoid hard rubbing. Grease marks may be removed with a paste made of Fuller's earth and cleaning fluid. Apply the paste to the spot; allow it to dry, and then brush it off. Some wallpapers are labeled "washable," but they may not hold up under frequent washings. It is always best to try out the effect of suds on a small inconspicuous space. Apply thick suds with a sponge to a small space, rubbing as lightly as possible, and rinse with a sponge wrung out of clear water. Use as little water as possible. There are some guaranteed washable wall papers, but they have an oil or synthetic surface which makes them cost more than ordinary wallpapers.

Other precautions in wall care

With radiant heat and air conditioning, walls will stay clean for several years. With registers and radiators, however, there are constant air currents, so that all walls near the heating units soil rapidly. To eliminate a great deal of wall washing and to keep your walls always looking fresh, avoid letting dirt collect.

With a broad soft lamb's-wool broom or with a long-handled T broom covered with cheesecloth or outing flannel, dust painted walls and ceilings over radiators every week and other walls and ceilings every two or three weeks. However, when the dirt is greasy, this is not recommended. If your vacuum cleaner has a wall-cleaner attachment use it for cleaning walls and ceilings.

Radiators and registers are dust collectors, and they require regular care to protect your furniture, walls, and draperies. Once every two weeks during the winter and always in the fall before turning on the heat, clean radiators or registers. The proper attachment for a vacuum cleaner is effective on both radiators and registers and for cleaning the opening to the shaft. If you do not have a vacuum cleaner, place a dampened newspaper over a dry newspaper, and put them under the radiator. Brush the dirt down between each radiator section. To clean registers, brush the grating, and collect the dirt on a dampened paper.

Keep the basement clean to avoid having dirt blow upstairs. Remove the dust from the floors every day, so that air currents will not carry it through the house.

✶ WHAT CARE DOES FURNITURE REQUIRE?

If you are buying new furniture, begin to take care of it the day it arrives. Avoid placing pianos, radios, tables, or any all-wood pieces, especially wood veneers, near a sunny window or a radiator. Avoid placing a piano on an outside wall. Provide mats for table lamps and flower bowls; use coasters for glasses when drinks are served, and avoid ash trays with rough edges that may scratch the furniture on which the trays are placed. Equip radiators and registers with moisture pans to add humidity to the air and to prevent furniture wood from drying out.

Wood furniture

In caring for wood furniture, the question arises whether to use wax or furniture polish. Wax requires more time because surfaces must be free of oil and dirt before wax is applied, but wax leaves a more durable finish with a lovely patina. Furniture polish may leave an oily looking surface if it is not properly applied. Furniture polish over a wax finish or wax over furniture polish usually gives a mottled effect. Determine which finish you plan to use. Then before applying either finish, wash the entire wood surface of the furniture with a sponge wrung out of a mild soap solution, rinse with a damp cloth, and dry.

To apply furniture polish, slightly dampen a soft cloth and apply a little polish to the cloth. Rub the cloth over the surface of the furniture, rubbing with the grain of the wood, and a few minutes later, polish with a soft dry cloth.

To apply paste wax, make a pad of some soft cloth, and use the pad to spread a thin coat of wax over the surface of the furniture. Allow to dry about 20 minutes, and buff with a soft cloth. Some of the newer self-polishing waxes may be used instead of paste wax. The frequency with which furniture needs cleansing and waxing will be determined by its use. A thorough cleaning and waxing will last a long time if sticky or oily fingers or water marks are not allowed to mar the surface.

Here are some other hints on the care of wood furniture. Keep carved areas free of dust by brushing them lightly with a baby's hairbrush. Dust at least all the top surfaces of furniture daily. Avoid spreading dust by folding the cloth over as you go along. Use a soft piece of outing flannel, old muslin, cheesecloth, or chamois for dusting, and do not continue to use the same dustcloth until it is badly soiled. Rubbing furniture along the grain of the wood with a soft cloth gives it a lovely patina.

If your wood furniture fails to take on a nice luster, revive the finish. Dust, remove wax with a wax solvent, and wash, adding just a little turpentine and mild soap to the water. Use as little water as possible. Rinse and rub dry. Mix a little powdered pumice or rottenstone with lemon oil or boiled linseed oil, and rub the mixture over a square-foot area of the furniture at a time. Using a piece of felt or flannel, rub the wood until it is warm. Wipe off excess oil and pumice, and repeat the process over the entire surface. With a soft chamois or flannel, go back over the entire surface, and rub until a luster appears.

A permanent luster may be maintained by rubbing the surface several times a week with a soft cloth and a few drops of oil. If a final coat of thinned waterproof varnish is applied, the surface may be waxed.

Occasionally accidents will happen which mar the surface of furniture. Some common accidents and their proper treatment are listed.

1. If a cigarette leaves a burn or if a rough object leaves a scratch, use a commercial blemish remover according to the manufacturer's directions. Then wash the entire surface of the furniture, and restore the finish with polish or wax, or revive the entire finish.

2. If perfume or alcohol is spilled on a piece of furniture and a white mark shows, wipe up the perfume, and wash the spot immediately with soapy water. If the mark is stubborn, moisten a cloth with camphorated oil and rub it lightly over the mark. Wash and restore the finish with wax or polish.

3. If a wet glass leaves a white circle on a piece of furniture, place a clean blotter over the mark and press very lightly with a warm (not hot) iron. If the mark remains, try camphorated oil or blemish remover.

4. If a sharp object leaves a scratch on a waxed surface, rub the scratch with a walnut or with a Brazil nut meat, or touch up the scratch with iodine or a matching stain. For deep scratches, first rub fine steel wool over the edges of the scratch until they are smooth. Fill the scratch with clear shellac, and then rewax the surface.

Upholstered furniture

If you live in a dirty city or if there are young children in the house, avoid upholstery that does not clean easily, or use washable slip covers. Cloth or lace protectors on the arms and backs of upholstered furniture are old fashioned and are likely to give a spotty appearance to the furniture. But protectors made of matching material will protect these areas of the furniture from oily hair and dirty hands.

Brush and vacuum-clean upholstered furniture once a week. A small hand cleaner is especially easy to use. Otherwise, use the proper attachment on a full-sized vacuum cleaner. Daily brushing with a soft long-haired brush prevents dirt from accumulating. Before any type of cleaning solution or powder is used, the upholstery should be thoroughly brushed and vacuum-cleaned.

It is usually unwise to attempt to clean upholstered furniture that is badly soiled, though milder soilure may be satisfactorily removed. A number of preparations are on the market. Those with a cleaning-fluid base may be inflammable, and thus hazardous to use indoors. If dry cleaners are used, they should be applied with a genuine sponge. Work on a small area at a time, and overlap each application. New coarse powdered cleaners are on the market, and these are good for slightly soiled furniture.

You may also use commercial lather preparations, or make your own lather solution. Those containing a detergent are much more satisfactory than those containing a soap. Beat 1 cup of a mild detergent into 1 gallon of boiling water until the water disappears. With a soft brush or sponge, rub the lather over a small area until the lather is soiled. Avoid wetting the upholstery any more than absolutely necessary. Lift off the foam with a spatula, and wipe the upholstery with a cloth wrung out of clear water. Overlap each area cleaned with a previously cleaned area. Dry the upholstery with an electric fan or a vacuum cleaner drying attachment. Water cleaners may be more apt to leave marks than dry cleaners, but there is no fire hazard in using them.

Any kind of stain is difficult to remove from upholstery without leaving a mark, but with care, some stains may be removed. *Grease* may be removed fairly well with carbon tetrachloride, benzine, or a commercial solvent. *Blood* may be removed fairly satisfactorily with several applications of raw starch paste. *Chewing gum* can be loosened with benzine or carbon tetrachloride. *Mud* may be brushed off if allowed to dry. *Candy* may be washed off with soapy water, but the

area should be wiped thoroughly with a cloth wrung out of clear water. Avoid letting water penetrate the fabric too deeply. If fresh, *paint* may be removed with turpentine. Avoid soaking the fabric. Remove the last traces of the paint and the turpentine with benzine.

✦ WHAT CARE DO VENETIAN BLINDS AND WINDOW SHADES REQUIRE?

Venetian blinds

Pull the blinds down and give them a surface dusting with a soft cloth, or open them level and dust them with a three-prong, lamb's-wool duster when dust becomes at all noticeable.

The frequency with which blinds should be washed will depend upon where you live. No matter how soiled slats and tapes may seem, never wash Venetian blinds in the bathtub. The slats are removable in some Venetian blinds, and of course this simplifies cleaning. Slats may be washed like any other painted surface. Some authorities do not recommend waxing slats because the sun may turn the wax yellow and it is apt to penetrate the wood.

Seasonal cleaning will include brushing tapes and cords, and if necessary, cleaning tapes and cords. Dry-cleaning fluids are not very effective on cotton twill tapes. When the tapes and cords become very soiled, the blind will have to be taken apart so that the tapes and cords may be laundered. It is not difficult to take Venetian blinds apart and reassemble them if you do one blind at a time, saving an assembled blind to examine when you are in doubt as to how to proceed. Soiled tapes may be covered with a special clamp-on tape if you are hesitant about taking your blinds apart. Investigate the cost of having Venetian blinds cleaned at a laundry equipped for that purpose. In some localities the cost is very reasonable.

Window shades

These may be removed from the window and cleaned with wallpaper cleaner. If the dirt remains, any liquid used for washing walls may be used. The liquid should not be allowed to soak into the shades. Paper shades cannot be washed.

SUGGESTED ACTIVITIES

1. Have a class debate on the subject "It is more satisfactory to rotate house cleaning through the year than to do regular fall and spring house cleaning."

2. List all the special house-cleaning jobs, such as wall cleaning, window washing, and floor polishing, which must be done in your home-making department, and make out a schedule for rotating these jobs through the year to avoid concentrated spring and fall house cleaning.

3. Make a plan for doing each of the special house-cleaning jobs in your home-making department so that other activities which must be carried on in the department are not completely upset.

4. List the daily, weekly, occasional, and seasonal house-cleaning jobs in your home, and make out a work schedule for such jobs. Check the jobs that you can take over.

5. On a dirty wall in a closet, make four experiments with cleaners. Divide the area into four parts, and clean each with a different cleaner, comparing cost and effectiveness of the cleaners. Use (a) trisodium phosphate prepared according to the directions on page 298, (b) a detergent compound like the one described on page 297, (c) a commercial cleaner that waxes as it cleans, and (d) a wallpaper cleaner.

6. Clean and wax some floor at home or at school.

7. Discuss with your mother her method of rug cleaning, and bring your findings to class. Make a class summary of all findings.

8. Repair a mark on a piece of furniture, or clean some small upholstered piece.

9. Clean your Venetian blinds or window shades.

CHAPTER 2

What general home repairs may you learn to make?

A HOUSE cannot be completely satisfying unless it is kept in good repair. Such satisfactions as comfort, convenience, safety, health, economy, and even friendship can be greatly reduced when a house and its equipment are in poor repair. Some repairs may require an expert, especially if they are neglected until much work and much money are involved in making them. But many repairs can be made by the family.

Since an ounce of prevention is worth a pound of cure, we shall consider first seasonal checkups a house should have to keep it running smoothly and to prevent large repair bills. We shall also consider repairs that may need attention at any time of the year. We group them under plumbing, carpentry, electrical, painting, and miscellaneous repairs. We must also consider the tools a family needs to make repairs. It may be surprising how many of the repairs on a house you can make. Help your family compile a list of needed home repairs, and determine which ones you can help with and which ones will require outside help.

★ **WHAT SEASONAL ATTENTION DOES YOUR HOME NEED?**

A regular checkup in the spring and in the fall will set a house in running order for the coming season. If your family plans house cleaning on a seasonal basis, the spring and fall checkups for repairs may well be done as a part of the spring and fall cleaning. But if house cleaning is done on a rotation basis throughout the year, special plans should be made for checking regularly on repairs that are needed.

The spring checkup

Here are some of the things your family will want to do as part of the spring checkup on your home. Study the list, and determine where you can help. If you live in a warm climate, some of the jobs listed may be unnecessary.

1. Check and if necessary clean the furnace and chimney.
2. Walk around the house and inspect the masonry. Plan to have necessary repairs made.
3. Inspect window and door frames, porch, and porch steps for loose or rotten boards. Plan to renew paint and to replace loose or worn boards.
4. Take down and store storm windows and storm doors. Repair and put up screens.
5. Clean and oil the lawn mower, and inspect the garden tools. Make necessary repairs.
6. Test the water hose and nozzle.

7. Repair and paint outdoor furniture.

8. Examine the basement for termites. If there is evidence of termites, ants, or other insects, consult an exterminator.

9. Inspect corners of floors and closets for mouse holes. Set traps if necessary, and repair holes with wood or metal patches.

10. Arrange for insulation if your home needs it.

The fall checkup

If the spring checkup has been thorough, there will be fewer jobs left for fall. However, certain jobs may be done only in the fall. Many of these duties apply to cold climates.

1. If the furnace was not checked and cleaned in the spring, attend to it now. Test out the furnace before the first cold day.

2. Take down screens; clean them, and if necessary paint them, and then store them in a dry place. Replace storm windows.

3. Check weather stripping around the windows, and if necessary supplement the original stripping with a flexible puttylike tape.

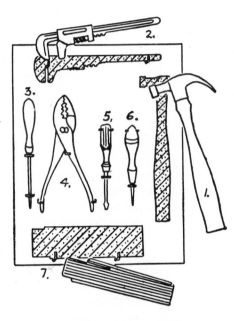

ILLUSTRATION 182A (above). *Minimum set of home tools, shown stored on a shadow panel*

1. Hammer   4. Pliers
2. Monkey wrench   5. Small screw driver
3. Medium screw driver   6. Awl
              7. 6' folding rule

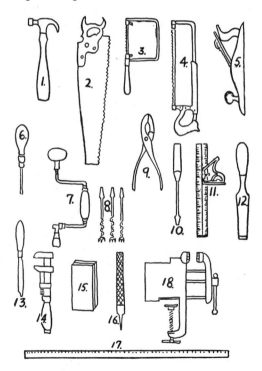

182B (left).   *A set for more extensive repairs*

1. Hammer   10. Screw driver
2. Crosscut saw   11. Combination square
3. Coping saw   and level
4. Hack saw   12. Chisel
5. Jack plane   13. Knife
6. Brad awl   14. Monkey wrench
7. Ratchet brace   15. Sharpening stone
8. Auger bits   16. File
9. Combination   17. Yardstick
   pliers   18. Vise

4. Check inside electric cords and plugs, and if wires or plugs need replacing, make these repairs now. Avoid stretching wires under rugs. Neglect or carelessness may cause a fire.

5. Drain pipes and faucets that are apt to freeze.

6. Examine the roof for leaks and loose shingles.

7. Examine guttering for worn places, and plan to make repairs. Clean out accumulated leaves.

8. Clean, store, and protect outdoor furniture.

9. Drain the hose, and store it.

★ WHAT TOOLS WILL YOU NEED FOR MAKING REPAIRS?

No good mechanic expects to get desired results with the wrong tools or with poor tools. If you plan to make extensive repairs, you will need the tools indicated in Illustration 182B. A tool panel with shadow pictures of each tool helps to keep tools in place. Check the list given to see whether you need additional tools. Many people have no interest in tools, and therefore, they know little about making repairs. They may consider it more economical to pay someone to do a job than to do it themselves and run the risk of its not being satisfactory. But if you are handy with tools and if you have the right ones, after a little experimenting, you should be able to make the following repairs.

★ WHAT PLUMBING REPAIRS CAN YOU LEARN TO MAKE?

A leaky faucet or a flush tank that will not shut off wastes many gallons of water a day. A stopped-up drain and a pilot light that does not function properly are not only annoying but are hazards to safety and health. As you study the directions for making these repairs, consult Illustrations 183–186 for further help.

To check a dripping faucet

First of all be sure that the water is turned off at the cutoff valve below the sink or bathroom lavatory. The cutoff valve may be in the basement. To prevent damage by the tools to the finish of the faucet, place a cloth over the cap nut below the handle, and remove the cap nut with a wrench. Turn the handle and lift out the inside mechanism. Locate the screw head that holds the washer in place, and with a screw driver, remove the screw and the washer. Replace the old washer with a new one, and if the screw threads are worn, replace the screw. Reassemble the parts; tighten the cap nut, and turn the water on.

To repair a flush tank

Check to see whether the float rests nearly on the surface of the water. If it is almost submerged, it has developed a leak and is thus unable to stop the flow of water. Unscrew the float, and replace it with a new one. The water level in the flush tank may be too low for satisfactory flushing or so high that water is wasted through the overflow pipe. In the former case, bend the float rod up, and in the latter case, bend the rod down.

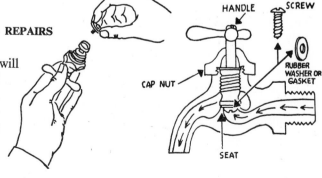

ILLUSTRATION 183. *How to check a dripping faucet*

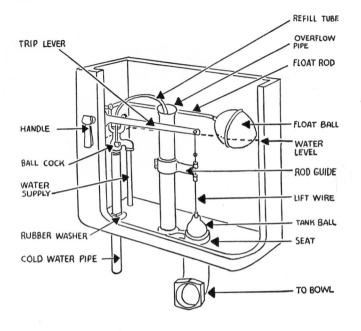

TRIP LEVER

REFILL TUBE

OVERFLOW PIPE

FLOAT ROD

HANDLE

FLOAT BALL

WATER LEVEL

BALL COCK

ROD GUIDE

WATER SUPPLY

LIFT WIRE

TANK BALL

RUBBER WASHER

SEAT

COLD WATER PIPE

TO BOWL

ILLUSTRATION 184. *Flush tank. Various parts which may need adjusting to make a flush tank operate correctly are shown.*

If the water level is low and water continues to run into the tank, the tank ball is at fault. Turn off the water at the cutoff valve, and flush the tank. Raise the lift wire carefully so as not to bend it. Hold it with pliers, and unscrew the tank ball. Replace the tank ball with a new one of exactly the same size. If a new float ball or if bending the float rod down has not stopped the wasting of water through the overflow pipe, the trouble may be due to a faulty ball-cock valve. Replacement parts are available at a plumbing-supply store.

To relieve a stopped-up drain

First of all with tweezers or with a crochet hook, remove the string or hair from the drain entrance in the sink or lavatory. If this does not unstop the drain, hold a suction plunger over the drain, nearly cover the bell cap of the plunger with water, and pump the plunger up and down until water will flow

through the drain. Flush the drain with a lye solution, following carefully the directions given on the can. If water still flows through the drain slowly, locate the cleanout plug under the bowl, and place a bucket under it to catch water. Unscrew the cleanout plug with a wrench. If the plug refuses to loosen, heat it with a lighted candle, and tap it lightly. With a stiff wire or long slender knife, clean out the trap. Pour a hot lye solution into the bowl to flush out dirt and grease. Replace the cleanout plug, and flush the drain again with a hot lye solution. Lye can be harmful; so be careful!

To adjust a pilot on a gas range

Turn off the gas at the handle back of the stove, and test the burners by turning them on and holding a lighted match to them to be sure that the gas is off. Locate the pilot, and with a wire, clean out the grease and dirt. Turn on the gas, and light the pilot. Adjust

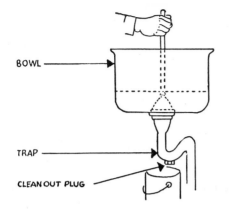

ILLUSTRATION 185. *To relieve a stopped-up drain*

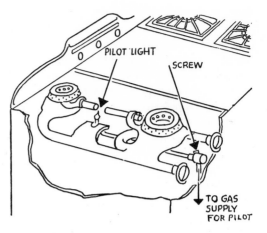

ILLUSTRATION 186. *Parts to locate when adjusting the pilot on a gas range*

the pilot flame by loosening or tightening the screw on the pilot pipe.

✴ WHAT CARPENTRY REPAIRS CAN YOU LEARN TO MAKE?

Carpentry repairs may sound easier than plumbing repairs because almost anyone can drive a nail if the occasion arises. However, it may be very annoying if the nail keeps bending or if the wood keeps splitting. Some carpentry jobs that are not difficult are outlined as follows.

To drive a nail or a screw, without splitting the wood

With a pencil, make a mark where you want to insert a screw or a nail. Select a nail or a screw of the proper thickness and length. With a drill and bit smaller than the nail or the screw, drill a small pilot hole. Hammer the nail evenly, or tighten the screw firmly in place. A little soap rubbed on the screw will make it go into the wood more easily.

To adjust a door that sticks

Check to determine where the door sticks. Tighten all screws on the hinges. If the screws

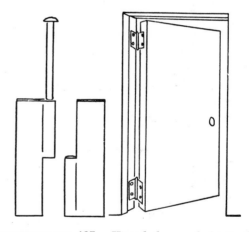

ILLUSTRATION 187. *Hinged door and detail of hinge*

have become very loose, remove them, and fill the screw holes with plastic wood before tightening the screws. If the door still does not close properly, use a piece of chalk and mark where the door sticks. If the offending place is on the top or front of the door and if the door is only slightly oversize, the excess wood may be removed by sandpapering. Cover a block of wood with coarse sandpaper, and rub it over the tight parts of the door. If the door sags, however, it may be necessary to remove the pins from the door hinges and lift off the door in order to remove the excess wood from the bottom. If the amount of wood to be removed from the door is more than $\frac{1}{16}$ of an inch, planing will be more satisfactory than sandpapering. When planing the top or the bottom of the door, be sure that you plane from the outside edge so as not to split the wood. Frequently a sagging door may be remedied simply by loosening the bottom hinge, slipping a piece of cardboard between the hinge and the door jam, and then tightening the screws. The same treatment may be used on the top hinge for a door that binds at the top.

To ease a tight window

Lubricate the runways with paraffin, soap, or candle wax. Raise and lower the window several times. If paint has dried around the windows, insert a chisel or a putty knife around the edges, and tap gently. Check the windows for loose or broken chains or cords.

★ WHAT ELECTRICAL REPAIRS CAN YOU LEARN TO MAKE?

Being able to make minor electrical repairs around the house will save much time, worry, and money. People who are unable to make simple repairs frequently suffer great inconvenience when a fuse blows out or when a faulty plug will not permit some piece of equipment to operate. Then too, it is important from the safety standpoint to keep cords and plugs in good repair. Illustrations 188–190 will help you understand how to make the following repairs.

To replace a fuse

While your lights are all working, make a chart of the fuse box indicating the areas in

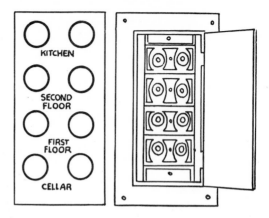

ILLUSTRATION 188.   *Fuse box and fuse-box chart*

the house that are controlled by the different fuses. Post this chart near your fuse box. When a fuse burns out, determine the cause — a loose wire, an overloaded circuit, a short circuit in an iron cord, and so forth — and avoid having a repeat performance. When replacing a fuse, first pull open the service switch to avoid shock hazard. Unscrew the burnt fuse. From your fuse storage box, select a new fuse of the right number, and screw it in to replace the old one. Pull on the service switch.

To rewire a plug

Make sure that the cord is not connected with the current. Remove the insulating disk which covers the binding posts. Loosen the screws, and pull out the worn ends of the wires. Cut off the burned or frayed ends of the wires; then strip the outer covering of cord so as to separate the two strands of wires about 2 inches from the end. Be careful not to cut the insulation that covers the two stranded wires. Slip the plug onto the cord, and tie the wires in an underwriters' knot as shown in Illustration 189. Scrape the insulation off the ends of the wires for about half an inch. Turn each set of wires clockwise

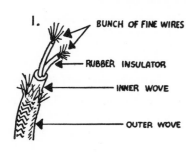

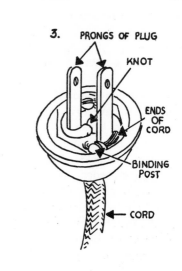

ILLUSTRATION 189. *To rewire a plug.*
Sketch 1 shows the construction of a cord;
2, an underwriters' knot; 3, cord ends
attached to plug.

around a binding post with no loose ends
showing. Tighten the screws.

To repair an electric cord

If the outside covering of the cord is broken
or damaged, buy a new cord. But if the
break has occurred inside the appliance plug,
it can be easily remedied. Remove the screws
in the appliance plug, and take it apart.
Loosen the terminal screws, and remove the
wire. Cut off the cord above the break. Peel
the outside covering of the wires back for
about 3 inches, and cut it off neatly. Carefully
bind the covering with a thread just above
the cut to prevent further raveling. Scrape off
the insulation on the ends of the wires,
exposing about $\frac{3}{4}$ of an inch. The insulation
above the exposed ends of each wire may be
wrapped with narrow strips of friction tape.
Twist the uninsulated end of each of the wires
around the screw in a clockwise direction,
and tighten the screws securely. Carefully
place the two terminals into the grooves in
the body of the plug. Slip the spring down the
cord and into the spring groove. Then replace

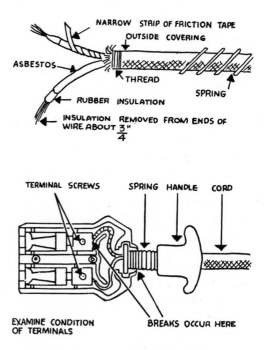

ILLUSTRATION 190. *To repair an electric cord. The*
sketch above shows how to prepare the cord;
below, the cord attached to the plug.

and tighten the screws holding the appliance plug together.

✴ WHAT PAINTING JOBS CAN YOU DO?

Painting can be fun if you have on clothes you do not have to worry about and if you have a good brush and a firm stepladder. There are many paint jobs about a house that you can tackle. Further suggestions as to supplies needed and procedures used in painting are given on page 136.

To renew the finish on radiators

Paint radiators during the season when you do not need heat. If possible, disconnect the radiator, and move it away from the wall. Clean it thoroughly with a vacuum-cleaner attachment. With a wire brush, loosen all dirt, rust, and loose paint, and with steel wool, rub the surface to be painted. Wash the radiator carefully with turpentine. Paint it with radiator enamel or flat wall paint for best results. Using as long strokes as possible, put on a thin coat of paint, and apply as many other thin coats as needed when the previous coat is thoroughly dry.

To paint woodwork

Inside woodwork painted for the first time requires two undercoats before enamel is applied. A first coat of shellac will make the undercoat go farther. If you are painting over old paint, the surface will have to be washed first, so that the new paint will not peel off. Tap off all loose paint, and smooth off the edges with steel wool or sandpaper. If the old paint is peeling or badly blistered, scrape it off. If large areas of paint must be removed, it is advisable to have an expert prepare the surface. Clean the entire surface with turpentine. Apply enamel, thinned to spreading consistency, with a good bristle

brush about 3 inches wide. If the finish is in bad condition, you will have to use two or three coats, but one coat will usually serve as a refresher coat.

To fill hairline cracks and paint walls

For walls, select a paint that will wash, and read the directions carefully before purchasing it. A semigloss is recommended for kitchen and bathroom walls, and a flat paint, for walls in other rooms. Wash the walls before painting them because paint over dirty or greasy walls will peel off. With a plaster stick or special compound available at any hardware store, go over all hairline cracks. Large plaster-repair jobs require an experienced person. Estimate the amount of paint needed, and buy enough for the entire job especially if you are mixing your own color. A gallon of paint will cover approximately 400 square feet. Mix enough color at one time for the entire job. Apply the paint with a firm bristle brush 4 inches wide. Allow each coat to dry 24 to 48 hours before applying a second coat.

To paint outside trim

Sand, scrape, or burn off peeled or blistered areas. Wipe well with turpentine to remove dirt and grease. If water is used in cleaning, the wood must be perfectly dry before applying the paint because oil or water will cause paint to peel and blister. Apply two coats of paint on all the trim unless the original coat is fairly smooth Apply three coats if you are changing the color.

✴ WHAT OTHER REPAIRS CAN YOU MAKE?

A number of little unexpected jobs present themselves in keeping a house in good working order. If the needed supplies are available, such jobs may take only a few minutes time. Some of the common, small, miscellaneous repairs which you can make are as follows.

To repair and adjust window shades

Reversing window shades will prolong their usefulness. Before reversing them, sponge the shade on both sides, rinse, and dry thoroughly. Lay the shade out flat on a long table or on the floor. Remove the tacks from the roller, and take the stick out of the hem. Trim off the upper and the lower edges of the shade with a single-edge razor blade. To do this, place the shade over a hard surface or on newspapers to protect the table, and hold a hardwood yardstick firmly along the edges to guide the razor blade. Fold a one-turn hem and hold it in place with paper clips. Stitch with double-duty thread, using a long stitch. Tack the other end of the shade onto the roller. With pliers, tighten the nubbin at top of the roller, and replace the shade in its brackets.

To repair a frayed rug

Examine small rugs for weak spots in the backing, and repair the weak areas with heavy press-on tape. Then repair frayed edges. On the backside of the rug, with a yardstick and chalk, draw a line below the frayed edges parallel with the warp or filling yarns. Cut off one end or one side at a time to prevent fraying. Then apply rug binding to the cut edge, holding the rug right side up with one edge of the binding on the cut edge of the rug and with the other edge of the binding toward you. With carpet thread, whip the rug edge and the binding edge together. Turn and fold the binding to the back of the rug, holding the binding in place with spring clothespins or heavy paper clips. Then whip the binding to the backing of the rug.

To repair holes in a screen

With wire snips or metal shears, trim a rectangular shape out of the rip or the tear in the screen. Cut a piece of similar mesh screen about $\frac{3}{4}$ of an inch larger on all four sides than the hole in the screen. Ravel the wire back half an inch on all four sides of the piece. Bend the raveled wires at right angles, and fit the piece over the hole. Press the wires down on the opposite side of the screen. Screen patches in assorted sizes may be bought in a ten-cent store.

SUGGESTED ACTIVITIES

1. Demonstrate before the class how to (a) replace a worn washer, (b) relieve a stopped-up drain, (c) adjust a gas pilot, (d) replace a plug in an electric cord, (e) repair an iron cord, (f) repair a screen.

2. Make a list of the equipment you will need for each of the above repairs.

3. Name some other repairs you can make or learn to make, and describe how to do them.

4. Discuss home repairs that members of the class have had experience in making.

5. With your father, give your house a spring or a fall checkup. List the repairs you can help with, and make a schedule for doing them.

6. Perform any of the following tasks which need to be done at school or at home: (a) ease a tight window, (b) make a fuse-box chart, (c) refinish a radiator, (d) paint the bathroom walls, (e) turn the window shades, (f) repair a rug. Prepare a report of your work, and present it to the class.

7. With help, make a tool panel for your home or for your homemaking department, and paint silhouettes of each tool on it, so that it will be easy to keep each tool in its place.

8. If your supply of tools at home or at school is inadequate, plan what tools are needed, investigate quality and price of the tools, and if possible make the purchases.

CHAPTER 3

How can you refinish and renovate old furniture?

MANY a room has been furnished very attractively on a mere shoestring in so far as money is concerned. With the "know how," a little determination, and plenty of time, you can achieve delightful results. An old family heirloom doomed to a life in the attic or in the garage may be refinished to become a prized possession. Furniture with no antique value may be altered to serve as useful and attractive pieces. An old washstand may make an interesting bookcase and radio cabinet; discarded wood-back chairs may be padded and upholstered to look like new; old tables may be lowered to make useful coffee tables. Look around your home and make a list of furniture that needs refinishing, redecorating, or redesigning, and see what you can do to add new interest to several rooms after studying this chapter.

★ HOW MAY YOU REPAIR SAGGING SPRINGS?

Springs may sag because the webbing has worn out or because the springs have broken loose from the webbing. If only the webbing is stretched or if only the cord holding the springs to the webbing has broken, you can make the necessary repairs yourself. Springs may have to be replaced if a chair is in bad condition, and an allover repair job should be done by a reputable upholsterer. To replace the webbing or retie the springs, use the following directions, referring frequently to Illustration 191.

1. Turn the chair upside down, and remove the cambric cover.
2. Remove the webbing, snipping it where it is caught to the springs.
3. If the springs are loose under the padding on the seat, the job should be done by an experienced person. If the cord or twine holding the bottom of the springs is loose or broken in places, retie these areas, using strong hemp twine. For the greatest strength, springs should be tied in eight directions as shown in Illustration 191 (1). Knot one end of the twine and tack it in place; tie each spring in position, holding the twine taut between the knots; knot the other end of the twine and tack it in place. Continue in this fashion until all the springs are tied in all directions.
4. Plan the placement of lengthwise and crosswise webbing strips so that they will intersect at the point where each spring touches them. There should be very little space between webbing strips. Tightly woven jute webbing 3 to 4 inches wide should be used. Place the end of the webbing so that it overhangs the outside edge of the frame by 1 inch. Tack the webbing securely to the frame. Turn back the overhanging piece, and tack it securely and

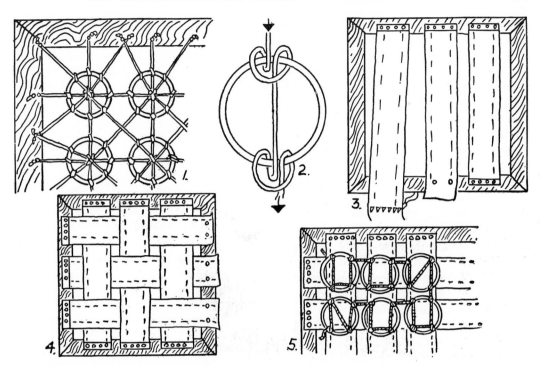

ILLUSTRATION 191.   *To repair sagging springs. Sketch 1 shows the springs tied 8 times; 2, detail of knot; 3, stretching webbing; 4, interlacing webbing; 5, sewing webbing to springs.*

neatly for additional strength. Using a webbing stretcher which may be bought inexpensively, pull the webbing across the frame. Hold the webbing taut, and tack it in place. Cut the webbing off an inch beyond the edge of the frame; fold the extension back, and tack again. Never cut the webbing until you have stretched it across the frame. Tack until all lengthwise strips are in place. Tack crosswise pieces in the same way, interlacing them as shown in Illustration 191 (4).

5. Using a curved upholsterer's needle and heavy linen thread, sew each spring to the four corners of the webbing intersection as shown in the illustration.

6. Replace the cambric cover. If the old cover is strong, it may be cleaned and used again. Otherwise a new cover should be used.

✴ WHAT SIMPLE UPHOLSTERING JOBS CAN YOU LEARN TO DO?

It is not advisable for beginners to attempt anything but the simplest of upholstering jobs. The process is slow, tedious, and laborious. For these reasons, we suggest that the amateur begin with a padded detachable chair seat. The next project may be an upholstered slip cover for an occasional chair where the back is separated from the seat. After mastering these two projects with some degree of skill, the next project may be an allover padded chair, such as a lounge or wing chair.

Only the experienced person should attempt to strip a chair down to the wood and do a complete reupholstering job. It requires patience, skill, and a great deal of physical exertion to renew springs, distribute padding, make edge rolls, and stretch the muslin covering firmly in place. If a piece of furniture needs reconditioning in addition to reupholstering, it will be less expensive in the long run to have a professional upholsterer do the work.

One rule is of major importance for even the simplest upholstering job. Observe carefully how the upholstery was put on piece by piece, jot down each step, and reupholster in reverse order. In addition to noting the sequence of the steps, carefully observe and note how corners are turned, how tacks are set in, how the narrow cardboard strips are set back of folds to give firm edges, and how edge rolls are attached to sharp wood edges to relieve pressure on the fabric.

We also add this warning. Never attempt to reupholster over old upholstery, and never rip or tear off the old covering and discard it. In the first place, the discarded pieces make good patterns for cutting new pieces, and in the second place, you may want to examine the old pieces to find out how corners are treated, where edges are snipped, or at what points cording is joined. Some people chalk mark all tack holes and notch all edges on the new cover, so that it is marked just like the old one.

✶ WHAT SUPPLIES AND EQUIPMENT WILL YOU NEED?

Illustration 192 on this page gives sketches of the main supplies and equipment needed for the upholstering jobs described. We list supplies and equipment as follows.

FROM YOUR WORKBASKET: Although a steel tape measure is more accurate, you may use an ordinary cloth tape measure. Get out your largest, sharpest shears, sharp pins, heavy-duty or carpet thread, thimble, and tailor's chalk.

WORKBENCH: This should be a firm bench, old table, or several wooden boxes about 21 inches in height. An ordinary table is too high to work on in comfort, and it is difficult to work on the floor.

WEBBING STRETCHER: This may be purchased, or you may make your own if you have

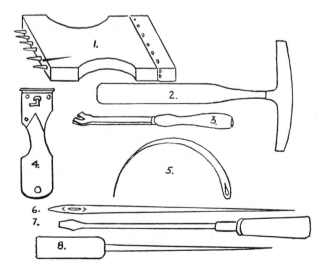

ILLUSTRATION 192. *Equipment needed for upholstering*

1. Webbing stretcher
2. Upholstery hammer
3. Tack puller
4. Razor blade and adjustable holder
5. 6″ curved needle
6. 8–10″ straight needle
7. Screw driver
8. Ice pick

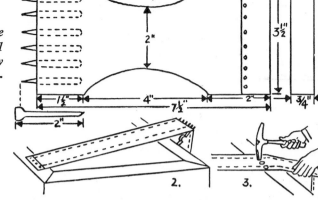

ILLUSTRATION 193. *How to make and use a webbing stretcher. Sketch 1 gives all the dimensions; 2 shows how to stretch the webbing; 3 shows tacking the stretched webbing in place.*

the time. The first sketch in Illustration 193 will give you all dimensions. Sand the edges of your block, and drive 6 two-inch nails into one end as shown, allowing half an inch to extend beyond the end of the block. Cut off the heads with the snipper side of a pair of pliers, and with a metal file, smooth each end down to a point. As a protection to the furniture, stretch a piece of leatherette or chamois over the end of the block opposite the nails, and tack the protector in place. Illustration 193 will show also how to use the stretcher when stretching webbing over the springs.

RAZOR BLADE: A single-edge razor blade and holder will be more useful for trimming edges in some places than scissors.

MAGNETIC UPHOLSTERER'S HAMMER: This type of hammer will save a great deal of time and also a few finger bruises. A hammer with a claw end will eliminate the need of a tack puller.

SCREW DRIVER: A screw driver with a very thin edge makes it possible to remove tacks easily and to avoid gouging the wood.

UPHOLSTERER'S NEEDLES: You will need both curved and straight needles. Curved needles for heavy materials should measure four to six inches along the curve, and for thin material such as chintz, two-and-a-half inches along the curve. Straight needles should be eight to ten inches long, and may be pointed at one or both ends.

ICE PICK: This is used to adjust the padding as the material is stretched. As you work, it is almost always necessary to add padding at chair corners and at the places where the arms join the chair back.

CARDBOARD STRIPS: Lightweight cardboard may be cut into half-inch strips for back-tacking. Be sure to cut these strips evenly, using a metal rule and a single-edge razor blade.

SPRING TWINE AND WEBBING: These will be needed for tying up sagging springs.

COTTON PADDING: This is a natural-colored heavy cotton padding that comes in rolls. Upholstery supply houses will usually sell any desired length.

UPHOLSTERER'S TACKS: These are flat-headed tacks resembling carpet tacks. Numbers 4 and 6 are recommended for tacking material to the frame. Numbers 8 to 12 are stronger for tacking webbing. For a secure edge and to avoid "tunnels," these tacks are often placed close together, almost touching each other.

With this equipment, you are ready to go to work beginning with something simple.

✶ HOW WILL YOU COVER A DETACHABLE CHAIR SEAT?

For this simple first job, it is not necessary to have all of the supplies and equipment listed. Follow the procedure outlined.

1. Turn the chair upside down, and remove the seat pad by releasing the screws. Place these screws where you can find them because it may be difficult to find others the right size.
2. Remove the tacks holding the covering in place, and lift off the cover. You will find a piece of cotton padding under the cover. If this is firm, use it again, but if not, replace it with one or two new layers cut exactly the same size.
3. Use the old covering for a pattern, but cut the new piece an inch larger all around to give you something to hold on to as you stretch the fabric. If the new fabric is expensive or if your supply is limited, you may be able to allow a little less surplus and still stretch the fabric smoothly. Draw threads, and straighten the ends of the fabric before cutting into it because you will not do a good job if your material is not perfectly straight. If you are using plastic leather, be sure to buy the kind backed with cloth. Turn the plastic over, and outline your covering with chalk, drawing along the threads of the cloth back. Remember that the warp must run straight from the front to the back.
4. Stretch the fabric or plastic leather from front to back, and partially insert a tack at center front, center back, and center sides to anchor the fabric. Tack the front edge in place working from the center out. If the fabric is inclined to stretch, the tacks will have to be close together. Remove the anchor tack at the back, and stretch the fabric in place, tacking from the center out. Do the same with one side and then with the other, smoothing the cloth out with the palm of the left hand and tugging with the right hand. Fold the edges back at the corners on the sides, and tack them in place.
5. Replace the seat pad, and screw it in place.

✱ HOW WILL YOU COVER AN OCCASIONAL CHAIR WITH A SEPARATED BACK?

Perhaps you have a chair in your home like the one pictured in Illustration 194.

This is one type of chair that may be an exception to the rule of never reupholstering over old upholstery. Often this style of chair has no muslin lining, and when you remove the upholstery, the cotton padding falls off.

ILLUSTRATION 194. *An occasional chair with a separated back*

Remove one corner of the upholstery fabric, and observe what is under it. If there is no lining and if the edges of the chair are all smooth, it will be safe to cover over the old material. However, the cambric covering on the bottom should come off. Proceed as directed in the following numbered items.

1. Remove the old covering in this order — cambric covering under the seat, seat covering, outside back covering, and inside back covering if there are muslin undercovers. Press all pieces and use them for patterns. Cut the new fabric 1 to 1½ inches larger all around — the outside back need not be this much larger — so that you will have something to hold on

to while stretching the fabric over the seat and inside back. Remember that the warp thread or straight of the goods must run straight from the top to the bottom and from the back to the front of the seat. If there is no muslin undercover on the back and the seat and you cannot use the old upholstery for a pattern, measure the chair and cut paper patterns according to directions given for cutting slip covers on pages 338–339.

2. If the seat padding is a little depressed in the center, it should be built up. Cut out two or three squares of cotton padding half the thickness of the piece and each about $\frac{3}{4}$ of an inch larger all around than the other. Lay the smallest square in place, then the next smallest, and finally the largest. This is called "terracing." With a coarse-tooth comb, pull the outside edges of the last square a little, so that the cotton patch will not show through the covering.

3. Place the new fabric over the seat so that it extends below the seat evenly on all sides. Turn the chair upside down, and insert a tack at center front, at center back, and at center sides, but do not hammer the tacks all the way in. If you are using figured fabric, make sure that your design is centered. Tack along the back edge, working from the center out to the sides. Stretch and tack along the front. You will not be able to tack all the way to the end of the cloth because the front arms and back side rails will be in the way.

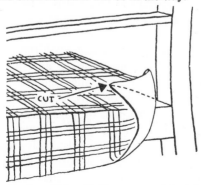

ILLUSTRATION 195. *Cutting corner into triangles*

4. Fold back the excess material at the front arms and back rails so that the warp yarns are at right angles to the filling yarns and the fold merely touches the corners at the back rails and arms. With sharp shears, cut from the corner of the cloth to the folded line as shown in Illustration 195. Fold under the edges of these triangular pieces so that the fabric fits around the rails and the arms. Trim off the excess turn-under to $\frac{3}{4}$ of an inch. Pull the folded edges into place, and tack them securely to the frame, so that the seat will not sag. The corners may need some padding. If so, adjust the bits of new padding before fastening the corners. Replace the lining under the seat, anchoring it first with tacks at the four centers.

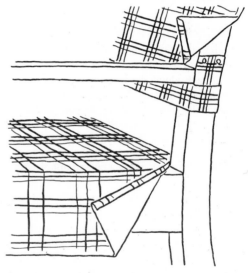

ILLUSTRATION 196. *Strip tacked to back rail at arm joint and seat cover ready for tacking*

5. On the back of the chair, you will notice that a piece of the back rail shows where the arm joins the rail. First of all, turn under the edges of a strip of fabric so that it is the width of the rail and an inch longer than the width of the arm. Tack it on the rail a half an inch above and below the width of the arm as shown in Illustration 196.

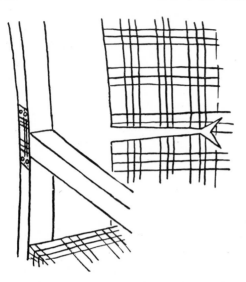

ILLUSTRATION 197. *Slashing back to fit around arm*

6. Stretch the inside back fabric in the same manner as you stretched the fabric for the seat. Tack along the top and the bottom on the wooden frame. Where the arms join the back rails, slash the fabric as you would the ends of a bound buttonhole. See Illustration 197. Crease back these edges, and stretch the fabric around the arm. Sew the edges to the fabric underneath, using a curved upholsterer's needle.

7. When you replace the outside back, you have your first opportunity to use a cardboard strip for backtacking. Place the upper edge of the outside back cover along the top of the chair with the right side of the fabric turned toward the inside chair back. Place the cardboard strip along the edge of the back cover as shown in Illustration 198. Use the larger size tacks here, and place them 1 to $1\frac{1}{2}$ inches apart. Drop the cover back in place. Fold under the raw edges at the sides and bottom; crease them, and trim them to $\frac{5}{8}$ of an inch. Turn them in again, and anchor the center sides and the center bottom. Pin along the sides and the bottom. With your curved needle and heavy duty or carpet thread, sew the sides and bottom in place, keeping the

stitches as inconspicuous as possible. Be sure that the back cover is stretched as taut as possible before stitching.

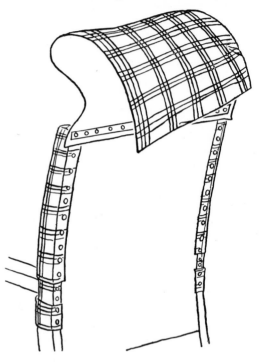

ILLUSTRATION 198. *Using cardboard in tacking the top of the chair back covering*

✶ **HOW WILL YOU REUPHOLSTER A LOUNGE CHAIR?**

Do not attempt to reupholster a lounge or a wing chair if the back, arms, or bottom sag very much. A good piece of furniture will outlast several upholsterings with the exception of perhaps the cushion and bottom springs. If the bottom springs only need new webbing, you may do this job yourself by following the directions on pages 312–313. If the cushion is bumpy, good economy may warrant sending it to an upholsterer for repairing. The cost for repairing cushion springs is reasonable. An upholsterer may even be willing to replace the cover with your new fabric for a small additional cost. It is often difficult to cover cord, insert it snugly, and stitch close to the cording on the average home sewing machine, especially if you are using very heavy fabric.

Our best advice here is to remove the old fabric one piece at a time, usually in the order given in the list which follows. Make note of any unusual problems you will meet in replacing the cover.

Gimp or braid if any
Cambric cover under bottom of chair
Side panels at back of chair if any
Outside back
Inside back
Chair arm panels if any
Outside chair arm
Inside chair arm
Chair seat (not cushion)

At this point, a well-built chair should still have a muslin covering. An inexpensive chair may have only cotton padding. A well-built chair may need no reconditioning. If there are slight depressions, terrace pad them as described on page 317. If the padding is apt to slip, cut out a muslin patch, stretch it over the cotton, pin it in place, and then sew it down with a curved needle.

If your chair has no undercovering, remove the top layer of old cotton padding. Cut new pieces the same shape, and lay them in place. These new pieces may be held in place while you are working by partially hammering in long tacks at strategic places and removing them as you work toward them.

Now you are ready for the new covering. Read the directions over at least twice before you begin, and reread them as you progress.

Cutting the pieces

Cut your new fabric from the old pieces. Watch the straight of the material and the effect of any patterned fabric. Allow at least an inch of extra material all around to give you a firm grip on the fabric when you begin to stretch it. It is a good precaution to run an uneven basting stitch in contrasting color down the center of each piece on the lengthwise thread. Remember that lengthwise threads or the warp must run from the top to the bottom of the back, the back to the front of the seat, and the inside to the outside over the arm (not back to front). With tailor's chalk, outline the shapes of the old pieces on the new pieces to help in placing them on the chair.

The chair seat

Place the upholstery fabric in position on the chair seat. You will have noticed that a chair with a separate cushion has a partial seat covering of a less expensive fabric than the upholstery fabric. This may be a matching or a neutral color of ticking, denim, or sailcloth.

Push the back of the seat cover down between the chair back and the seat, and well into the back crevice. Push the sides of the seat cover down between the arms and the seat. If the chair has a separate corded panel along the front, allow the seat cover to come about $\frac{5}{8}$ of an inch below the top of the panel. Otherwise, drop the front seat cover to extend at least an inch under the chair.

Anchor as described before at the center front, center back, and center sides. Slash the back corners of the seat covering as described in item 4 for covering an occasional chair. Tuck the ends back into the crevices, and hold them in place by sewing with a long straight upholsterer's needle. Pad the corners or snip the material before sewing to make sure that the surface is taut and smooth. Stretch and tack the seat cover in place along the back. Unless you are an experienced person it is a good idea not to hammer the tacks all the way down until you have the entire seat cover stretched in place. You may want to remove a few tacks and make some adjustments. If your material is firm, you may find a webbing stretcher useful in stretching the seat cover, but do not use it on soft or loosely woven fabrics. Pushing the cloth with the left palm and tugging with the right hand should give a firm taut covering. Trim off all edges to a width of about an inch.

If there is a separate strip across the front of the chair below the seat, set it on now with a cardboard strip as described in covering the back of an occasional chair.

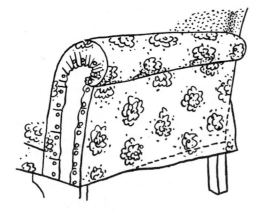

ILLUSTRATION 199. *Covering the chair arms. Edges at the lower right have not yet been tacked.*

Inside chair arm

Place the material over the arms so that the chalk outline of the old cover is in the same position as the original cover. Excess fabric will be trimmed off later. Keep the warp threads on a line with an imaginary line through the center of the chair arm. Tuck the material down into the crevice between the seat and inside arm. Snip at points where wrinkles occur, and pad where depressions occur. Pull taut along the frame-

work on the front side of the chair, and tack as shown in Illustration 199. Hammer the tacks in only partially. Stretch the fabric over the arms, and tack it in place working from the center toward the back and front. If the front side needs no adjusting, hammer the tacks all the way in. The curved section where the back joins the arm will be snipped as directed for snipping a slip cover, step 4 on page 339 and step 8 on page 340. Tuck all excess material between seat and arm, and pull through crevice to outside. Tack and trim edges.

Outside arm

Treat the outside arm according to directions for covering the outside back of an occasional chair, item 7, page 318. Before doing this, it is well to experiment a little first. Fold the top edge under, and pin the entire section in place on the outside arm of the chair. A little time spent this way may avoid ripping later. Run a chalk line along the folds at the top, bottom, and sides, so that you are sure the outside arm covering will fall into place after you have tacked the cardboard strip from the inside at the top and dropped the side covering into position for stretching. Trim off all creased edges to a width of one inch. Stretch and tack as directed for all pieces.

Chair arm panels

When you removed these wood panels, you noticed that there were four or five nails in them. Leave them in. If you pulled them out, replace them before covering the panel. If you do not have the nails, use long slender flat-headed new ones. At the four or five points, nail the wood panel in place. Remove it, circle the nail holes, and be sure later to insert the nails into these same holes.

ILLUSTRATION 200. *Replacing the arm panels. The sketch at the near right shows the back of the wood panel, nails in, front covered, and cord tacked on. At the far right the smoothly covered panel has been nailed in place over the eased-in fabric on the front of the arm.*

Stretch a cover over the wood panel; snip or fold in the edges when necessary to make a smooth covering, and tack the edges in place. Recover the old cord if cord was used, and tack it in place along the edge of the panel as shown in Illustration 200. Trim the raw edges to $\frac{5}{8}$ of an inch. Hold the panel in position making sure that the nails are inserted in the holes marked. Hold a flat board on top of the panel, and hammer the board (not the panel) until the panel is in place.

Inside back

Place the fabric in position; tuck in the lower edge between the back and the seat, and clip around the arms as described for slip covers on page 339. Stretch and tuck in excess material around the arm curves. Cut the creased edges to a width of one inch, and tack the covering in place.

Outside back

Finish the outside back according to directions for covering the back of an occasional chair, item 7, page 318. Or if the back is a wood panel, treat it in the same way that the wooden chair arm panels were treated.

Cushion

If the seat cushion has a muslin covering, remove the old upholstery fabric. If it does not have a muslin covering, cut off the cording with a single-edge razor blade, clipping away excess material but being careful not to rip the seams. Cover according to directions for making a slip cover for a chair cushion on pages 342–343. However, eliminate the zipper or other means of opening, and allow the boxing to extend around all four sides. Sew the boxing to the corded edge using a curved needle.

✷ HOW CAN YOU REFINISH OLD FURNITURE?

Really good old furniture is lovelier finished in the natural wood than lacquered or enameled. Redesign, paint, or decorate discarded modern furniture, heavy mission furniture, or ugly pieces of Victorian furniture if you want to, but restore the original finish on Early Colonial, eighteenth century, or beautiful Victorian pieces.

To refinish furniture, assemble the following items before you begin.

ILLUSTRATION 201A. *A discarded bureau. A piece of furniture like this discarded bureau need not be forever unused. Instead this piece became the Welsh cupboard shown below.*

201B. *A Welsh cupboard. Plywood was fastened to the back all the way to the floor. Shelves and scalloped sides were added. Wood knobs replaced metal hardware. After the cupboard was painted, the decoration was applied.*

Plenty of old rags and newspapers

Medium ($\frac{1}{2}$ or 0) and fine (00 or 000) sandpaper

Wood block about 1 by 2 by 4 inches in size

Paint scraper or putty knife

Paint remover

Medium and fine steel wool

Powdered pumice or rottenstone

Medium heavy lemon or linseed oil

Benzine or denatured alcohol

Good bristle brush about 2 inches wide for shellac

Good varnish brush

Clear or orange shellac or clear varnish with a synthetic resin base

Wax

Other supplies and equipment may be needed, such as *strong glue, plastic wood,* an *oil stain,* and the like, if furniture must be repaired or if a stain is necessary. The steps in refinishing are described as follows.

Remove old finish

Use a good paint and varnish remover. Ask your paint dealer to recommend a good one because some paint removers are much better than others. It is not safe to work with varnish remover unless the room is well ventilated. If possible work out of doors. Follow the directions on the can. Some people use lye to remove an old finish. If you use lye, read the directions on the can and be careful. When the paint or varnish begins to blister, scrape it off with a putty knife, being careful not to mar the wood. Use a wire brush, an old toothbrush, or steel wool saturated in the remover to remove the finish from carved sections. Work fast with veneered woods. Apply enough separate coats of the remover to reach the original wood. On veneered surfaces, wipe off all traces of the remover with a soft cloth saturated in denatured alcohol or benzine. If there is no veneering, scrubbing with soap and water is satisfactory for removing all traces of film.

The furniture should then be rinsed thoroughly to remove the soap. Allow the furniture to dry completely.

Fill in holes or cracks

When there are large nicks in the surface, trim them in a rectangular shape along the grain of the wood, and clean them well. From a matching piece of wood, cut a patch exactly the same size and shape. Apply synthetic resin glue to the patch, and set it into the hole. The school shop teacher may be willing to help with this step. For small dents, use plastic wood. You may make your own plastic wood by mixing fine sawdust with furniture glue to form a stiff paste, or you may buy it readymade. Fill in the crevice; allow the plastic wood to dry, and then sandpaper the surface. Colored sealing wax may be used instead of plastic wood.

Repair broken parts

If any parts, such as drawer slides, handles, or legs are loose, glue and screw or nail them in place. Allow glued repairs to stand 24 hours before continuing with the refinishing process.

Prepare the surface for the finish

Wrap the medium sandpaper over a block of wood and sand the surface, drawing the block with the grain of the wood. Wipe off the dust, and rub the surface with 00 and then 000 sandpaper along the grain of the wood until the surface is very smooth. Use medium and fine steel wool on intricate leg parts and carved sections. Wipe with a cloth saturated in benzine until all traces of sawdust and dirt have disappeared.

Apply a stain and a filler if desired

If much of the original stain has been removed with the old finish or if you prefer a darker finish, apply an oil stain. Remember, however, that shellac will darken a little, especially if orange shellac is used, and that all woods darken with age. A good mahogany finish is produced with rose-lake stain. Match the color of the old stain as nearly as possible, and apply one light coat with a flat bristle brush. Wipe off the surface with old rags as soon as the stain begins to look dull in places. Allow the stain to dry for 24 hours.

Open-grained woods, such as mahogany, oak, and chestnut, may require a filler coat if much of the old filler has been removed in sanding. Buy a paste wood filler slightly darker in color than the color of the wood you are refinishing. Thin it with turpentine or benzine to paint consistency, and brush it on with and across the grain of the wood. When the filler begins to look dull, wipe the surface with a piece of burlap, rubbing across rather than with the grain of the wood. Allow the filler to dry for 24 hours, and then sand the surface with fine sandpaper. A thin coat of shellac, sanded when it is dry, will act as a filler for fine-grained woods, such as gum and basswood.

Finish with shellac and wax, with varnish, or with oil

You may choose one of three finishes. The *shellac and wax finish* will give a durable surface with a lovely patina. Use white shellac on light woods and orange shellac on dark woods. It may be necessary to thin the shellac with denatured alcohol. With a clean, good bristle brush, apply the shellac lightly over the surface following the grain. Wipe off drops at the edges. In making brush strokes, do not scrub or work over the surface. Allow the shellac to dry thoroughly for 12 to 24 hours. Sand the surface lightly with 000 sandpaper until smooth, and then wipe with benzine.

Mix a little pumice and oil in a saucer until you have a smooth thick paste. Rub the paste into the wood with a soft piece of wool or cotton cloth until the wood is slightly warm. Dust off any leftover particles. It is the rubbing that produces the lovely finish. Wipe lightly with a cloth dampened with benzine. Apply a second coat of shellac. Apply a second paste coat of pumice or rottenstone, and rub well again. Wipe off with benzine. For a rich patina and a good surface, you may repeat this process one or two more times. When entirely dry after the last wiping with benzine, wax with stained, paste furniture wax, and rub well. If you want a table top to have extra protection against heat and water marks, you may give it two coats of thinned *spar varnish* before waxing. Rub lightly with extra fine sandpaper after each application to obtain a smooth surface.

For a *varnish finish* apply a sealer coat of shellac, sanding it when it is dry. Then brush on a light coat of thin varnish with a synthetic resin base. Brush the varnish on with the grain of the wood. Remove any excess varnish at the edges. Allow to dry 24 to 36 hours, and sand with 000 sandpaper along the grain of the wood. Repeat varnishing and sanding two more times. Varnish should never look heavy like paint. Wipe off the surface with benzine, and rub with pumice and oil as previously described. Wipe with benzine, and wax.

For an *oil finish*, partially saturate a soft cloth with boiled linseed oil, and rub the cloth briskly over the surface until the wood becomes warm. Wipe off well. Rub with an old Turkish towel until a luster appears. Repeat the oiling and rubbing 10 to 12 times, being careful not to let the wood soak up too much oil at any one time because excess oil in any one spot will make blotches. Never shake oil onto the surface because it will leave blotches.

Many people prefer this finish on antique furniture.

✳ HOW MAY YOU REDESIGN OLD FURNITURE?

With a little ingenuity, a lot of time and effort, and a little money, you can work wonders with seemingly worthless furniture. You are probably familiar with some of the furniture redesigned and decorated by Peter Hunt, the noted Provincetown artist and decorator. His imagination and skill have worked magic with many a piece of furniture headed for the junk pile. Illustrations 201–208 show a number of pieces of rejuvenated furniture in the before and after stages, and brief explanations under each illustration tell how the work was done. Perhaps you will be inspired to transform into usefulness some discarded phonograph cabinet, coat rack, washstand, sideboard, rocking chair, kitchen table, school desk, picture frame, or bed.

In planning to redecorate furniture, be sure that the redecorated piece will fit into your decorating scheme. Gay, informal pieces require an informal setting, and conversely, formal pieces require a formal setting. If you plan to paint designs on furniture, be sure that there will not be too much pattern in the room. Also be sure that the design is in keeping with the character of the room. If the piece you are redesigning is made of beautiful wood, you will probably want to give it a natural finish like one of those just described, so that the grain of the wood can be seen through the finish. But if the wood is not beautiful or if a different type of finish would fit in better with your decorating idea, you may decide to finish the piece with paint.

✳ WHAT SHOULD YOU KNOW ABOUT PAINTING FURNITURE?

Before attempting to paint, be sure that you understand the following suggestions in re-

ILLUSTRATION 202. *An old marble-top washstand becomes an interesting hall chest. The back was removed, the wood refinished, and the brass hardware replaced by carved pear pulls.*

ILLUSTRATION 203. *A three-quarter spool bed becomes Hollywood twin beds. Matching spool sections were cut from the head and foot of the old bed to fit as head pieces behind the twin beds.*

gard to the choice of supplies and the application of the paint.

Paints

You will need a flat paint for the undercoat and an enamel or a semienamel for the finish. For painting designs, you will need tubes of paint in red (American vermilion), yellow (chrome yellow, medium), blue (cobalt or ultramarine), and green (chrome green, medium). You may prefer Japan oils, the type of paint used for outdoor advertising, because these oils dry very quickly. Regular oil paint requires about 24 hours to dry. White undercoat as it comes from the can may be used to lighten colors. Mix the tube paints to obtain variations in hue. Mix a few drops of clear varnish with your tube paint to make the dried surface more durable.

Brushes

Buy genuine hog's-hair brushes marked "pure bristle," and give them your best care. You will need a 1-inch brush for small surfaces and a 1½- or 2-inch brush for larger surfaces. For painting designs on furniture, you will need round camel's-hair brushes with good tips — numbers 4, 8, and 12. One number 4 brush will do, but you should have two or three of the other sizes to avoid having to clean your brush so often. Unless you are very careful, using a brush for too many colors may make the colors muddy. Redsable brushes for painting designs are excellent but very expensive.

Other items

You will need plenty of turpentine, old rags, and newspapers. You will also need number ½ or number 0 sandpaper to roughen the surface of the old finish. New paint will chip off if it is used on a smooth enamel or varnish finish. After each coat of paint or

ILLUSTRATION 204. *A console table from a discarded dining table. The table was sawed off beyond the center, leaving three legs, and then refinished.*

varnish, you will have to sandpaper the surface lightly with number 00 or number 000 sandpaper. The final coat of finish need not be rubbed with sandpaper.

Procedure

New wood will need an undercoat of flat paint. If you want to paint light colors over dark wood, two undercoats may be necessary. Previously finished furniture should be thoroughly clean, and then it should be wiped with benzine or with one of the commercial grease solvents to remove old wax or oil. The old finish should be sanded with number ½ or 0 sandpaper until the surface is dull. One coat of good enamel should be sufficient on new or previously finished furniture. If the old finish is badly chipped or blistered, remove the finish as described on page 310,

ILLUSTRATION 205.
A bookcase from a washstand, and side chairs from kitchen chairs. Doors on washstand were removed, shelves rearranged and painted, frame upholstered in plastic leather edged with tape and tacks. Posts on chairs were sawed off, exposed parts enameled, back and seat padded and then upholstered to match bookcase.

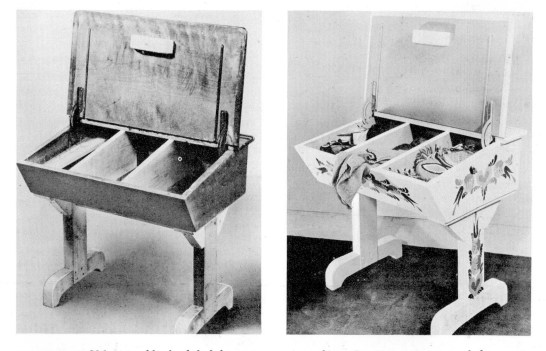

ILLUSTRATION 206.   *An old school desk becomes a sewing cabinet. Partitions separate work from equipment. In a 1″ by 2″ board, nails with points filed down hold spools. Decoration is gay.*

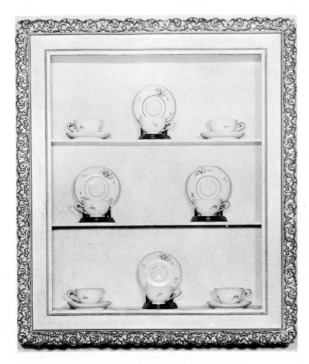

ILLUSTRATION 207 (left). *A shadow box from a picture frame. The frame is boxed to give shelves about $3\frac{1}{2}''$ deep. An antique finish may be used on the frame, and the shelves painted a suitable color for the room. Metal rings to hang over picture hooks are attached to the top back of the box.*

ILLUSTRATION 208 (below). *An old-fashioned chiffonier becomes a modern chest. Removing the mirror, cutting out the door, changing the hardware, removing the legs, and painting cause the change.*

CHAPTER 4

How may you save by making your own curtains, draperies, and slip covers?

NEXT time your mother talks about needing new slip covers, curtains, or draperies, you might volunteer to make them. Perhaps you might earn a little money if your mother plans to pay someone for making them. Curtains and draperies are easy to make. The greatest difficulty is in handling so much material. Slip covers are more difficult to cut and fit, but once you understand how to proceed, you will find that making them is not much different from any other type of construction.

Attractive draperies and curtains add greatly to the appearance of a house. Slip covers protect fine upholstery or hide worn-out places at a cost of much less money and effort than new upholstery would demand. Being able to make your own slip covers, draperies, and curtains will lower their cost, and will give you the satisfaction of having contributed to the achievement of beauty in your home.

★ HOW WILL YOU PLAN AND MEASURE FOR CURTAINS AND DRAPERIES?

Before you attempt to make curtains or draperies, study pages 145–158, and determine what window treatment you want to use — plain draperies to the floor or window sill with or without glass curtains; draperies with a valance, cornice, lambrequin, or swag and cascades; or tailored or ruffled curtains without draperies. Here are some general rules to follow before buying or making either curtains or draperies.

1. Study your windows and decide whether or not you must make them appear wider or narrower, lower or higher. In old houses where windows are very broad and high, curtains and draperies may have to fit inside the frame. In more recently built homes, a board may have to be added at the top or side of a window frame, so that draperies may be hung to give the appearance of additional height or width, or to avoid cutting out needed light. A doorway onto a porch may look better treated as a window.

2. Place your fixtures before measuring for draperies or curtains. Illustration 98 shows various types of drapery and curtain fixtures.

3. Take measurements and record them. Use a yardstick rather than a tape measure, and measure flat on the window frame. The window sketch in Illustration 88, page 147, will familiarize you with the terms used in describing window parts. Measure from the upper edge of the fixture to the desired curtain or drapery length. To this measurement, add allowances for hems, for a heading if one is desired, and for shrinkage if necessary.

and then treat the wood as new wood. If you desire a less glossy finish than an enamel finish, mix one part of enamel with one part of undercoat.

When you paint, wear old clothes and old shoes. Paint where you cannot harm anything and where there is no dust. Dust will settle on the paint and give it a rough surface. Assemble all supplies before you begin. Stir your paint thoroughly. If you expect to be painting over a period of several days and do not want to stop to clean your brush, put it in a jar of turpentine to keep it soft. You can prevent a film from forming over your can of paint by keeping it tightly covered. When your brushes become saturated with old paint, purchase a commercial paintbrush cleaner and restore them. Be sure to burn your old rags because many fires are started from old paint rags piled up in corners.

Antique finish

If you want to scatter painted furniture among natural-finish pieces, an antiqued surface may blend in better with the natural wood finishes. To antique a painted piece, apply an antique glaze when the painted surface is thoroughly dry. For the glaze, mix 1 tablespoonful of clear varnish, 3 tablespoonfuls of turpentine, and 1½ teaspoonfuls of raw umber, raw sienna, or burnt sienna. Very dark colors will require lampblack. Brush the glaze well over one area at a time — for instance, over a table top, a section of an extension table top, a drawer front, and so on. With a dry lint-free cloth, wipe the glaze immediately, rubbing most of it off near the center and patting it along the outside edges. If you are applying an antique finish over a carved surface, wipe up the excess paint with a small brush. A little lampblack mixed with the brown glazes will produce a darker outside edge on a piece of furni-

ture if edges of this type are desired. Blend the dark glaze toward the center, and pat the surface with cheesecloth. Rub it again if necessary to bring up the high lights. If you are not pleased with the effect, wipe off all the glaze with turpentine, and try again. If the glaze seems to dry too fast, add a few drops of linseed oil. When the glaze is entirely dry, cover the surface with a thin coat of clear varnish.

Designs

If you want to use designs on painted furniture, consult current magazines or art books for suggestions. You may also be able to secure at paint stores booklets showing painted furniture designs and explaining how to apply them. Plan your design carefully on paper; sketch it lightly in pencil on the dry painted surface, and then fill in the colors. Some designs are applied with colored powders onto wet paint through a cut out stencil.

SUGGESTED ACTIVITIES

1. Visit an upholsterer's workshop, and give a report on his work.
2. Repair sagging springs in a chair at home or at school.
3. Remove the finish from a discarded section of furniture wood, and have it sawed into three pieces. Walnut, cherry, mahogany, or maple wood is preferable. Finish each piece according to a different one of the three natural-finish methods described on pages 324–325. Compare your results.
4. Refinish an old piece of furniture at home or at school.
5. Mount on the bulletin board pictures showing old furniture redesigned and refinished.
6. Redesign an old piece of furniture for your home or for your homemaking department.
7. Arrange an exhibit of class projects on renovated or refinished furniture for school or community display.

Hems and Headings

Allowances for top and bottom hems on *tailored curtains* should be 3 inches wide, so that the finished hems will measure 2¾ inches. Having top and bottom hems alike permits reversing the curtains when the lower part begins to wear. A row of stitching 1 inch below the top of the top hem will give a heading and a casing, but will necessitate the addition of 1 inch to the drapery length. If double hems in sheer materials are desired, twice the hem allowances should be added. For *ruffled curtains*, allow a quarter of an inch at the bottom rather than 3 inches for the bottom hem. For *draperies* with a pleated heading, allow 6 inches for 3-inch top and bottom hems plus 2 inches for the heading.

Other allowances

For *shrinkage* in curtains or draperies, roughly 3 inches per length or 1 inch per yard should be allowed. However, other considerations enter in. Nylon curtains will not shrink; so the extra length need not be allowed. Shrinkage in Sanforized materials is negligible, amounting to no more than 1 per cent. You may need to allow additional length in *figured* materials, so that the design in all drapery lengths will match. This may mean losing several inches on each length. You may be able to save several inches on each length by facing the top hem.

As you remember from your previous study of window treatments, curtains and draperies should start at the top of the window frame (very large or very handsome frames are exceptions) and extend to the sill, to the bottom of the apron, or to the floor. With floor-length draperies, glass curtains may be floor, sill, or apron length. All these points are discussed in Unit 5, Chapter 2, pages 145–158.

Width

Don't skimp on the width of curtains or draperies. Curtains should be 2 to 3 times the width of the window. For average windows, one width of 48-inch drapery material or one-and-one-half widths of 36-inch drapery material should be used. Yard-wide material may be wide enough for small windows, provided the drapery is lined. Never make the mistake of cutting narrow material through the middle to save yardage. Draperies must be full to be attractive.

Lining

As a rule draperies hang better if they are lined. Natural-colored sateen may be used for the lining material. Homespun materials and monk's cloth need not be lined. Lining materials may be 4 or 5 inches narrower than drapery materials. Each lining length should be 8 inches less than the length allowed for each drapery.

✶ HOW WILL YOU CUT AND MAKE CURTAINS?

Tailored curtains

First of all, you will need to straighten the ends of the material. To do this, draw a thread as near the two cut edges as possible but across the entire width. Trim off the uneven portions, using the place where the thread was drawn as a cutting guide. Before cutting any of the pieces, you should measure your material to be sure that you have enough for the total number of lengths. Lay the material flat on a large table or on the floor, and measure off each complete curtain length with a yardstick. Lay the yardstick on the material without stretching the material along the yardstick. If you stretch the material, your curtain lengths will be too short. Insert a pin at the end of each length, and count

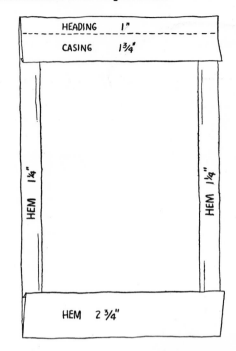

ILLUSTRATION 209. *Hemming tailored glass curtains. The sketch at the left shows hem allowances. At the right, using a $\frac{1}{4}''$ turn-under, side hems, then bottom hem, and then casing and heading are turned to the wrong side.*

your pieces. Check again, and then pull a thread on each pin line. Cut the curtain lengths, and trim off all selvages. If the corners of the material do not coincide when the cloth is folded down the center, have someone hold an opposite corner for you, and pull on the bias. Pull both opposite corners until the yarns are back in line.

Make a paper gauge $1\frac{1}{4}$ to $1\frac{1}{2}$ inches wide to use in marking side hems. If both sides have hems of the same width, the curtains may be reversed for longer wear. Pin and press hems on the wrong side of the material. Make a quarter-inch turn; insert pins at right angles about 5 inches apart; press lightly, and stitch.

Make a 3-inch gauge, and mark and press top and bottom hems. Turn under a quarter of an inch, and pin, press, and stitch the hems. Backstitch or tie the ends of the thread. With another gauge, mark a line 1 inch down from the outside edge of the top hem. Stitch on this line to make a casing; fasten the thread ends. Press the curtains, and hang them at the window to check their length. With a long machine stitch, run in a tuck back of the top hem to take care of any extra length allowed for shrinkage. Before laundering, pull out the temporary stitching that holds the top tuck.

ILLUSTRATION 210. *Making a curtain with a headed ruffle. From right to left, inside edge and bottom are double-turn hemmed on the right side; ruffle is hemmed and gathered; ruffle is attached to inside edge and bottom. Outside edge is hemmed on the wrong side; casing and heading are made.*

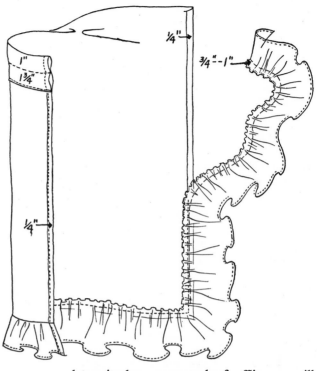

Ruffled curtains

Ruffled curtains may extend to the sill, to the bottom of the apron, or to the floor. Allow a quarter of an inch at the bottom rather than three inches for a bottom hem. Otherwise, measure for ruffled curtains and cut them as directed for tailored curtains. When *ruffles with a heading* are to be used, press or baste a quarter-inch, double-turn hem along the bottom and inside edges of each curtain length, but turn this hem toward the right side of the curtain.

Ruffles are usually cut along the lengthwise threads of the material to avoid as many seams as possible. A strip 6 inches wide will give a deep ruffle after the hems and a heading are taken off. For small windows, a 3- to 5-inch width will be wide enough. Measure the length and width of one curtain. Allow $1\frac{1}{2}$ to 2 times this measurement for ruffling, and

determine how many yards of ruffling you will need. One pair of curtains 72 inches long and 36 inches wide would require two yards of material 36 inches wide for a 6-inch ruffle twice as full as the length and width of each curtain. A narrow French seam should be used for joining the ruffle strips. Trim off the selvages on the outside strips. Unless the allowance for each curtain falls at the end of one of the strips, join all the strips and hem and gather them in one piece. With the machine hemmer, hem both edges of the strips if you want a heading — one edge if you do not. Before gathering the ruffling, tie a colored thread at the length you have allowed for each curtain. This will save worrying about whether or not curtain and ruffling lengths will come out even.

Test a piece of cloth about 8 inches long until you have the machine gatherer set at the proper gauge. If you have allowed twice as much ruffling as the length it is to cover, the sample should gather into 4 inches. But if only one-and-a-half times as much ruffling was allowed, the sample should gather into 6 inches.

For a heading, gather ¾ or 1 inch below one of the hems. Pin the ruffling on top of the pressed or basted hem along the bottom and inside edge of the curtain so that the gathering line in the ruffle is directly over the inside edge of the hem. Be sure that there is sufficient ruffle fullness at the square corner of the curtain to permit the ruffle to lie flat. Stitch the ruffling to the curtain, stitching just inside the line of ruffling stitches.

For a ruffle without a heading, use either a fell seam or a variation of the French seam

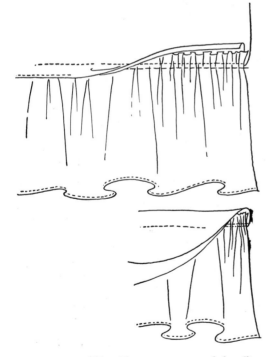

ILLUSTRATION 211. *Two ways to attach headless ruffles — above, fell seam; below, variation of French.*

to join the ruffling to the curtains. For the latter, gather ¼ of an inch from the unhemmed edge of the ruffling. With the wrong sides of the material together, pin the gathered edge of the ruffling to the bottom and inside edge of the curtain. Stitch as near the ¼-inch gathering line as possible, Trim the seam to ⅛ of an inch, and press it open. Working from the wrong side of the material, fold and pin the curtain side of the seam over the ruffling side. Stitch on the wrong side of the material as nearly over the first line of stitching as possible. If the ruffling is to be joined to the curtain with a fell seam, gather the ruffle ⅜ of an inch from the unhemmed edge. With the wrong sides of the material together, place the gathered edge of the ruffling along the bottom and inside edge of the curtain, pinning ⅜ of an inch from the edge. Stitch just inside the line of ruffling stitches. Press the seam open. Trim the ruffling side of the seam to ⅛ of an inch. Turn under ⅛ of an inch on the curtain side of the seam. Pin or baste and stitch it flat to the ruffle.

Make a quarter-inch, double-turn hem along the outside edge of each curtain length. Make a top casing and heading as directed for tailored curtains, stitching through the ruffle on a line with the crosswise threads of the material.

✦ HOW WILL YOU CUT AND MAKE LINED DRAPERIES?

Cut the draperies and the lining

Straighten the drapery material; mark off the lengths according to the allowances (see page 331); cut the lengths, and trim off the selvages as described for tailored curtains. If the design repeat is definite, the design on every drapery length must match. Straighten the lining material; mark off the lining lengths (8 inches shorter than the drapery lengths);

cut the lengths, and trim off the selvages, making each lining 5 inches narrower than the width of the draperies.

If the drapery material is not Sanforized, it is advisable to *shrink* it before cutting. To shrink the material, dampen it with a sponge on the wrong side and iron it dry. Or cut each length, being sure to add the one inch per yard allowed for shrinkage, and wash and then iron each separate length. As a rule, sateen will not need shrinking. However, to be sure, test it. See page 269.

Stitch the lining to the drapery

With the right sides of the material together, place a lengthwise edge of the lining along a lengthwise edge of the drapery so that the top of the lining is 5 inches below the top of the drapery. Thus the bottom of the lining will be 3 inches above the bottom of the drapery. Pin the edges together at 5-inch intervals, placing the pins at right angles to the edges and allowing $\frac{1}{2}$ an inch for the seam. Pin the other lengthwise edge of the lining to the other lengthwise edge of the drapery in the same way. Stitch from the top down on each side. Clip the seam edges at 4- or 5-inch intervals, and press the seams open. Turn the drapery right side out. Flatten the lining to the drapery so that 1 inch of the drapery extends beyond the seam on both sides. Pin and press with a damp cloth.

Hem the top of the drapery

Cut a strip of drapery stiffening as long as the width of the drapery after the side turnbacks are pressed in place. As a rule, drapery stiffening comes in a standard 3-inch width. Pin stiffening in place, putting the upper edge of it along the top edge of the drapery. Stitch along the lower edge of the stiffening. Turn back the hem the full width of the stiffening

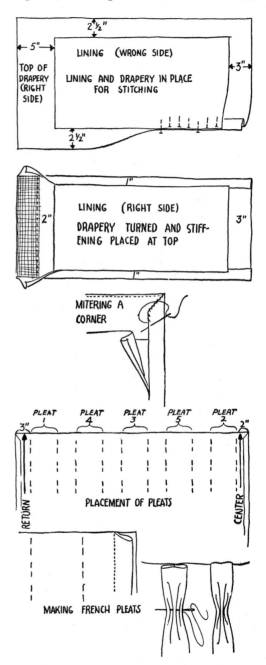

ILLUSTRATION 212. *Making lined draperies. From top to bottom, steps in construction are shown.*

and press. Fold the side hems in place and press. Miter the corners, as shown in Illustration 212. Cut out the surplus material, and whip the corners in place. Press a $\frac{1}{2}$-inch turn in the top of the lining; pin the lining to the drapery hem, and whip the lining to the hem.

Make French pleats

Always make an uneven number of groups of pleats — five or seven or even nine, depending on the amount of fullness to be taken up. A simple way to arrive at spacing is shown in Illustration 212. Determine the distance on the rod which the drapery must cover including the curve of the rod or its return to the wall. This return is usually about 3 inches. The width of the curtain minus these two measurements is to be taken up in pleats. Suppose the finished drapery measures 43 inches in width, and must cover 20 inches on the rod plus a 3-inch return which equals 23 inches, thus 23 from 43 leaves 20 inches for the pleats. Divided by 5, each pleat can be 4 inches in depth. The first pleat is placed at the curve of the rod or 3 inches from the outside edge of the drapery. The second pleat is placed 2 inches from the center edge of the drapery. For the third pleat, find the exact center between the first and second pleats; for the fourth pleat, the exact center between the second and third pleat, and so on as shown in Illustration 212.

With pencil, mark these spaces lightly on the back of the top hem of the drapery, and check all measurements carefully. Pick up the first pleat section, holding the two parallel lines together with the fold out, and stitch through these lines. Do this for each pleat. After stitching, pick up each pleat, and with your fingers adjust 2 or 3 folds in each pleat. Tack the folds in place on the right side at the bottom of the stitching.

Make the bottom hems

Hang your draperies for at least a day before marking the bottom hem. Turn, pin, press, and hem the drapery by hand. If the material is heavy, use seam binding to finish the hem. Miter the corners of the hem; tack in weights if needed, and whip the corners in place. Hem the lining by machine. The bottom edge of the lining hem should cover the top edge of the drapery hem by about one inch.

✶ HOW WILL YOU MAKE SLIP COVERS?

Anyone who can make and fit a dress can make a slip cover. Even though a person with experience in making slip covers can drape the fabric over the chair and cut and fit as he or she goes along, it is advisable for the amateur to work from a muslin or a paper pattern. If you prefer to work with muslin, cut and fit only half the chair, and then place your pattern on the fold of the fabric when you cut. If you work with a paper pattern, take measurements and cut laundry or wrapping paper full size. The directions on pages 338–343 are based on using a paper pattern.

Equipment for working will include the following:

Unbleached muslin, an old sheet, or laundry paper
String or yarn for marking lines
Box of pins
Tape measure
Shears
Ruler or yardstick or T square
Long slender needles
Soft lead pencil or hard chalk sharpened to a point
Heavy duty thread (4 spools for a chair)
Cording (uncovered cable cord or readymade covered cord)
Button tape, zippers, snaps
Cording foot for machine

YARDAGE CHART FOR SLIP COVERS

Type	Number of cushions	50-Inches Wide		36-Inches Wide		Cord covering	Cord
		Plain	Figured or striped	Plain	Figured or striped		
Sofa	3	14 yds.	15½ yds.	23 yds.	27 yds.	1½ yds.	40 yds.
	1 long	12	13½	21	25	1½	36
	0	10	11	16	19	1¼	25
Love seat	2	10	11	16	19	1¼	25
	1	10	11	16	19	1¼	23
	0	8½	9½	11½	13¾	1	16
Armchair	1	7½	8¼	11	13¼	1	18
	0	6	7	9	10¾	1	13
Boudoir chair	1	5	6	8½	10¾	1	15
	0	4	4¾	6½	7¾	⅔	12
Wing chair	1	8	9	10	12	1	18
	0	6½	7¼	8½	10¼	1	13
Cogswell chair	1	7	8	10	12	1	16
	0	5½	6	8½	10¼	1	11
Day bed and mattress	3	14½	16	21	25	1½	42
	0	10	11	14	16¾	1¼	25
Day bed	3	11	12	15½	18½	1¼	32
	0	7½	8½	11	13	1	14
Ottoman		2½	2¾	3	3⅓	½	7
Chaise longue	1	10	11	16	19¼	1¼	23
	0	7	8	11	13¼	1	16
Dining room chair		1½	1¾	1¾	2	⅓	6
Extra cushion		1½	1¾	2	2¼	⅓	5

The chart on this page will help you to determine how much slip cover material you will need. The amounts are rather generous. You will notice that a sofa with no cushions will require 10 yards of plain fabric or 11 yards of figured fabric, whereas a sofa with three cushions will require 14 yards of plain fabric or 15½ yards of figured fabric in order to center and match the pattern. If you are using uncovered cable cord and covering it yourself, you will need 1¼ to 1½ extra yards of the slip cover material or of a contrasting material. If you are buying cable cord already covered, you will need 40 yards for a three cushion sofa.

Since the procedure for making other types of slip covers is similar to that for slip-covering a chair, directions are given in the following numbered steps for covering the type of chair shown in Illustration 213.

Step 1

Establish a valance line on the perimeter of the chair; pin yarn or cord around the chair where the top of the valance or pleating is to come. Establish the center line of the chair from the center of the lower edge of the back through the center of the lower

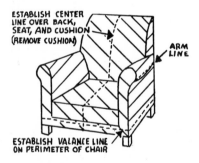

ILLUSTRATION 213A.   *Step 1. Marking guide lines*

edge of the front and through the center of the cushion. Mark the center line by pinning yarn or cord in place. Establish an arm line on the outer ridge of the arm by pinning yarn or cord in place.

Step 2

Take the following sets of measurements and record them. Do not write in this book.

A. Top of chair to valance line at side back, and width of back on the outside at its widest part

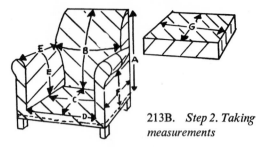

213B.   *Step 2. Taking measurements*

B. Top of chair to seat with cushion out, and width of back on the inside at its widest part

C. Length and width of seat

D. Distance from edge of seat to valance line, and width across front from inside arm to inside arm

E. Distance from seat to established arm line, and length of arm at its longest part

F. Distance from arm line to valance line, and width of the side at its widest part

G. Length and width of cushion

Step 3

To make your pattern, draw on wrapping paper the rectangles formed by the length and width measurements secured in Step 2. These rectangles are shown in Illustration 213C. To outside back, outside arm, cushion, and front strip, add one-inch seam allowances on all sides. To inside back and inside arm, allow a four-inch seam allowance on the bottom and one-inch seam allowances on the top and sides. To seat, add four-inch seam allowances on the back and the two sides and a one-inch seam allowance on the front. Label each piece, and record measurements on it. Since two fabric pieces are needed for inside arm, outside arm, and cushion, label these pattern pieces accordingly.

Lay the pattern pieces on your material so that the design in the fabric is placed to the best advantage. Center the design on the seat and on the inside and outside backs. Match stripes or plaids if either of these types

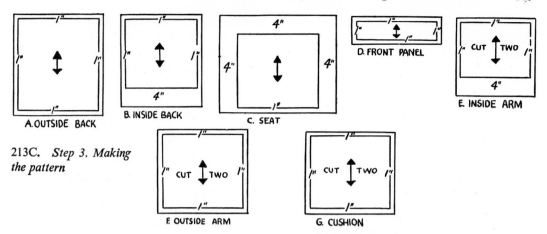

A. OUTSIDE BACK
B. INSIDE BACK
C. SEAT
D. FRONT PANEL
E. INSIDE ARM
F. OUTSIDE ARM
G. CUSHION

213C. *Step 3. Making the pattern*

of materials are used. When the pieces are laid on the cloth, you should have left at least 1¼ yards of 36-inch material or ¾ of a yard of 50-inch material for the pleating or ruffling and for the boxing around the cushion. The small panels for arm fronts and side backs (two of each) will also come out of this remainder. See Step 8.

Cut the fabric, and label each piece indicating its lengthwise center.

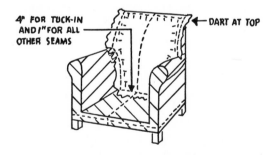

213D. *Step 4. Placing the inside back*

Step 4

Center and pin the inside back onto the chair. Place the material right side out on the chair. Fold in a dart at the top corner on both sides of the inside back, pointing the darts toward the center of the chair back. To

fit the inside back over the arm, slash the inside back just enough to ease the surplus over the arm of the chair. With a blunt knife, tuck in the material where the arm joins the back. Sharpen chalk or a soft lead pencil, and tuck it into the crease, dotting the curve for the seam line. Pull out the material around the curve on both sides; trim for a one-inch seam, and slash again at one-inch intervals almost to the chalk line.

Step 5

Place and pin the outside back, allowing a one-inch seam across the top where the outside and inside backs are joined. Pin the seam as a plain seam.

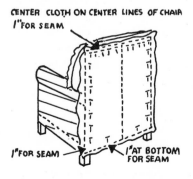

213E. *Step 5. Placing the outside back*

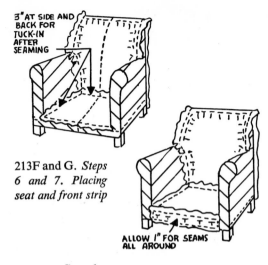

3" AT SIDE AND BACK FOR TUCK-IN AFTER SEAMING

ALLOW 1" FOR SEAMS ALL AROUND

213F and G. *Steps 6 and 7. Placing seat and front strip*

darts and the seams which were pinned on the right side. Baste all darts and seams, and stitch and press the darts. Try on right side out, and make any corrections needed in the fit. Remove, stitch seams, and press.

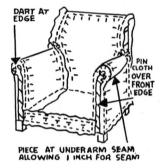

DART AT EDGE

PIN CLOTH OVER FRONT EDGE

PIECE AT UNDERARM SEAM, ALLOWING 1 INCH FOR SEAM

213H. *Step 8. Placing inside and outside arm*

Step 6

Place and pin the seat. Pin a one-inch seam where the seat joins the inside back, allowing a three-inch surplus for a tuck-in.

Step 7

Place and pin the front strip, allowing an inch for seams on all sides. Pin the seam where the front strip joins the seat.

Step 8

Pin inside arm in place, allowing a one-inch seam on all sides and providing a three-inch tuck-in where the inside arm joins the seat. Fit around the inside back of the arm in the same way that you fitted the inside back (see Step 4). Pin the seams joining the inside arm to the seat and to the inside back.

Pin the outside arm in place. Pin the seam joining the outside arm to the inside arm. Fold in darts to take out the fullness around the curve at the front of the arm. Point the darts toward the center of the arm-front curve.

At this point, remove the slip cover from the chair. Transfer to the wrong side the

Step 9

Cut a paper pattern for the arm-front panel and for the side-back panel by fitting the paper to the chair. Allow a quarter-inch seam around the edges and a one-inch seam at the bottom. Cut two cloth panels by each of the patterns. Trim the seam of the cording to a quarter of an inch, and baste the cording around the panels with the raw edges of

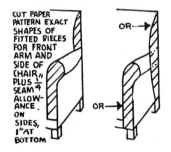

CUT PAPER PATTERN EXACT SHAPES OF FITTED PIECES FOR FRONT ARM AND SIDE OF CHAIR, PLUS $\frac{1}{4}$ SEAM ALLOWANCE ON SIDES, 1" AT BOTTOM

OR→

OR→

213 I. *Step 9. Making arm-front panels*

each coinciding. Use a cording foot to stitch the seam. To join the two ends of the cord, pull the cord out of the binding the width of the seam, and cut it off. Following the grain of the material, seam the binding together on the wrong side; press the seam open and replace the binding over the two ends of the cord. Press neatly. As shown in Step 9 of the illustration, the slip cover pattern may be cut so that the arm-front panel extends only to the front strip rather than to the valance or pleat line. Likewise, the side-back panel may extend to the valance or pleat line rather than to the arm line.

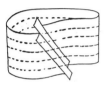

213J. *Joining bias strips for covering cord*

When several yards of bias are needed for covering the cord, join a wide bias strip on the straight edges extending one of the straight edges beyond the other the desired width of the covering strip as shown in Illustration 213J. Thus all the small strips are correctly joined on the straight of the material with only one seaming. Cut the strip the desired width around the tube thus formed. The strip should be $1\frac{1}{2}$ to $1\frac{3}{4}$ inches wide for covering the cord. Place the cord in the center of the strip. Fold the strip over the cord, bringing the edges of the strip together. Stitch close to the cord using a cording foot on the machine.

Step 10

Select the style of valance best suited to the chair. Cut the valance so that it is wide enough to extend from the valance or pleat line to within half an inch of the floor plus two inches — one inch for a seam and one inch for a hem. For a pleated or gathered valance, the length of the strip should be one-and-a-half to two times the perimeter of the chair. If you choose a box-pleated valance, plan the pleats so that the center of a pleat or the space between two pleats will come at

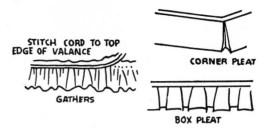

213K. *Step 10. Choosing and making a valance*

the center front and at the center back of the chair, and so that the edge of a pleat will fall at each corner. Experiment with several paper pleats until the desired spacing is obtained and then notch each crease. Open out and make a gauge for all the pleating. The gauge may have to be adjusted a little to make pleats come out as desired on all four sides. Hem the bottom edge of the pleating with the hemming foot; and pleat the strip. Press the pleats in place. Stitch cording around the top of the pleats as shown in Illustration 213K.

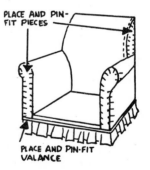

213L. *Step 11. Placing panels and valance*

Step 11

Put the slip cover on the chair. Pin the seams joining the outside back to the sides. When all other pieces have been pinned in place and stitched, the side seam on the

right side of the chair will be stitched, but
the side seam on the left will be made into a
closing as indicated in Step 12.

Place and pin-fit the arm-front and the side
panels. Slip pins through the back of the cord,
forcing the raw edges under, and catch a few
threads in the slip cover. If this is done
correctly, the seams will be pinned for basting
on the inside.

Mark the valance line with a yardstick as
you would mark the hem of a dress. With
an inch seam allowance taken off, the
hemmed pleating should come to within half
an inch of the floor. Pin the pleating in place,
using the pinning technique described for
pinning the panels in place. Remove the slip
cover from the chair; baste the pleating to the
slip cover, and stitch the pleating in place.

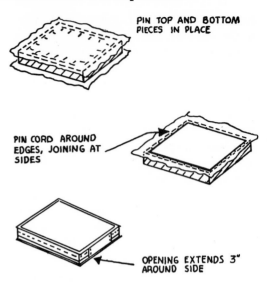

213N.   *Step 13. Covering the cushion*

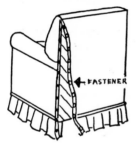

213M.   *Step 12. Making a closing*

Step 12

On the unstitched seam line at the left side
of the slip cover, stitch a zipper or strips of
button tape in place, or hem or bind both
sides of the seam and sew on snaps.

Step 13

Pin the cushion pieces to the top and
bottom of the cushion, and pin covered cord
around the edges with the raw edge of the
cord toward the raw edge of the pieces.
Corners should be square, and opposite sides

should measure the same. If the cushions are
slightly irregular in shape, disregard the
irregularities, and try to make even sides
and square boxed corners in the cover. Join
the ends of the cord, and baste and stitch the
cording in place. Press the seam. Cut a strip
of material as wide as the thickness of the
cushion plus two inches for seams, and long
enough to extend around the front and sides
of the cushion to within two inches of the
back. Turn one inch under at both ends of
the strip. For the closing, cut two strips as
long as the back of the cushion plus eight
inches and as wide as half the thickness of
the cushion plus one inch for a seam allowance and two inches for a lap if the closing
is to be fastened with button tape or with
snaps. If the closing is to be fastened with
a zipper, add one inch for the zipper seam
rather than two inches for a lap. Hem the
edges for a lap, and apply button tape or
snappers, or insert the zipper. Pin the closing
strip to the back and side ends of the top
and bottom of the cushion. Pin the strip for

the front and sides in place. Lap the turned-under ends of this strip over the ends of the closing strip, and stitch these ends together. Baste the strips or boxing in place; check the fit of the cover on the cushion; stitch the seams, and press.

Some people prefer not to use a center-back closing like the one just described. In this case, box the cushion all the way around, leaving one seam at the back and side backs open. Face the boxing edge of the seam, and bind the corded edge. Use snaps on the closing, or sew the cushion covers in place. With a closing of this type, the covered cushion may be reversed from bottom to top.

SUGGESTED ACTIVITIES

1. Collect pictures of interesting curtain and drapery styles.

2. In order to gain more confidence in your work or to provide illustrative material for your homemaking department, you may want to make good-sized samples of the following: (a) a tailored curtain, (b) a ruffled curtain, and (c) a lined drapery with French pleats.

3. Visit a department store and investigate the types of curtain fixtures available. Find out what kinds of fixtures may be used for hanging stationary draperies, draw draperies, draperies with valances or swags, draperies with curtains, curtains without draperies, and curtains and draperies around a bay window.

4. Make curtains or draperies for some room at home or at school. Decide on the best style of draperies or curtains for the room; select the fabric; place the fixtures if necessary; estimate the amount of material needed; buy the material; and then make the curtains or draperies as an individual or class project.

5. Visit a department store or an interior decorator's shop, and observe the making of slip covers.

6. Make a slip cover for some piece of furniture at home or in your homemaking department.

CHAPTER 5

What furnishings may you create from discarded materials?

It's fun to create something from almost nothing, and after your first experience, many ideas may come to you. Old tables, orange crates, spools, old lamp shade frames, and a variety of other discarded materials may be turned into useful and attractive home furnishings or accessories. However, let us consider a few cautions to be observed. Be sure that the article you plan to make will be attractive within itself, and that it will be harmonious with the decorative idea of the room in which you intend to use it. Be sure that the article will be durable, and that it can satisfactorily fulfill the purpose for which it is intended. And last but not least, be sure that it will be worth the time, effort, and money involved in making it.

A few ideas for articles you can make are given in this chapter. For additional ideas, consult such books and materials as *101 Home Furnishings and How to Make Them* by Lucina Wakefield, *It's Fun to Make Things* by Martha Parkhill and Dorothy Spaeth, *Home Decoration with Fabric and Thread* by Ruth Spears, *750 American Home Patterns*, published by the *American Home* magazine, and others. These books and the patterns are listed in the Suggested References for Unit Nine on pages 350–351.

★ MAKING A DRESSING TABLE

A dressing table may be made from a variety of discarded materials. Any old table of suitable size, a shelf fastened to the wall, an old washstand, or two orange crates turned on end and connected by a strip of plywood for a top make a suitable foundation for the dressing table. The top may be varnished or enameled, and the sides covered by an apron or a skirt. The fullness in the apron is frequently gathered or pleated at the top, but many variations in style are possible as Illustration 214 indicates. The apron is usually made in two sections which come together at the center front, so that the drawers or shelves in the foundation may be easily reached. The apron should extend to within half an inch of the floor, and an allowance for fullness should be made of from two to three times the measurement across the sides and front of the foundation. If the apron is attached to the foundation with snap tape, it may be easily removed for washing. The socket side of the snap tape is tacked to the foundation, and the ball side is sewed to the apron.

By studying the suggestions given in Illustration 214, it should be fairly easy to make a satisfactory dressing table.

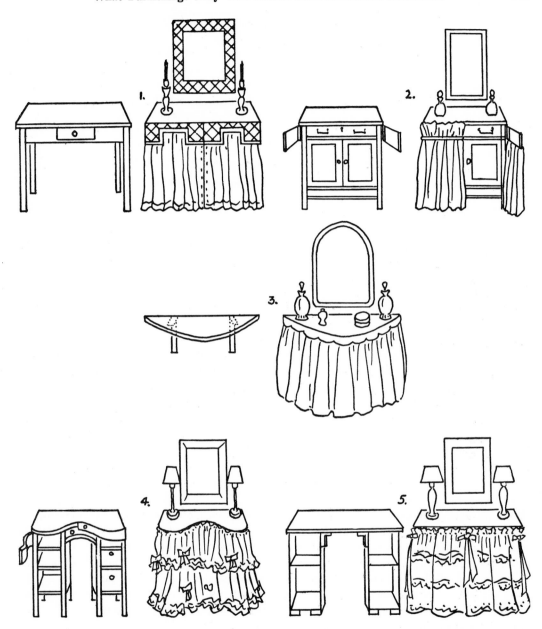

ILLUSTRATION 214.   *In sketch 1, a kitchen table, in 2, a washstand, in 3, a shelf, in 4, a ready-built frame, and in 5, orange crates are converted into dressing tables. Notice the variety shown in the style of dressing table skirts.*

✱ A SPOOL SHELF

A hanging shelf for small plants and other decorative objects may add a note of interest to your room or to some other room in the house. Such a shelf may be made for a corner or for a flat wall surface. How to make an oblong shelf will be discussed here. You will need to assemble the following:

Plywood, packing-box wood, or masonite for 3 shelves
4 quarter-inch dowel rods
40 small spools or 32 large spools
Wood button molds for each end of the dowels
8 round-headed screws
Paint and paint brushes
Hand drill
Synthetic resin glue
2 fence staples

Cut three pieces of wood or masonite 8 by 18 inches, and drill $\frac{1}{2}$-inch holes $1\frac{1}{2}$ inches from the edges at each corner. To make sure that the holes will be in a corresponding position on each shelf, nail the three shelves together temporarily with three long thin nails, and drill all the holes at one time. Experiment on an old piece of wood until you are sure that the hole will accommodate the $\frac{1}{4}$-inch dowel. Assemble the shelf to determine how long to cut the dowels. Each dowel must be long enough to fit through the three shelf pieces and through ten small spools or eight large ones. After cutting the four dowels the proper length, glue the ends and insert them in the four holes of the lower board so that they are even or as near even as possible with the bottom of the board. Glue the bottom of a spool and slip it over the dowel. If the spaces between the shelves are to be equal, glue and slip into place five small or four large spools on each dowel before gluing another shelf in place. If the ends of the dowels do not fit evenly with the bottom of the bottom shelf and the top of

the top shelf, smooth them down with rough sandpaper. Over the ends of each dowel, glue a wooden button mold or a flat disk sawed from a broom handle and sanded smooth. Insert a round-headed screw of the proper size through each disk and into the dowel as shown in Illustration 215. At both sides of the back of the top shelf, partially insert a fence staple by which to hang the shelf. Finish the shelf with flat paint and enamel. Hang it on heavy picture hooks.

✱ DECORATED PIE TINS FOR THE KITCHEN

Pie tins painted and decorated by hand or with decal transfers may add interest to plain kitchen walls or shelves. Use only those tins which have a smooth surface. Give the tins one or two coats of a flat paint that will adhere to tin. Enamel may be used for the second coat, but it is easier to decorate over flat paint than over enamel. When the paint is thoroughly dry, apply the design. For hand-painted designs, trace the outline lightly. Heavy carbon lines will make the paint cloudy. Paint with quick-drying Japan oils to avoid smearing the paint. If a glazed finish is desired, brush with one coat of clear spar varnish. To apply decals, follow the instructions given on the package.

If the decorated tins are to be hung on the wall, some method of hanging them may have to be worked out. Pie tins with rings already on them may be available. If not, perhaps the industrial arts teacher in your school or some of his students will solder metal rings on the tins for you. Or perhaps you can purchase wire plate hangers, and use them.

✱ LAMP SHADES FROM DIS-CARDED FRAMES

If you have a good wire frame with upright spokes, you may cover it easily with buck-

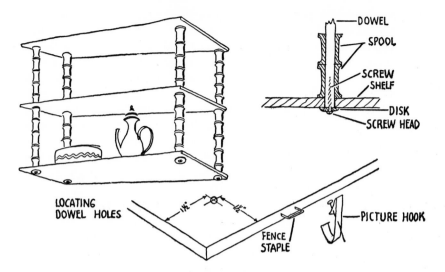

ILLUSTRATION 215. *A spool shelf. The finished shelf, a detail drawing of the support for the shelves, locating the dowel hole, and how to hang the shelf are shown.*

ILLUSTRATION 216. *Decorated pie tins for kitchen walls or shelves. After the tins are painted with a paint that will adhere to tin, designs are applied by hand painting or with decal transfers.*

ram, heavy wallpaper, or parchment paper. A pleated cloth covering requires more skill and time, but even that you can master.

Making a pattern

First, make an approximate paper pattern by outlining the wire frame as it is rolled over smooth wrapping paper as shown in Illustration 217(1). Dab a little nail polish on the frame at the top and the bottom of one spoke to indicate where to start and where to stop the rolling. When you have outlined the frame on the paper, add half an inch for overlap at one end. Cut out the pattern, and test it on the frame, holding it in place with spring-type clothespins.

Paper and buckram shades

Cut the parchment paper or the buckram from this pattern. If you are using wallpaper, you will need to paste a backing of heavy white paper, available at drafting supply counters, to the wallpaper before you cut it. To do this, cut out a rectangle of wallpaper large enough to accommodate your pattern, and spread wallpaper paste very evenly over the back side of it. A paste made of a fourth of a cup of flour, a fourth of a cup of sugar, and 1 cup of water, cooked to the consistency of mayonnaise, will do. Blend the flour and the sugar, and add the cold water gradually. Cook until thickened, stirring constantly. Beat out all lumps in the paste with an egg beater, or strain the paste through a fine strainer. When the paste is made and applied, place the pasted side of the wallpaper on the drawing paper, and press the sheets flat with a clean cloth. Place waxed paper over the surface, and dry flat under a rug over night. Cut out the pattern when the paper is thoroughly dry.

Hold the shade in place around the frame with spring-type clothespins to fit the side overlap or seam together. Glue the seam in place on the wallpaper or the parchment paper shade, and place a weight on the seam until it is dry. Sew the seam in place on the buckram shade. Whip the edges of the buckram shade over the frame as shown in 2 of Illustration 217. Attach the parchment paper or the wallpaper shade to the frame with special glued lamp-shade tape or passe-partout binding, available at a stationery store. Fold the binding through its center as shown in 3 of Illustration 217; dampen and paste one side of the tape along the top of the shade, overlapping the tape at the joint. Snip both sides of the binding every half inch if the shade flares so much that the tape will not go on without puckering. Dampen the other side of the tape; press it over the wire frame, and tuck it inside the wire rim of the shade. Fasten the bottom of the shade to the bottom of the frame in the same way.

Decorations

Various types of decorations, as suggested in Illustration 218, may be added to either paper or buckram shades. Glue the applied paper decorations to the paper shades before the overlap or seam in the shade is glued, and dry the pasted pieces thoroughly under a weight. Braid, ball fringe, ruffles, and the like may be sewed or glued with upholsterer's glue to buckram shades after the shade has been attached to the frame.

Pleated cloth shades

If you wish to cover the frame with pleated cloth, first of all wrap the two wire circles with rayon seam tape to give something to sew the cloth to. For the lining, make a paper pattern as described in Illustration 217. Lay it on a piece of rayon taffeta or other lining material, with the center of the pattern on

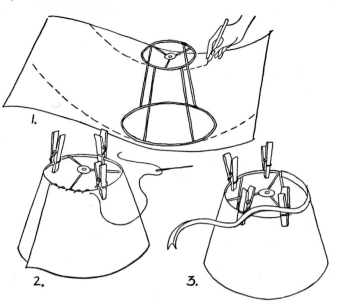

ILLUSTRATION 217. *Making lamp shades. Sketch 1 shows how to make a paper pattern; 2, how to whip a buckram shade over the frame; 3, how to attach a paper shade to the frame with glued lamp-shade tape.*

a lengthwise thread of the taffeta. Cut the taffeta about half an inch larger on all edges than the pattern. Pin the taffeta in place on the inside of the frame, turning the raw edges over the top and bottom rings. Fit and pin the joining seam. Remove the taffeta, and stitch the seam on the machine. Trim the seam evenly, and press it open. Pin the lining in place again, with the seam along one of the wire spokes. Whip along the top edge of the shade, stitching through the binding. Whip along the lower edge of the shade, stretching the lining taut as you go.

For the outside cover which may be satin, taffeta, or any leftover drapery fabric, cut and join enough straight lengths of cloth to go around the lower edge of the frame three times. These lengths should be at least half an inch wider than the width of the frame. Divide this long strip into four equal parts, marking the divisions with pins. Locate points on the upper ring of the frame which divide it into four equal parts. Pleat the strip along the top ring of the frame, holding each

pleat in place with a pin, and letting the edge of the strip extend a fourth of an inch above the frame. When you pleat each quarter, whip it in place. When the pleats are all sewed in place, using sharp shears, trim off the top edge even with the ring. Stretch and pin the pleats in place along the lower edge, and sew one quarter at a time. Trim off raw edges. Finish the top and bottom with braid.

Plain cloth shades

If you wish a plain stretched cloth shade, fit and stretch the outer covering as you did the lining, making sure to have the seams coincide over a spoke. Trim at the top and at the bottom with fringe or braid.

SUGGESTED ACTIVITIES

1. As a class or as an individual project, make as many of the following articles as are needed at school or at home: (a) a dressing table, (b) a spool shelf, (c) a set of decorated pie plates, and (d) a fresh lamp shade. Evaluate the articles made by class members, and list ways of improving them.

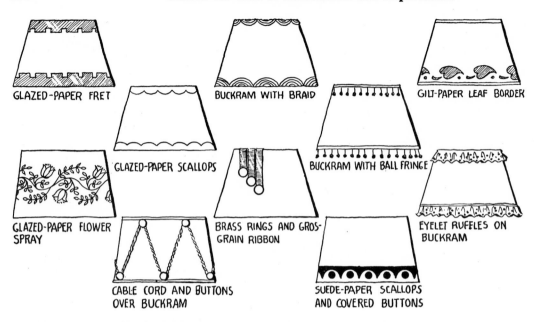

GLAZED-PAPER FRET

BUCKRAM WITH BRAID

GILT-PAPER LEAF BORDER

GLAZED-PAPER SCALLOPS

GLAZED-PAPER FLOWER SPRAY

BRASS RINGS AND GROS-GRAIN RIBBON

BUCKRAM WITH BALL FRINGE

EYELET RUFFLES ON BUCKRAM

CABLE CORD AND BUTTONS OVER BUCKRAM

SUEDE-PAPER SCALLOPS AND COVERED BUTTONS

ILLUSTRATION 218. *Ideas for decorating paper and buckram shades. Designs are glued to paper shades before the overlap is made. Decorations may be sewed or glued to buckram shades.*

2. Collect ideas for other articles for the home which may be made from discarded materials. Have a class evaluation of these ideas, and paste pictures or sketches of the satisfactory ones on the bulletin board.

3. Make a collection of supplies available at home, such as spools, cans, boxes, and the like, and plan articles which can be made from them for Christmas, birthday, or special gifts for family and friends.

4. Collect ideas for making dressing tables and dressing table skirts. Find pictures of dressing table skirts, or sketch your own designs.

5. Compare workmanship and cost in a ready-made lamp shade and in one re-covered at home. In estimating the cost of the re-covered shade, place a fair valuation on the time which would be required to cover it.

6. Arrange an exhibit of articles made for the home, listing supplies needed to make each article, any cost involved in making it, and the approximate time required to construct it.

SELECTED REFERENCES
FOR UNIT NINE

BOOKS

Better Homes and Gardens Handyman's Book. Meredith Publishing Company, Meredith Building, Des Moines 3, Iowa, 1951

Brostrom, Ethel, and Sloane, Louise, *Revive Your Rooms and Furniture.* The Viking Press, Inc., New York, 1959

Dodd, Marguerite, *America's Homemaking Book.* Charles Scribner's Sons, New York, 1957

Evans, M., and Associates, *Complete Home Improvement Handbook.* McGraw-Hill Book Company, Inc., New York, 1957

Family Handyman's Book of Built-ins You Can Make, editors of *Family Handyman Magazine*, Harper & Brothers, New York, 1956

Family Handyman's Book of Painting and Redecorating, editors of *Family Handyman Magazine*, Harper & Brothers, New York, 1956

Fitzsimmons, Cleo, and White, Nell, *Management*

for You. J. B. Lippincott Company, Philadelphia, 1958

Gilbreth, Lillian, Thomas, Orpha Mae, and Clymer, Eleanor, *Management in the Home.* Dodd, Mead & Company, New York, 1959

Grice, Harry Lee, *Interior Decorating Simplified.* Pageant Press, Inc., New York, 1960

Hochman, Louis, *Home Improvements You Can Do.* Arco Publishing Company, Inc., New York, 1956

House Beautiful Home Maintenance and Building Manual. House Beautiful, New York, 1960

Hunt, Peter, *Peter Hunt's How-to-Do-It Book.* Prentice-Hall, Inc., Englewood Cliffs, N.J., 1952

Livingstone, Jeffrey, *Make-It-Yourself Furniture for the Home Craftsman.* McGraw-Hill Book Company, Inc., New York, 1956

Nickell, Paulena, and Dorsey, Jean Muir, *Management in Family Living.* John Wiley and Sons, Inc., New York, 1959

Popular Mechanics Home Improvement Guide. Popular Mechanics, Chicago, 1956

Starr, Mary Catharine, *Management for Better Living.* D. C. Heath and Company, Boston, 1956

Whitman, Roger B., *First Aid for the Ailing House.* McGraw-Hill Book Company, Inc., New York, revised 1958

CURRENT PUBLICATIONS

Write to the following addresses for current lists of literature and prices:

Bissell, Inc., Grand Rapids, Michigan (*Betty Bissell Book of Home Cleaning*)

Hoover Home Institute, The Hoover Company, North Canton, Ohio (*cleaning and home care*)

S. C. Johnson Company, Racine, Wisconsin (*cleaning and home care*)

National Institute of Dry Cleaning, Silver Spring, Maryland (*quarterly bulletin*)

Pittsburgh Plate Glass Company, Pittsburgh 19, Pennsylvania (*paints and glass*)

U.S. Government Printing Office, Washington 25, D.C.:

Carpet and Rug Repair, 1944 (Farmers' Bulletin No. 1960)

Clothes Moths and Carpet Beetles: How to Combat Them, 1957 (Home and Garden Bulletin No. 24)

Detergents for Home Laundering, 1956 (Home and Garden Bulletin No. 49)

How to Prevent and Remove Mildew, 1960 (Home and Garden Bulletin No. 68)

Silverfish and Firebrats: How to Control Them, 1957 (USDA leaflet 412)

Stain Removal from Fabrics, 1959 (Home and Garden Bulletin No. 62)

ACKNOWLEDGMENTS

IN addition to credits given in the text, the authors wish to express their appreciation to the librarians at the Mellor Library in Edgewood (Pittsburgh, Pennsylvania), the Wilkinsburg Public Library, Pennsylvania, and the Carnegie Library of Pittsburgh. Special acknowledgment is also made to Miss Pauline Fish, teacher of homemaking at the Mount Lebanon High School, Mount Lebanon, Pennsylvania, for her critical appraisal of the revised manuscript and the *Charts*, as well as to Mrs. Marguerite Donaldson for her untiring efforts in preparing the manuscript.

Grateful acknowledgment is made to the following sources from which charts have been adapted.

PAGE

116   E. I. du Pont de Nemours & Company
216   Westinghouse Electric Corporation
337   Consolidated Trimming Corporation

Credit for reproducing drawings is as follows.

PAGE

29, 51–53   Federal Housing Administration
57 (lower right)   Curtis Companies
99 (lower left)   The Magee Carpet Company
157   Consolidated Trimming Corporation
196–197   Bigelow Sanford Carpet Company
225   The Coca-Cola Company
258   American Walnut Manufacturers Association and the Mahogany Association
261   Money Management Institute of Household Finance Corporation

Grateful acknowledgment is made to the following sources for their kind permission to reproduce black and white photographs.

PAGE

2, 40 (lower), 41 (lower), 63   National Gypsum Company
6   American Mutual Liability Insurance Company
10, 139 (photo by Beacon Photography Company)   Masonite Corporation
14   New Castle Products Incorporated (Modernfold Doors)
26   (photo by Bill Hedrich, Hedrich-Blessing), 40 (upper)   National Homes
30   H. Armstrong Roberts
35   Hedrich-Blessing Studio
39 (upper and lower)   Pittsburgh Plate Glass Company (upper photo by Bill Hedrich, Hedrich-Blessing)

41   Harnischfeger Homes, Incorporated
54   *House and Home* magazine (photo by Joseph W. Molitor)
55   Swift Homes, Incorporated
64   American Radiator and Standard Sanitary Corporation
66, 79, 219, 242, 244 (right)   General Electric Company
67, 81, 245   Westinghouse Electric Company
68, 76, 91, 102 (lower), 137, 155, 156, 195, 203 (upper), 210 (upper), 222, 250   *Better Homes and Gardens* magazine
84   St. Charles Kitchens (photo by Hedrich-Blessing Studio)
92   *Good Housekeeping* magazine (photo by Hans Van Nes)
96, 160, 251 (left), 252 (center)   Alexander Smith and Sons Carpet Company
102 (upper)   Molla, Incorporated
112, 200 (upper)   Rooks Photo
128, 187   Joseph Horne Company
130, 131   Kroehler Manufacturing Company
133   *Stylist Magazine* and Rooks Photo
140   American–Saint Gobain Corporation
142–143   Fawcett Publications
166 (all except lower center), 167 (all except lower row)   Imperial Furniture Company
166 (lower center), 167 (lower left and lower right)   Paine Furniture Company
167 (lower center)   Boston Museum of Fine Arts
200 (lower)   Grand Rapids Chair Company (photo by Southwick-Andrews)
203 (lower), 207 (lower)   Andres, Incorporated
207 (upper)   The Wallpaper Institute (photo by William Gilchrist)
210 (lower)   Dunbar Furniture Corporation and Harold J. Siesel Company

212   Alfred Assid
213   Colonial Manufacturing Company
220   Brach-Allen Studio
221 (left)   Chelsea Clock Company
221 (upper right and lower right)   Seth Thomas Clocks
226–229   The Coca-Cola Company
232   Bakersfield, California, High School, Esther D. Shellman
234 (left), 236 (lower), 243 (upper)   Hotpoint
234 (below)   Tappan (photo by O'Keefe and Merritt)
236 (upper)   Whirlpool Corporation
238   Speed Queen
240, 241, 296 (right)   The Hoover Company
243 (lower), 244 (left)   The Hobart Manufacturing Company (Kitchenaid)
249   The American Carpet Institute
251 (right), 252 (lower)   The Firth Carpet Company
252 (upper)   The Magee Carpet Company
259   Money Management Institute of Household Finance Corporation
265, 297 (right), 322, 327 (lower left and lower right), 328 (lower left and lower right)   E. I. du Pont de Nemours & Company
271   *American Fabrics* magazine
274, 276   Cannon Mills, Educational Department
284–285   Fostoria Glass Company

286–287   Sterling Silversmiths Guild of America and Towle Silversmiths
292 (upper)   Highland Park, Michigan, Homemaking Laboratories, Eunice E. Herald
292 (lower)   S. C. Johnson & Son, Inc.
296 (left)   *Dupont Magazine*
297 (left)   The Cleanliness Bureau

Especially grateful acknowledgment is made to the following sources for their kind permission to reproduce the Color Plates appearing in this book.

Facing page 88, Color Plate 1, *Living for Young Homemakers* magazine
Facing pages 89, 184, 216, 217, Color Plates 2, 11, 13, 14, *Better Homes and Gardens* magazine
Facing pages 120, 121, Color Plates 3 (photograph by *House Beautiful*), 7, 8, Carpet Institute, Incorporated
Between pages 120–121 (right), Color Plate 6, Dunbar Furniture Corporation and Harold J. Siesel Company
Facing page 136, Color Plate 9, Williamsburg Restoration Approved Reproductions
Facing page 137, Color Plate 10, *McCall's* magazine
Facing page 185, Color Plate 12, Consolidated Trimming Corporation

INDEX

PI a

Regular exercise

The automobile and labor-saving equipment have caused the average American citizen to neglect regular exercise. Several years ago the *Kraus Physical Fitness Tests* were given to 7000 children from European countries and the United States. In the six basic tests for strength and flexibility, six out of ten children from the United States failed one or more of the tests, in contrast to only one out of ten among European children.

Walking is one of the best forms of exercise. Outdoor games, regular gym classes, and setting-up exercises at home help to keep a person physically fit.

✶ **WHAT PREVENTIVE MEASURES INSURE SAFETY?**

Every year there are between 27,000 and 30,000 fatal accidents in the home — twice as many as on the job. This high death rate is exceeded only by highway accidents.

Accidents are the fourth major cause of death, surpassed only by heart disease, cancer, and nervous disorders. They cause more deaths among children than the nine most deadly diseases combined — polio, pneumonia, cancer or leukemia, tuberculosis, kidney diseases, intestinal infections, and meningitis. Children can be *immunized* against communicable diseases but they can only be *protected* against accidents.

Causes of accidents

Suffocation in bed accounts for the largest number of accidents among children under one year of age. (Statistics and reports on suffocation may include some fatalities from undetected respiratory diseases.) Older children have suffocated in unused refrigerators or by pulling thin plastic bags over their heads. Choking on food or on foreign objects also causes a large number of deaths among infants and small children.

From age two, motor vehicle accidents take the heaviest toll among young children. In the home, fires and explosions claim the most lives. As children grow older, drowning becomes responsible for more deaths. Firearms, left loaded and accessible at home, and hunting accidents take an unnecessary toll.

Falls account for about half of all accidental deaths in the home, and over eight out of ten victims are 65 and over. The most dangerous areas in the average home are the bedroom, kitchen, stairs, and bathroom. In the *bedroom* people trip on scatter rugs or electric light cords, slip on highly polished floors, bump into open drawers. Children fall out of unprotected windows. In the *kitchen*, clothes catch fire over open burners, people become asphyxiated when pilot lights fail to operate, children are burned when pot handles are within reach or the water temperature is too high. When electric cords are frayed or worn, when sharp objects are laid about carelessly, or when spilled food is not wiped up, a serious accident can occur suddenly. *Stairways* with poor lighting, no handrails, objects left in the way, loose carpeting or pads cause accidents that could easily be avoided. The *bathroom* that has outlets near the tub or electric cords that are not covered with rubber can become an electrocution booth. Medicines and razor blades left loose are a great temptation to children. A tub without a place to grasp while getting out may cause many falls.

People are often careless about keeping poisons in the bathroom and kitchen. Aspirin, turpentine, gasoline, and ammonia mistakenly consumed account for many deaths.

One in every five home accidents occurs on the premises *outside the home*. Such accidents often happen to outsiders. If the person who delivers the milk, mail, laundry, newspaper, or groceries is injured or dies as a result of an accident caused by a roller skate or wagon on a walk or an unmarked hole in the yard, a lawsuit may follow. Lawsuits can run into many thousands of dollars. One protection is to be careful, and another is to carry public liability insurance.

Accident prevention

Some of you may be baby sitters or perhaps you have younger brothers and sisters. If so, you are aware of how much watching and protection young children need. Many accidents can be avoided. Here are some trouble spots to check in your own home:

Loose screens in windows
Absence of rails on stairs
Basement doors left open
Unshielded heaters and electric fans
Unprotected electric outlets
Frayed electric wires
Leaks in gas pilot lights or heaters
Unsteady chairs
Poisonous or inflammable fluids accessible to
    children
Tablecloths to pull down
Pot handles within reach
Loose or frayed rugs
Knives, scissors, and other sharp tools lying
    around or left within reach of children
Old and unlabeled medicines kept in medicine
    cabinet for possible future use
Cluttered stairs
Open drawers and closet doors
Needles and pins on furniture or floor
Electric cords in room traffic lanes
Absence of two-way switches
Overloaded electric circuits

Careful housekeeping can prevent many accidents. You should wipe up all spilled food, liquid, or grease immediately. One little grape or an apple peeling can cause a serious fall. Use skidproof scatter rugs, keep electric cords well out of the way, avoid high-luster floor polishes, and stand only on firm chairs and ladders. Keep litter off stairs, and remove children's toys, garden tools, and lawn mowers from outside areas before dark.

Never transfer medicine from its original bottle. Throw away all old medicines. Keep poisons and combustible liquids safely separated from food. Never plug in an electric cord with wet hands or while you have one hand on the faucet. Use rubber cords in kitchen and laundry areas.

Home fires account for a very large number of accidental deaths. Spontaneous combustion and the careless use of matches are not the major causes. *Electrical fires* now destroy more property than fires of any other origin. Homes built before World War II were wired for lighting and a few laborsaving appliances; their circuits were not meant to take today's electrical load. It is estimated that wiring is inadequate in four out of five homes.

When overloaded wires are forced to carry too much current, they become hot. A blown fuse or a tripped circuit breaker is a warning signal. Instead of installing adequate wiring, many people resort to using a stronger fuse. The fuse may not blow out but the wires will continue to get hotter *inside the walls*. Eventually the wires will disintegrate, cause the wall to smolder, and may cause the home to become an inferno. Studies indicate that defective television sets cause seventeen times as many fires as defective Christmas tree lights. If the motor in the refrigerator, television or hi-fi set, washer, or any other equipment begins to smoke when there is no one in the room, a fire can start quickly.

You will learn more about wiring in Chapter 5, Unit 2.

ILLUSTRATION 5.   *Hazards to home safety. Using a cleaning fluid near a fire in a closed room, cluttered steps, a dangling iron cord, an electric heater that may cause shock or burn, and standing on a rocking chair to hang curtains invite serious accidents.*

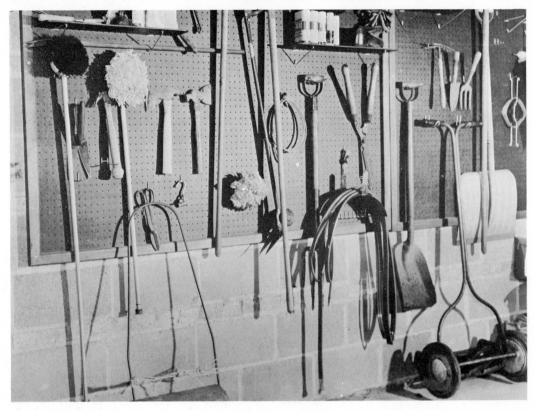

ILLUSTRATION 6. *Tools are readily available when you need them, and the home is safe from accidents caused by sharp tools when all tools are hung on a pegboard storage wall.*

✳ HOW CONVENIENT IS YOUR HOME?

If the modern homemaker were suddenly projected back several generations, she could scarcely endure the inconveniences of keeping house. Try to imagine your kitchen with an open fireplace for cooking, with no convenient cabinets except a big kitchen cupboard, and with a springhouse instead of a refrigerator. Modern kitchen, laundry, cleaning, and storage equipment is providing for the homemaker more hours to enjoy the aesthetic values of the home.

Even with modern equipment, we often do not make the best use of work areas. How to arrange these areas efficiently and conveniently is discussed in Unit 3, pages 77–87. However, you may want to make a preliminary check of the arrangement of work and storage areas in your home. When you want to use simple tools for minor repair jobs, can you find the tools easily? When you help with the laundry, are laundry supplies within easy reach? Have you enough convenience outlets for all your laborsaving equipment? Is the cleaning closet organized so that you can always find dustcloths, polishes, and other supplies?